PRAISE FOR *APPROACHING THE MIDDLE CHAMBER*

"Before he may complete his rite of passage, the Craftsman must first climb a series of symbolic steps; a journey which will ultimately lead him to the middle chamber of King Solomon's temple, where the Fellow is entitled to a Craftsman's wages. Jaime Paul Lamb has carefully ascended those steps and, having reaped the rewards of his harvest, has expanded upon what those steps entail for all who would dare to follow him up that winding path. An instant classic, *Approaching the Middle Chamber* should be placed in the hands of every Fellowcraft."

—P.D. Newman, author of
Alchemically Stoned: The Psychedelic Secret of Freemasonry

"When I was initiated into the degrees of Masonry, my favorite was the Fellow-Craft; though I was never given a satisfactory explication of the degree, or its symbolism, from the Masons of my Lodge. I wish I would have had this book at that time. Jaime Paul Lamb has done an excellent job with his explanation and understanding of the Fellow-Craft lecture and its esoteric import. I highly recommend this book."

—Darcy Küntz, author of
The Complete Golden Dawn Cipher Manuscript

"When Passed to the Second Degree, the new Fellowcraft is told to study the seven liberal arts and sciences. Today, this comes across as admonishment to obtain a good education, or advice from a time where open scientific investigation was a perilous pursuit. However, Lamb's work draws out the similarities of these studies to the Masonic lodge and more ancient traditions. As such, *Approaching the Middle Chamber* has all the hallmarks of what will become a seminal introduction to the subjects."

—Frater YShY, author of
Adept Magic in the Golden Dawn Tradition

"*Approaching the Middle Chamber* is a whirlwind exploration of the philosophies underlying Freemasonry's central teachings. The philosophical disciplines contained at the Fraternity's core are decoded in a manner both surgical and irrefutable, leaving the reader simply awe-inspired. Jaime Paul Lamb has set a new standard in discourse on the Middle Chamber Lecture."

—Robert H. Johnson, host of *WCY Podcast*

APPROACHING THE MIDDLE CHAMBER

THE SEVEN LIBERAL ARTS IN FREEMASONRY & THE WESTERN ESOTERIC TRADITION

JAIME PAUL LAMB

THE LAUDABLE PURSUIT PRESS

Published by The Laudable Pursuit Press.
2020

Edited by Jason E. Marshall, 32°

Book design and layout by Matthew D. Anthony, 32°

ISBN: 978-1-7326214-1-1

The Laudable Pursuit
www.thelaudablepursuit.com
Email: editor@thelaudablepursuit.com

Printed by Lulu.com

ACKNOWLEGDEMENTS

I would like to thank the Brethren of my Mother Lodge, Old Well-Saint John's Lodge no. 6, F.&A.M., Norwalk, Connecticut, the Brethren of Ascension Lodge no. 89, F.&A.M., Phoenix, Arizona, the Brethren of Arizona Research Lodge no. 1, the *Fratres* of the Arizona College of the *Societas Rosicruciana in Civitatibus Foederatis*, and the *Fratres et Sorores* of the Hermetic Society of the G∴D∴, for their inspiration, support and Light. Many thanks to P.D. Newman, Dan Hawkins and Jake Trayer, my *Fratres* in Masonic Rosicrucianism, for proofreading my manuscript; to William S. Burkle for providing scans from his personal copy of the 1909 pre-U.S. Games Rider-Waite Tarot; and to Piers Vaughan for his invaluable insight as well as the contribution of his brilliant Foreword to the present volume. Thank you to Jason Marshall, Matt Anthony and The Laudable Pursuit for all their hard work and their unceasing dedication to advancing Masonic thought and letters. Lastly, I would like to thank my wife, Stephanie, for her patience, love and support.

This book is dedicated to those seeking Further Light in Freemasonry and the Western Esoteric Tradition.

Sincerely & Fraternally,
Jaime Paul Lamb
Phoenix, Arizona
Anno Lucis 6020

CONTENTS

The Winding Staircase, from Mackey's Manual of the Lodge, 1891

FOREWORD

Most Lodges suffer from a problem when it comes to education: either it is focused on pure ritual performance, or the learning of catechisms, the *ring-pass-not* for admission to the next Degree. Even Jurisdictions with a comprehensive educational system tend to focus on ritual excellence, Masonic protocol, history (most often what I term "famous dead Masons" talks) and management skills ("how to run your Lodge"). All useful, no doubt; but none of these really focus on the core *purpose* of Freemasonry.

Therefore, most Masons have to rely on books to supplement their knowledge. Now there is no doubt that there is a plethora of books on Masonry out there, ranging from great classics to the less-than-useful. The problem is: sifting through the vast amount of written words to find the parts relevant to one's interests at that time. This normally means scouring through a number of books, the internet, libraries and other sources, in order to put together a Gestalt of what one is seeking. With the advent of Observant Masonry and other systems of education (including the excellent Masonicons and similar events popping up across the country), a deeper level of themed education is becoming more available; but even if a Lodge is fortunate enough to have a comprehensive educational system which delves into the sources, the symbolism and the esotericism of ritual, what is offered will most likely focus on the personal interests of the Education Officer.

One of the greatest misunderstandings in Freemasonry arose when the leaders of the Craft declared that "there are no secrets in Masonry," thereby guaranteeing the demise of the Order. Thankfully, more enlightened heads have muted that call, either for the sound reason that they know it to be patently false; or for the more cynical reason that, by saying nothing they can attract more members and refill their investment portfolios. For some, Masonry will never be more than an opportunity to get together and break bread with friends and enjoy a clam bake or pancake breakfast while raising money for local charities. These are certainly worthy reasons to participate. But we must not forget that our roots (and by this

I am referring to the 17ᵗʰ Century and not to any particular theory of our primitive origins) are steeped in esoteric theory, and that our founders had a far more profound objective in mind than writing a few simple plays to stress our need to be charitable, to care for widows and orphans, and to be nice to furry animals. The founding (or, for some, the *resurrection*) of Masonry in England was inspired by members of the Royal Society, who, while embracing the new experimental approach to science, still harbored strong interests in the Pre-Enlightenment sciences of Astrology, Alchemy and Numerology alongside Astronomy, Chemistry and Physics; and while they ordered their scientific experiments around hypothesis, controls, visible results and repeatability; nevertheless, they still harbored a deep interest in what could not be controlled in a test tube, might not be repeatable in an identical manner for all people, and that which might not even be visible to human eyes. Similarly, in mainland Europe, Masonic Lodges exercised their minds on the mysteries of ancient civilizations (Memphis and Mizraïm), Alchemy (the Gold und Rosenkreuzer), the Templar legacy (Rite of Strict Observance) and even the practice of Theurgy (The Order of Elus Cohen of the Universe). However, it should be stressed that this was still only a lesser stream in the universal current which is Freemasonry; yet just as the injunction to "make a daily advance in Masonic knowledge" means little more to many Masons than sharing a joke in an email or message with their friends, there are a large number who seek enlightenment in the way envisaged by our founders over 300 years ago.

This book is therefore a breath of fresh air for anyone who is seeking to find a comprehensive review of the key lessons of the Fellowcraft Degree. Perhaps some will ask why a book of this magnitude is focused on what many see as a minor step sandwiched between the two key Degrees of Entered Apprentice, when one is first initiated, and the Master Mason Degree, when one becomes a fully functioning member of the Lodge? Indeed, the very verb used for this Degree – *passing* – suggests something which is both ephemeral and unimportant!

However, that misses the point entirely. While the First and Third Degrees are clearly significant in the status they afford to the seeker, it is the Second Degree which really contains the education for the entire edifice. Even a casual glance at the rituals will show the Reader that the First and Third Degrees are focused on ritual, while the Second Degree contains the sublime teachings encapsulated in the extraordinary *tour de force* which is the Middle Chamber Lecture. Remember also that, before Speculative Masonry determined to add a Third (and a Fourth, for that matter) Degree, the Fellowcraft was the culmination of the apprenticeship in the Craft, and the title of Master was simply a title given to the *primus inter pares* of an Operative Lodge. It is therefore high time that the Fellow-craft Degree take back its place as perhaps the greatest of all the Degrees.

With a view to how the early Speculative Freemasons viewed their rituals and lectures through the lens of a society both excited about the coming Age of Enlightenment with its discoveries, inventions and its ex-perimentation, and a desire to maintain links with the swirling currents which both emphasized their national heritage and the mysterious teach-ings of the Renaissance, including Hermeticism, Kabbalah, and later Ros-icrucianism, the author has put together an extraordinary book which will enable the Mason keen to expand their knowledge to find the materials they need in one place. There is also enough material to attract the atten-tion of a non-Mason who is versed in these topics as well. For anyone who questions the relevance of Centuries-old teachings to modern times, let me simply quote that old adage: "those who do not learn history are doomed to repeat it", which is why every religion values their ancient texts, and studies them for solutions to contemporary problems. Anyone with a passing understanding of the Holy Scriptures, for example, knows that numbers are used as keys to important truths. Is it surprising, therefore that in the Historical Lecture from the Royal Arch Degree, the number '3' is mentioned no less than twenty-eight times?

The author has provided a fascinating review of the Middle Chamber Lecture and draws together threads as apparently diverse as Kabbalah, the Art of Memory, modern musical theory, Hermeticism, techniques of exe-gesis, and even an experiment in alchemy which can be performed at home with no unusual equipment. His breadth of knowledge is demonstrated by his ability to draw from a number of traditions – both Western and Eastern – to illustrate his points, yet his style is easy to follow and flows comfortably. Each Chapter begins with a passage from Duncan's *Masonic Ritual and Monitor* to provide the text which will subsequently be analyzed in depth. I will draw the Reader's attention to one significant comment in the author's introduction: "it is demonstrable that the use of occult herme-neutics yields access to [the seven liberal art's] esoteric substratum and, thereby, previously inaccessible insight, understanding and Light may yet be gained, even if only at the subjective level." So, applying tools from other schools – be they scientific or occult – to try to unravel the meaning behind certain passages is by no means a pointless exercise if the process results in our mind making a connection or establishing a relationship of two ideas between which we had previous seen no connection. As an ex-ample, the application of historical analysis, archeology and the process of exegesis to the Scriptures – as opposed to the former approach of simply accepting them as written by God's finger and incapable of being analyzed in any manner – has brought to light many insights and understandings of the texts which would otherwise have gone unperceived. And the author's application of van Gennep's theory on Rites of Passage to Freemasonry provides a rationale for the structure of Masonic ritual which might otherwise have gone unnoticed.

That said, this is not an easy read: in an age of sound bites and tweets, we are reminded of the great Masonic books of Waite, Pike, Wilmshurst and Leadbeater, where close study was rewarded with many insights and points for meditation. Indeed, one might call this book a college course in the Fellowcraft Degree. To expand on the teachings, a number of Appendices and a Suggested Reading list are included to give the reader all the tools they need to understand the book and to continue their studies in areas of particular interest to them. The author also returns to topics several times during the course of the book, thereby reinforcing the messages he wants to communicate especially. In reading it I am reminded of one of the most influential books of my youth, Hofstadter's monumental *Gödel, Escher, Bach: An Eternal Golden Braid* (which incidentally has 777 pages). The scope of the book is monumental, and I believe the author has succeeded in his endeavor.

I recommend this book to anybody – Mason or non-Mason – who wishes to explore the symbols and intention of the Second or Fellowcraft Degree. It is appropriate both to the solitary reader wishing to make a true advance in knowledge; and to those Study Groups which are appearing in increasing number, as a very suitable book to study together.

Piers Vaughan
January 22nd, 2020

INTRODUCTION

At a period [...] when few were instructed in the trivium, and very few studied the quadrivium, to be master of both was sufficient to complete the character of a philosopher. The propriety, therefore, of adopting the seven liberal arts and sciences as a symbol of the completion of human learning is apparent. The candidate, having reached this point, is now supposed to have accomplished the task upon which he had entered — he has reached the last step, and is now ready to receive the full fruition of human learning. So far, then, we are able to comprehend the true symbolism of the winding stairs. They represent the progress of an inquiring mind, with the toils and labors of intellectual cultivation and study, and the preparatory acquisition of all human science, as a preliminary step to the attainment of divine truth, which, it must be remembered, is always symbolized in Masonry by the Word. [...] The middle chamber is therefore symbolic of this life, where the symbol only of the Word can be given, where the truth is to be reached by approximation only, and yet where we are to learn that that truth will consist in a perfect knowledge of the G. A. O. T. U. This is the reward of the inquiring Mason; in this consist the wages of a Fellow Craft; he is directed to the truth, but must travel farther and ascend still higher to attain it.[1]

I would like to state, forthwith, that it is my belief that the entirety of what we recognize as Masonic literature[2] is but a series of commentaries on an experiential system which can only be viably transmitted in the form of symbolism, ritual and allegory – *and that these are the sole means by which the Hidden Mysteries of Freemasonry are conveyed.* Supplementary literature may be of immense value in elucidating certain perspectives

---

1 Mackey, *An Encyclopedia of Freemasonry and its Kindred Sciences*, Everts & Co., 1884, p. 885

2 The only admissible exception being the several editions of William Preston's *Illustrations of Masonry*, with Oliver's commentary; and only then because our ritual and lectures are so dependent upon the work.

through analogy and comparison, but it is just that – *supplementary* – the personal insight of others, compared and synthesized with our own. To be sure, many eminent Masons who have come before us have done much to illuminate the path, but "the map is not the territory", as Korzybski observed.[3] No matter how canonical or authoritative the work may seem to be – such as that of Oliver, Mackey, Pike, Wilmshurst, et al. – it merely represents the interpretation of an individual Mason; not an uncolored view of Freemasonry itself, but an impression. The current volume is no different; it was composed in an effort to expand and buttress the Mason's theoretical perspective, vis-à-vis Western Esotericism, in the hope of making more meaningful those experiences he has in our work – *but it is not a substitute for the work*. Again, Freemasonry is experiential, initiatic; it is transformative and vital; it is an experience that defies explanation and, in that sense, constitutes a truly ineffable and occult transmission.

While it is fairly obvious that Freemasonry's Mysteries are experiential in nature, there is also an often-overlooked *intellectual* transmission in the work of the Craft. All those who have been passed to the degree of Fellow Craft have, however fleetingly, encountered the seven liberal arts and sciences, as these are referenced in the lecture pertaining to that degree (see Appendix D). Outside of established academia, Freemasonry is one of the few remaining societies prescribing the arts and sciences as a means toward moral, intellectual and spiritual development. It is somewhat lamentable, however, that more time and attention isn't paid to these seven fundamentals of a classical education – in addition to the other subjects raised in the lecture – after their cursory introduction in the Fellow Craft lecture. This book was composed in an effort to help rectify this deficiency by inspiring the reader to peer further into those Mysteries contained within the seven liberal arts and sciences; that such an endeavor might widen their scope, deepen their experiences and, ultimately, make their lives more meaningful.

Another large part of the impetus for writing the present volume arose from my decision to finally undertake this syllabus, in earnest, for my own benefit. I had spent too many years dabbling in various subjects with fleeting interest, cherry-picking information from here and there, in an effort to cobble together some semblance of applicable knowledge and understanding; yet these fragmented bits of, well, *trivia* would not seem to coalesce into anything like a practical system. I was looking for a way to synthesize this information that it might become accessible as a means to enrich my experiences in and of the world. It wasn't until I had begun

---

3   Korzybski, *Science and Sanity: An Introduction to Non-Aristotelian Systems and General Semantics*, The International Non-Aristotelian Library Pub. Co., 1933, p. 58

to develop a conceptual schema, a unifying theoretical framework, within which I could organize the material, that the arts and sciences began to provide a practical frame of reference. I have found Freemasonry and the greater Western Esoteric Tradition to be that schema, that organizational system or foundation of fundamental principles, upon which I could begin to erect an intellectual and metaphysical edifice – "that house not made with hands" – which is, I believe, the primary objective of Freemasonry.

Though a thorough study of the seven liberal arts and sciences is emphatically recommended, it is not within the scope of the present volume to practically instruct the reader in the minutiæ of these disciplines – again, the reader will not be academically or formally instructed in the subjects contained herein. This book is meant to function neither as a textbook nor a workbook – it is a broad overview of the subjects raised in the Fellow Craft lecture, *with the express purpose of highlighting their esoteric and occult significance*, particularly through the critical lenses of Western astrology, comparative mythology, Neoplatonism, Hermeticism, Qabalah[4], Rosicrucianism, Tarot symbolism and, of course, Freemasonry. The basic, exoteric curriculum associated with the seven liberal arts and sciences has been catalogued many times over by others more qualified for the task than myself. However, the subject, or rather subjects, have to my knowledge yet to be thoroughly worked up from the perspective of the greater Western Esoteric Tradition – a tradition of which Freemasonry may be said to be a subcategory. Again, it is the object of this book to uncover and present those aspects of the Fellow Craft lecture that are of immediate interest to the esoterically-inclined Freemason, as well as the Western occultist who may not yet have approached the Fraternity's West Gate. To that end, I have applied a decidedly esoteric theoretical critique throughout.

In order to facilitate the development of this critical frame of reference, as well as for the benefit of the reader who may not as yet be well-versed in occult theory, I have included three appendices detailing the most commonly accepted Hermetic correspondences (qabalistic, astrological and tarotic), the arrangement of the *Etz Chaim*, or "Tree of Life", and Agrippa's table of planetary hours (see Appendices A, B and C). I have given the Hebrew and Greek for many of the proper names, as these will facilitate the reader's independent analysis, should they decide to calculate

---

4   Note that I will be using the spelling Q-A-B-A-L-A-H throughout this volume; I do this for two reasons: first, because I believe it best fits as an English transliteration of the Hebrew Q-B-L-H (Hebrew: קבלה; meaning "reception" or "correspondence") and, second, to differentiate Hermetic Qabalah, as it is promulgated in the highly syncretized Western Esoteric Tradition, from that of the strictly Christian (Cabala) or Judaic (Kabbalah) systems.

their numerological values. I have given some of these values – *gematria* for the Hebrew, *isopsephy* for the Greek – in order to illustrate points I wished to make in context. That being said, I have left plenty of room for the reader to apply their own interpretation, qabalistic or otherwise – as it is neither my aim nor desire to proselytize for a certain methodological orientation nor to indoctrinate the reader into the manner of a particular perspective. Although, I do maintain that these established hermeneutic and exegetical methods, which are representative of those most commonly applied in the Western Esoteric Tradition, are immensely valuable tools for those wishing to examine the occult substrata of the subjects addressed herein.

In my highlighting of symbolical motifs, apropos Western Occultism, it is not my intention to imply that these are necessarily inherent in the work of Freemasonry. In other words, I am not arguing for the objective presence of, say, Tarot symbolism in the ritual and symbolism of the Craft, as I understand that this may be anachronistic. However, I believe that there is great value in fostering and promoting a living exegetical dialogue with the material, which may include the introduction of interpretive methods foreign to the work itself, much as one might apply a mythologically based critical theory to modern cinema, for example. Taking Abrahamic scripture and its relationship to qabalistic analysis as another example, we find that qabalistic method appears at a later date than that which is set for the composition of scripture – however, the value of applying a qabalistic exegesis is not undermined by this deficit, as it still serves as a valid and fruitful interpretive method, regardless of its concepts not being inherent or preexistent in the source work. It is simply not plausible to imply that qabalistic concepts exist in scripture, *in situ*, nor that these were cryptically deposited by early Abrahamic scribes – but, conversely, it is demonstrable that the use of occult hermeneutics yields access to scripture's esoteric substratum and, thereby, previously inaccessible insight, understanding and Light may yet be gained, even if only at the subjective level.

Regarding the form and sequence of the present volume, I have, for the sake of thoroughness, devoted a chapter to the operative and speculative denominations of Freemasonry and the Brazen Pillars on the porch of K∴S∴T∴, both of which being anterior to the Winding Staircase in the lecture. I have also included a chapter on the wages and jewels of a Fellow Craft, which are posterior, and are to be received in the Middle Chamber of K∴S∴T∴. Thus, a culmination of all the subjects addressed in the Fellow Craft lecture, from beginning to end, is presented herein. On the Winding Staircase itself, I have addressed the three principal stages of human life, the three principal supports of the Lodge and the three principal officers of the Lodge, all three triads are represented by the course of three steps, and also to the five orders of architecture and the five human senses, represented by the course of five steps on the Winding Staircase. In this book, we will be paying particular attention to the third course of seven steps, consisting of the seven liberal arts and sciences, as these form the weightiest subjects of our curriculum.

During the process of outlining and writing the initial drafts of this book, it had become obvious to me that each of the subjects had to be studied in their prescribed order, as each are contingent upon their predecessor. Taking a couple subjects from the trivium, for example, it became immediately apparent that one would need to have a firm grasp of grammar in order to properly construct a rhetorically sound discourse. Just as in the quadrivium, one must digest the abstract concept of number (arithmetic) in order to extrapolate the concept into multi-dimensional space (geometry). Digesting the seven liberal arts and sciences in the sequence in which they are prescribed in the Fellow Craft lecture is imperative to any rigorous course of their study. It is in this way that proficiency in any one of them is best attained. Analogously, in the degrees of Freemasonry, we do not confer the Master Mason degree on one who has yet to experience and show proficiency in the Entered Apprentice and Fellow Craft degrees. In cases such as these, *sequence is everything*.

I have cited *Duncan's Masonic Ritual and Monitor* (1866) and Morgan's *Illustrations of Masonry* (1827) to support ritual passages (with the omission of any signs, grips, words or any material other than that which supports the Fellow Craft degree lecture) as opposed to referencing the actual ritual of any particular Grand Jurisdiction, which I felt would be imprudent. *Duncan's* and Morgan's infamous exposé are both readily available to the general public and I personally feel that I am under no obligation to keep something so easily obtainable inviolate, as it is not within my power to protect it from the eyes of the *profani*. That being said, they are both as general a representation of Preston-Webb Masonic ritual as any currently being practiced by the various American Jurisdictions and will thereby serve to support such passages as needed. I have also referenced the 1956 edition of *Masonic Treatise with an Elucidation on the Religious and Moral Beauties of Freemasonry*[5] by William Finch and, most especially, the 1867 edition of *Illustrations of Masonry*[6] by William Preston throughout, since

5   Finch, *Masonic Treatise with an Elucidation on the Religious and Moral Beauties of Freemasonry*, Fellow Craft Degree, Chapter II, 1802, reprint of 1956 edition

6   Preston (Oliver, commentary), *Illustrations of Masonry*, New York: Masonic Publishing and Manufacturing Co., 1867

the various editions of this document essentially form the foundation of our ritual as currently practiced in the United States.

In the absence of the temporal and monetary resources necessary to peruse the dusty libraries of the Earth, with gloved hands, poring over rare antiquarian volumes, I have done a great deal of my research virtually – that is to say, online. Hardcopy volumes from my personal library have been consulted in addition to innumerable pdf's and material from online archival and academic databases. I have tried my best to use primary sources and have carefully cited them; my apologies, in advance, if the reader finds anything amiss in this regard. This work, however, contains a great many original observations for which there are no precedents in Masonic or occult literature; I have done my best to support the terms of these observations but, at times, conjecture was unavoidable. When I did venture into these more speculative areas, I tried to make it evident that I was doing so. My personal belief is that we must continue to push the boundaries beyond that which has already been established in order to gain new insight and, therefore, I support an intrepid spirit and a sense of the *avant garde* in research of this kind, particularly in the domain of the Western Esoteric Tradition, as so much of its history is inextricably bound to a more numinous sort of "heirohistory". Though I have endeavored in this spirit, I feel that it is equally important to approach Masonic research responsibly and to avoid perpetuating errors – I have done my best.

The interpretation of ancient megalithic sites may serve as an apt analogy to illustrate the point of an interdisciplinary approach to research. My wife and I have, over the years, visited several such world heritage sites, such as those found in and around Upper and Lower Egypt, the greater Angkor complex in Cambodia, Stonehenge in the United Kingdom, Machu Picchu and Sacsayhuamán in Peru, and Tiwanaku and Puma Punku in Bolivia. In researching these structures, we have noted that the common academic practice is to send a team of archeologists, alone, to gather data specifically pertinent to the objects of their domain of research (that is, after all, how financial support in academia is distributed); this is in opposition to sending a more comprehensive team, consisting not only of archeologists, but also an archeoastronomer, a mythologist, a philologist, etc., in an effort to arrive at an interdisciplinary vantage point from which to interpret the data. When interpreted from the perspective of a single discipline, biases are merely confirmed or refuted, while a holistic picture of these sites remains elusive. Conversely, by the application of a polymathic, or interdisciplinary interpretive perspective, such as that with which we will presently survey the Fellow Craft lecture, one may begin to assemble a multifaceted picture of the object of inquiry, as opposed to that which is offered by a limited and relatively myopic interpretive approach. It is in this interest that I have endeavored to scrutinize the data made available to us in the Fellow Craft lecture from the broader perspective of the Western Esoteric Tradition (simultaneously ancient, medieval, Renaissance, Victorian and modern), as opposed to a strictly historical, linear or domain-confined approach, in an effort to develop a more penetrating critique of the material contained therein.

In a sentence, the present volume is a work of occult philosophy, using as its structure and formal frame of reference, the Fellow Craft lecture as presented in the second degree of Freemasonry, toward the development of a synthetic interpretation of the work vis-à-vis Western Esotericism.

That being said, we will be taking our subjects in their order of appearance in the Fellow Craft lecture, starting at the symbolic porch of K∴S∴T∴ and up to the Middle Chamber of the same. The presentation of the lecture occurs at the beginning of the second section of the Fellow Craft degree, after the candidate has taken his Obligation as such. The candidate is first conducted, generally by the Senior Deacon, to a place representing the porch of K∴S∴T∴...

CHAPTER I

∴

THE OPERATIVE AND SPECULATIVE DENOMINATIONS OF MASONRY

Masonry is considered under two denominations – namely, Operative and Speculative. By Operative Masonry, we allude to the proper application of the useful rules of architecture, whence a structure will derive figure, strength, and beauty; and whence will result a due proportion and a just correspondence in all its parts [...] it demonstrates that a fund of science and industry is implanted in man, for the best, most salutary, and beneficent purposes. By Speculative Masonry, we learn to subdue the passions, act upon the square, keep a tongue of good report, maintain secrecy, and practise charity [...] It leads the contemplative to view with reverence and admiration the glorious works of creation, and inspires him with the most exalted ideas of the perfections of his Divine Creator. Our ancient brethren worked at both Operative and Speculative Masonry; they worked at the building of King Solomon's Temple, besides numerous other Masonic edifices. They wrought six days, but did not work on the seventh (7th), for in six days God created the heavens and the earth, and rested on the seventh day; therefore our ancient brethren consecrated this day as a day of rest from their labors; thereby enjoying frequent opportunities to contemplate the glorious works of creation, and to adore their great Creator.[1]

While still standing, without the door, upon the symbolic porch of K∴S∴T∴, the newly-obligated Fellow Craft is thus instructed as to the difference between the operative and speculative denominations of Masonry. He is informed that the prime defining factor of the operative

1 *Duncan's Masonic Ritual and Monitor* (1866), New York: Crown Publishers, 1986, pp. 72-73

craft is "[…] the proper application of the useful rules of architecture", while speculative Masons are to "[…] learn to subdue the passions, act upon the square, keep a tongue of good report, maintain secrecy, and practise charity." [2] The Fellow Craft is urged to develop an appreciation of the "glorious works of creation"; an awareness which will allow him to humbly discern the handiwork of the Creator in His Creation. The modes of this appreciation, in both the Masonic and the broader philosophical sense, may be said to include the same criteria by which one may measure the *good* (ethics), the *true* (logic) and the *beautiful* (aesthetics), such as number, ratio, proportion, harmony, symmetry or any other means by which the human mind may uncover the underlying order in the abstract (noumenal) as well as in the concrete (phenomenal). He is then told that our ancient brethren practiced both operative and speculative Masonry and is given a brief description of the workmen on the site of K∴S∴T∴. These workmen are said to have wrought for six days and rested on the seventh, in imitation of the labor/leisure distribution enacted by God over the seven days of Creation.

It should be stated forthwith that the decision to take literally the accounts of the building of the Temple – a Temple for which we have merely anecdotal evidence in support of its historicity[3] – or, conversely, to interpret the narrative allegorically, are at the discretion of the individual. Within the Masonic Fraternity, there is no requirement as to which interpretation – literal or figurative – one must subscribe. Neither perspective in-itself appears to be detrimental to the efficacy of the Masonic experience, as Brethren of both inclinations populate the Lodge. The lion's share of the lessons inculcated in the speculative craft are conveyed by ritualism, allegory and symbol in conjunction with lectures providing further elucidation, rather than merely by the sort of standard, explicit pedagogy one encounters in academia, as Freemasonry's lessons are designed to be simultaneously perceived by the mind (mentally/intellectually; the *mercurial* modality), body (experientially/empirically; the *saline* modality) and soul (emotionally/imaginatively; the *sulfuric* modality). In light of this tendency in Masonic initiation, a synthesis of the literal and the figurative is essential to a sufficiently developed and nuanced perspective on the material. In a sense, the differences between the literal and figurative interpretations of Masonic symbolism – not to mention those of scripture, mythology, or the arts in general – are akin to the operative and speculative denominations of

2   *Duncan's Masonic Ritual and Monitor* (1866), New York: Crown Publishers, 1986, p. 72

3   Milstein, "King Solomon's Wall Found – Proof of Biblical Tale?", *National Geographic*, retrieved at: nationalgeographic.com

Masonry. The operative, or literal interpretation emphasizes the historicity and material causality of such events; while the speculative, or figurative interpretation stresses the value of allegorical allusion, *hierohistory* ("holy history"; an abstract history which is not confined to a deterministic, linear narrative – an organic, impressionistic and mytho-theologically historical model, accounting for lore and fable), and one's subjective relationship with the narrative or symbol presented. In the following, we will further elucidate the origins of, and the relationship between, both the operative and speculative craft; we will also attempt to trace both the historical and quasi-historical lineages of each denomination.

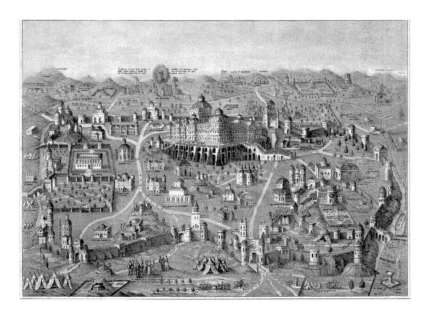

Jerusalem and King Solomon's Temple, print circa 1871

Stonemasonry, or operative Masonry, may be defined as the quarrying, hewing, raising, dressing, carving, finishing and setting of free stone in accordance with architectural designs. Quarrymen first locate the site of the desired material and split sheets of rock into irregular blocks, hewn from living stone, which are then raised for transport. Sawyers will then dress these stones into six-sided cuboids, prepared for the banker masons, who will then finish the stones for either further carving or for setting into an edifice. Some stones, requiring further ornamentation, are sent to carvers who will execute these more detailed operations such as carving floral, figurative or abstract designs, thus blurring the line between art and craft. Fixer masons will then set the completed stones, according to the architectural plans, usually by means of lifting tackle. The fixers will often apply lime mortars and grouts. Each of these positions in the operative craft, whether viewed as permanent specializations or as temporary stages of advancement, require comprehensive training. Often, this training takes the form of a hierarchical structure based on the craftsman's degree of proficiency. These degrees are believed to have been first established in the medieval cathedral builder's guild and are as follows, from bottom to top: *Apprentice* (known in speculative Masonry as *Entered Apprentice*), *Journeyman* (known as *Fellow Craft*) and *Master Mason*.[4]

Considering the definition established above, and the findings from archeological sites of the period – such as Çatalhöyük (Turkey), the Wall and Tower of Jericho (West Bank, Israel), Göbekli Tepe (Turkey), Khirokitia Choirokoitia (Cyprus), Theopetra Cave (Greece), etc. – we may safely conclude that the origin of operative stonemasonry can be traced at least to the Eurasian Mesolithic (Greek: μέσος, *mesos* meaning "middle" and λίθος, *lithos*, meaning "stone") period[5], which was an archeological era straddling the end of the Upper Paleolithic and the dawn of the Neolithic, roughly occupying the years 15000-5000 BCE. It is in this remote prehistoric period that we begin to see the remnants of megalithic structures composed of quarried and worked stone.[6] Some of these structures, particularly those found slightly later in the Neolithic, betray a degree of technical sophistication that would be difficult or impossible to execute today, often requiring the modern archeological intelligentsia, and greater academia, to revise long-standing paradigms in their fields, as was the case following the discovery of Göbekli Tepe in Turkey's Southeastern Anatolian region.[7] Correspondingly, it is in this period where we find the emergence of agriculture and animal husbandry – two innovations which signaled the decline of the nomadic hunter-gatherer cultures and the subsequent onset of civilization. A surplus of grains and livestock meant that

---

4   Akande, "Medieval Masons and Gothic Cathedrals", *Society of Architectural Historians*, 2016, retrieved at: sah.org

5   See also: the Epipaleolithic (Greek: επί, *epi* or "above", παλαιός, *palaiós* or "older, ancient", and λίθος, *lithos* or "stone") period in the ancient Near East, which spanned from about 20000-8000 BCE in the Levant and Caucasus.

6   Scham, "The World's First Temple", *Archaeology Magazine*, Dec. 2008, p. 23

7   Symmes, "Turkey: Archeological Dig Reshaping Human History", *Newsweek*, 2010, retrieved at: newsweek.com

it was in the best interest of these previously nomadic societies to settle into localized communities, thus necessitating civilizing patterns such as urbanization, art expression, social stratification and labor specialization. Due to this specialization, it is around this time that we see the emergence of the class of stonemasons – those who had raised living stone from the quarries and fit them for use in the construction of edifices and monuments – and the further hierarchical stratification within that class, such as the overseers (*Menatzchim*), craftsmen (*Ghiblim*) and bearers of burden (*Ish Sabal*), as mentioned by Josephus in his *Antiquities of the Jews*.[8]

There is ample reason to suspect that the speculative denomination of Masonry, particularly those within the architectural subset of the whole, had its influence even at this early stage of the Craft's evolution. Aside from an obviously very high proficiency in geometry and a consideration of religious and mythological motifs, perhaps the most conspicuous signs of the influence introduced by the speculative craft may be found in the astronomical orientation of ancient megalithic structures.[9] By considering celestial events, stellar configurations and other cosmic phenomena in their architectural designs, these ancient builders were not only erecting temples and monuments but they were fixing temporal markers by which to gauge equinoctial and solstitial events while simultaneously drawing upon the subtle influences of cosmic sympathies, concentrated by mirroring macrocosmic stellar formations in the microcosmic terrestrial arrangements of their structures. Perhaps the most notable modern example of this phenomenon, Robert Bauval's Orion correlation theory addresses the arrangement of the pyramids on Egypt's Giza Plateau as being a deliberately conceived microcosmic model of the macrocosmic stellar arrangement of Orion's belt.[10] It is not by chance that the tendency to erect monuments which helped to chronicle the cycles of nature coincided with the agricultural taming of the land, as knowledge of these cycles was essential to early agrarian and pastoral societies. With the advent of agriculture, we also see the development of an accompanying *agrotheology*[11], specifically pertaining to those Mysteries that allegorized the annual agricultural cycle in ritual similarity, thus drawing upon the influence of a sort of sympathetic magic.

8   Flavius Josephus, *Antiquities of the Jews*, 94 CE, retrieved at: gutenberg.org

9   Hiebert, *Celestial and Mathematical Precision in Ancient Architecture*, University of Manitoba, pdf retrieved at: unmanitoba.ca

10   Bauval & Gilbert, *The Orion Mystery: Unlocking the Secrets of the Pyramids*, Broadway Books, 1995

11   An especially handy term for this phenomenon which, I believe, was coined by Brother P.D. Newman in reference to the theologizing of agricultural cycles in the ancient world.

First theorized by Sir J.G. Frazer in his study of comparative religion, *The Golden Bough* (1890), the concept of sympathetic magic may be divided into two subsets: the law of *similarity* and the law of *contagion*. Presently, we are concerned with the law of similarity, which posits that like produces like, effects resemble their causes and, by extrapolation, that a microcosmic action or ritual corresponding to a natural phenomenon or event – in this case, the agricultural cycle – will have a causal effect on the macrocosmic cycle. This form of imitative magic may be discerned in the Mysteries of Dionysus (concerning the grape) and those of Demeter and Persephone (i.e., the Eleusinian Mysteries, concerning grains), as well as other agrarian cults. To a similar end, astronomical alignments and sympathetic stellar configurations may be observed at many sites spanning the globe, over an extremely vast period of time; a few of the more notable examples of these phenomena being the Giza Plateau[12], Stonehenge[13], Teotihuacan[14], Angkor Wat[15], Göbekli Tepe[16], and literally hundreds more. When we begin to see evidence of the utilization of astronomical alignments as a means to draw cosmic sympathies in the domain of architecture and stonemasonry, we also begin to observe the influence of the astrotheological and agrotheological aspects associated with the speculative denomination of the Craft.

12   Magli, *Topography, astronomy and dynastic history in the alignments of the pyramid fields of the Old Kingdom*, 2009, pdf retrieved at: ariv.org

13   Lockyer, *Stonehenge and Other British Stone Monuments Astronomically Considered*, 1909, p. 62, retrieved at: sacred-texts.com

14   Šprajc, "Astronomical Alignments at Teotihuacan, Mexico", *Latin American Antiquity*, 11(4), 2017, retrieved at: cambridge.org

15   Sparavigna, "Solar Alignments of the Planning of Angkor Wat Temple Complex", *Philica*, 2016, p. 591

16   Sweatman & Tsikritsis, "Decoding Göbekli Tepe with Archeoastronomy: What Does the Fox Say?", *Mediterranean Archaeology and Archaeometry*, Vol. 17, No 1, 2017, pp. 233-250

Bust of Posidonius of Apameia from the Naples National Archaeological Museum

Though it was predicated on a very ancient concept, the theory of cosmic sympathy (Greek: συμπάθεια, *sumpatheia*) was first documented by Posidonius of Apameia (135-51 BCE), a Greek Stoic philosopher, geographer and astronomer. In his physics, the terrestrial and celestial spheres were interconnected and reciprocally influential – the actions of one had a causal effect on the other – thus underpinning their sympathetic relationship.[17] Posidonius also extended his theory into the domains of meteorology and divination – concepts which he had extrapolated from Aristotelean physics. This is an early version of an idea which had resurfaced in both Neoplatonism and Hermeticism a century or two later, and again in medieval qabalistic thought and in the Renaissance astrology of the Florentine Neoplatonists, wherein the macrocosm was reflected in the microcosm and vice versa. This sympathetic relationship is, in fact, the very principle which differentiates the disciplines of astrology from astronomy, alchemy from chemistry, and speculative from operative Masonry. Astrology and astronomy both observe, measure and chronicle the movement of celestial bodies – but, in astrology, there is the accompanying belief that these cycles have an effect on man, his disposition and fate. Alchemy and chemistry both study the combinations and transformations of substances

17   Luz, *Cosmic Sympathy: The Teachings of Posidonius*, Berkeley Hills Books, 2004

and elements – but, in alchemy, there is the accompanying belief that these operations in the external macrocosm have a transformational effect in the alchemist's internal microcosm. Speculative and operative Masonry both utilize the working tools, the hierarchical degrees and the vernacular of stonemasonry – but in speculative Masonry, there is the accompanying belief that, through the philosophical application of these tools, degrees and vernacular, the Mason is himself hermetically transformed.

We are informed by eminent Masonic scholars, such as Oliver[18], Mackey[19] and Da Costa, that the first organization of operative builders and architects emerging from the mists of the ancient world were known as the Dionysian Artificers. Of this society, Da Costa said "[…t]his sect or society was now called the Dionysian Artificers, as Bacchus was supposed to be the inventor of building theatres; and they performed the Dionysian festivities […f]rom this period, the Science of Astronomy which had given rise to the symbols of the Dionysian rites, became connected with types taken from the art of building."[20] With varying degrees of plausibility, these authors have attempted to establish a lineal succession from these ancient builders, through the *collegia* of the Roman Empire, into the guilds of the medieval cathedral builders, and finally to the accepted Masonry of the 17th century speculative Lodges. This may very well prove to be the case but, as it stands, a few crucial and definitive links have yet to be forged into this chain of reasoning and, alas, the truth of the matter may be forever lost to the ages. It is also somewhat problematic that nearly all the historical documentation available on this elusive cadre of architects, presumably functioning from within the greater body of Dionysian *mystes*, may be solely found in Masonic literature.

> [T]*he Dionysiacs of Asia Minor were undoubtedly an association of architects and engineers, who had the exclusive privilege of building temples, stadia, and theatres, under the mysterious tutelage of Bacchus, and were distinguished from the uninitiated or profane inhabitants by the science which they possessed, and by many private signs and tokens by which they recognized each other.*[21]

---

18   *The Masonic Trowel* vol. 6, Reynolds & Son, 1867, p. 38

19   Mackey, *The Symbolism of Freemasonry,* Clark & Maynard, 1869, pp. 45-57

20   Da Costa, *The History of the Dionysian Artificers,* 1820, pdf of a 2002 redaction

21   Robison, *Proofs of a Conspiracy,* London. edit., 1797, p. 20 – as cited in Mackey's *Symbolism of Freemasonry,* 1882

The City Dionysia at Athens

A central theme in the collective Masonic commentary on the Dionysian Artificers is that they were an organized body of builders and architects who have their origin in the Mystery cult of Dionysus (Greek: Διόνυσος), the god of the grape harvest, wine-making, fertility and *ekstasis*. The Dionysian Mysteries, which also formed the basis of the later Roman *Bacchanalia* – annual festivals dedicated to Bacchus, who was the Roman syncretization of the Greek Dionysus – were ecstatic rites utilizing intoxicants such as wine and/or mead. The rites themselves were essentially agrotheological, or vinicultural, in that the process of wine-making was ritually allegorized in a chthonic, death-and-resurrection initiatory cycle, representing the annual circuit of the agricultural cycle. These Mysteries, which have been speculated to be of either Thracian, Anatolian or even Minoan origin[22], were diffused throughout the ancient world with centers in Greece, Rome, Syria, Asia Minor and elsewhere. Mackey had described the Dionysian *mystes* as both a speculative and operative society – speculative in their esoteric theology and initiatory rites, and operative in their architectural labors[23] – and also argues for their participation in the building of K∴S∴T∴ due to the cult's presence in Asia Minor, specifically at Tyre, and the consequent procurement of skilled workmen from the region.

22 Rostovtzeff, *Rome* (Duff, trans.), Oxford University Press, 1960, pp. 93-94
23 Mackey, *The Symbolism of Freemasonry*, Clark & Maynard, 1869, p. 47

According to Abrahamic scripture[24], the ancient Phoenician city of Tyre (founded 2750 BCE, according to Herodotus), now in modern-day Lebanon, was the home of King Hiram I (regnal years 980-947 BC) and a particular worker in brass also called Hiram (or *Huram Abi*; Hebrew: ם אבי ריח), who was said to be a widow's son from the Tribe of Naphtali. Hiram's tribal affiliation is significant in that the zodiacal sign of Virgo is attributed to the Tribe of Naphtali and, furthermore, that Virgo is associated with Isis, the sister-wife of Osiris and mother of Horus. Horus, upon the death of his father Osiris, came to be known by the epithet "the widow's son".[25] In his *Morals and Dogma of the Ancient Accepted Scottish Rite*, Albert Pike, in reference to the Knight of the Brazen Serpent (25° of the Scottish Rite system), said that "Virgo, the domicile of Mercury, is borne on the flag of *Naphtali*, whose eloquence and agility Jacob magnifies, both of which are attributes of the Courier of the Gods". The attribution of Virgo to Naphtali is further established in Mathers' *Twelve Signs and Twelve Tribes*. Hiram was further described as "a man filled with wisdom and understanding"[26]; a passage which is qabalistically notable, as it is a pairing of *Chokmah* (Hebrew: חכמה; meaning "Wisdom") and *Binah* (Hebrew: בינה; meaning "Understanding"), which are the supernal *sephiroth* atop the qabalistic pillars of Mercy and Severity, respectively. As each *sephirah*, or "emanation", is said to be *filled* by its predecessor and to overflow into its successor on the cosmogonical *Etz Chaim* (Hebrew: עץ חיים; meaning "Tree of Life"), it is significant that *Kether* (Hebrew: כתר), the "Crown" and topmost *sephirah*, overflows into *Chokmah* which itself overflows into *Binah* (see Appendix B). This Tyrian craftsman, Huram Abi, is presumed to be none other than Hiram Abiff, the protagonist in an extra-scriptural Masonic narrative encountered in the third, or Master Mason degree. Mackey further advances an interesting theory that the Hiramic Legend – Freemasonry's central allegory – is a reworking of the Dionysian mythological cycle by those Jewish workmen who may have wanted to cleanse the rite of its unsavory, paganistic character. [27] Mackey's hypothesis necessarily presupposes that this Hiramic recasting of the Dionysian initiatory cycle – a sort of Masonic syncretism – was secretly passed through both operative and speculative Lodges, over nearly three millennia in a relatively intact form, and is the origin of the ritual as currently practiced today. One glaring issue with

---

24   *The Holy Bible*, KJV, 1 Kings 5

25   Petrie, "The Ceremony of Anba Tarabo", *Ancient Egypt*, Macmillan, 1921, p. 113

26   *The Holy Bible*, KJV, 1 Kings 7:13-14

27   Mackey, *The Symbolism of Freemasonry*, Clark & Maynard, 1869, pp. 56-57

this hypothesis is the documented practice of Noachite Masonry[28], which pre-dates the Hiramic Legend in Masonic ritual. Also, there is no mention of the Legend in Anderson's *Constitutions* of 1723 – the first document of Masonic history, charges and regulations written after the formation of the Grand Lodge of England in 1717. This document contains a history of Freemasonry which reaches as far back as antediluvian times, including the stories of Noah and Lamech, both of whom were subjects in pre-Hiramic Masonic ritual. The Hiramic legend, and its use in the third degree, is explicitly mentioned by the time of the publication of the *Constitutions* of 1738. Ergo, sometime within the fifteen-year interim between the *Constitutions* of 1723 and those of 1738, we encounter the first appearance of the Hiramic Legend being used in the ritual of some Lodges.[29]

Da Costa and Mackey seem to be in agreement that, in addition to practicing the operative crafts of stonemasonry and architecture, the Dionysian Artificers superimposed the initiatory, mystical and esoteric elements of the Mysteries onto the framework of the physical craft, thereby synthesizing a very early form of speculative Masonry. Da Costa similarly attributes practices associated with speculative Masonry to the artificers:

> [...] *they extended their moral views, in conjunction with the art of building, to many useful purposes, and to the practice of acts of benevolence* [...] *It is essential to observe, that these societies; had significant words to distinguish their members; and for the same purpose they used emblems taken from the art of building.*[30]

As was the case with nearly all of the Mystery traditions of the ancient world, the Dionysian Artificers and their associated cult disappeared into oblivion with the advent and spread of Christianity throughout the Mediterranean, Near-East and North Africa. In fact, the decline of Greco-Roman polytheism, in general, was inversely proportionate to the rise of Christianity, as persecution from the newly-instituted state church of the Roman Empire gained power and influence after the First Council of Nicaea in 325 CE. That there was no longer any room in Christendom for divergent beliefs meant that adherents to those alternative systems which weren't entirely extinguished were forced to operate clandestinely. It is at this time that we find clues pointing to the possible survival of some of the elements associated with the Mysteries in the burgeoning *collegia*, in

---

28   *Graham Manuscript*, 1726

29   Pritchard, *Masonry Dissected*, 1730

30   Da Costa, *The History of the Dionysian Artificers*, 1820, pdf of 2002 redaction

which they may have found refuge and insulation from persecution.

The first historically documented occurrence of trade organization among stonemasons is found in the *collegia* (plural form of *collegium*) of the ancient world. These organizations are believed to have had their origins in the Hellenistic Period (commencing in 323 BCE with the death of Alexander the Great and terminating in 31 BCE with the rise of the Roman Empire) of the Mediterranean, North Africa and the Near East. Though collegiate predecessors had existed in many other countries – such as the Greek *thiassoi*, their immediate antecedent – *collegia* became a regular societal fixture in the Roman Empire. Various guilds, clubs and societies were established as *collegia*, a central feature of which was a legal presence, thus allowing them to own property and have collective representation. A *collegium* could be formed by as little as three citizens and, at this smaller level, often served as a means of ensuring a decent sepulcher for its members. A *collegium* met in a hall or meeting place called a *schola*, or *curia*. Dues were collected and stored in a chest called an *arca*. Largely, membership was transferred hereditarily and transfer from one *collegium* to another was forbidden. From their inception in the first century BCE until their dissolution in the fifth century CE, the *collegia* of the Roman Empire had intermittently fallen in and out of favor, depending on their political influence; they were banned in 56 BCE by Julius Caesar but were championed by the emperor and Stoic philosopher, Marcus Aurelius, for instance. Under Nero's rule, and going forward, the *collegia* were strictly regulated and extorted for their power and influence in the trades, politics and the military – the three great supports of the Empire. Masonry's connection to the Roman *collegia* is best made evident through the lineage of the *Collegia Fabrorum*, or builder's guilds.

Frieze from the College of the Fabri Tignarii, Rome

Between about 406 and 455 CE, the Roman Empire was beset by invading barbarian hordes, such as the Huns, Visigoths and Vandals, which ultimately caused the Western Empire to disintegrate. In the ensuing chaos, many *collegia* were dismantled, with the exception of a few in Rome and Constantinople, which maintained monopolistic control over their areas of specialization. Largely thanks to the scholarship of a woman named Lucy Baxter, writing under the name Leader Scott, we owe the compelling theory of the Comacine Masters being the last vestige of collegiate culture surviving into the medieval period which formed after the ebb of the barbarian invasions.[31] According to her theory, an unknown *collegium* of builders and architects escaped the ravages of the barbarian invasions by cloistering themselves in Northern Italy's Lombard kingdom near Lake Como, hence the moniker *Magistri Comacini*, or Comacine Masters. This name appears in print for the first time in King Rotharis' (regnal years 636-652 CE) laws numbered CLXIII and CXLV, wherein the Comacines "[...] figure as Master Masons with full and unlimited powers to make contracts and subcontracts for building works; to have their collegantes or 'colleagues' partners, members of the guild or fraternity, call them what you will - and lastly, their serfs (*servi*) or workmen and labourers."[32] Whether or not the *Comacini* are to be considered an irrefutable link between the *collegia* and the medieval craft guilds – and, thereby, contributors to the stream of a proto-Masonic lineage, eventually culminating in Freemasonry proper – is subject to debate and may forever remain so. Their legend is certainly worthy of our consideration and is well-represented in Masonic histories.[33, 34]

> *Like one ship crossing a stormy sea into which all its sister vessels had sunk, the organization of the Comacine masters preserved the ark of civilization until such time as the hurricane cleared from Europe and the seething barbarian tribes themselves became ready for peace and communal life. If there is any unbroken continuity in the history of architecture, if builder guilds of a more modern period can trace any of their arts, traditions and customs back to ancient times, it is through the Comacines that the chain was kept unbroken in the Dark Ages.*[35]

31 Scott, *The Cathedral Builders: The Story of a Great Masonic Guild*, Sampson Low, Marsten & Co., 1899

32 Rivoira & Rushforth, *Lombardic Architecture*, Nabu Press, 1923

33 Mackey, *An Encyclopedia of Freemasonry and its Kindred Sciences*, Everts & Co., 1884, p. 163

34 Newton, *The Builders*, Torch Press, 1914, p. 86

35 Haywood, "Freemasonry and the Comacine Masters", *The Builder Magazine*, Vol. 9, No. 10, 1923

As Europe began to stabilize after the barbarian invasions and the fall of the Roman Empire, we begin to observe the formation of craft guilds. These organizations – which, like the *collegia*, offered their members mutual support, fellowship, communal banking, burial funds, etc. – were differentiated by their trade or specialization. Some of the crafts organized into guilds were those of the carpenters, painters, tanners, cobblers, apothecaries, candle makers and, of course, the stonemasons. While essentially secular in nature, these guilds were typically allied with the church and were often assigned a certain biblical narrative – such as the Creation, the Fall of Man, the Fall of Lucifer, the Raising of Lazarus or the Last Judgement – to portray in Church-sanctioned mystery plays. Often, the subject matter was chosen in keeping with the guild's craft, as was the case with the Feeding of the Five-Thousand (assigned to the baker's guild) and the Building of Noah's Ark (assigned to the carpenter's guild).[36] These dramatizations, apart from being a major contributing influence on later developments in theater and the cinema in general, could comfortably be presumed to be the direct antecedent to the extra-scriptural dramas performed in Freemasonry and its appendant bodies, as the stonemason-specific narratives performed by the Fraternity are centered upon those pertaining to the building of K∴S∴T∴.

The Cathedral Builders, 15ᵗʰ Century Miniature

36   Gassner & Quinn, *The Reader's Encyclopedia of World Drama* (England: middle ages), London: Methuen, 1969, pp. 203-204

The craft guilds were typically supervised by wardens, whose object it was to maintain standardization. These officers were elected annually and met in assemblies one to four times *per annum*. These assemblies were filled out by oath-bound members of the guild. As mentioned above, it is within the medieval craft guilds that we begin to see the hierarchical stratification of the workmen into the following classes (in ascending order): apprentices, journeymen (or, fellow crafts), and masters. Though this system can be traced back to 1260 CE, it was in 1563 CE that the duration of apprenticeship was formally fixed at seven years[37], a duration that is still imposed to this day in some Masonic Jurisdictions, such as Australia. An apprentice was to be compliant, faithful and of sound body. Upon his graduation to journeyman, or "fellow of the craft", the apprentice was entitled to the privileges afforded that class and considered an equal – *on the level*, as it were. The passage from apprentice to journeyman was predicated on the completion of the workman's masterpiece and/or examination by the wardens. Journeymen were free to travel and receive wages; they generally worked under various masters until, in some cases, they were able to open a shop of their own, take on apprentices and hire journeymen. It was thereby that the fellow craft attained the title of master. In time, civil problems arose, particularly those between the greater guilds and the lesser artisanal guilds; issues also emerged regarding a proto-unionization which may have negatively affected quality and innovation in the crafts. Political criticism was levelled at the guilds, arguing that they hindered free trade and advancing capitalism until, in England in 1835 CE, the privileges enjoyed by the craft guilds were permanently abolished by Parliament. Further industrialization forced artisans to find employment in the ever-growing manufacturing industries.

It was during the reign of the guild system that we begin to see the first legitimately documented cases of admission of speculative members in the operative craft of Masonry – though there are a few earlier accounts of the admission of an accepted, or speculative masons, one of which may be found in the Cooke Manuscript dating from 1450 CE – making it the second-oldest of the Old Charges, next to the *Halliwell Manuscript* (aka, the *Regius Poem*, the composition of which has been dated sometime between 1390[38] and 1425 CE[39] at Shropshire, England) – wherein it is stated that Prince Edwin, who has alternately been said to be King Athelstan's

---

37   Haywood, "Freemasonry and the Guild System", *The Builder Magazine*, Vol. 9, No. 11, 1923

38   Halliwell

39   Prescott, *The Old Charges Revisited*, from Transactions of the Lodge of Research No. 2429 (Leicester), 2006, Pietre-Stones Masonic Papers

(regnal years, 925-939 CE) son or brother and was not an operative Mason, was said to have become a Mason himself:

> *And after that was a worthy kynge in Englond, that was callyd Athelstone, and his yongest son lovyd well the seiens of Gemetry, and he wyst well that hand craft had the praetyke of the seiens of Gemetry so well as masons; wherefore he drew him to eonsell and lernyd [the] practyke of that scions to his speculatyf. For of speculatyfe he was a master, and he lovyd well masonry and masons. And he bicome a mason hymselfe.[40]*

Judging by the regnal years of his father (or brother, in some accounts), King Athelstan, one could comfortably confine Prince Edwin's Masonic career to the 10th century CE – a very early date for accepted Masonry, indeed. Certainly, laymen who were patrons of the craft were accepted into the fraternity as honorary Masons, as it were; and these most likely for political reasons, coming from a royal bloodline or for their proficiency in the speculative aspects of the Craft, such as displaying aptitude in geometry, astronomy, or some other member of the seven liberal arts and sciences. What trade secrets or Mysteries might be conveyed to one who had neither formally apprenticed nor produced a master's piece is subject to conjecture. The operative guilds were reaching their nadir, however, and the ever-increasing number of accepted Masons were poised to, in time, inherit full custodianship of the ancient Craft.

Due largely to the Protestant Reformation, particularly in England, the guild system began to decline sharply throughout the first half of the 15th century, being finally being suppressed by Henry VIII (regnal years, 1509-1547 CE). Cathedral building was halted, as these edifices were associated with the Papacy and therefore regarded as anathema by the Puritans. Job prospects for operative masons, then working independently, were bleak and many sought employment in private palatial construction for the affluent gentry and aristocracy. During this socially and politically tumultuous period, we begin to see the first documented instances of accepted Masonry in the form of Lodge records reflecting speculative attendance among the Brethren. Lyon's *History of the Lodge of Edinburgh* mentions minutes from that Lodge from 1600 CE naming one John Boswell, Laird of Auchinleck as a member. Other speculative Masons in Scotland, particularly Edinburgh and Kilwinning Lodges, are named at this time,

---

40   Matthew Cooke Manuscript, lines 611-626, 1450 CE, according to Hughan

among them: William Schaw (1598 CE), Lord Alexander (1634 CE), his brother Sir Anthony Alexander (1634 CE), and Sir Alexander Strachan of Thornton (1634 CE) – these men also appearing to be relatively active in Lodge affairs.[41] A short time later, in England, we encounter the more popular examples of speculative admission, such as that of Robert Moray (raised at Newcastle, 1641 CE) and Elias Ashmole (raised at Warrington, 1646 CE).

Elias Ashmole by William Faithorne, 1656

In many ways, Ashmole epitomizes the eventual transition to the almost purely speculative Craft we know today, in that his extra-Masonic pursuits mirror many of those associated with Masonic-related esoterica. Elias Ashmole (1617-1692 CE) was a prominent English antiquary,

41   Haywood, "How Operative Masonry Changed to Speculative Masonry", *The Builder Magazine*, Vol. 9, No. 11, 1923

polymath, alchemical commentator, astrologer and a "zealous Rosicrucian".[42] He was a founding fellow of the Royal Society (elected in 1661 CE), which was granted a royal charter from King Charles II in 1660 CE; the Society was the premier intellectual order in England at the time, with an emphasis on Baconian natural philosophy. In 1650 CE, four years after becoming a Freemason, Ashmole, under the anagrammatic pseudonym "James Hasolle", published *Fasciculus Chemicus* – an English translation of two alchemical codices, one of which was composed by Arthur Dee, the son of John Dee, the famed Elizabethan occult philosopher. Two years later, he then went on to publish *Theatrum Chemicum Britannicum*, a compendium of annotated metaphysical poems. The object of his alchemical work, which was studied by the natural philosopher Isaac Newton, was to form a theoretical synthesis of the Galenic and Paracelsian traditions. In 1853 CE, Ashmole was given an edition of *The True Matter of the Philosopher's Stone*, bequeathed him by his mentor and "spiritual father", alchemist, astrologer and Rosicrucian William Backhouse, though it is thought that Ashmole's interests in alchemy were purely speculative, as were his interests in Masonry.[43]

Both alchemy and Rosicrucianism may be counted among the many tributaries to what would become speculative Freemasonry. Considering that alchemy may be divided into operative (practical) and speculative (theoretical) denominations – a distinction that is also made evident in Freemasonry – one may understand how these two systems would be synergistic, particularly as it pertains to their common methods of symbolizing and allegorizing their work. Alchemy and Freemasonry are both rife with elaborate symbol sets and either allegorical prose or dramatizations representing certain craft-specific processes. Furthermore, as we have shown, the work of both of these traditions share a belief in a core Hermetic principle centered on the sympathies between the microcosm and the macrocosm, in that an operation performed in a particular domain may have a causal effect in another corresponding domain – also a central feature of sympathetic magic. Though the case had been left to go cold for most of the last century, the dynamic between alchemy and Freemasonry has again been receiving much needed attention in Masonic thought and literature of the 21st century.[44] There is tremendous value for the Freemason of today in developing this critical perspective.

---

42   De Quincey, "Historico-Critical Inquiry into the Origin of the Rosicrucians and the Freemasons", *Confessions of an English Opium-eater*, London: Walter Scott, 1886, p. 207

43   Beresiner, "Elias Ashmole: Masonic Icon", *Masonic Quarterly*, UGLE, 2004

44   See: Newman, *Alchemically Stoned: The Psychedelic Secret of Freemasonry*, The Laudable Pursuit, 2017 and Hogan, *Alchemical Keys to Masonic Ritual*, Lulu Press, 2007

If in no other form than nominally, Rosicrucianism has also been perpetuated in speculative Freemasonry and its appendant bodies, such as the Rose-Croix degrees of the Ancient and Accepted Scottish Rite and in the *Societas Rosicruciana*, or the Masonic Rosicrucian Society; the latter of whose grades are patterned on those of the *Orden der Gold und Rosenkreuzer* ("Order of the Golden and Rosy Cross"). Founded by Samuel Richter in 1710 CE and reconstituted in the mid-18th century by Hermann Fictuld (1700-1777 CE), the *Orden der Gold und Rosenkreuzer* was a German Rosicrucian society peopled exclusively by Freemasons and alchemists. The qabalistically-sequenced grade structure of the Order would be adopted by many Rosicrucian and Hermetic orders to follow, including the Masonic *Societas Rosicruciana* and, through them, to the Hermetic Order of the Golden Dawn. Arguments have been made to the effect of attributing the origin of speculative Freemasonry as issuing from the milieu of European Rosicrucianism.[45] One thing is clear: other than perhaps the work of the Florentine Neoplatonists of the Renaissance, the Rosicrucian *furore* of the early 17th century was the most developed synthesis of esoteric Christianity, Hermeticism, alchemy, astrology, sympathetic magic and qabalistic thought in the early-modern era – and, perhaps not coincidentally, all of these subjects have since been considered as to their relationship to the speculative Craft. This leaves us, in the absence of concrete evidence one way or another, to consider three possibilities: 1. interest in the Hermetic Arts was infused into speculative Freemasonry due to deliberate Rosicrucian influence, which would have likely been due to their finding the Masonic system a suitably inconspicuous host for their aims and doctrines; 2. interest in these subjects spontaneously generated in Freemasonry due to its conflation with other traditions, such as Rosicrucianism, Theosophy and Templarism; or 3. the occult sciences have, since their inception, been in the keeping of Freemasonry – under the category of the "Hidden Mysteries" (which the Entered Apprentice is obligated to "forever conceal and never reveal"), or speculative aspects of the Craft – and, conversely, found their temporary outward expression in the form of Rosicrucianism.

Thus we have traced the lineages of both operative and speculative Masonry from their most primitive origins, disappearing into the mists of prehistory, through their various synergistic periods which have occurred over the course of several millennia, and on through the final transition into the edifice we have inherited in our time; an edifice which represents a

---

45   De Quincey, "Historico-Critical Inquiry into the Origin of the Rosicrucians and the Freemasons", *Confessions of an English Opium-eater*, London: Walter Scott, 1886

synthesis of the vernacular, tools and hierarchical structure of the operative Craft, the retention of the allegorical narrative and personages surrounding the building of K∴S∴T∴ and its extra-scriptural Mystery play (i.e., the Hiramic Legend), along with the fibers of those arcane systems – such as Hermeticism, Neoplatonism, astrology, alchemy, Qabalah, Rosicrucianism, etc. – which have been woven into the greater fabric of the speculative Fraternity's philosophical and theoretical heritage.

CHAPTER II

∴

THE BRAZEN PILLARS

Brother, the first thing that particularly attracts our attention are two large brazen pillars, one on the right and one on the left hand. The name of the one on the left hand is Boaz, and signifies strength; the name of the one on the right is Jachin, and denotes establishment; they, collectively, denote establishment and strength, and allude to a passage in Scripture: "In strength shall this house be established." These are representations of the two pillars erected at the outer porch of King Solomon's Temple. [...] These chapiters were ornamented with a representation of net–work, lily-work, and pomegranates, and are said to denote Unity, Peace, and Plenty [...] These chapiters have on the top of each a globe, or ball; these globes are two artificial spherical bodies; on the convex surfaces of which are represented the countries, seas, and various parts of the earth, the face of the heavens, the planetary revolutions [...] The principal use of these globes, besides serving as maps, to distinguish the outward parts of the earth, and the situation of the fixed stars, is to illustrate and explain the phenomena arising from the annual revolution and the diurnal rotation of the earth around its own axis. They are the noblest instruments for improving the mind, and giving it the most distinct idea of any problem or proposition, as well as enabling it to solve the same. Contemplating these bodies, we are inspired with a due reverence for the Deity and his works and are induced to encourage the studies of astronomy, geography, navigation, and the arts dependent on them, by which society has been so much benefited. The composition of these pillars is molten or cast brass [...] They were cast hollow the better to withstand inundation and conflagrations, and are said to have contained the archives of Masonry.[1]

---

[1] *Duncan's Masonic Ritual and Monitor* (1866), New York: Crown Publishers, 1986, pp. 73-74

In the lecture pertaining to the Fellow Craft degree (see Appendix D), the newly-obligated Fellow Craft is conducted to a site representing the porch of K∴S∴T∴. Thereupon, the first objects to which his attention is drawn are the Brazen Pillars, *Jachin* (Hebrew: יָכִין) and *Boaz* (Hebrew: בֹּעַז), which are said to be representations of those that stood on the porch, flanking the entrance to the Temple. The word *Jachin* is said to denote establishment, and *Boaz* signifying strength. Taken together, they may be interpreted as "In strength shall this house be established." During the lecture presentation, it is further explained that Jachin is on the right and in the south, and that Boaz is on the left and in the north – though this is in opposition to the biblical record as to how the pillars stood on the porch of K∴S∴T∴. The most conclusive evidence for an eastern orientation of K∴S∴T∴ may be found in Ezekiel:

> *And he brought me into the inner court of the LORD's house, and, behold, at the door of the temple of the LORD, between the porch and the altar, were about five and twenty men, with their backs toward the temple of the LORD, and their faces toward the east; and they worshipped the sun toward the east.*[2]

The porch of the Temple was on the eastern side of the edifice while the *Sanctum Sanctorum* lay in the west. This orientation would have allowed the rising Sun to penetrate the Temple through the east gate and illuminate the *Sanctum Sanctorum*, or Holy of Holies. In other words, one would have been facing west and had their back to the rising Sun if one were knocking on the door of the Temple at dawn. Ergo, the pillar Jachin, which is said to have stood on the right, would have been on the north side of the door, and Boaz, on the left, would have stood on the south side. That the orientation of a Masonic Temple is diametrically opposed to that of K∴S∴T∴ poses an interesting problem, worthy of our contemplation. We know that the Masonic Temple is a place where men develop and apply moral and ethical principles that they may become more perfected by virtue of their own good works – thus fostering humanistic endeavors – and is thereby a Temple of Man. We know also that K∴S∴T∴ was the House of God, wherein man's fate is strictly governed by the Will of YHVH (Hebrew: יהוה, the *Tetragrammaton*). This discrepancy may prompt one to wonder whether the opposition in orientation was indeed deliberate and, if so, was it possibly meant to serve as a partially concealed commentary on

2   *The Holy Bible*, KJV, Ezekiel 8:16

man's station vis-à-vis Deity?

The idea that man is instrumental in, and ultimately responsible for, his own personal salvation is considered heretical by most denominations of Christianity. This is an aspect of the greater Gnostic heresy. The early Gnostic sects believed that man could attain salvation and union with God through the direct experience of *gnosis* (Greek: γνῶσις – a knowledge of the Divine spark in man). This is in direct opposition to the central Christian tenet that salvation is only possible through faith and the intercession of Christ. Similarly, in the Hermetic and Neoplatonic traditions, it is believed that man may attain *henosis* (Greek: ἕνωσις – a mystical oneness with Reality) through the practice of *theurgy* (Greek: θεουργία – a magical practice involving ritualism and invocations designed to secure the favorable intervention of preternatural, cosmic, angelic or divine entities). There are those who interpret Freemasonry's emphasis on personal development as fundamentally being a survival and extension of Gnostic, Hermetic and Neoplatonic philosophies. A notable example of this principle in Masonic ritual – one so plain that it could easily escape notice – may be found in the Entered Apprentice degree, wherein the recently-obligated apprentice is told that, "Accepted Masons [...] are taught to make use of [the Common Gavel] for the more noble and glorious purpose of divesting our minds and consciences of all the vices and superfluities of life, thereby fitting us, as living stones, for that spiritual building, that house not made with hands, eternal in the heavens."[3] The implication is that the Freemason may, by the application of the Working Tools of the Craft, prepare himself for his ascent into Heaven, engendering his own salvation by the application of his will and intellect – *even in the absence of divine intercession.* Another example of this may be found in the Mason's professed desire for Light. Masonic Light is not differentiated as being either intellectual or spiritual in nature, though both are implied. However, as is the case with many of the symbols we encounter in Freemasonry, the individual is left to make sense of this enigma for himself, as he should.

Moving on in the Fellow Craft lecture, we are informed of the dimensions of the Brazen Pillars that "[t]hey are said to have been in height thirty-five (35) cubits, twelve in circumference, and four in diameter; they are said to have been adorned with two large chapiters of five cubits each, making their entire height forty (40) cubits."[4] Taking a closer look at the possible symbolic import of these dimensions, we may first consider their individual numerological significance. The number thirty-five is the septe-

---

3   *Duncan's Masonic Ritual and Monitor* (1866), New York: Crown Publishers, 1986, p. 46
4   Ibid., p. 73

nary quintupled (7 x 5 = 35) and was called "the eternal residence of the soul" by German philosopher and Christian mystic Jakob Böehme (1575-1624 CE).[5] Taken separately, the numbers three and five represent the Trinity (symbolized by the triangle) and man, the Pythagorean/Vitruvian microcosm (symbolized by the pentagram). Thereby, the number may be interpreted as a commentary on man's relationship to the threefold manifestation of God. In Hebrew *gematria*, thirty-five is one of the scriptural enumerations of *Hod* (Hebrew: הוד; meaning "Glory" or "Splendor"; as it is spelled in Psalms 8:1). Qabalistically, *Hod* is the eighth (3 + 5 = 8) *sephirah* on the *Etz Chaim*, representing the base of the Pillar of Severity, and corresponds to all things mercurial and/or Hermetic (see Appendix B). The mention of "twelve in circumference" immediately brings the to mind the twelve zodiacal signs, spanning 30° each, and dividing the 360° circle of the ecliptic – thereby, being twelve in circumference. Twelve is also the number of the "simple letters" of the Hebrew alphabet (*heh, vau, cheth, zayin, teth, yod, lamed, nun, samech, ayin, tzaddi* and *qoph*), which qabalistically correspond to the twelve zodiacal constellations, beginning with Aries (see Appendix A). The number twelve may also be said to represent the approximate number of synodic lunar months (each being 29.53 days) per year and the twelve years of a completed Jupiterian return.[6] Duodecuple symbolism is pervasive in scripture, encompassing the twelve Tribes of Israel, the twelve stones in Aaron's breastplate (Hebrew: וְהַתֻּמִּים הָאוּרִים, the *Urim* and *Thummim*), the twelve loaves of shew-bread, the twelve apostles, and many other appearances – in total, the number twelve occurs 189 times in the Bible, making it one of scripture's most ubiquitous integers. In classical mythology, we encounter the number twelve in the Olympic Pantheon and in the Labors of Hercules, the latter of which may be interpreted as being allegorical of the Sun's apparent passage through the signs of the zodiac in one annual circuit. Taken separately, the numbers one and two may be said to represent the juxtaposition of unity (1, the *monad*) and duality (2, the *dyad*). The pillars were said to have been "four [cubits] in diameter"; we need but enumerate a few symbolic quartets to illustrate our point: the classical elements (fire, air, earth and water), the Four Living Creatures (bull, lion, eagle and man – which comprise the fixed quadriplicity of the zodiac and also the component parts of Babylonian sphinxes – the *Lamassu* who guarded the portals), the cardinal directions, the four lunar phases, etc. In Hebrew gematria, the number four is the value of the letter

---

5 "Properties of the Number 35", *Riding the Beast*, 1998, retrieved at: ridingthebeast. com

6 NASA, "Solar System Exploration", *Jupiter*, 2019, retrieved at: solarsystem.nasa.gov

daleth (Hebrew: ד), meaning "door", thereby qabalistically conflating the above-mentioned symbolic quartets with a liminal passage, as if to imply that *through a trial of the elements and the stellar Guardians, one may pass onward through the portal, initiated.* If the reference "two large chapiters of five cubits each" is considered as representing a totality of ten (2 × 5 = 10), we may consider the ten *sephiroth* which comprise the *Etz Chaim*, and are, like K∴S∴T∴, flanked by two pillars. Lastly, we learn that these pillars are forty cubits in height, in their entirety. In many ancient traditions, the number forty is used figuratively as a non-numerical signifier – a substitute for any large, approximate number. This could mean that the pillars were simply "very high". Biblically, transitionary periods of forty days and nights, or forty years, are used to mark a liminal passage from one epoch to another.[7] Forty is also the ordinal value of *Netzach* (Hebrew: נצח; meaning "Victory") using the *Mispar Siduri* method of gematria, which assigns the numbers one through twenty-two to the Hebrew alphabet. *Netzach* is the seventh *sephirah*, occupying the symmetrically opposite position on the *Etz Chaim* as the aforementioned *Hod*, thereby representing the base of the Pillar of Mercy – thus both pillars are represented in the numerical symbolism of their dimensions. This is by no means an exhaustive analysis of the wealth of numerological symbolism in the dimensions of the Brazen Pillars, but we have addressed enough to illustrate the immense value in the application of a qabalistic and gematriac hermeneutic, which we will be applying to the pillars in further detail below.

Glass bowl fragment depicting the Pillars Jachin and Boaz, ca. 3rd century CE

---

7   Coogan, *A Brief Introduction to the Old Testament: The Hebrew Bible in Its Context*, Oxford, 2008, p. 116

When cross-referencing the Masonic and Biblical accounts of these pillars, however, we encounter a discrepancy as to their height. The dimensions of these pillars are dealt with in considerable detail in 1 Kings:

And king Solomon sent and fetched Hiram out of Tyre. He was a widow's son of the tribe of Naphtali, and his father was a man of Tyre, a worker in brass: and he was filled with wisdom, and understanding, and cunning to work all works in brass. And he came to king Solomon, and wrought all his work. For he cast two pillars of brass, of eighteen cubits high apiece: and a line of twelve cubits did compass either of them about. And he made two chapiters of molten brass, to set upon the tops of the pillars: the height of the one chapiter was five cubits, and the height of the other chapiter was five cubits: And nets of checker work, and wreaths of chain work, for the chapiters which were upon the top of the pillars; seven for the one chapiter, and seven for the other chapiter. And he made the pillars, and two rows round about upon the one network, to cover the chapiters that were upon the top, with pomegranates: and so did he for the other chapiter. And the chapiters that were upon the top of the pillars were of lily work in the porch, four cubits. And the chapiters upon the two pillars had pomegranates also above, over against the belly which was by the network: and the pomegranates were two hundred in rows round about upon the other chapiter. And he set up the pillars in the porch of the temple: and he set up the right pillar, and called the name thereof Jachin: and he set up the left pillar, and called the name thereof Boaz. And upon the top of the pillars was lily work: so was the work of the pillars finished [...] The two pillars, and the two bowls of the chapiters that were on the top of the two pillars; and the two networks, to cover the two bowls of the chapiters which were upon the top of the pillars; And four hundred pomegranates for the two networks, even two rows of pomegranates for one network, to cover the two bowls of the chapiters that were upon the pillars.[8]

---

8   *The Holy Bible*, KJV, 1 Kings 7:13–22, 41–42

And, again, in Jeremiah:

Each pillar was eighteen cubits high and twelve cubits in cir-
cumference; each was four fingers thick, and hollow. The bronze
capital on top of one pillar was five cubits high and
was decorated with a network and pomegranates of bronze all
around. The other pillar, with its pomegranates, was similar.[9]

We are told in the lecture that the chapters of the pillars were adorned with network, lilywork, and pomegranates. Taking each of these symbols in their turn, we first note that the word *network* may be variously understood as "a fabric or structure of cords or wires that cross at regular intervals and are knotted or secured at the crossings [...], a system of lines or channels [... or as] an interconnected or interrelated chain, group, or system."[10] Taken literally, the first definition seems to fit most snugly, as this is generally how the network is depicted in the pillar's physical construction. It is the third definition, however, which is most relevant to the network's symbolic application in Masonic ritual, for it is said that the network denotes unity. Thus, by this network of unity, all Freemasons are connected through their shared initiatory experiences and the binding ties of their Obligations.

Exoterically, the lilywork is said to denote purity and peace, due to its whiteness and the retired places in which it grows. Looking a little further into the symbolism of the lily (genus: *lilium*), we find that this flower has had a long-standing position in the greater symbolism of classical mythology. Carvings, frescoes and friezes have been found on the Greek island of Crete, dating as far back as 1580 BCE, when the island was home to the Minoan civilization. The lily, whose name is derived from the Greek *leiron*, was believed by the ancients to have had its very origin among the Olympian pantheon. Zeus was said to have once brought Hercules, the product of one of the god's many extramarital trysts, to suckle at his wife, Hera's breast. Knowing of Hercules' illegitimacy, Hera refused to nurse the child. Waiting until she was fast asleep, Zeus introduced the baby Hercules to his wife's breast. Angrily, Hera awoke, pushing her husband and the infant away, but not before a few drops of her milk fell to the earth – and it was upon this site that the first lilies were said to have sprouted.[11] The

9   *The Holy Bible* KJV, Jeremiah 52:21–22
10   Entry: "Network"; *Webster's Collegiate Dictionary*, retrieved at: merriam-webster.com
11   Diodorus Siculus, *Library of History*, Book IV, 9

lily is also a prominent funerary flower, owing to the state of peace and innocence to which the deceased has returned.

The pomegranate (genus-species: *punica granatum*), which is said to denote plenty in the Fellow Craft lecture, has a very developed history in the symbolism of ancient near-east religion and myth. The fruit itself is thought to have first been cultivated in Iran and Afghanistan[12], where it was revered by the ancient Zoroastrians as a holy symbol, representing the immortality of the soul and the perfection of nature. In Iranian mythology, the pomegranate is associated with Esfandiyar, who became invincible after eating the fruit.[13] In Greek mythology, the pomegranate was thought to have risen from the spilled blood of Adonis.[14] The pomegranate's most notable appearance is in a mythological narrative known as the Rape of Persephone.[15] Persephone (Greek: Περσεφόνη), also called the *Kore* (Greek: Κόρη; meaning the "maiden"), was the daughter of Zeus and Demeter (Greek: Δημήτηρ), the goddess of the grain, agriculture and the harvest. In the myth of her abduction by Hades (Greek: Ἅιδης), the god of the underworld, Persephone was said to be gathering flowers with the Oceanids when Hades suddenly burst through the earth and carried her off to the underworld. Her mother, Demeter, was so distraught that she neglected the earth, ceasing the cycles of agriculture. The starving denizens of the ancient world beseeched Zeus to intervene. Hades complied to Zeus' command to produce Persephone but not before tricking her into eating the food of the underworld – pomegranate seeds. Having eaten the pomegranate seeds, Persephone was obliged to remain in the underworld for one-third (in later tellings, six months) of the year, during which Demeter, despondent, neglected her duties to the earth; these are the winter months, when the agricultural cycle ceases for a time. "The Rape of Persephone", by which the myth is traditionally known, is briefly mentioned in Hesiod's *Theogony*, and in further detail in the anonymous *Homeric Hymn to Demeter*, in which Persephone is reunited with Demeter near Eleusis, whereupon Demeter promised to establish her Mysteries.

---

12   Morton, "Fruits of Warm Climates", Entry: "Pomegranate (Punica Granatum)", *Purdue New Crops Profile*, 1987, pp. 352-355

13   Sina, "The Legend of Fesenjān", *Medium*, 2014, retrieved at: medium.com

14   Graves, *The Greek Myths*, Penguin Books, 1992, p. 95

15   Ovid, *Metamorphoses*, Book V, 462

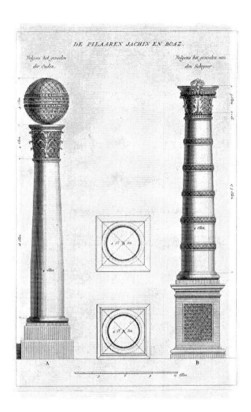

The pillars Jachin and Boaz, Calmet ca. 1725

Though their presence is structurally inconsistent with the Biblical description, topping the Brazen Pillars of the Masonic Lodge are two globes – the celestial and the terrestrial. The terrestrial sphere is assigned to Jachin, and the celestial to Boaz. The Fellow Craft is told, in the lecture, that...

> [...t]he globes are two artificial spherical bodies, on the convex surface of which are represented the countries, seas, and various parts of the earth; the face of the heavens, the planetary revolutions, and other important particulars. The sphere, with the parts of the earth delineated upon its surface, is called the terrestrial globe; and that with the constellations and other heavenly bodies, the celestial globe. Their principal use, besides

serving as maps to distinguish the outward parts of the earth, and the situation of the fixed stars, is to illustrate and explain the phenomena arising from the annual revolution, and the diurnal rotation of the earth round its own axis. They are the noblest instruments for giving the most distinct idea of any problem or proposition, as well as for enabling us to solve it. Contemplating these bodies, Masons are inspired with a due reverence for the Deity and his works; and are induced to apply with diligence and attention to astronomy, geography, navigation, and all the arts dependent on them, by which society has been so much benefited.[16]

He is also told that "[t]hey are the noblest instruments for giving the most distinct idea of any problem or proposition, as well as for enabling us to solve it"[17], it is easy to, at first, dismiss this lofty claim as mere hyperbole – until we begin to unpack its inferences and extrapolations in other disciplines and domains. The above passage from is particularly meaningful from the geometrical, astronomical and Hermetic perspectives. Since we will be dealing with the two former subjects later in the present volume, in the chapters devoted to geometry and astronomy, we will address the Hermetic significance here. There is a central underlying tenet, running its way through the course of Hermetic thought spanning from (at least) the first few centuries of the Common Era up to today; namely, that microcosmic operations are reflected in those of the macrocosm and vice versa. This dynamic is most notably exemplified in a 6th century document called *Tabula Smaragdina*, or Emerald Tablet.[18] The oft-quoted axiom "that which is above is like that which is below" may be found in this early-medieval, Arabic piece of *Hermetica*. This notion, as it is found in Neoplatonic and Hermetic writings, is an extension of the thought of the aforementioned Posidonius of Apameia, who is credited with codifying the concept of cosmic sympathy, wherein the terrestrial and celestial spheres represented the microcosmic and macrocosmic domains of causal action; they were considered interconnected and reciprocally influential. All magical and astrological ideas regarding the manipulation of subtle planetary and stellar

16   Webb, *The Freemason's Monitor*, Salem: Cushing & Appleton, 1818, pp. 49-50

17   Preston (Oliver, commentary), *Illustrations of Masonry*, New York: Masonic Publishing and Manufacturing Co., 1867, p. 49

18   Goodrick-Clarke, *The Western Esoteric Traditions: A Historical Introduction*, Oxford University Press, 2008, p. 34

influences may be traced to the concept of cosmic sympathy, whether emanating from the astral magic of the Mesopotamians, Egyptians, Greeks, Arabs, the magi of the Renaissance or the modern practitioner.

Further concerning the structure of the pillars, we are met with this intriguing passage: "They were cast hollow the better to withstand inundation and conflagrations, and are said to have contained the archives of Masonry." This is almost certainly in reference to the antediluvian story of Lamech.[19] Lamech had four children (Jabal, Jubal, Tubal-cain and Naamah) by two wives (Adah and Zillah). His children are said to have founded many of the useful arts and sciences, with architecture and animal husbandry attributed to Jabal, music to Jubal, and metallurgy to Tubal-cain. In the anonymously composed *Mason's Constitutions* of 1701[20], these attributions are slightly expanded to include stonemasonry and weaving, and all are placed under the jurisdiction of geometry, itself said to be "accounted above any of the seaven [sic] sciences".[21] The children of Lamech knew that God would exact his apocalyptic wrath either by fire or by water, so they constructed two pillars in which to preserve the records of their arts, in hope that they might be found after the coming Deluge or Conflagration. One pillar, made of stone, they called *Marbell*, which was said to be impervious to the conflagrations of fire; the other pillar, *Laturus*, was resistant to inundation by water. The *Constitutions* then go on to describe how Hermes – said to be the Father of Wisdom and grandson of Noah – found one of the two pillars after the Deluge. Hermes, after recovering this antediluvian body of knowledge, taught these civilizing arts to man. These students of Hermes went on to found the civilization of the Mesopotamians (Sumerians, Akkadians and Assyro-Babylonians) and, later, that of the Egyptians.

---

19   *The Holy Bible*, KJV, Genesis 4:18-24

20   Anonymous, *Mason's Constitutions*, 1701, reprinted in Hughan's *Masonic Sketches and Reprints*, Masonic Publishing, 1871, pdf retrieved online

21   Ibid, p. 174

Luxor Temple with one of originally two obelisks flanking the entrance,
photo ca. 19th century

The Brazen Pillars have much in common with the obelisks (Egyptian: *tekhenu*; Greek: *obeliskos*) of Dynastic Egypt, as pairs of obelisks could regularly be found flanking the portals of the pylons in ancient Egyptian temple architecture. Like the Brazen Pillars, obelisks were not load-bearing or necessary for any material support. Ergo, it may be assumed that these objects were meant to symbolize a concept, action or phenomenon. It has been suggested that the impetus behind the design of obelisks was to create a microcosmic representation of the effects of macrocosmic astronomical phenomena such as zodiacal light and Sun pillars.[22] This sort of terrestrial mirroring of celestial events was evidently very common in the region.[23] Another possible scenario necessitating the erection of a pair of perpendicular columns could be that of orienting the edifice solstitially or equinoctially. There is a method by which the shadows produced by two closely-arranged poles (raised perpendicularly by means of a *plumb* line to stand at a *right angle* to a *level* plane – which may be accomplished by

22   Gary and Talcott, "Stargazing in Ancient Egypt", *Astronomy*, June 2006, pp. 62-67

23   See: Robert Bauval's Orion correlation theory; Bauval & Gilbert, *The Orion Mystery: Unlocking the Secrets of the Pyramids*, Broadway Books, 1995

means of the Working Tools of a Fellow Craft Mason) may be observed in diurnal sunlight – or, more accurately, by the biannual solstitial events – to produce the north/south axis. Then, by the square-producing application of a 3:4:5 triangle – a process we will discuss in greater detail in the section of geometry – the north/south axis may be intersected by the east/west axis, thus producing the cardinal directions.[24] Once this orientation is established, the foundation of the edifice may be surveyed and geometrically demarcated. Because of their employment in temple orientation, these non-load-bearing obelisks – and, by extension, the Brazen Pillars on the porch of K∴S∴T∴ – may have been left as monuments or *proofs* that the builder's work was indeed square and true. In this sense, the Brazen Pillars may have functioned as gnomons to trace *analemmata* whereby the orientation of the cardinal directions may be obtained.[25]

It is in their most solstitial context that the Brazen Pillars relate to both the Saints John and, thereby, to the Point Within A Circle diagram. The diagram is of a circle with a point at its center, bordered by two parallel, perpendicular lines. If the circumpunct is thought of as a solar symbol – which it usually is, outside of Freemasonry – then these parallel lines which are appended to it may be thought of as solstitial markers, like the Brazen Pillars. That the parallel lines are attributed to Saint John the Baptist (whose feast is held on June 24th, very near the summer solstice) and Saint John the Evangelist (whose feast is held on December 27th, very near the winter solstice)[26], does much to support the diagram's interpretation as representing an annual solar circuit, as these Saints have been associated with the Tropic of Cancer and the Tropic of Capricorn, respectively.[27] As we've already mentioned, the pillars, like their Egyptian obelisk predecessors, may have also been used to mark the solstices in ancient temple construction – thereby meriting our examination as to their relationship to the two perpendicular lines in the Point Within A Circle diagram. Analogues to this motif may also be found in the Royal Arch banner, upon which the fixed zodiacal signs (Taurus, Leo, Aquila-as-Scorpio-proxy, and Aquarius) are flanked by two androsphinxes, representing the solstices, and also in the Mithraic tauroctony, wherein Mithras, as a personification of the vernal equinox in Taurus, is flanked by Cautes and Cautopates, themselves representing the solstices.

24   Plutarch, *Moralia*, Vol. V, "On Isis and Osiris", Loeb Classic Library, 1936, p. 135

25   See: Vitruvius' *De architectura*, Book IX, Chapter 1, for the classical perspective on gnomons and *analemmata*.

26   Knoop, *The Genesis of Freemasonry*, Manchester University Press, 1947

27   Lamb, *Myth, Magick & Masonry: Occult Perspectives in Freemasonry*, The Laudable Pursuit, 2018, Section II

As briefly discussed above, in reference to their dimensions, the Brazen Pillars have also been utilized in qabalistic symbolism, as they flank the Middle Pillar of the *Etz Chaim*. Boaz is associated with the Pillar of Severity – the passive, feminine pillar – and Jachin is associated with the Pillar of Mercy – the active, masculine pillar. As we have already briefly touched upon, each letter of the Hebrew alphabet is assigned a numerical value. In qabalistic theory, this alpha-numeric correspondence is called *gematria* (Hebrew: גמטריא, or גימטריה). Gematria, along with other qabalistic methods such as *notariqon* and *temurah*, was initially employed by medieval qabalists as a means of scriptural exegesis (see Appendix A). It was thought that, by these qabalistic methods, the esoteric subtext of exoteric writings could be decoded and, thereby, the deeper meaning could be gleaned from the work. For instance, by calculating the gematriac value for the word *Jachin* (Hebrew: יָכִין), we produce the number 740 (*yod*/10 + *kaph*/20 + *yod*/10 + *nun final*/700 = 740). When we do the same for *Boaz* (Hebrew: בֹּעַז), we produce 79 (*beth*/2 + *ayin*/70 + *zayin*/7 = 79). These numbers may be analyzed individually or when added together, producing the sum of 819. When two words share the same gematriac value, these words are thought to share a qabalistically synergetic relationship – one complementing or elucidating the other. Bearing this in mind, some other words that have a gematriac value of 740 are: *Egyptian* (Hebrew: מצרית) and *two* (Hebrew: לשתי) – the dual obelisks flanking the portal of the temple. Words having a gematriac value of 79 are: *wisdom* (Hebrew: וחכמה) and *brethren* (Hebrew: אחיכם). When we consider words that share the gematriac sum of the two pillars, 819, we find: *sanctify* (Hebrew: הקדשתי) and *forsake* (Hebrew: נטשתני). The qabalist may then contemplate the relationship between these words and utilize their findings in an overall hermeneutic. Another method may be employed in the case of multi-digit numbers thereby affording us other avenues of qabalistic exegesis involving less cumbersome figures. By utilizing an occult numerological process known as "theosophical addition" (which we will address in further detail in Chapter VIII, in the section dealing with arithmetic), multi-digit numbers may be reduced to a single digit. When this method is applied to the number 819, the number 9 is produced (8 + 1 + 9 = 18; 1 + 8 = 9). Nine is the number of the *sephirah Yesod* (Hebrew: יסוד; meaning "Foundation"); nine is also the gematriac value of the Hebrew letter *teth* (ט; meaning "serpent"); furthermore, the letter *teth* is attributed to the Strength VIII Tarot card. Analyzing this data – "strength" and "foundation" – within the context of the two Brazen Pillars, we find supportive echoes of the interpretation we are given of their meanings: "In it is strength" and "he shall establish".[28] The letter *teth* is attributed to the 19th path on the *Etz Chaim* (see Appendix B), which connects the *sephiroth* of severity (*Geburah*) and mercy (*Chesed*), from which the two qabalistic pillars derive their names, further solidifying the synthesis of these polar opposites implied by *teth*, the Strength VIII Tarot and the number nine, apropos the Brazen Pillars. The presence of the letter *teth* also seems to allude to the hidden wisdom contained in the symbolism of the pillars, as the Ophite Gnostic sect regarded the serpent as being representative of the wisdom transmitted by Sophia. This wisdom transmission may be seen as being qabalistically encrypted in the Brazen Pillars silently standing in Masonic Lodge rooms, awaiting those who would apply the interpretive keys by which their occult import is made clear.

Another notable appearance of Jachin and Boaz occurs on Justice XI, the Hierophant V cards and, most conspicuously, on the High Priestess II card in the Rider-Waite Tarot deck[29], which we will address in further detail below. It is not uncommon among Freemasons to dismiss the association with such superstitious divinatory playthings out of hand – however, there is a long and established connection between the Tarot and the Fraternity. Before we address the Brazen Pillars' presence in Tarot symbolism, it is first necessary that we endeavor to briefly establish the Tarot within the context of Freemasonry.

While Tarot had already been in use for divination and fortune-telling for some time, the beginnings of Tarot esotericism can be traced to the publication of *Le Monde Primitif, analysé et comparé avec le monde moderne* (1781) by Swiss Freemason Antione Court de Gébelin (initiated 1771 at *Lodge Les Amis Réunis*). In his book, de Gébelin interprets the Marseilles Tarot to contain survivals of arcane religious symbolism, ultimately concluding that the origins of the mysterious deck point back to ancient Mystery Traditions, particularly those of Isis and Osiris. De Gébelin was also the first to propose that the Tarot was composed as a distillation of the collected wisdom contained at the Library of Alexandria (destroyed by fire in 48 BCE) and that the deck was, thereby, a compendium of the cryptic philosophical arcana of the ancient world. This arcana, however, was encoded in symbolism meant only to be deciphered by those of a certain attainment in the language of symbols – a challenge which seems to have attracted many Freemasons.

The attribution of the twenty-two letters of the Hebrew alphabet

28   Pike, *Morals and Dogma of the Ancient and Accepted Scottish Rite of Freemasonry,* Supreme Council of the Southern Jurisdiction, A.A.S.R., U.S.A., 1871, p. 9
29   Waite, *Rider-Waite Tarot,* Rider & Sons, 1910

to the twenty-two trump cards in the Major Arcana was first made in an essay by the Comte de Mellet which was included in volume XIII of Antoine Court de Gébelin's *Le Monde primitif*. In 1854, French occultist, Rosicrucian and Freemason, Éliphas Lévi (1810-1875; a Hebrew transliteration of his given name, Alphonse Louis Constant; initiated 1861 at *Lodge Rose du Parfait Silence*) further advanced the occult application of the Tarot. Lévi's magnum opus, *Dogme et Rituel de la Haute Magie* (English: *Dogma and Ritual of High Magic*, published in two volumes in 1854 and 1856), is divided into twenty-two chapters, each corresponding to a letter of the Hebrew alphabet and to the cards of the Tarot's Major Arcana. Other correspondences relating to Qabalah, alchemy, astrology, Hermeticism and, of course, ceremonial magic are made throughout the work and attributed to their corresponding Tarot card and Hebrew letter. The book was especially influential to Albert Pike (1809-1891), who cribbed large uncredited passages of Lévi's work for inclusion in his *Morals and Dogma of the Ancient and Accepted Scottish Rite of Freemasonry* (1871). Lévi's chief translator and commentator latter in the 19th century and into the 20th was Arthur Edward Waite (1857-1942) – a Mason whose shadow continues to loom large over the world of the Tarot.

Freemason and Masonic Rosicrucian, Arthur Edward Waite (initiated 1901 at Runymede Lodge No. 2430) was also a member of the Hermetic Order of the Golden Dawn – a Victorian magical society founded in 1887, which had a focus on Hermetic Qabalah, whose curriculum and Outer Order rituals were based on cipher manuscripts which had most likely been procured from the property of Freemason Kenneth Mackenzie (1833-1886) after his death.[30] Due to his research and experience in the Order, Waite undertook the revision of the Tarot in accordance with Hermetic and Qabalistic correspondences. Enlisting fellow Golden Dawn member, artist Pamela Colman Smith (1878-1951) – who rendered the original images in gouache and ink on paper, Waite irretrievably altered the landscape of the Tarot and, to this day, the *Rider-Waite Tarot Deck*, as it has come to be known, is the most recognizable deck in the world. There are also several allusions made in the imagery that, while they may escape the notice of the profane, most Masons would be able to discern. Later in the 20th century, Freemasons such as Paul Foster Case (1884-1954; initiated 1926 at Fairport Lodge No. 476) and Manly P. Hall (1901-1990; initiated 1954 at Jewel Lodge No. 374), among others, have contributed to the evolution of this strange pack of cards – a pack of cards which continue to

---

30   Küntz (editor), *The Complete Golden Dawn Cipher Manuscript*, Holmes Publishing, 1996

fascinate both the initiated and the profane, but seem to have a particularly strong resonance with Freemasons.

The High Priestess II, Rider-Waite Tarot, Rider & Son, 1909,
from the private collection of William S. Burkle

Turning our attention back to the symbolism depicted on the High Priestess II card, we immediately notice the presence of the Brazen Pillars – one marked with the letter *B*, the other with the letter *J*, in reference to the Holy Saints John; that these letters are in reference to the pillars of K∴S∴T∴, is beyond reasonable doubt. The orientation of the pillars is such as to suggest that the viewer is on the porch of the Temple, with his back to the east, facing the *Sanctum Sanctorum*. This is also the orientation one has when looking at the *Etz Chaim* (see Appendix B), with the Pillar of Severity on the left and the Pillar of Mercy on the right. In personal application, however, the *Etz Chaim* corresponds to the human body as if one were to back into the image – with *Geburah* at the right shoulder and *Chesed* at the left – this is the orientation one has when performing the Qabalistic Cross component of the Golden Dawn's Lesser Ritual of the Pentagram, for example. The Hebrew letter attributed to the High Priestess is *gimel* (ג), which means "camel" and is represented by the letter *G* in the Latin alphabet. This brings to mind the central position of the ever-present letter *G* found in American Masonic Lodges. The gematriac value of the letter *gimel* is three, which is particularly significant apropos the preponderance of trinary symbolism found in Freemasonry, much of which will be addressed in the chapters devoted to the course of three steps on the Winding Staircase. Qabalistically, the High Priestess II occupies the thirteenth path on the *Etz Chaim* – this is the path on the Middle Pillar which unites *Kether* with *Tiphareth*. The Marian appearance of the Priestess seems to allude to the hidden nature of this path, as it flows from the macroprosopus (Hebrew: אריך אנפין, *Arich Anpin*, representing God the Father in *Kether*) into the microprosopus (Hebrew: ר: יעֵן יִפְנַא, *Ze'ir Anpin*, representing the Son of God in *Tiphareth*) and may be seen as the vehicle by which the Holy Spirit descends from God, through the Virgin's Immaculate Conception, and manifests in the sphere of the Son (Sun). The High Priestess II card also corresponds to the Moon, as evidenced by the crescent Moon at her feet, and also to the element, water. These lunar and aquatic correspondences allude to memory and the unconscious mind and, thereby, to reflectivity and depth, strengthening the Hermetic concept of the macrocosm being reflected in the microcosm and vice-versa. The Priestess is depicted with a Hathor-esque headdress which, in its bovine symbolism, may be read as a nod to the Taurian precessional age – both Bat and Hathor being Taurian age deities. This is masonically significant in that the *Anno Lucis* of Freemasonry, which adds four-thousand years to the Gregorian year, roughly marks the beginning of the Taurian age, a 2,160-year period when the vernal equinox occurred in the sign of Taurus.[31] The attributes of the ancient Egyptian cow-goddess, Bat, were subsumed by Hathor during the Middle Kingdom; and, in time, Hathor's attributes were largely subsumed by Isis. This mythological evolution is somewhat represented in the High Priestess II card in that the Priestess, in Isiac fashion, appears to be guarding the veil which separates the viewer from the

---

31   Lamb, *Myth, Magick & Masonry: Occult Perspectives in Freemasonry*, The Laudable Pursuit, 2018, Section II

Mysteries of the *Sanctum Sanctorum*. Pomegranates, another motif found on the chapiters of the Solomonic pillars, are depicted on the veil, perhaps as an allusion Persephone in her chthonic aspect, or possibly to the plenitude of the Mysteries contained therein. Lastly, we will address the scroll in the Priestess' hand, which reads "TORA". This may be interpreted to be in reference to the Jewish Torah (Hebrew; תּוֹרָה; meaning "law" or "teaching") which, most specifically, refers to the Pentateuch, or the first five books of the Tanakh. Another interesting interpretation involves the word TORA in its anagrammatic modes: ROTA, TARO, ORAT, TORA, ATOR (which is somewhat corroborated by the Wheel of Fortune X Tarot card). These modes, if read sequentially as a quasi-Latin sentence, may be interpreted to read: "The wheel of Tarot speaks the law of Hathor".[32]

After passing through these pillars, and being instructed in their exoteric significance, the Fellow Craft is conducted to the foot of the Winding Staircase, which leads to a place representing the Middle Chamber of K∴S∴T∴.

---

32   Greer, *Tarot for Your Self: A Workbook for Personal Transformation*, Weiser, 1984, p. 27

CHAPTER III

∴

THE WINDING STAIRCASE
&
THE NUMBER FIFTEEN

THE WINDING STAIRCASE

[…] we are now about to make an ascent through a porch, by a flight of winding stairs, consisting of three, five, and seven steps, to a place representing the Middle Chamber of King Solomon's Temple, there to receive instructions relative to the wages due, and jewels of a Fellow Craft.[1]

We are thus introduced to a certain Winding Staircase in the lecture accompanying the Fellow Craft degree of Freemasonry (see Appendix D). This staircase is utilized as a symbolic mode of instruction; and to each step, a certain emblem, concept and/or subject is attributed. Symbolically, the Winding Staircase represents a journey – it implies motion, evolution and transformation. That the staircase *winds* is symbolic of the time, effort and dedication required of the Fellow Craft in his pursuit of knowledge; oppositely, a straight staircase would signify a direct, less-convoluted passage. The use of the staircase, which is the mode by which one is elevated – in the most literal sense – to a higher plane, is fitting because the pursuit of knowledge it represents is the true means by which the Fellow Craft ascends to the sublime degree of Master Mason. Staircases also allude to the anthropological concept of liminality (from the Latin *limen*, or "threshold") in that they consist of three distinct

---

1   *Duncan's Masonic Ritual and Monitor* (1866), New York: Crown Publishers, 1986, p. 72

parts: a beginning, a middle and an end. Initiatory rites of passage are also said to consist of three parts: separation (pre-liminal rites), transformation (liminal rites) and reintegration (post-liminal rites). The middle section – represented, in this case, by the staircase itself, since it is preceded by the porch and succeeded by the Middle Chamber – represents the liminal space wherein the transformational element of the initiation is to occur.[2] From a broader perspective, the Fellow Craft degree as a whole could be seen as the liminal, transformational stage in the three-part suite of Blue Lodge degrees; the Entered Apprentice is differentiated from the rest of society, and thereby *separated*, by means of his Obligation; the Fellow Craft is *transformed* by his experiences on the porch, Winding Staircase and in the Middle Chamber of K∴S∴T∴; and the Master Mason – a good man who has been made better by the symbolic application of the working tools – is *reintegrated* into society, charged to "cultivate assiduously the noble tenets of our profession – brotherly love, relief, and truth".[3] We will be returning to the concept of liminality in its initiatory context in Chapter IV, in the section dealing with the Three Principal Stages of Human Life.

Masonic Fellow Craft Degree Symbolic Chart, Sherer, 1856

2 The reader is directed to the work of anthropologists Arnold van Gennep (1873-1957), who first posited liminality as a component of rites of passage, and Victor Turner (1920-1983), who developed the concept further. This is a tremendously valuable perspective from which to appreciate initiatory ritualism, such as that found in Freemasonry.

3 *Duncan's Masonic Ritual and Monitor* (1866), New York: Crown Publishers, 1986, p. 132

In their tripartite nature, staircases also allude to the three domains which are commonly found to be underlying qabalistic, Neoplatonic and Hermetic cosmological models: the terrestrial, the celestial and the super-celestial, or supernal. The terrestrial, or sublunary world, consists of the elements; the celestial world consists of the planetary spheres; the super-celestial world is that mysterious domain which lay beyond the sphere of the zodiac and fixed stars. In the cosmology of Paracelsian physician and astrologer, Robert Fludd (1574-1637 CE), the three spheres are differentiated by the lowest sphere containing the elements, the middle sphere containing the planets, and the higher sphere corresponding to the pseudo-Dionysian angelic hierarchy. Similarly, in the cosmology of Heinrich Cornelius Agrippa (1486-1535 CE), we find the Three Worlds expressed as the terrestrial world (consisting of the elements; their study and manipulation through natural philosophy and alchemy), the celestial world (consisting of the planetary influences; their study and manipulation through astrology and astral magic) and the intellectual world (consisting of ideas, the *mens*, and the archetypes, or Platonic forms; their study and manipulation through qabalistic and angelic magic).[4] The Winding Staircase is similarly sequenced in that the *elementary* rudiments of knowledge occupy the foot of the Staircase; the seven liberal arts and sciences, with all of their septenary and planetary correspondences, occupy the middle of the Staircase; and at the top, the Fellow Craft is allowed to alight the Staircase and partake of the Mysteries of the Middle Chamber of K∴S∴T∴, there to receive the wages and jewels of a Fellow Craft.

Staircases, ladders and other modes of ascent have been symbolically employed in a number of allegories and in the rites of several Mystery traditions. For instance, the seven Mithraic initiatory grades (in ascending order: *corax, nymphus, miles, leo, perses, heliodromus* and *pater*) were arranged in steps corresponding to the planetary spheres and thereby prefigured the ascent of the soul after death.[5] Each of these steps were separated by a gate and, like the Neoplatonic cosmological schema, led to the firmament, or the sphere of the fixed stars (corresponding to the second *sephirah, Chokmah*, in the qabalistic *Etz Chaim*). There was also a certain test or ordeal accompanying each grade, through which the initiate must pass in their elevation.[6] Hieroglyphically, steps denote ascension and have been linked to an appellation of Osiris as "he who stands at the top of the steps".[7]

4   Agrippa, *Three Books of Occult Philosophy*, 1531, Bk. I, Chap. 1
5   Clauss, *The Roman Cult of Mithras*, Routledge, 2001, p. 102
6   Ibid., p. 103
7   Cirlot, *Dictionary of Symbols*, Routledge, 1962, p. 312

Generally, nine is the number of steps in the Egyptian usage, probably in reference to the Great *Ennead* (Greek: Ἐννεάς; phonetic Egyptian: *Pesedjet*) of Heliopolis: Atum, Shu, Tefnut, Geb, Nut, Osiris, Isis, Seth and Nephthys.[8]

In general, staircases represent spiritual ascension; they are symbolic of the connection between the terrestrial and the celestial planes, similar to the biblical account of Jacob's ladder, whereupon the angels of God ascended and descended.[9] Angelic beings were also a central feature of the celestial hierarchies of the Neoplatonic Christian mystic Pseudo-Dionysius the Aeropagite (Greek: Διονύσιος ὁ Ἀρεοπαγίτης, 5-6th century CE), who posited three spheres, each containing three angelic groups (in ascending order: angels, archangels, principalities, powers, virtues, dominions, thrones, cherubim and seraphim). We are told that, in a foundational qabalistic work known as the *Zohar* (Hebrew: זֹהַר; meaning "Splendor" or "Radiance"), Jacob's ladder consisted of seventy-two steps which disappeared into the heavens.[10] The number seventy-two immediately brings to mind the seventy-two angels of the *Shem HaMephorash* (Hebrew: המפורש שם; meaning "the Explicit Name") and their corresponding seventy-two astrological quinances. The quinances, as the name implies, are 5° arc segments of the total 360° of the ecliptic. There are seventy-two of these arc segments (360 ÷ 5 = 72), two for each decan (a 10° arc segment; three per zodiacal sign), and each of them are assigned an angel and a göetic dæmon. Note that, in this instance, the word *dæmon* denotes the personification of an astral or cosmic sympathy and not an evil entity, *per se*. That these angels and dæmons have been assigned to the seventy-two rungs of Jacob's ladder illustrates a motif that is similar to that of the Neoplatonic and pseudo-Dionysian celestial hierarchies, the strata of mediating forces between man and the Creative Intelligence. Additionally, step pyramids and ziggurats, such as the Great Ziggurat at Ur in southern Iraq, the Pyramid of Djoser at Saqqara, Egypt, and the Pyramid of the Moon at Teotihuacan, Mexico, utilize this same symbolic motif – forming a bridge between terrestrial life and the celestial afterlife, between man and his gods.

8　Clifford, "Creation Accounts in the Ancient Near East", *Catholic Biblical Quarterly*, 1994, pp. 99-116

9　*The Holy Bible* KJV, Genesis 28:10-17

10　Cirlot, *Dictionary of Symbols*, Routledge, 1962, p. 312

Kircher's Shem HaMephorash from Œdipus Ægyptiacus, 1652

Often, modes of ascent are employed to symbolize the gradual accumulation of knowledge, which is particularly fitting, apropos the staircase's Masonic application. Staircases may also signify the movement of one toward their goals – each step representing advancement in a particular area. In dream analysis, staircases are considered auspicious omens, indicative of incremental progress of either the intellectual or spiritual varieties. Straight staircases may be interpreted to connote an uncomplicated ascent, with few obstacles, whereas spiral or winding staircases often imply mystery and disorientation. Staircases are also a ubiquitous symbolic device employed in cinema, wherein they may be used to convey anything from tension and complication to grandeur and excess. Taken literally, a staircase connects the lower level of an edifice with the upper. Figuratively, it may connect ideas or even states of being.[11] And, of course, in the dream symbology of Sigmund Freud "[s]taircases, ladders, and flights of stairs, or climbing on these, either upwards or downwards, are symbolic representations of the sexual act".[12] While this interpretation may, at first, seem overly simplistic and/or inaccurate, there is obviously great value in zooming out the lens of interpretation to include broader biological and reproductive perspectives in the frame of reference, particularly if one wishes to examine the symbol's import, *in situ*, as constellated among a greater suite of symbols.

The Winding Staircase, as it pertains to the architecture of K∴S∴T∴, is mentioned but once in scripture – in the context of the Temple's dimensions and floorplan:

> *And it came to pass in the four hundred and eightieth year after the children of Israel were come out of the land of Egypt, in the fourth year of Solomon's reign over Israel, in the month Zif, which is the second month, that he began to build the house of the LORD. And the house which king Solomon built for the LORD, the length thereof was threescore cubits, and the breadth thereof twenty cubits, and the height thereof thirty cubits. And the porch before the temple of the house, twenty cubits was the length thereof, according to the breadth of the house; and ten cubits was the breadth thereof before the house. And for the house he made windows of narrow lights. And against the wall of the house he built chambers round about, against the walls of the house round about, both of the temple and of the oracle: and he made chambers round about: The nethermost chamber was five cubits broad, and the middle was six cubits broad, and the third was seven cubits broad: for without in the wall of the house he made narrowed rests round about, that the beams should not be fastened in the walls of the house. And the house, when it was in building, was built of stone made ready before it was brought thither: so that there was neither hammer nor axe nor any tool of iron heard in the house, while*

---

11   Bellmore, *Stepping on Symbols*, retrieved at: reelclub.wordpress.com

12   Freud, *The Interpretation of Dreams*, Franz Deuticke, 1900; p. 222 of the Dover Publications, 2015 edition

it was in building. The door for the middle chamber was in the
right side of the house: and they went up with winding stairs
into the middle chamber, and out of the middle into the third.[13]

In the Masonic lecture, the Winding Staircase is said to be divided
into three courses, consisting of three, five and seven steps, respectively,
from bottom to top. We should first note that all of these numbers are odd,
as is fifteen, their sum. These numbers are central to the preponderance of
odd-number symbolism found in the speculative, or philosophical, craft
of Freemasonry – but odd numbers also have made an imprint on the
operative craft. In ancient temple architecture, as well as in the secular
architecture of today, staircases consisting of an odd number of steps are
vastly more common than those with an even number. In addition to this
being considered an auspicious omen, staircases were and are generally
rendered with an odd number of steps because most people will step off
with their dominant foot and having an odd number of steps allows them
to also alight the staircase on their dominant foot, thereby lessening the
possibility of a misstep.

The number of steps in front should always be odd, since, in
that case, the right foot, which begins the ascent, will be that
which first alights on the landing of the temple.[14]

According to the pre-Socratic philosopher and mathematician, Pythagoras (580-500 BCE), odd numbers were considered more perfect than
their even counterparts.[15] We learn from the commentaries of the Greek
Pythogorean, Philolaus (470-385 BCE), that Pythagoras classified numbers in three groups: odd, even and evenly-odd; the latter being the product of an even and an odd number added together, which would include
the numbers three, five, seven and fifteen. We will be dealing with the
numbers three, five and seven in greater detail further in our study, but we
will address the significance of the number fifteen in the following section,
since we are now dealing with the Winding Staircase as a whole, which is
comprised of a total of fifteen steps.

13   *The Holy Bible* KJV, I Kings 6:2-8
14   *Vitruvius, De architectura, Book III, Chapter 4*
15   Mackey, *The Symbolism of Freemasonry*, Clark & Maynard, 1882

THE NUMBER FIFTEEN

In Pythagorean number symbolism, we learn that the number fifteen is a triangular number; it being next in a sequence of triangular numbers after the number ten, which the Pythagoreans represented as the *Tetraktys*. The number fifteen has also anciently been associated with the lunar phases, in that it is the approximate number of days (precisely, 14.76 days) between a new and a full moon, a first and third quarter, etc. This is evidenced in an archaic German unit of measure known as a *mandel*, meaning "little moon" or "part of a moon", which consisted of fifteen items; much like the word *dozen* denotes twelve items.[16]

The number fifteen is significant for several religious and mythological reasons. The ancient Assyrian city of Nineveh was surrounded by a colossal stone and mudbrick wall that was over fifty feet high and forty-five feet thick, and could only be accessed through one of the city's fifteen gates. The Assyrian goddess Ishtar (who was a manifestation of the earlier Sumerian goddess, Inanna, and later associated with the Greek Aphrodite through syncretization and her association with the planet Venus) was worshipped at Nineveh by the service of fifteen priests.[17]   Fifteen is also the number associated with the Holy Name, Jah (Hebrew: יה).[18] Jah, or Yah, is a shortened form of Yahweh or Jehovah (Hebrew: יהוה – in its consonantal spelling, YHWH is most often referred to as the *Tetragrammaton*). When rendered for their numerical, or gematriac, value, the letters *J* and *H* become *yod* (י – gematriac value: 10) and *heh* (ה – gematriac value: 5) which, when taken together, have a numerical value of fifteen. In Psalms, the Levites were said to have climbed the fifteen steps which led to the Temple of King Solomon by singing the fifteen Songs of Ascent.[19] Among these Songs of Ascent may be found the following passage, with which Freemasons will be familiar:

> *Behold, how good and how pleasant it is for brethren to dwell together in unity! It is like the precious ointment upon the head, that ran down upon the beard, even Aaron's beard:*

---

16   Schimmel, *The Mystery of Numbers*, Oxford University Press, 1993, p. 213

17   Ibid., pp. 213-215

18   *The Holy Bible*, KJV, Psalm 68:4

19   *The Holy Bible*, KJV, Psalms 120-134

that went down to the skirts of his garments; As the dew of Hermon, and as the dew that descended upon the mountains of Zion: for there the LORD commanded the blessing, even life for evermore.[20]

Egyptian alchemist, Zosimos of Panopolis (3rd century CE; Greek: Ζώσιμος ὁ Πανοπολίτης), in his *Visions of Zosimos*, a collection of dreams which have been interpreted as alchemical allegories, wrote of his encounter with a "priest of the Adytum" called Ion. This dream entity who, in the *Visions*, goes on to be dismembered, decapitated and burned to ashes before being resurrected in spirit, introduced the alchemist to a mysterious staircase consisting of fifteen steps...

And saying these things, I slept, and I saw a certain sacrificing priest standing before me and over and altar which had the form of a bowl. And that altar had fifteen steps going up to it. Then the priest stood up and I heard from above a voice say to me, "I have completed the descent of the fifteen steps and the ascent of the steps of light. And it is the sacrificing priest who renews me, casting off the body's coarseness, and, consecrated by necessity, I have become a spirit."[21]

2	9	4
7	5	3
6	1	8

Kamea of Saturn

20   *The Holy Bible*, KJV, Psalms 133
21   *Zosimos of Panopolis, Visions of Zosimos, 3rd century*

The number fifteen is also representative of the magic square, or *kamea*, of Saturn – a symbol also associated with the aforementioned Ishtar. Each row, column and diagonal of the nine-celled, three-by-three *kamea* of Saturn has a sum of fifteen, a number known as the square's "magic constant".[22] Saturn is the seventh celestial sphere in the Hermetic and Neoplatonic cosmological models, which was based on the Chaldean-Ptolemaic order of planets (in ascending order: the Moon, Mercury, Venus, the Sun, Mars, Jupiter and Saturn), which moved against the canopy of the fixed stars. Heinrich Cornelius Agrippa (1486-1535 CE) referred to the Saturnal *kamea* square as the "spiritual seal" because of the planet's position between the sphere of Jupiter and that of the firmament. In this sense, the number fifteen represents the seventh and last *seal* before the spirit may ascend to the sphere of the fixed stars. Qabalistically, the sphere of Saturn is associated with *Binah* (Hebrew: בינה; meaning "Understanding") and that of the fixed stars is associated with *Chokmah* (Hebrew: חכמה; meaning "Wisdom"), both of which, along with *Kether* (Hebrew: כתר; meaning "Crown"), comprise the supernal triad. The number fifteen may also be interpreted as representing the Divine Androgyne, in that the sum of seven – the number of the *sephirah Netzach* (Aphrodite) – and eight – the number of the *sephirah Hod* (Hermes) – is fifteen (Herm-Aphrodite).

The etymological root of the word *Saturday* is the Latin *Saturni Dies*, or "day of Saturn".[23] Saturday is also the Sabbath (Hebrew: שבת; *Shabbat*), the holy day in Judaism.[24] The Hebrew word for Saturn is *Shabtai* (Hebrew: שבתאי), which is the root of the Sabbath, the day of "rest" or "cessation".[25] This is because Saturday was the seventh day of Creation – the day Deity rested from His labors…

> *And on the seventh day God ended his work which he had made; and he rested on the seventh day from all his work which he had made. And God blessed the seventh day, and sanctified it: because that in it he had rested from all his work which God created and made.*[26]

22   Mackey, *An Encyclopedia of Freemasonry and its Kindred Sciences*, Everts & Co. 1884; Entry: "Magic Squares"

23   Entry: "Saturday"; *Online Etymological Dictionary*, retrieved at: etymonline.com

24   Mueller, *Oxford Encyclopedia of Ancient Greece and Rome*, Oxford University Press, 2010, p. 221, Entry: "Saturn"

25   Sela, "Saturn and the Jews", *Katz Center*, University of Pennsylvania, 2017, retrieved at: katz.sas.upenn.edu

26   The Holy Bible, KJV, Genesis 2:2-3

Interpreting the *kamea* of Saturn as a microcosm of the Temple, we find the numbers three, five and seven occupy what amounts to its "Middle Chamber". The *kamea* is divided into nine cells – three on the bottom, three in the center and three on top – the numbers three, five and seven are attributed to cells in the middle of this magic square. Fifteen is simultaneously the "magic constant" of the *kamea* of Saturn and the sum of the steps on the Winding Staircase.

> *The parallel between the Hebrew god and Saturn is of considerable importance as regards the alchemical idea of the transformation of the God of the Old Testament into the God of the New. The alchemists naturally attached great significance to Saturn, for, besides being the outermost planet, the supreme archon (the Harranites named him "Primas"), and the demiurge Ialdabaoth, he was also the spiritus niger who lies captive in the darkness of matter, the deity or that part of the deity which has been swallowed up in his own creation. He is the dark god who reverts to his original luminous state in the mystery of alchemical transmutation.*[27]

---

27 Jung, "Hebrew God and Saturn", CW11, *The Archive for Research in Archetypal Symbolism*, retrieved at: aras.org

CHAPTER IV

∴

THE THREE PRINCIPAL STAGES OF HUMAN LIFE, THE THREE PRINCIPAL SUPPORTS OF THE LODGE, THE THREE PRINCIPAL OFFICERS OF THE LODGE
&
THE NUMBER THREE

THE THREE PRINCIPAL STAGES OF HUMAN LIFE

The first three [steps on the Winding Staircase] allude to the three principal stages of human life, namely, youth, manhood, and old age. In youth, as Entered Apprentices, we ought industriously to occupy our minds in the attainment of useful knowledge; in manhood, as Fellow Crafts, we should apply our knowledge to the discharge of our respective duties to God, our neighbors, and ourselves; so that in old age, as Master Masons, we may enjoy the happy reflections consequent on a well-spent life, and die in the hope of a glorious immortality.[1]

---

1   *Duncan's Masonic Ritual and Monitor* (1866), New York: Crown Publishers, 1986, p. 74

As we learn in the Masonic Fellow Craft lecture (see Appendix D), the three steps allude to the three stages of human life: youth, manhood and old age.[2] Again, we see the tripartite division of the whole – in this case, a human life – three aspects emanating from the one. This differentiation of youth, manhood and old age corresponds to the ancient Roman life stages of *pueritia, juventus* and *senectus*, respectively, thus illustrating the antiquity of this threefold distinction. Though they may be seen purely as biological designations, it is important to note that all cultures have marked these phases – and, most significantly, the passage from one to the next – by rites of passage and ceremonies of initiation. Initiations such as these are an anthropological constant, as they define the status of the individual within the hierarchical stratification of their society – the social organism within its societal ecosystem – and, thereby, help to maintain the equilibrium of a community. Arnold van Gennep famously referred to this social stratification as "a kind of house divided into rooms and corridors."[3]

Van Gennep's metaphorical "house" is one with which Masons should find resonance, apropos the metaphorical "house not made with hands, eternal in the heavens".[4] For it is in the Mason's microcosmic, terrestrial temple that the macrocosmic, celestial temple is hermetically mirrored. A similarly sympathetic dynamic is also referenced in the Working Tools section of the Entered Apprentice degree: "[…] thereby fitting our bodies, as living stones, for that spiritual building, that house not made with hands, eternal in the heavens," and constitutes one of the many examples of concepts associated with Hermetic philosophy being present in the ritual and symbolism or Freemasonry. We should note that, in Van Gennep's metaphor, the "rooms" of the "house" contain those members who are established in their particular subset of the society, while the "corridors" represent those liminal portals, by means of which the individual is advanced, or *passed*, from one station in life to another. These corridors, or initiatory portals, are represented in the West by such diverse developmental milestones as baptism, circumcision, *quinceañera*, First Communion, *Bar* or *Bat Mitzvah*, graduation, "jumping in" a street gang, white coat ceremonies, receiving a black belt in a martial art, retirement parties, etc. The symbolic exchange of such Hermetic concepts with those of classical initiatory systems may also be detected in the ancient use of *hermai* (Greek: ἑρμαῖ; plural of *herm*), which were stone sculptures, often depicting the head and

---

2   *Duncan's Masonic Ritual and Monitor* (1866), New York: Crown Publishers, 1986, p. 74

3   Van Gennep, as cited in Journet, "Les rites de passage", *Sciences Humaines*, 2001

4   *The Holy Bible*, KJV, 2 Corinthians 5:1

phallus of Hermes, atop and upon a squared lower section. These *hermai* functioned as boundary markers and, thereby, delineated liminal passages – much like the passages through which the initiate would be conducted by Hermes, the archetypal *psychopompos* and initiator.[5] One common critique of most Western initiatory systems is that they lack one or more of the tripartite liminal functions – this, however, is not the case in Freemasonry, as it is one of the few intact systems fulfilling all three of Van Gennep's initiatory phases.

In the Fellow Craft lecture, the three principal stages of human life are attributed to the three craft degrees of Freemasonry; youth to the Entered Apprentice, manhood to the Fellow Craft, and old age to the Master Mason. The attribution of these phases to the Masonic degrees explicitly frames these life-stages in an initiatory context, much like the aforementioned liminal rites of passage. The Entered Apprentice degree ceremony *separates* the aspirant from his former peer group by means of his Obligation to the Fraternity, thus fulfilling the pre-liminal aspect; in the Fellow Craft degree, the initiate is *transformed* by the absorption and application of the arts and sciences encountered in the lecture which accompanies the degree (to which this book may be viewed as a supplement), thus fulfilling the liminal requirement; finally, the Master Mason is *reintegrated* into his Lodge – on the level, as it were – and also into society at large, in the form of a "better man", thus fulfilling the post-liminal initiatory element. In a sort of fractal sense, the three craft degrees individually display these three classic phases of initiation. While it would be imprudent to reveal specific details here, suffice it to say that the pre-liminal elements (rites of separation) occurring in each of the three degrees would be fulfilled by features such as the Chamber of Reflection, the preparation room, and hoodwinking; the liminal elements (rites of transition) are illustrated by features such as the Obligation, the lecture accompanying each degree, and the portrayal of the central Masonic allegory (the Legend of G∴M∴H∴A∴.); and the post-liminal (rites of incorporation) would be fulfilled by features such as the administration of the Charge, the rite of Investiture, and the communal Agape feast (also known as a Harmony, or Festive Board). All of these are merely examples, expressed in the vaguest terms, but the astute Mason should be able to discern the hallmarks of these three initiatory stages both within the suite of craft degrees as a whole, as well as in the degrees when examined individually.

---

5 Dodd & Faraone, *Initiation in Ancient Greek Rituals and Narratives: New Critical Perspectives*, Routledge, 2013

The Riddle of the Sphinx, frontispiece from Kircher's Œdipus Ægyptiacus, 1652

The three principle stages of human life also bring to mind the "riddle of the sphinx" scene in Sophocles' *Oedipus Rex*. Upon his arrival to Thebes, Oedipus is accosted by a terrible, man-eating sphinx who asks the riddle: "What walks on four feet in the morning, two in the afternoon, and three at night?" Oedipus' answer: "Man: as an infant, he crawls on all fours; as an adult, he walks on two legs and; in old age, he uses a walking stick". His answer being correct, the traveler was allowed to enter the city and become its king. Tragically, Oedipus' enthronement turned out to be a rather dubious honor, but that is another matter…

THE THREE PRINCIPAL SUPPORTS OF THE LODGE

[The first three steps on the Winding Staircase] also allude to the three principal supports in Masonry, namely, Wisdom, Strength. and Beauty; for it is necessary that there should be wisdom to contrive, strength to support, and beauty to adorn all great and important undertakings.[6]

The three steps on the first course of the Winding Staircase are also attributed to the three principal supports of the Masonic Lodge, which are Wisdom, Strength and Beauty; "[…] wisdom to contrive, strength to support, and beauty to adorn all great and important undertakings,"[7] as it is stated in the lecture. They are often represented by three columns, each of which being rendered in a classical Greek architectural style: an Ionic order column denoting Wisdom, a Doric order denoting Strength and a Corinthian order denoting Beauty. We will be visiting the classical orders of architecture in greater detail in Chapter V of the current volume dealing with the course of five steps, to which the Orders are attributed. However, it is worth presently illustrating why the Ionic, Doric and Corinthian columns have been respectively assigned to the supports of Wisdom, Strength and Beauty. The Ionic column, which is characterized by the use of volutes (spiral, scroll-like ornaments) on its capital and is the narrowest of all the three canonical orders, is associated with Athena ('Aθῆνα), the goddess of *Wisdom*. Consequently, this order is most often employed in houses of learning, such as libraries, schools and academies. The Doric column, which was the earliest conceived and least adorned of the classical orders, was considered the strongest and most indicative of the masculine virtues. Ergo, this order is associated with Ares ("Aρης), the god of war, and used to convey *Strength*. The Corinthian column, which is the most ornate of the orders, replete with capitals adorned with acanthus leaves and slender fluted columns, is associated with Aphrodite ('Aφροδίτη) and is thereby representative of *Beauty*.

Wisdom, Strength and Beauty also respectively correspond to the mind, body and spirit; Wisdom being the product of a well-tempered *mind*, a sound *body* providing Strength and support, and the aesthetic

6   *Duncan's Masonic Ritual and Monitor* (1866), New York: Crown Publishers, 1986, p. 74
7   Ibid

spirit which inspires all things of Beauty. In Greek, these three qualities are known as *psyche* (ψυχή), *soma* (σῶμα) and *pneuma* (πνεύμα); for the cultivation and maintenance of these three components of a well-rounded life should always be considered in due measure and proportion. In Freudian terms, the psyche is further divided into three parts: the *id*, *ego* and *superego* – another common example of the tripartite division of the singular whole. Similar to the three principal stages of human life, Freud's model of the psyche, which he developed in 1923, saw the id, ego and superego as developing sequentially according to the psychic maturity of the individual. The id, which is primitive and instinctual, is the first component to emerge; next, the ego forms as the subject's personal consciousness finds equilibrium with external reality; finally, the superego finds expression as the inner voice of the subject's relative set of morals and ethics. When the id, ego and superego are integrated into a proportionally-balanced whole, the byproduct is Wisdom; for the thoughts and actions of one with so tempered a *psyche* could only be called *wise*. The body, or *soma*, finds its fullest manifestation in Strength, which may only be attained through discipline. The spirit, or *pneuma*, reaches its fullest and most realized expression in the arts. In a 1964 diary entry, writer, filmmaker and philosopher Susan Sontag once wrote that "Art is a form of nourishment (of consciousness, the spirit)"[8] – echoing a sentiment found in the work of Russian painter and art theorist Wassily Kandinsky (1866-1944), who wrote:

> *[In great art] the spectator does feel a corresponding thrill in himself. Such harmony or even contrast of emotion cannot be superficial or worthless; indeed the Stimmung [German; spirit, or mood] of a picture can deepen and purify that of the spectator. Such works of art at least preserve the soul from coarseness; they 'key it up,' so to speak, to a certain height, as a tuning-key the strings of a musical instrument.*[9]

The spiritual conception of art may be found in the remotest periods of human history. In ancient Egypt, for example, wooden or stone statues were created in the image of the recently deceased for the express purpose of housing their *ka*, or spirit, after death. In fact, it was a common practice to draw celestial spirits into Egyptian statuary by specific rites of astral magic – thus, literally *inspiring* them. Renowned British Egyptologist,

8   From a 1964 diary entry, parentheses hers
9   Kandinsky, *Concerning the Spiritual in Art*, Courier Corp., 1977, p. 2

E.A. Wallis Budge (1857-1934) had said that "from time immemorial the people of Egypt believed that every statue possessed an indwelling spirit."[10] Ancient Egyptian statuary was said to be "animated" by spirits to such an extent that the stone figures were said to have actually moved and even prophesized. Astral spirits were invoked into the statues by means of "words of power" and magical rites. In one such rite, the Egyptian magus exhorted the disembodied spirit "Inhabitant of the tomb! Inhabitant of the tomb! [...] now inhabit your statue." Once the spirit was invoked, the magus then held a sacred amulet to the eyes, nostrils and mouth to the statue and said "Now are thine eyes made. Horus has opened thy mouth, he has opened thine eyes; he has given breath to thy nostrils with the divine amulet that opens the eyes," thereby rendering the statue *inspirited*, completing this ancient magical operation.[11] This practice, and other similar operations, did not die with the ancient Egyptian magi – during the Renaissance, for example, several theologians, astrologers and magicians adopted the practice into their own syncretic magical systems. Drawing upon the wealth of Neoplatonic, Gnostic and quasi-Egyptian Hermetic literature which had recently made its way into the West, in addition to the medieval grimoire tradition – a tradition including works of primarily astrological magic such as *Picatrix* (Arabic: Ghāyat al-Ḥakīm, غاية الحكيم, 10th or 11th century) and the Solomonic *Claviculi* (מלשה חתפמ, including the *Lesser Key*, or *Lemegeton*, and the *Ars göetia*) – with which they were already familiar, Pico della Mirandola (1463-1494), Heinrich Cornelius Agrippa (1486-1535) and Giordano Bruno (1548-1600), among others, had written much about the drawing down of these spirits celestial or angelic hierarchies (not to mention the dæmons of the thirty-six decans, or 10° arc segments of the ecliptic, and the göetic dæmons associated with the seventy-two quinances, or 5° arc segments of the ecliptic)[12] into magically-operative works of art such as statues, amulets and talismans.

> *This beneficent magic, in calling forth, as it were, from their hiding places into the light the powers which the largess of God has sown and planted in the world, does not itself work*

10   Budge, *Cook's Handbook for Egypt and the Sudan*, T. Cook & Son, 1906
11   Mayet, "Le Destin, la Divination Egyptienne ell'Oracle d'Antinous", as cited in *Atlantis Rising Magazine*, April, 2012
12   I have chosen to use the word *dæmon*, as opposed to *demon*, in order to differentiate the personifications of the quinances and decan images from the common association with the word, which implies a malevolent entity and carries an obviously negative connotation.

*miracles, so much as sedulously serve nature as she works her
wonders. Scrutinizing, with greater penetration, that harmony of the universe which the Greeks with greater aptness
of terms called sympatheia and grasping the mutual affinity
of things, she applies to each thing those inducements (called
the iugges of the magicians), most suited to its nature. Thus
it draws forth into public notice the miracles which lie hidden in the recesses of the world, in the womb of nature, in the
storehouses and secret vaults of God, as though she herself were
their artificer. As the farmer weds his elms to the vines, so the
"magus" unites earth to heaven, that is, the lower orders to the
endowments and powers of the higher.[13]*

Wisdom, Strength and Beauty, frontispiece of the Builder's Jewel londres, 1741

13   Pico della Mirandola, *De hominis dignitate* (English: *Oration on the Dignity of Man*),
1486

There are several ways in which one may orient Wisdom, Strength and Beauty within the greater schema of Hermetic Qabalah. One may begin by using their correspondences on the *Etz Chaim* (see Appendix B) and attributing them to the appropriate *sephirah*, whereby Wisdom would be assigned to *Chokmah* (which means "Wisdom" in Hebrew), Strength to *Geburah* (which is associated with Ares/Mars), and Beauty to *Tiphareth* (which means "Beauty" in Hebrew). Interestingly, this particular sephirothic distribution finds each principal on one of the three pillars of the tree; *Chokmah* is the uppermost *sephirah* on the Pillar of Mercy, *Geburah* is the middle *sephirah* on the Pillar of Severity, and *Tiphareth* is the central *sephirah* on the Middle Pillar, or Pillar of Mildness – thereby, the three principal supports of the Lodge are represented on the *Etz Chaim*.

The celestial correspondences attributed to these three *sephiroth* are, respectively: the fixed stars, Mars and Sol, the Sun. The paths which unite these three *sephiroth* are that of *lamed* (ל, path 22, gematriac value: 30, meaning: "ox goad"), and that of *heh* (ה, path 15, gematriac value: 6, meaning: "window"); their total gematriac value being thirty-six (see Appendix A). Considering this data, the qabalist may note that Mars' Strength is prodded into activity by the Beauty of the Sun in order to achieve balance, represented by the Scales of Libra; and also that the fiery Sun is given visual access to the supernal vistas of the fixed stars, its immediate ruler, the Emperor. As we learned in Chapter II, which dealt with the Brazen Pillars, words that share the same gematriac value are said to resonate with each other in an occult manner; with this in mind, we find that the words *tabernacle* (Hebrew: להא) and *Babylon* (Hebrew: לבב) share the total value of the paths connecting Wisdom, Strength and Beauty. The reader is invited to interpret the significance of this data in their own qabalistic analysis.

Utilizing the Tarot attributions associated with these two paths, we find that Mars (Strength) and the Sun (Beauty) are united by Justice XI and that the fixed stars (Wisdom) and the Sun (Beauty) are united by the Emperor IV. This is an astrological significant configuration in that Justice XI corresponds to Libra, the scales, and the Emperor IV corresponds to Aries, the ram. In tropical astrology, these cardinal signs host autumnal and vernal equinoxes, respectively. This equinoctial configuration could not be more representative of temperance, balance and equilibrium, particularly since Sol is at their fulcrum – just as the Earth is at the fulcrum of the Sun's rays at the equinoxes. Elementally, Aries represents fire, while Libra represents air – fire and air being the two upper, more rarified classical elements, as opposed to their denser counterparts, water and earth. The Tarot cards Justice XI and the Emperor IV also represent an axis, at the extremes of which lay mercy and severity, but in a reversed polarity than that of the pillars to which they are tethered. The tempered mediation of Justice XI unites the Pillar of Severity with the Middle Pillar, whereas the severe authority of the Emperor IV unites the Pillar of Mercy with the Middle Pillar (see Appendix B).

THE THREE PRINCIPAL OFFICERS OF THE LODGE

The three steps on the first course of the Winding Staircase are also said to denote the three principal officers of the Masonic Lodge, also known as the pedestal, or dais officers. Often, the jewels of these three officers are emblematically depicted on this course of steps. Their jewels are the plumb, the level and the square and they represent the Junior Warden, Senior Warden and Worshipful Master, respectively. For those readers who may be unfamiliar the titles, duties and general hierarchical structure of Freemasonry's officers, we will provide some clarification. The Masonic officer's roles are symbolic representations of those used by the medieval craft guilds of cathedral builders in Europe, as discussed in Chapter I. Freemasonry, which to some extent stems from the medieval stonemason guilds, uses some of the vernacular and instruments of the operative trade. However, in Freemasonry, these designations and tools are applied symbolically, thereby highlighting the distinction between operative stonemasons – those who physically quarry, raise, dress and fit worked stone into architecturally conceived edifices – and speculative, accepted Masons – those who philosophically apply the working tools of the craft to their own hearts, minds and consciences in an effort to better fit, as living stones, that "house not made with hands, eternal in the heavens".[14]

Taking the three principal officers, in their ascending hierarchical order, are the Junior Warden, the Senior Warden and the Worshipful Master. We will begin by examining their duties within the context of speculative Masonic work. We read in Morgan's *Illustrations of Masonry*, of the Junior Warden's duties:

> *As the sun in the south at high meridian is the beauty and*
> *glory of the day, so stands the Junior Warden in the south, the*
> *better to observe the time, call the crafts from labor to*

---

14   *The Holy Bible*, KJV, 2 Corinthians 5:1, a passage frequently employed in Masonic ritua

refreshment, superintend them during the hours thereof, see that none convert the hours of refreshment into that of intemperance or excess; and call them out again in due season, that the Worshipful Master may have honor, and they profit and pleasure thereby.[15]

The Senior Warden's duties:

As the sun sets in the west to close the day, so stands the Senior Warden in the west to assist the Worshipful Master in opening his lodge, take care of the jewels and implements, see that none be lost, pay the craft their wages, if any be due, and see that none go away dissatisfied.[16]

And the Worshipful Master's duties:

As the sun rises in the east to open and adorn the day, so presides the Worshipful Master in the east to open and adorn his lodge, set his crafts to work with good and wholesome laws, or cause the same to be done.[17]

The diurnal solar symbolism of these three officer's stations is, of course, obvious; the station of Worshipful Master, which is in the East, represents sunrise; the station of the Junior Warden, which is in the South, represents midday; and the station of the Senior Warden, which is in the West, represents sunset. This brings to mind the Hindu Trimurti (Sanskrit: त्रिमूर्ति, meaning "three forms"), a tripartite solar division personified by the gods Brahma (the creator), Vishnu (the preserver) and Shiva (the destroyer), as the Sun could be said to be created at sunrise, preserved at meridian height, and destroyed at sunset. Taken together, these divinities, like those of Christian trinitarianism, also represent three modalities of one Supreme Deity – a recurring concept in the present study. The apparent path of the Sun on its diurnal course along the ecliptic has been mythologized in many cultures, notable examples being the Atet solar barque of

15 *Morgan, Illustrations of Masonry, Ezra A. Cook, 1827, p. 13*
16 Ibid
17 Ibid, p. 14

Ra, the Trundholm Sun chariot of the Nordic Bronze Age, and the chariot of Helios (Phoebus-Apollo), the vehicle which drew the Sun along its daily path and upon which Phaëthon, the son of Helios and the Oceanid nymph Clymene, took his ill-fated ride.

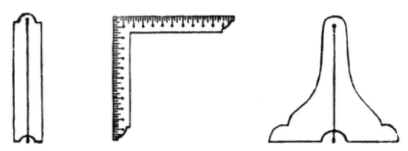

The Working Tools of a Fellow Craft, from Mackey's Manual of the Lodge, 1891

There is a set of working tools associate with each degree in Freemasonry, just as there is a jewel associated with each office. The working tools for the Entered Apprentice are the twenty-four-inch gauge and the common gavel, and are explained in the lecture of that degree; the working tools of the Master Mason are all the tools of Masonry, but most especially the trowel, also explained in the accompanying lecture. It is the working tools of the Fellow Craft with which we are presently concerned – these are the plumb, the level and the square. Their operative and speculative applications are explained thus:

> *The plumb is an instrument made use of by operative masons to raise perpendiculars, the square to square their work, and the Level to lay horizontals; but we, as Free and Accepted Masons, are taught to make use of them for more noble and glorious purposes; the plumb admonishes us to walk uprightly in our several stations before God and man, squaring our actions by the square of virtue, and remembering that we are traveling upon the level of time, to "that undiscovered country, from whose bourne no traveler returns."[18]*

In the lectures accompanying the Blue Lodge degrees, the explanations of the working tools are primarily representative of either their operative usage or their moral and ethical speculative applications – the

18   *Duncan's Masonic Ritual and Monitor* (1866), New York: Crown Publishers, 1986, p. 82

plumb is generally understood as symbolizing integrity and moral rectitude; the level, fairness and equality; and the square, honesty and truthfulness. Emblematically, the plumb, level and square appear on the first three steps of the Winding Staircase because, as Masons, our first concern is to begin to improve our character before we may effectively begin to improve our mind. We will now take a detailed look at the three working tools, individually, which are also the jewels of the three pedestal officers: the plumb, the level and the square.

The plumb (alternately, plumb bob or plummet) is a cord with a non-magnetic, usually lead, weight at one end, and sometimes affixed to a wooden frame. Operatively, the plumb is used to indicate a vertical direction, to prove a vertical line, or to measure depth, particularly of a body of water – to "plumb the depths", as it were. It thereby represents the vertical axis, corresponding to the vertical Cartesian coordinate z (the *applicate*), which we will discuss in further detail later. The instrument has been in use at least since ancient Egyptian times.[19] The plumb bob is still in wide usage throughout the building trades though, recently, laser instruments have come into favor. The etymological root of the word plumb is the Latin *plumbum*, which means lead.[20] It is from the word *plumbum* that the ascription of the initials *Pb* was attributed to lead on the Periodic Table of Elements. In its form as an adjective, the word shares its etymology with the word *aplomb*, which means confidence or poise, especially in trying times, alluding to the ability to remain *upright* and true.

The plumb bob describes a vertical reference line, pointing to the center of gravity, thereby proving a perpendicular. It is in this aspect that the plumbline, or plummet, has long been used as a metaphor for justice and righteousness. The instrument is employed in this metaphorical sense several times in the Bible. We read in the book of Amos, for instance, the following passage with which every Fellow Craft will be familiar:

> *Thus he shewed me: and, behold, the Lord stood upon a wall made by a plumbline, with a plumbline in his hand. And the LORD said unto me, Amos, what seest thou? And I said, A plumbline. Then said the Lord, Behold, I will set a plumbline in the midst of my people Israel: I will not again pass by them any more.*[21]

---

19   Stocks, *Experiments in Egyptian archaeology: stoneworking technology in ancient Egypt*, Routledge, 2003, p. 180

20   Entry: "Plumb"; *Online Etymological Dictionary*, retrieved at etymonline.com

21   *The Holy Bible*, KJV, Amos 7:7-8

And another pertinent passage, wherein the plummet is employed in a similarly metaphorical context, in Isaiah:

> *Judgement also will I lay to the line, and righteousness to the plummet.*[22]

In Hebrew, the word for plumb is rendered as אנך, or *anak*, and it contains the letters *aleph*, *nun* and *kaph* final. With this information, we may employ Hermetic and Qabalistic exegetical methods (see Appendix A) to arrive at the potential occult significance of the word. The gematriac value of *aleph* is one (1); that of *nun* is fifty (50); and that of *kaph* final is five-hundred (500). The total gematriac value for the word *anak* is five-hundred-fifty-one (551). As we had previously discussed, words sharing the same gematriac value are believed to have a synergetic relationship, in that one word may help to elucidate the other, or otherwise reveal the word's occult subtext. Other scriptural words with a gematriac value of five-hundred-fifty-one are: *qowmah* (קומתה) which means "height", *tequwmah* (תקומה) which means "stand", *pasha* (ומפשעיהם) which means "transgression", and *qin'ah* (קנאת) which means "jealousy". Examining the juxtaposition of each of these words with the concept of the plumb, we find that the words *height* and *stand* clearly support the implied uprightness and moral rectitude; but what affords us even greater opportunities for contemplation are the antithetical connotations of *transgression* and *jealousy*, which are obviously in opposition to these qualities. Just as the Pillars of Mercy and Severity stand in polar opposition on the *Etz Chaim* and are ultimately synthesized in the Middle Pillar (see Appendix B), we find that the dialectic introduced by our jealousies and transgressions may be rectified by the plumb.

---

22   *The Holy Bible*, KJV, Isaiah 28:17

The Fool, Death and the Wheel of Fortune, Tarot de Marseilles

The letters *aleph*, *nun* and *kaph* correspond to the Tarot cards: The Fool 0, Death XIII and Wheel of Fortune X, respectively. Interpreting these cards in a sequential, linear narrative, we again observe the tripartite, liminal rites of initiation. The Fool 0 represents new beginnings, the quest for adventure, and the spirit of hopefulness and of improvisation that define the aspirant. Hounded by restlessness and ennui, he leaves his home, of his own free will and accord, on a quest for meaning. In the Death XIII card, he experiences the transformational quality of initiation, old paradigms are torn asunder. He is faced with a grim ordeal and the confusion of cognitive dissonance inspires him to seek psychic resolution. In the Wheel of Fortune X, the initiate again encounters the nagging dog which clawed at his back when he began his journey as the Fool, but this time in the form of the bloodthirsty sphinx. However, his travels and trials have equipped him with the answer to her dreaded riddle – for the initiate has learned the answer by passing the three stages of initiation, themselves representing birth, manhood and old age.

The plumb was also an integral component of instruments used in early astronomical observation, such as the T-crossbar, quadrant and astrolabe, as well as instruments of navigation and surveying. Only by establishing an accurate vertical reference point, at a 90° angle from a level plane, could one calculate the aspects and relative positions of the stars and other celestial bodies. The same is true for navigation, which was contingent upon the stars and their positions. Accuracy in surveying was also dependent on fixed coordinates, as it is currently. We will address these subjects in greater detail in Chapter XIII, wherein we will investigate the quadrivial subjects of geometry and astronomy.

Lead, or *plumbum*, is sometimes associated with the *prima materia*, or first matter, in alchemical processes. This is partly because alchemical lead is considered "cold and moist" in opposition to alchemical gold being considered "hot and dry". Lead is seen as requiring perfection through a series of metallurgical, or mineral kingdom alchemical operations which would elevate this base metal to its exalted and incorruptible state. Thus, lead and gold are theoretically seen as representing the two extremes on an alchemical segment. In some alchemical and magical systems, the planetary glyph for Saturn is associated with the element lead. Interestingly, lead is sometimes personified as an old man bearing a scythe in some alchemical codices – not unlike Father Time or the titan Cronus, with whom Chronos was conflated due to their sharing the name Κρόνος, in the Greek. This can be seen to tie back to Masonic symbolism in several ways. In the suite of symbols known as the Weeping Virgin of the Third Degree, an image of Father Time, holding a scythe and an hourglass at his feet, is seen undoing the ringlets of the virgin's hair as she weeps over a broken pillar. The scythe also appears in the Master Mason degree lecture in which it is referred to as an emblem of time, "which cuts the brittle thread of life, and launches us into eternity."[23]

As a transitive verb, "to plumb" may also mean "to seal with lead". In this form, we may consider the *plumbing* of the chest into which Set tricked his brother, Osiris. An abridgement of this ancient Egyptian myth, as told in Plutarch,[24] runs roughly as follows: Set and the queen of Ethiopia, along with seventy-two accomplices, conspire to kill Osiris. The presence of the number seventy-two in mythological narratives, or elsewhere in literature, should always prompt the attentive reader to be conscious of a possible astrological allegory; as this is the number of the quinances, or 5° arc segments of the ecliptic, and is sometimes employed in astro-mythological lore. Set produces a chest made to fit Osiris' measurements, and offers the chest to any of the banquet guests who best fits inside of it. Of course, Osiris is a perfect fit and, while he is inside the chest, Set *plumbs* the lid, trapping Osiris within. The chest was then thrown into the Nile river, by which it was borne to Byblos, a coastal Phoenician city, where it became lodged in a tamarisk tree trunk. In some versions of the myth, the

23   *Duncan's Masonic Ritual and Monitor* (1866), New York: Crown Publishers, 1986, p. 130
24   Plutarch, *Moralia*, "On Isis and Osiris", 1874, ch. 12

tree into which the chest becomes embedded is an acacia.[25] The tree was later cut down and used as a pillar in the palace of the king of Byblos; this is the origin of the Djed Pillar, or "Pillar of Stability". Isis, who had been diligently searching for signs of her brother-husband, hears of the pillar and travels to Byblos to retrieve Osiris' remains.

Papyrus depicting Osiris and Isis

The level is the jewel of the Senior Warden of the Masonic Lodge and, as such, it is assigned to the second step of the course of three steps upon the Winding Staircase. In the operative sense, the level is an instrument with a straight horizontal surface and a perpendicular plumb bob affixed to a wooden frame. It is used to prove horizontals – if the plumb line, which runs at a 90° angle to the horizontal surface, is centered in its vertical guiding channel, then the horizontal surface is true, or "level".

---

25   Two common species of the acacia tree in North African and the Levant are *acacia senegal* and *acacia nilotica*, both of which contain the psychoactive compound *dimethyltryptamine* (DMT). The reader is again directed to the work of Brother P.D. Newman, whose work explores this subject in great detail.

Because the instrument, like the plummet, also employs a plumb bob, the level is sometimes referred to as a "plumb level". Both the plumb and the level utilize the Earth's gravity to prove their respective surfaces, via the lead weight suspended from the cord. Modern levels most commonly use a bubble of air in an enclosed glass or clear plastic tube of a colored liquid, and are consequently referred to as "bubble levels", though laser levels have been increasingly popular as of late. In its metaphorical or figurative applications, the word *level* is in common usage and can carry connotations of equality, calmness, consistency, self-control, evenness, equanimity, composure, or can imply honesty and frankness, as in to "level" with someone. The idiom "on the level", which likely has its origin in Freemasonry, has made it into common Western vernacular and is used to imply honesty, authenticity or genuineness.

The etymological root of the English word *level* is the Latin *libella*, which is the diminutive form of the Latin *libra*, meaning "scales" or "balance".[26] The symbolism of the scales harken back to the Greek *Themis* (Θέμις), who personified law and justice – though her form of justice was thought to be more of an expression of Divine Justice, as opposed to a representation of legal justice conceived of by mankind. Themis was also included among the Delphic Oracles, due to her ability to see the future.

> *Themis is untranslatable. A gift of the gods and a mark of civilized existence, sometimes it means right custom, proper procedure, social order, and sometimes merely the will of the gods (as revealed by an omen, for example) with little of the idea of right*[27]

Considering the rampant Egypto-Hellenic syncretization which occurred during the Ptolemaic Kingdom (323 – 30 BCE), Themis may be seen as an extension of the Egyptian concept and persona of Ma'at. In its conceptual form, Ma'at denoted truth, justice, morality, harmony and the very equilibrium of the Universe. In keeping with the concept of Ma'at, the Old Kingdom-era (2686 – 2181 BCE) Egyptian citizenry were expected to conduct themselves by this set of morals.[28] As a personification in the New Kingdom (1569 – 1081 BCE), Ma'at was the daughter of Ra,

---

26   Entry: "Level"; *Online Etymological Dictionary*, retrieved at etymonline.com

27   Finley, *The World of Odysseus*, rev. ed., Viking Press, 1978, p. 78 note, retrieved online

28   Martin, "Maat and order in African Cosmology: A Conceptual Tool for Understanding Indigenous Knowledge", *Journal of Black Studies*, 2008, p. 951

and the goddess who represented the principles associated with the earlier concept of Ma'at, while also regulating the movement of the stars and the procession of the seasons. She was most-often depicted as a young woman, often with an ostrich feather protruding from her head and had temples dedicated to her at Karnak, Memphis and Deir el-Medina.[29] Probably the most notable appearance of the goddess Ma'at is in the "weighing of the heart" sequence found in the *Egyptian Book of the Dead*, an ancient funerary text in use since the beginning of the New Kingdom (1550 BCE) and into the Ptolemaic period (50 BCE). The texts were used to guide the recently deceased in their passage through the Duat, or underworld. The weighing of the heart was officiated by the *psychopompos*, Anubis (later to be syncretized with the Greek Hermes), and featured the scales upon which the heart of the deceased (Ani) was weighed against the Shu-feather of Ma'at. During the weighing, the deceased was to recite the Forty-two Negative Confessions ("I have not commited sin. I have not commited robbery with violence. I have not stolen." etc.[30]); and if the heart weighed the same or less than the feather of Ma'at, then the deceased was allowed to pass on – but, if the it outweighed the feather, then the heart was devoured on the spot by the demoness, Ammitt, who was part lion, pert crocodile and part hippopotamus, thereby denying the deceased of an afterlife.[31] The examples of both Themis and Ma'at before her illustrate that the very idea of the level has been linked, through the scales, to the concepts of justice, law and ethics from very ancient times.

The Weighing of the Heart, from the Papyrus of Ani, 1300 BCE

29   *The Essential Guide to Egyptian Mythology: The Oxford Guide*, Berkeley Reference, 2003, p. 190

30   *Papyrus of Ani*, 1250 BCE, Budge translation

31   Budge, *Death in Ancient Egypt: Weighing the Heart*, British Museum, Retrieved online

In Western astrology, Libra is the zodiacal sign spanning from September 23rd to October 22nd, and from 180° – 210° celestial longitude, inhabiting a 30° arc segment of the ecliptic. Tropically, the sign of Libra signals hosts the autumnal equinox and thereby ushers in the Fall season. The autumnal equinox, which we will go over in greater detail in the astronomy section of Chapter VIII, is one of two points, along with the vernal equinox, when the ecliptic (the Sun's apparent path through the heavens, from the perspective of the Earth) and the celestial equator (an imaginary projection of the Earth's equator onto the so-called celestial sphere) intersect. The scales of Libra may also be seen to represent the balance of the diurnal and nocturnal hours which occurs at the equinoxes. Fittingly, the Tarot card associated with the zodiacal sign of Libra is Justice XI (see Appendix A). In the Rider-Waite Tarot,[32] the figure is depicted as being seated between two columns, denoting the concepts of balance and law; she holds a sword in her right hand – the sword is double-edged and thereby illustrates the balance between knowledge and power. The scales are suspended by her left hand, symbolizing her impartiality – for if they were in the right hand, human biases and active meddling would be implied. There is a small square on her crown, which alludes to the organization of her thoughts – the square being a symbol of order and stability.[33] The element corresponding to the Justice XI card is air, which is symbolized by the sword, which represents the intellect and reasoning powers necessary to mete out a judgement that tempers *mercy* and *severity* – again, represented by the pillars on the card as well as those of the *Etz Chaim* (see Appendix B). The Hebrew letter attributed the Justice XI card is *lamed* (ל), corresponding to the Latin and English letter *L*, as in Libra, libella and level. The gematriac value of *lamed* is thirty, which has been said to "[r]epresent the perfect balance in the cosmic organization".[34]

In our examination of the jewels representing the three principal officers of the Masonic Lodge, we will now turn our attention to the square, which is the jewel of the Worshipful Master. A square is "an instrument having at least one right angle and two straight edges used especially to lay out or test right angles"[35] and may be described as an angle of 90°, representing "the fourth part of a circle". As a verb, to "square" is to make two or more people, events, facts or ideas agree or concur – alluded to by

---

32   Waite, *The Pictorial Key to the Tarot*, Illustrated by Pamela Colman-Smith, US Games, 1911, "XI Justice"

33   Entry: "Square", *The Penguin Dictionary of Symbols*, Penguin Books, 1997

34   Entry: "*30*", Number Symbolism, *Riding the Beast*, retrieved at: ridingthebeast.com

35   Entry: "Square"; *Webster's Collegiate Dictionary*, retrieved at: merriam-webster.com

the phrase: "who best can work and best agree". The square also denotes a delineated space (e.g., Pershing Square, Times Square, etc.) and, as such, may be seen as the unfolding of a point into the four cardinal directions. In operative Masonry, the square is a tool used for trying or proving a right angle, to affirm the right-angularity of a horizontal surface to that of a vertical surface, or vice-versa, so that stones may be fitted together, or agree, with exact nicety. As a polygon, a perfect square may be defined as a regular quadrilateral tetragon, in that it has four equal sides (it is a *quadrilateral tetragon*) meeting at four right angles (it is *regular*). In mathematics, to square a number is to multiply that number by itself – it is the same as raising a number, or an algebraic expression, to the power of two, which is usually denoted by an exponent in superscript ($G^2 = G \times G$). Interestingly, if we square the first four numbers: 1, 2, 3, 4, we produce: 1, 4, 9, 16, then subtract each from the next ($4 - 1, 9 - 4, 16 - 9$), we produce 3, 5, 7.[36] We will further address the mathematic and geometrical qualities of this, in the Masonic and esoteric context, and other figures in Chapter VIII.

For the most part, perfect squares do not occur in nature. Though there are anomalous examples such as the cuboid crystals of iron pyrite ($FeS2$) and sodium chloride ($NaCl$), these are rarely, if ever, perfect quadrilateral tetragons. The square, we must remember, is a mathematical concept – like the point, the line and the circle, which have no exact manifestation in nature – and, as such, represents man's theoretical view of creation, *not creation itself.* It is for this reason, the square may be seen as a symbol of mankind, as so many of man's structures, devices and creations, from time immemorial, have contained right angles, squares and cuboid shapes. Masons, in the most primitive operative and speculative sense, have especially employed the square and the right angle as far back as history allows us to survey. Cities, ancient and modern, are replete with right angles, squares and cubes. Anciently, the world was even conceived by man as being an *oblong square.*[37] Peering backward into prehistory, and certainly into modern times, we see that all the civilizations of mankind have utilized the square, almost fractally, at every level. It is for this reason that the square denotes order and stability imposed on nature by man.

The square polygon also symbolizes materiality, in that it represents the four corners of the Earth; the four cardinal directions: north, south, east and west; the four seasons: winter, spring, summer and fall; and, perhaps

---

36   I have diligently searched for the origin of this observation to no avail. The earliest source I was able to find, by the time of the publication of the present volume, was an uncredited post to www.themasonictrowel.com from 2/1/2001 entitled *The Meaning of the Square.*

37   Haywood, *Symbolical Masonry*, George H. Doran Co., 1923, p. 180

most significantly, the four classical elements: fire, air, water and earth.[38] Overall, the stability and fixity of this shape lends itself to the permanency mankind has associated with material existence on the Earth which, until the Apollo 11 Moon landing in 1969, is all he has ever known. When we consider the square as a symbol of materiality, we must necessarily consider its compliment – the circle. The circle symbolizes timelessness, spirituality, idealism and the numinous. In Freemasonry as in geometry, the working tool that describes a circle is the compasses. Being complimentary to the 90° of the square, the compasses are generally depicted in their Masonic context as being opened at 60°– this being an allusion to either the individual degrees of an equilateral triangle (180° divided by three equals 60°), or perhaps to the sexagesimal, or base-60, system, which was developed by the ancient Sumerians in the 3rd millennium BCE. The origin of this system refers to the divisions of the total 360° of the ecliptic – a very foundational circular quantification, forming the basis of our seconds, minutes, hours, etc.[39] The square and compasses thus marry the spiritual and the material. The pairing of the square and the circle is a fairly ubiquitous symbolic motif found in alchemical symbolism, the union of opposites, the concept of squaring the circle, the Hermetic Marriage, the union of the masculine and feminine, Vitruvian Man, mandalas and, of course, the Masonic square and compasses.

---

38   Entry: "Square", *The Penguin Dictionary of Symbols*, Penguin Books, 1997

39   Neugebauer, *The Exact Sciences in Antiquity*, Dover, 1969, pp. 17-19

Luna.

4	9	2
3	5	7
8	1	6

Mercurius.

4	14	15	1
9	7	6	12
5	11	10	8
16	2	3	13

Jupiter.

8	58	59	5	4	62	63	1
49	15	14	52	53	11	10	56
41	23	22	44	45	19	18	48
32	34	35	29	28	38	39	25
40	26	27	37	36	30	31	33
17	47	46	20	21	43	42	24
9	55	54	12	13	51	50	16
64	2	3	61	60	6	7	57

Sol.

6	32	3	34	35	1
7	11	27	28	8	30
19	14	16	15	23	24
18	20	22	21	17	13
25	29	10	9	26	12
36	5	33	4	2	31

Saturnus.

37	78	29	70	21	62	3	45	5
6	38	79	30	71	22	63	14	46
47	7	39	80	31	72	23	55	15
16	48	8	40	81	32	64	24	56
57	17	49	9	41	73	33	65	25
26	58	18	50	1	42	74	34	66
67	27	59	10	51	2	43	75	35
36	68	19	60	11	52	3	44	76
77	28	69	20	61	12	53	4	45

Venus.

11	24	7	20	3
4	12	25	8	16
17	5	13	21	9
10	18	1	14	22
23	6	19	2	15

Mars.

22	47	16	41	10	35	4
5	23	48	17	42	11	29
30	6	24	49	18	36	12
13	31	7	25	43	19	37
38	14	32	1	26	44	20
21	39	8	33	2	27	45
46	15	40	9	34	3	28

Planetary magic squares, from Girolamo Cardano's Practica
arithmetice et mensurandi singularis, 1539

A magic square is a square divided into an equal number of cells, each of which containing a different integer, that when added together, either by row, column or diagonal, total to an equal number. The sum of each row, column or diagonal is called the "magic constant" of that particular magic square. The number of cells on one side dictates the order of that square, for example, a nine-celled square is of the order three. Though magic squares are largely considered to fall under the purview of recreational mathematics, they have been associated with both Freemasonry and the greater Western Esoteric Tradition. In the 11th century, magic squares were introduced to Europe by Ibn Zarkali of Toledo.[40] His text, *Kitāb tadbīrāt al-kawākib* (*Book on the Influences of the Planets*), was primarily concerned with what are called "planetary squares", which are sigils, or *kameas*, corresponding to each of the seven classical planets, each planetary square having a different number of cells and a unique magic constant. These planetary squares were primarily used in the construction of sigils, amulets and

---

40   Comes, *The Transmission of Azarquiel's Magic Squares in Latin Europe*, pp. 159-198, pdf retrieved online

talismans, designed for the purpose of drawing down the subtle cosmic influences of a particular planet. Magic squares were first framed in a qabalistic context in the 12th century by Abraham ibn Ezra of Toledo, who considered the gematriac relationships of the magic constants.[41] By the 15th century, planetary squares were present in Northern Europe, appearing in an edition of *Picatrix* printed in Kraków, Poland. These squares, from the Kraków *Picatrix* later appear in the works of Paracelsus (*Archidoxa Magica*, 1567) and Heinrich Cornelius Agrippa (*De ccculta philosophia*, 1531). Arguably, no one has done more to codify the *kameas* than Agrippa, who in Chapter 22 Book II of his *De occulta philosophia* laid out the definitive version of the squares to be referenced by nearly every magus, astrologer and Western occultist since. The magic constant and order for each of the seven planetary squares are as follows:

Planet	Constant	Order
Saturn	15	3
Jupiter	34	4
Mars	65	5
The Sun	111	6
Venus	175	7
Mercury	260	8
The Moon	369	9

The qabalist will immediately note the significance of this distribution, as it is that of the *sephiroth* on the *Etz Chaim*, from *Binah* to *Yesod* (see Appendix B), with the order corresponding to the number of each *sephirah* and the planets in the classic Neoplatonic, or Chaldean arrangement. Magic squares continued into the 17th century, appearing in the work of Athanasius Kircher (*Œdipus Ægyptiacus*, 1652) and Freemason, Benjamin Franklin (1706-1790), whose interest in the subject appears to have been largely recreational. Brother Albert Mackey, in his *Encyclopedia*, had said of magic squares:

---

41   Cammann, *Islamic and Indian Magic Squares*, part II. "History of Religions", 1969, pp. 271-299

There was no talisman more sacred than this among the Ori-
entalists [...] Thus designed, they called it by the name of the
planet Saturn, ZaHaL, because the sum of the 9 digits in the
square was equal to 45 [...] which is the numerical value of
the letters in the word ZaHaL, in the Arabic alphabet. The
talmudists also esteemed it as a sacred talisman because 15 is
the numerical value of the letters of the word JaH, which is
one of the forms of the Tetragrammaton. The Hermetic Philos-
ophers called these magic squares Tables of the Planets, and at-
tributed to them many occult virtues. [...] These magic squares
and their values have been used in the symbolism of numbers
in some of the advanced Degrees of Freemasonry.[42]

As we have shown, these squares have been employed astrologically,
as in the Arabic *Picatrix*; qabalistically, as in the work of Abraham ibn Ezra
and Athanasius Kircher; alchemically, as in the work of Paracelsus; magically, as in the work of Agrippa; recreationally, as in the work of Franklin;
and referenced in their Masonic context, due to their inclusion in the symbolism and composition of the "high degrees", by Mackey.

Taken together, the jewels of the three principal officers – the plumb,
the level and the square – may be seen as representing three-dimensional
space. The Cartesian coordinates: x (the *abscissa*), y (the *ordinate*), and z
(the *applicate*) are the coordinates of three-dimensional, Euclidean space.
The x axis represents a line going from side-to-side, the y axis represents a
line from front-to-back, and the z axis represents a line running up-and-
down. These coordinates are represented by three, mutually perpendicular
axes, which meet at a point called the *origin*. The three working tools – the
plumb, the level and the square – may be used to "try" each of these di-
mensional coordinates. The plumb proves the z axis, or *applicate*, in that it
tries a vertical line; the level proves the x axis, or *abscissa*, in that it tries the
horizontal; and the square proves the y axis, or *ordinate*, in that it bisects
the x axis at the *origin*, thereby forming a 90° angle, which is of course a
square. By this we find that the three principal officers' jewels, which are
also the working tools of a Fellow Craft, may be seen to represent three-dimensional, Euclidean space. We may extend this analogy a bit further to
add the fourth dimension of *time*, which is represented both by the plumb
– vis-à-vis *plumbum*, or lead, and its attendant Saturnal correspondences
– and by the level – the "Level of Time", as to which it is referred in the

---

42   Mackey, *An Encyclopedia of Freemasonry and its Kindred Sciences*, Everts & Co., 1884;
Entry: "Magic Squares"

working tools lecture of the Fellow Craft degree. One may consider the dimension of time (in the context of the spacetime continuum) to be that point, or *origin*, through which the mutually perpendicular lines of width, depth and height must pass. We are, of course, also reminded of the *signs* of Freemasonry, which are right angles, horizontals and perpendiculars; these are respectively represented by the square, which tries right angles, the level, which proves horizontals, and the plumb, which proves perpendiculars. In summary, there is ample reason to interpret the jewels of the three principal officers of the Lodge, when taken together, as representations of three-dimensional space, or perhaps even four-dimensional spacetime.

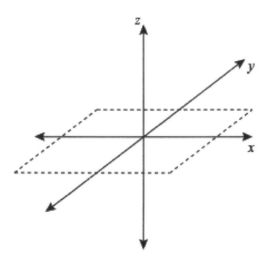

The Cartesian coordinates: x (the abscissa), y (the ordinate), and z (the applicate)

Having traversed the first course of three steps on the Winding Staircase, and having examined both the exoteric and esoteric correspondences of each, we are now prepared to begin the second stage of our ascension. Before we move on to the course of five steps, however, we will use this opportunity to first address the symbolism associated with the number three in general.

THE NUMBER THREE

Freemasonry is replete with ternary symbolism; this becomes abundantly clear when one considers the Fraternity's three Blue Lodge degrees, three dais officers, Three Great Lights, Three Lesser Lights, three burning tapers, three principal supports of the Lodge, the three squares of the 47th Problem of Euclid, three movable and three immovable jewels, etc. The number three, however, also finds its symbolic expression in myriad cultures and in all ages. To enumerate even a fraction of the instances of the number three occurring in the various traditions of the world would likely require multiple volumes. Keeping within the scope of the present inquiry, we will limit our investigation to an abridged account of the appearances of the number three in mythology, religion, philosophy, psychology, alchemy and the Western Esoteric Tradition, in general. These examples are presented solely for the purpose of providing the Freemason and occultist with a more developed reference point when encountering ternary symbolism in their initiatory experiences or in their personal study.

The most immediately conspicuous example of this triune distinction is found in the three Euclidean spatial dimensions – length, width and height – which we had considered in some detail vis-à-vis their correspondence to the jewels of the three principal officers, the working tools of a Fellow Craft and the Cartesian coordinate system, in the preceding section of this Chapter. These dimensions are mankind's way of spatially orienting himself and other objects in the material world of phenomena, and of describing such events. Whether these dimensions exist as things-in-themselves, external of our mentation, or whether they are merely the abstract means by which mankind theorizes, organizes and understands space, is beyond the scope of the present work – but certainly worthy of our consideration. A consideration such as three-dimensionality, however, is so central to our experience that it can, at times, be difficult to conceptualize; suffice it to say that the experience of these three dimensions – in addition to time and the penetration of our imagination – are all we have to go on, in terms of experiencing the world.

Our very lives seem to present themselves as a three-act play: birth, life and death; or youth, manhood and old age, as discussed in the foregoing section on the three principal stages of human life. It seems that nearly everything could be said to have a beginning, a middle and an end, from a novel to the Universe itself. Temporally, mankind, individually and collectively, experiences a past, a present and a future; the past being a collection of thoughts and actions having occurred before now; the present being the fulcrum of existence and the only thing we can ever wholly experience; and the future being uncertain, the realm of both fear and hope, representing the causal sum of the terms defined by the past and present. From the earliest times, life and the world have been expressed as tripartite manifestations. One example from classical Greek mythology dealing with this division is the myth of the brothers Zeus, Poseidon and Hades who, after overthrowing their titanic (and cannibalistic) father, Cronus, drew lots to decide what parts of the cosmos they would rule. Zeus won the draw and was awarded the skies; Poseidon, coming in second, was given the seas; while Hades, losing the draw, was left to rule over the dead in the underworld. Thereby, we observe the classical tripartite division of land, sea and air. This distinction was similarly delineated by the Tiwanakan culture of the Bolivian Andes, whose divine realms were stratified into three planes: the Alakpacha, the domain of the sky gods; the Acapacha, the land of living beings; and the Manquepacha, the underworld – this arrangement being depicted in the step pattern of a figure known as the Andean cross. There are copious other examples of ternary symbolism liberally distributed throughout the collective body of world myth and folklore, such as the three Assyro-Babylonian creator entities, Anu, Bael and Ea; Djinn granting three wishes; the Three Graces, followers of Aphrodite; the Three Erinyes, goddesses of revenge; Cerberus, the three-headed dog and guardian of Hades; the tripod upon which sat the oracular Pythia at Delphi; the three faces of Hecate, lunar goddess of magic and the crossroads; the three attempts to create mankind – from clay, wood and, finally, maize – as written in the *Popol-Vuh* (1550 CE) of the Mayans; the three eggs of the Sumatran Manuk Manuk; Shakespeare's three Weird Sisters in *Macbeth*; and on, and on, and on…

The Chakana, or Inca cross, Pisac, Peru

In world religion, we find this same ternary division expressed as the *Hu-mata*, *Hukhta* and *Huvarshta* (good thought, good words, good deeds) of Zo-roastrianism; the three patriarchs of Judaism – Abraham, Isaac and Jacob; the Christian Trinity (Πατρὸς καὶ τοῦ Υἱοῦ καὶ τοῦ Ἁγίου Πνεύματος); the qabalistic Supernal Triad, consisting of *Kether*, which overflows into the duality of *Chokmah* and *Binah*; the aforementioned Hindu *Trimurti* of Brahma, Vishnu and Shiva; the triple goddess of Wicca – the Maiden, the Mother and the Crone – represented by the waxing crescent, the full, and the waning crescent Moons;

The Pythagoreans held the number three in high regard, referring to it as the "triad" and considering it the noblest number because it is the sum of all the terms below it when added together.[43] Also, their *Tetraktys*, the symbol upon which they swore their solemn oaths, was arranged in the form of an equilateral triangle. The Pythagorean Theorem states that the square of the hypotenuse (*c*) of a right triangle is equal to the sum of the squares of the two other sides (*catheti a & b*), and is sometimes written as the equation $a^2 + b^2 = c^2$. Though geometrical and algebraic proofs of the theorem have been presented for millennia, by both professional and recreational mathematicians, Euclid's proof[44] is the version most frequent-

---

43   Hemenway, *Divine Proportion: Phi in Art, Nature, and Science*, Sterling Publishing Company Inc., 2005, pp. 53-54

44   Euclid, *Elements*, Book I, Proposition 47

ly employed in Masonic symbolism. We will further discuss the immense importance of this theorem and equation in Chapter VIII, in the Geometry section, of the present volume – particularly, as it pertains to ancient Masonry. The symbol of the equilateral triangle, or the delta (the Greek character: Δ), may also be found in Freemasonry; of this symbol, Albert Mackey says:

> *The equilateral triangle is to be found scattered throughout the Masonic system. It forms in the Royal Arch the figure within which the jewels of the officers are suspended. It is in the Ineffable Degrees the sacred Delta, everywhere presenting itself as the symbol of the Grand Architect of the Universe. In Ancient Craft Masonry, it is constantly exhibited as the element of important ceremonies. The seats of the principal officers are arranged in a triangular form, the three Lesser Lights have the same situation, and the Square and Compasses form, by their union on the greater light, two triangles meeting at their bases. In short, the equilateral triangle may be considered as one of the most constant forms of Masonic symbolism.[45]*

Though the tripartite division of *body*, *mind* and *spirit* is a fairly common theme in modern metaphysical circles, holistic medicine and New Age culture, it is in fact a very ancient model with roots in the medieval Scholasticism of Thomas Aquinas, early Christianity, Judaism and the Classical Pagan World.[46] The ancient Greeks illustrated this distinction by the words *psyche* (Greek: ψυχή, "soul" connoting *mind*), *soma* (Greek: σῶμα, "body") and *pneuma* (Greek: πνεῦμα, "spirit"). In Hebrew, these concepts are rendered in the words *nephesh* ("soul", נֶפֶשׁ), *basar* ("flesh", בָּשָׂר) and *ruach* ("spirit", רוּחַ). In the medieval Thomist and Aristotelian traditions, as well as in alchemical codices of the period, we find these components represented in the Latin *anima* ("soul" or "mind"), *corpus* ("body") and *spiritus* ("spirit"). Though the unity of the human existence is recognized in this model, man's triune nature is considered in order to philosophically compartmentalize certain aspects of his being; it was by this trisection that the early natural philosopher could individually contemplate the materiality of the body; the abstractions of the mind; and the nature and destiny of

---

45   Mackey, *An Encyclopedia of Freemasonry and its Kindred Sciences*, Everts & Co. 1884; Entry: "Triangle"

46   White, *Max Sheler's Tripartite Anthropology*, 2001, retrieved at: academia.org

the spirit. Due to the realization that one could not effectively apply the same methods of inquiry in all domains, the ancient philosopher thereby isolated these components. Consequently, the mind was considered under the purview of the philosopher; the body under the scope of the physician; and the spirit allotted to the care of the theologian. So advantageous did this frame of reference prove to be that it is still, for better or worse, commonly employed.

In Platonic philosophy, there exists the tripartite distinction of the "properties of being", otherwise known as the *Trancendentals*; these are the *true*, the *beautiful* and the *good*. These were anciently prescribed as the three areas of human inquiry. But, before we begin to unpack these, it is first important to place these three domains of philosophical inquiry in the context of the generally accepted branches of Western philosophy as a whole; these include: Epistemology, Logic, Ethics, Aesthetics and Metaphysics. Taking these in their turn, we understand Epistemology to encompass the theory of knowledge; what we can learn and what can we know. Logic studies the rules of reasoning and valid argumentation. Ethics, or moral philosophy, is concerned with human values and behavior. Aesthetics deals with the idea of beauty, particularly its objectivity and subjectivity. Metaphysics inquires as to the nature of being and the notion of reality. Each of these major branches divide further into subsets of inquiry; for instance, Metaphysics may be expanded to encompass ontology, cosmology and eschatology. The philosophical domains encompassing the True, the Beautiful and the Good are logic, aesthetics and ethics, respectively; for logic is the means by which we develop sound reasoning to accurately discern the True; aesthetics teaches us to recognize proportion, symmetry and harmony in creation, thereby perceiving the Beautiful; and the study of ethics guides us in forming a morally sound framework by which to conduct ourselves individually and in society, thereby realizing the Good.

Philippus Aureolus Theophrastus Bombastus von Hohenheim, Paracelsus, by Hirschvogel, 1538

In his *Liber Paragranum*, Paracelsus (Philippus Aureolus Theophrastus Bombastus von Hohenheim, Swiss, 1493-1541 CE) likely coined, and certainly popularized, the term *spagyria*. The word, which comes from the Greek *spao* (σπάω), to "draw out", and *ageiro* (ἀγείρω), to "gather", is most commonly used to describe alchemical operations performed in the Vegetable Kingdom for the production of medicinal or magical tinctures. In this sort of spagyric alchemical process, the plant material is separated into its constituent parts: salt alkaloids, essential oils and alcohol content – these components are represented by the three philosophical principles of alchemy: salt, sulfur and mercury. The processes involved in the operation are: distillation, which yields the essential oils (the sulfur, or "soul" of the plant); fermentation which renders the alcohol content (the mercury, or "spirit" of the plant); and extraction from the calcined ash, yielding the mineral content (the salt, or "body" of the plant). We will be returning to the three philosophical principles of alchemy in greater detail in Chapter

IX of the present volume, where they will be addressed particularly as to how they pertain to the wages of a Fellow Craft, which are corn, wine and oil.

Hermes Trismegistus was said to have known "the three parts of the philosophy of the whole world".[47] Hermes Trismegistus (Greek: Ἑρμῆς ὁ Τρισμέγιστος, Latin: *Mercurius ter Maximus*), or "Thrice-greatest Hermes" an epithet that was found at the Thoth Temple at Esna, Egypt[48], was the (likely pseudepigraphic) author of the *Corpus Hermeticum* (3-7th century CE) – the sacred texts forming the basis of Hermeticism. Hermes Trismegistus represented a Ptolemaic syncretization of the Egyptian Thoth with the Greek Hermes, both gods of communication, wisdom and writing, through the *interpretatio græca*. In the context of Hermeticism, the three parts of philosophy of the whole world are astrology, alchemy and theurgy, as the *Corpus Hermeticum*, and the later *Tabula Smaragdina*, address subjects such as the theurgical conjuration of spirits for the animation of statues, post-Babylonian, or Chaldean astrology, and the practice of alchemy. Because of Hermeticism's esoteric purview, it has become a major tributary to the greater Western Esoteric Tradition, as we may observe vestiges of its influence in Qabalah, Renaissance Neoplatonism, Rosicrucianism, alchemy, magical societies such as the Hermetic Order of the Golden Dawn and, of course, Freemasonry.

---

47   *Tabula Smaragdina*, or *Emerald Tablet*, 6-8th century CE, Isaac Newton translation
48   Hart, *The Routledge Dictionary of Egyptian Gods and Goddesses*, second edition, Routledge, 2005, p 158

CHAPTER V

∴

THE FIVE ORDERS OF ARCHITECTURE, THE FIVE HUMAN SENSES
&
THE NUMBER FIVE

THE FIVE ORDERS OF ARCHIRECTURE

By order, in architecture, is meant a system of the members, proportions, and ornaments of columns and pilasters; or, it is a regular arrangement of the projecting parts of a building, which, united with those of a column, form a beautiful, perfect, and complete whole. Order in architecture may be traced from the first formation of society. When the rigour of seasons obliged men to contrive shelter from the inclemency of the weather, we learn that they first planted trees on end, and then laid others across, to support a covering. The bands which connected those trees at top and bottom, are said to have suggested the idea of the base and capital of pillars; and from this simple hint originally proceeded the more improved art of architecture. [...] The original orders of architecture were no more than three; the Doric, Ionic, and Corinthian. To these the Romans added two: the Tuscan, which they made plainer than the Doric; and the Composite, which was more ornamental, if not more beautiful than the Corinthian. The first three orders alone show invention and particular character, and essentially differ from each other; the two others have nothing but what is borrowed, and differ only accidentally; the Tuscan is the Doric in its earliest state; and the Composite is the Corinthian enriched with the Ionic. To the Greeks, and not to the Romans, we are indebted for what is great, judicious, and distinct, in architecture. [...] These observations are intended to induce the industrious craftsman to pursue his researches into the rise and progress of architecture, by consulting the works of the best writers on the subject.[1]

When speaking of the orders of architecture, or of classical architecture in general, one is usually[2] referring to the decorative and structural conventions employed by the Greek and Roman civilizations of classical antiquity.[3] The classical orders were five variations on a simple post and lintel, or column and entablature system; these components were wrought from stone – usually marble or limestone; and each was replete with a distinct set of design motifs, dimensions, ratios and proportions.[4] Each column consisted of, from bottom to top, a base, a shaft, and a capital. The height of each column was measured in diameters of the lower base of the column; so, for example, one would say that a column was seven lower diameters high. The various orders are most easily differentiated by the décor found at their capitals – the unadorned simplicity of the Doric; the volutes, or scrolls, of the Ionic; and the acanthus leaves of the Corinthian, for example, are immediately distinguishable elements. The entablature likewise consisted of three parts: the architrave, the frieze, and the cornice. From the bottom to the top of the entablature, we find the architrave, which was the supportive lintel, resting atop the colonnades; the frieze, which was an often ornamented, unmolded strip; and the cornice, which was a protruding strip of molding, just beneath the pediment, or gable.

As we are informed in the lecture of the Fellow Craft degree (see Appendix D), we are indebted to the Greek architects for the genuine-

1   Preston (Oliver, commentary), *Illustrations of Masonry*, New York: Masonic Publishing and Manufacturing Co., 1867, pp. 41-43

2   I say "usually" because the term "classical architecture" is sometimes, though less commonly, applied to other refined and sufficiently developed architectural styles such as that of the ancient Egyptian, Chinese and Mayan civilizations.

3   Fleming, Honour & Pevsner, *Dictionary of Architecture*, 3rd Ed., Penguin Books Ltd, 1986, p. 76

4   Gwilt, *An Encyclopædia of Architecture: Historical, Theoretical, and Practical*, Longman, Brown, Green, and Longmans, 1842, p. 680

ly innovative contributions to this architectural vocabulary of aesthetics, forms and proportions. The Roman Empire continued to employ Greek architecture, introducing very few products owing to their own originality. As mentioned in the lecture, the Roman's two main stylistic contributions were the Tuscan and the Composite orders, which were hardly original innovations, as they were patterned on established Greek forms and consisted of slight variations on Doric and Corinthian themes. True Roman innovation could be seen slightly later, however, with the introduction of concrete, which allowed for a more seamless appearance and finish. The Greek and Roman traditions continued until the collapse of the Western Empire (476 CE) when they began to wane in favor of the Byzantine influence from the East.[5] A resurgence of the classical styles occurred in the 8th and 9th centuries, resulting from the Carolingian Renaissance in Northern Europe. The Romanesque movement, which retained the flavor of the Byzantine and was characterized by its semi-circular arches and its domes, eventually gave way to the more intricate Gothic style in the High and Late Middle Ages.

Much of the ancient classification and documentation of the three Greek orders come to us through the work of Vitruvius (Marcus Vitruvius Pollio, 80?-15? BCE) as presented in his book *De architectura* (also known as *The Ten Books on Architechture*), which was dedicated to his patron, Augustus Caesar.[6] The treatise is the only extant major work on the subject of classical architecture surviving since antiquity and was an influence on many early Renaissance artists, architects and philosophers.[7] Vitruvius was a 1st century BC Roman architect, civil and military engineer, and author. Among his many innovations, Vitruvius is thought to have been among the first to have conceived and designed architectural acoustics, having situated *echeas* (something like a large pot, similar in function to a "bass trap") in his theater plans.[8] Another one of his areas of research and discourse dealt with the mirroring of the human body, and other elements of nature, in the dimensions and perfect proportions of architecture; this field of study was the impetus for Leonardo da Vinci's Renaissance-era drawing, *Vitruvian Man* (1490? CE). In what could certainly be read as commentary on the sympathetic relationship between the microcosm and the macrocosm, and on the universal distribution of Divine Order throughout creation, Vitruvius wrote that...

5   Adam, *Classical Architecture*, Viking, 1992, p. 16

6   Entry: "Vitruvius", Chisholm (editor), *Encyclopædia Britannica*, 11th ed., Cambridge University Press, 1911

7   Liukkonen, *Books and Writers*, "Vitruvius", kirjasto.sci.fi, 2015

8   Reed Business Information, *New Scientist*, 1974, p. 552

[...] in the human body the central point is naturally the navel. For if a man be placed flat on his back, with his hands and feet extended, and a pair of compasses centred at his navel, the fingers and toes of his two hands and feet will touch the circumference of a circle described therefrom. And just as the human body yields a circular outline, so too a square figure may be found from it. For if we measure the distance from the soles of the feet to the top of the head, and then apply that measure to the outstretched arms, the breadth will be found to be the same as the height, as in the case of plane surfaces which are perfectly square.[9]

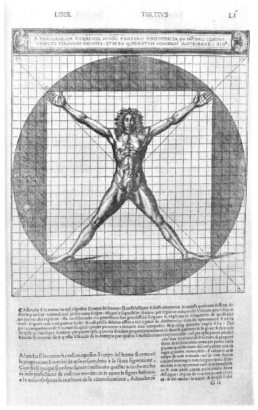

Vitruvius, De architectura, Book III, Cesariano, 1521

---

9   Vitruvius, *De architectura*, Book III, Chapter 1

One of Vitruvius' most lasting and frequently referenced contributions is found in *De architectura*, wherein he asserted that every structure, in order to be whole, must display three indispensable qualities: stability, utility and beauty (Latin: *firmitatis, utilitatis et venustatis*).[10] These three qualities, which are sometimes referred to as the "Vitruvian Virtues", may be likened to – and perhaps even informed – the Masonic triad of Wisdom, Strength and Beauty, in that wisdom is needed to contrive a useful structure, thus meeting the requirement of *utilitatis*; strength to support said structure directly corresponds to *firmitatis*; and beauty to adorn an expedient and durable edifice satisfies the quality of *venustatis*. Thus the three principal supports of the Lodge – Wisdom, Strength and Beauty – speculatively mirror these operative virtues of temple architecture.

In a passage which could just as well be read from the speculative perspective as from the operative, Vitruvius said of classical temple architecture: "in the members of a temple there ought to be the greatest harmony in the symmetrical relations of the different parts to the general magnitude of the whole."[11] While, operatively, relationships between the various components must be proportionate, symmetrical and balanced; speculatively, the members of a Lodge must be well-tempered and harmonious – reflecting the disposition of those "who best can work and best agree".[12]

Before moving on to an individual exposition of each order, it would be prudent to note that the ancient Greeks, and even the Romans such as Vitruvius, did not recognize the Tuscan and Composite styles as distinct architectural orders but as subsets of the Doric and Corinthian, respectively. Ergo, when we speak of the five orders of architecture, we must be conscious of the fact that the ancient, classical world knew of only three orders; the canonization of the Tuscan and the Composite orders occurred during the Italian Renaissance, and was likely motivated by Italian nationalism. The first appearance of both the Tuscan and Composite as distinct orders, alongside the original Greek orders, occurs in the treatise *I sette libri dell'architettura* (*The Seven Books of Architecture*) by the Italian Mannerist architect Sebastiano Serlio (1475-1554 CE). The fourth of the seven books was entitled *Regole generali di architettura sopra le cinque maniere de gli edifici* (1537); it was in this work that Serlio laid out the five orders of architecture in the manner with which we are familiar today. The Seven Books are sequenced in such a way as to proceed from abstractions

---

10   Vitruvius, *De architectura*, Book I, Chapter 3
11   Vitruvius, *De architectura*, Book III, Chapter 1
12   Sickels, *General Ahiman Rezon*, 1868, p. 194

and generalities to practical design and construction…

> [F]irst, the Euclidean 'heaven' composed of the definitions of
> geometry comprising point, line and perfect (square) planes;
> second, the underlying, three-dimensional forms of Nature
> represented through the theory of perspective; third, the archi-
> tectural embodiment of perfect form reflected in the Pantheon
> and the 'idealised' monuments of antiquity; fourth, the rules
> of the Orders, progressing from Tuscan to Composite, as ev-
> idenced in antique ruins and the text of Vitruvius, and the
> universality of the Orders in composing doors, fireplaces and
> palace façades; fifth, the use of the Orders in temples of Serlio's
> invention; sixth, the use of the Orders in house designs [...][13]

The Tuscan order is somewhat of a composite of the earlier Doric and
Ionic styles, in that the Tuscan fuses the simple columns and plain round
capitals of the Doric with the column-to-base-diameter ratio and other
proportions of the Ionic. Tuscan columns were usually unfluted and had
plain unornamented friezes. Being considered rustic in nature, the Tuscan
order was widely used in domestic architecture, such as the peristyle halls
and verandas of private residences, as well as in docks and warehouses.
Sebastiano Serlio highlighted the martial quality of this later subordinate
extension of the Doric order when he said that the Tuscan style was "suitable to fortified places, such as city gates, fortresses, castles, treasuries, or
where artillery and ammunition are kept, prisons, seaports and other similar structures used in war."[14] During the Renaissance, Italian commentators dubiously claimed that the Tuscan order predated the three canonical
Greek orders. This order, having originated in Tuscany region of central
Italy, would give the Romans architectural primacy over the Greeks – but,
from the perspective of accepted archeological records, their claim is demonstrably false.[15]

Having its origin in the western Dorian region of ancient Greece, the
Doric order is the earliest of the three canonical orders. One theory posits
that 7th century BCE Greek traders brought this influence back with them

---

13   Hart & Hicks, *Sebastiano Serlio on Architecture*, Vol. I, Books I-V, *Tutte l'opere
d'architettura et prospetiva*, 1996, p. *xxvi*

14   Serlio, *Regole generali di architettura sopra le cinque maniere de gli edifice*, 1537

15   Ackerman, "The Tuscan/Rustic Order: A Study in the Metaphorical Language of
Architecture", *Journal of the Society of Architectural Historians*, March, 1983, pp. 15-34

from their sojourns in Egypt.[16] This theory is somewhat corroborated by the founding Western Egyptologist, *Jean-François Champollion (1790-1832), who remarked that the Tombs of Beni Hassan (2055-1650 BCE), on the East Bank of the Nile near Al Minya, were rendered in a proto-Doric, or Egypto-Doric style.*[17] The Doric was the shortest of the orders, usually measuring only four to seven lower diameters in height, and was raised directly atop the stylobate, or foundation, without a base. Doric entablature usually contained a decorative frieze and its columns were often fluted. This order has most notably been used in peripteral (Greek: *peripteros*, περίπτερος) temple design. A *peripteros*-type temple consists of a central *naos* (Latin: *cella*; "inner chamber", such as the *sanctum sanctorum*) surrounded by a portico, or porch, with a colonnade, creating a four-sided arcade, or peristyle. Interestingly, the Doric order has retained skeuomorphic vestiges of its wooden predecessors, such as ornamental allusions to wooden joists fitted together by pegs, notable in the stone *triglyph* and *guttae* of the Doric frieze.[18] In Freemasonry, the Doric column is associated with the Senior Warden and, thereby, with principal support of Strength. This attribution is especially fitting since the Doric order is dedicated to Ares (Latin: Mars, the god of war) and has classically been associated with masculine virtues.[19] This order may be seen in the Temple of Ares (Ἄρης) at the northern section of the Ancient Agora, and the Temple of Hephaestus (Ἥφαιστος), both are from the 5th century BC and located in Athens, Greece. A notable modern example of the Egypto-Doric style may be seen at "the Tomb" of the Skull and Bones secret student society, built in 1856 on the Yale University campus at New Haven, Connecticut.

16   Jenkins, *Greek Architecture and Its Sculpture*, Harvard University Press, 2006, pp. 16-17

17   *Baedeker, Egypt: Handbook for Travelers, Part I, 1895, p. clxvi*

18   Summerson, *The Classical Language of Architecture*, World of Art series, Thames and Hudson, 1980, pp. 13-14

19   Ibid., pp. 14-15

The Five Orders of Architecture, from Mackey's Manual of the Lodge, 1891

The Ionic order is perhaps the most easily recognizable of the classical orders, in that it has clearly distinguishable volutes (scroll-like designs on the capitals), a thinner columnar shaft, and shares very little aesthetic similarity to the Tuscan and Composite orders, unlike the Doric and the Corinthian, respectively. This order is said to have originated in Ionia (600-480 BCE), which was located on the central western coast of Anatolia, in what is now present-day Turkey.[20] According to an obscure passage in Vitruvius, the Ionic volute could be accurately described with only a straight edge, a square, a compasses and a length of string.[21] Having the thinnest shaft of all the orders, the Ionic column almost always has a base, whereas columns of other orders may rest directly on the stylobate. Ionic columns were generally eight, and sometimes nine, base-diameters high and are almost always fluted. Through the Italian Renaissance, the Ionian was the natural order employed in the design of libraries, academies, courthouses and other houses of wisdom and justice.[22] The Ionic column

20   Vitruvius, *De architectura*, Book IV, Chapter 7

21   Andrey & Galli, "Geometric Methods of the 1500s for Laying Out the Ionic Volute", *Nexus Network Journal*, vol. 6 no. 2, 2004, pp. 31-48

22   Summerson, *The Classical Language of Architecture*, 1963, MIT Press, retrieved online

is associated with the Worshipful Master of the Masonic Lodge and, fittingly, alludes to the principal support of Wisdom. Temples composed in the Ionian style may be seen at the Artemision (Ἀρτεμίσιον, "Temple of Artemis", 7th century BCE) at Ephesus, near modern day Selçuk, Turkey, and the Erechtheion (Ἐρέχθειον, 421-406 BCE), a section of the greater Acropolis complex of Athens, which was fittingly dedicated to Athena, the goddess of wisdom.

Widely considered the most elegant of the classical orders, the Corinthian was the last of the original Greek orders to be developed, with earliest known example dating from 427 BCE at the Temple of Apollo Epicurius at Bassae. This style was conceived in the ancient city-state of Corinth, located at the base of a narrow strip of land connecting the Peloponnese to mainland Greece.[23] Featuring slender, fluted columns, this order was comparatively tall, standing at ten base-diameters high. The most remarkable component of this order is its ornate capital, which is copiously adorned with carvings of acanthus leaves. In Mediterranean countries, the acanthus is regarded as a symbol of enduring life and immortality, hence its traditional use as a display in funerary celebrations.[24] The acanthus motif of the Corinthian capital was said to be designed by Callimachus (Καλλίμαχος, 5th century, Athens or Corinth) who, after observing the acanthus growing around the votive basket at the head of the tomb of a young "freeborn" maiden, was struck by inspiration…

> *Just then Callimachus, whom the Athenians called katatêx-itechnos for the refinement and delicacy of his artistic work, passed by this tomb and observed the basket with the tender young leaves growing round it. Delighted with the novel style and form, he built some columns after that pattern for the Corinthians, determined their symmetrical proportions, and established from that time forth the rules to be followed in finished works of the Corinthian order.[25]*

Master Masons may note the similarities between the symbolism of the acanthus to that of the acacia, particularly in the context of how the acacia is employed at the head of the grave of G∴M∴H∴A∴. By extension,

---

23   Wilson-Jones, "Designing the Roman Corinthian Order", *Journal of Roman Archaeology*, 1989

24   "Acanthus", *Buffalo as an Architectural Museum*, retrieved at: buffaloah.com

25   Vitruvius, *De architectura*, Book IV, Chapter 1

it is also significant that the principal support of Beauty is attributed to the station of the Junior Warden – the office of G∴M∴H∴A∴ at the building of K∴S∴T∴ – and that the Corinthian style is said to be the most beautiful of the three original Greek orders. Upon their adoption of the Greek orders, the Corinthian style was an early favorite of the Romans and, therefore, may be seen at several site in the former Roman Empire such as the Pantheon (Πάνθειον, 126 CE), the Temple of Mars Ultor (2 BCE), both in Rome, and at the Temple of Vesta (1st Century BCE) in Tivoli, Italy.

The Composite order, as its name implies, was an amalgamation of the Ionic and the Corinthian styles – retaining both the volutes of the Ionic and the acanthus motif of the Corinthian.[26] The columns, like those of the Corinthian, were usually ten base-diameters in height, slender and fluted. Like the Tuscan, the Composite was not recognized as an independent order until the Renaissance and it is not found in ancient Greek architecture. The first known example of this order is in the Arch of Titus (82 CE) in the Roman Forum, though it has been suggested that the order was developed as much as a century earlier, "a little before Augustus' reign".[27]

As we have seen, the architects of antiquity, in employing the classical orders in temple building, were concerned with the relationships and proportions of each element as they fit together in a harmonious and unified whole. To this end, the components of classical architecture could be reduced to one unit of measure which acted as the organizational key to the design of each temple – this unit was known as a *module*.[28] The module was expressed in ratios throughout the entire structure and could thus be seen as a fractal unit of the whole. Usually, the base diameter of the column's shaft served as the module by which the structure was proportionally organized.[29] In this regard, we again see an observance to the sympathetic relationship of the microcosm and the macrocosm in both form and function. Vitruvius noted this convention under the categories of *eurythmia* and *symmetria* in his Six Principles of Design, which were: *ordinatio* (order), *dispositio* (arrangement), *eurythmia* (proportion), *symmetria* (symmetry), *decor* (propriety) and *distributio* (economy). By *eurythmia* was meant a harmonious rhythm or flow in design; whereas *symmetria*, in its ancient connotation, was closer in meaning to "mathematical

26   Henig (ed.), *A Handbook of Roman Art*, Phaidon, 1983, p. 50
27   Ibid.
28   Curl (ed.), *Oxford Dictionary of Architecture*, 2nd ed., 2006, pp. 606-607
29   Ibid., p. 496

harmony" than it was to what we think of as symmetry today.[30]   In this sense, we see vestiges of the Pythagorean current in the architectural concerns of classical antiquity, in that harmonious numerical relationships are recognized as being a central consideration.

Modern examples of ancient Greek and Roman classical architecture may still be found in presumably every city in the Western world to the present day. These forms and styles, now referred to as neoclassical architecture, began to reappear around the middle of the 18th century in response to the exceedingly ornate Rococo movement.[31] The return to the classical styles and ancient orders of architecture was indicative of a return to the perceived purity of the Greco-Roman world and, to a lesser extent, the early Renaissance. This resurgence in architecture was mirrored theologically (in the *prisca theologia*, meaning "ancient theology") in the early Renaissance by the Florentine Neoplatonists, again in the Enlightenment, and most recently during the 19th century occult revival – all periods during which the return to classicism was concurrently reflected in philosophy (in the *philosophia perennis*, meaning "perennial philosophy"). A few notable examples of neoclassical architecture in the United States include the Baltimore Basilica (1863 CE) in Maryland, the Lincoln Memorial (1922 CE) in Washington D.C., and the Ancient and Accepted Scottish Rite's House of the Temple (1915 CE), which was modeled after the Mausoleum at Halicarnassus, also in Washington, D.C.[32]

THE FIVE HUMAN SENSES

The objects of human knowledge are innumerable; the channels by which this knowledge is conveyed, are few. Among these, the perception of external things by the senses, and the information we receive from human testimony, are not the least considerable; the analogy between them is obvious. In the

---

30   Jones, *Principles of Roman Architecture*, Yale University Press, 2000, pp. 33-46

31   Entry: "Neoclassical architecture", *Encyclopedia Britannica*, retrieved at: britannica. com

32   The reader is encouraged to enter: "list of Masonic buildings in the United States" into their preferred search engine. A search such as this yields a wealth of information and images that are an irrefutable testament to Freemasonry's preference for the architecture of classical antiquity.

testimony of Nature given by the senses, as well as in human testimony given by information, things are signified by signs. In one as well as the other, the mind, either by original principles or by custom, passes from the sign to the conception and belief of the thing signified. The signs in the natural language, as well as the signs in our original perceptions, have the same signification in all climates and nations, and the skill of interpreting them is not acquired, but innate.[33]

As human beings, our senses are the first means by which we begin to interface with the external world of phenomena. Through the media of sound, sight, touch, smell and taste, we gradually begin to accumulate a body of experiential data by which we orient ourselves in the world, with others, and with our very sense of self, as our inner lives may be said to be informed by our outer experiences. This happens when sensory data, representative of outer objects and events, is gathered from the circuitry of our peripheral nervous system and transmitted along synaptic pathways which connect neurons in the body with those in the brain.[34] In slightly greater detail, the process of sensation begins when our bodies detect stimulus energy through receptor cells in our sensory organs; this stimulus energy is transduced into electrical energy which triggers a process known as action potential; through the process of action potential, electrical currents are converted into chemical codes; when this chemical information reaches the brain, it is distributed by the *thalamus* to specific regions of the cerebral cortex; finally, this information is collated in a process known as perception, which is the means by which we organize, interpret, and give meaning to sensory data.[35] The importance of the final stage of perception in this sequence cannot be overstated, as it forms the very fulcrum of being and consciousness…

[…] perception always intercedes between reality and ourselves.[36]

---

33   Oliver, *The Antiquities of Freemasonry*, Philadelphia: Hyneman, 1854, p. 633

34   Sumners, "How Do Synapses Work?", *Texas A&M Today*, 2018, retrieved at: tamu. edu

35   "How Do We Sense and Perceive the World?", *General Psychology*, retrieved at: general-psychology.weebly.com

36   Barry, *Visual Intelligence: Perception, Image, and Manipulation in Visual Communication*, pp. 15-16, in reference to the surrealist art of Rene Magritte

In addition to the five "traditional" senses, there are several others at work gathering data to help complete the picture of human sensation; a few of the most commonly considered are the *vestibular sense*, *thermoception* and *proprioception*. The vestibular sense allows us to perceive our head and body in space and to remain gravitationally oriented; thermoception is the sense by which we perceive changes in temperature; and proprioception tells us the relative position of our body parts and how much force or acceleration to use in physical operations. It is also important to consider the roles that cognition and imagination play in interpreting and making meaningful this empirical data from the sense organs and creating a consistent map of the world. In this regard, our imagination has an analogous function to the Masonic working tool, the trowel, in that it spreads the cement which binds our sensory data into "one common mass" – a coherent picture or map of reality.

There is a caveat, however, as the Polish-American scientist and philosopher Alfred Korzybski once famously noted when he said, "the map is not the territory".[37] That is to say that, though we receive stimuli from our sensory organs and organize these into a *perception* of the external world – this internal *representation* of the world is not the world-in-itself – it is but a simulacrum; a platonic shadow play; a replica of an approximate reality. This argument extends not only into the metaphysical domains of epistemology, which studies what we can *know*; ontology, which studies what can *be*; cosmology, which studies from *whence* came the world; and eschatology, which studies *whither* the world will go; but also into arena of modern social and cultural criticism.

The idea that our individual synthesis, or perception, of the world and the world itself are two different things is a central ontological problem. Our personal idea and experience of the world is formed through our five (plus) human senses, imagination and cognition. Our senses report to our brains through synaptic connections and our sensory nervous system; our imagination fills in the blanks by positing various creative hypotheses that color the empirical data with our ideas, thoughts and images; and it is by cognition that we try the consistency and truthfulness of the amalgam of our senses and imagination, thereby forming a reasonably complete mental model of the events and things of the outer, phenomenal world that is consistent with our past experiences and the general narrative of reality to which we subscribe. But is the external world a thing-in-itself, independent of our perception? Or, rather, is the world an outward projection of our

---

37   Korzybski, *Science and Sanity: An Introduction to Non-Aristotelian Systems and General Semantics*, The International Non-Aristotelian Library Pub. Co., 1933, p. 58

imagination? Is it the representation of a concept? A hologram? A dream?

While it may be a difficult prospect to accept and deeply digest, it is crucial that we understand that our senses are not infallible. For example, if you have ever – *even once in your life* – turned around because you thought someone called your name, but were mistaken; or if you have ever waved at someone you thought you knew, only to find them a stranger; or have had any other experiences of mistaken perception; then, you can never say that your senses faithfully report the external world with one-hundred percent accuracy. For it is by recognizing this deficiency in sensation and perception – along with its ideological analogue in conception – that we may begin to develop the sort of healthy skepticism (or, perhaps, something closer to the transcendental fulcrum of empiricism and rationalism?) necessary to defend us from the vices of naiveté and intransigence, as well as from the creeping tentacles of indoctrination.

Immanuel Kant, Becker, 1768

When Sickels wrote: "In the testimony of Nature given by the senses, as well as in human testimony given by information, things are signified by signs",[38] he raised two of the central features of the act of perception which had initially been addressed in the work of the German, Enlightenment-era philosopher, Immanuel Kant (1724-1804); namely, *a posteriori* and *a priori* knowledge. *A posteriori*, or synthetic knowledge, is gained from the "testimony of Nature given by the senses"; it is constituted by what we may observe through the senses; it is empirical and concrete. Conversely, *a priori*, or analytic knowledge, is that which may be known through reason alone; it is not contingent on verification by nature or phenomena; it is truly the "human testimony given by information"; it is rational and abstract. Kant, in his *Critique of Pure Reason* (1781), endeavored to develop a dialectical synthesis of these two epistemological modes, which resulted in his transcendental idealism – an admixture allowing for certain aspects of both rationalistic idealism and empirical materialism to be synthesized in "ideas of sense", and that knowledge is formed from both sense impressions and universal concepts, which Kant referred to as *categories*.[39]

The Irish Masonic writer, the Reverend Jonathan Ashe, D.D., M.M., raised another interesting proposition when he spoke of the *sign* and that which it *signifies*…

> *All knowledge beyond our original perceptions is got by experience. The constancy of Nature's laws connects the sign with the thing signified, and we rely on the continuance of that connection which experience has discovered.*[40]

In essence, this distinction has its origin in the work of Plato who, in his *Theory of Forms*, posited that the physical world consists of imperfect imitations, or shadows, of their archetypal, noumenal progenitors, the *Forms* or *Ideas*.[41, 42] In other words, the Form would constitute the abstract, archetypal template of a perceivable object. For example, if one were to consider a fork: as a thing in the world, a fork may be silver, plastic,

---

38   Sickels, *The General Ahiman Rezon and Freemason's Guide*, New York: Macoy, 1887, p. 143

39   Entry: "Transcendental Idealism", *Encyclopedia Britannica*, retrieved at: britannica.com

40   Ashe (Oliver, commentary), *The Masonic Manual; or, Lectures on Freemasonry*, New York: Leonard & Co., 1855, p. 89

41   Diogenes Laërtius, Πλάτων ἐν τῇ περὶ τῶν ἰδεῶν ὑπολήψει, "Plato", *Lives of Eminent Philosophers*, Book III, paragraph 15

42   In this case, the word *Form* is capitalized to differentiate it from the physical manifestation, or *form*, such as the "shape of a thing".

wooden, two-tined, three-tined, four-tined, new, tarnished, broken, or have any number of specific qualities – yet, there still remains the universal characteristics by which we recognize a fork, *despite its myriad manifestations*, though there is no concrete object in the world that could irrefutably be described as *the* quintessential fork without negating the validity of a number of other objects that also clearly present as forks. That is to say that there is no physical fork on Earth, no matter how simple or complex, that may be said to be the universal exemplar of what we mean when we say "fork" but, conversely, all perceivable objects that present as "a fork" may be said to share in the heterogeneous expression of *forkness*.

This concept of the signified and the signifier, to which Kant, Ashe and Sickels make reference, has been a constant concern in metaphysical philosophy for millennia; the basic tenet of which having been expressed, under one name or another, in Plato's Forms, Aristotle's hylomorphism, Descartes' *cogito* argument, Hume's skepticism, Kant's transcendental idealism, Hegel's *Phenomenology of Spirit* (1807), Heidegger's *Dasein*, and all manner of critiques and commentaries apropos the subject/object dichotomy. Most recently, the problem was further developed through in the work of the 20th century semioticians Charles Sanders Peirce (1839-1914) and Ferdinand de Saussure (1857-1913) and critical theorists such as Jean Baudrillard (1929-2007) and Guy Debord (1931-1994), who applied this model to the social sciences and cultural criticism, positing that the signs, or representations of things, have survived that which they once signified, leaving us only with a universe littered with bland simulacra, or imitations of real life, devoid of any inherent meaning. It is not the purpose of the present work to persuade the reader in favor of any particular philosophical position – it is merely to set the words of these 19th century Masonic writers, which are extremely weighty in their implications, within the context of epistemology, ontology and the broader metaphysical stage.

That the senses are highlighted in the Masonic initiatory experience is significant, particularly when considered vis-à-vis the accentuated role the senses have played in the Mystery traditions of the ancient world. In some cases, the deprivation of a certain sense for an interval of time was employed. To deny a critical sense such as sight, for instance, is to heighten those senses which remain available to the initiate. Trance-like states may be induced through sensory deprivation and through other means of disorientation, such as circumambulation. This disorientation is specifically cultivated in order to facilitate an altered state of consciousness and to thereby heighten the receptiveness of the initiate to an empirical appreciation of the sensory data. In 1994, J. Nigro Sansonese hypothesized that the extremely popular and long-running Eleusinian Mysteries (Greek: Ἐλευσίνια Μυστήρια), an ancient Greek Mystery cult said to have been perpetuated for over a thousand years, utilized the manipulation of the senses, in addition to a pranayama-like control of the breath, to induce trance-like states and the phenomenon of proprioception. Sansonese also theorized that the sacred lights and sacred sounds that the initiate was said to have experienced within the *kisté*, a chest which held the *sacra* of the cult, were inner psychological or neurological phenomena and that the *kisté* itself was in fact symbolic of the initiate's skull.[43] Any sensory channel which stimulated the initiatory experience was employed in the ancient Mysteries; the eminent French Mithraic scholar, archeologist and historian Franz Cumont (1868-1947) highlighted the role of the senses when he said that "[t]hese religions gave greater satisfaction first of all to the senses and emotions, in the second place to the intelligence, and finally and chiefly to the conscience".[44] All of the five human senses, individually or in concert, have long been exploited in the Mysteries; of this initiatory convention, authority on the ancient Mystery cults, Samuel Angus (1881-1943) wrote...

> *No means of exciting the emotions was neglected in the passion-play, either by way of inducing careful predispositions or of supplying external stimulus. Tense mental anticipation, heightened by a period of abstinence, hushed silences, imposing processions and elaborated pageantry, music loud and violent or soft and enthralling, delirious dances, the drinking of spirituous liquors, physical macerations, alternations of dense darkness and dazzling light, the sight of gorgeous ceremonial vestments, the handling of holy emblems, auto-suggestion and the promptings of the hierophant— these and many other secrets of emotional exaltation were in vogue.*[45]

---

43 Sansonese, *The Body of Myth*, Rochester, 1994, pp. 195-215
44 As quoted in Angus, *The Mystery Religions*, London: Murray, 1928, p. 141
45 Ibid., p. 49

Demeter, Triptolemus and Persephone, triad of the Eleusinian Mysteries, 440 BCE

The cultivation of this sort of sensory disorientation was central to the Mysteries – particularly those of the ecstatic (Greek: ἔκστασῃ) or enthusiastic (Greek: ενθουσιασμός) varieties. These states of heightened sensitivity, mystical receptiveness and altered consciousness were achieved by the physical and sensual means of the alternate deprivation and inundation of light; frenzied dancing to spirited music; the inhalation of fumes and of incense; the drinking of certain potions, such as the (probably entheogenic) *kykeon*; the visual and tactile beholding of the *sacra*, or sacred objects; and all manner of sensory involvement and derangement. These rites often began with prescribed fasting for a period of time and culminated in a sacred feast (such as the early Christian *agape*), at which the initiates were restored to physical homeostasis.[46] Nor are these sensory motifs confined to any particular corpus of initiatory rites belonging to any certain society, as universal parallels may be drawn across all ages and cultures.

For the purposes of our present study, we will be confining our study to the five "traditional" senses: hearing (audition), seeing (vision), feeling

---

46   Angus, *The Mystery Religions*, London: Murray, 1928, p. 83

(somatosensation), smelling (olfaction) and tasting (gustation), as these are the five human senses made reference to in the Masonic Fellow Craft lecture. The sensory organs that gather this empirical data are the ears, eyes, skin, nose and tongue, respectively. Taking each of the five senses individually, we first encounter that of hearing, or audition, of which Preston said…

> *Hearing is that sense by which we distinguish sounds, and are capable of enjoying all the agreeable charms of music. By it we are enabled to enjoy the pleasures of society, and reciprocally to communicate to each other, our thoughts and intentions, our purposes and desires; while our reason is capable of exerting its utmost power and energy. The wise and beneficent Author of Nature seems to have intended, by the formation of this sense, that we should be social creatures, and receive the greatest and most important part of our knowledge by the information of others. For these purposes we are endowed with Hearing, that, by a proper exertion of our rational powers, our happiness may be complete.*[47]

The ability to hear is a widely distributed characteristic among the members of the Kingdom Animalia and approximately 99.75% of human beings are born with a fully developed capacity to hear sounds.[48] With a wide variance on an individual basis, the human ear is equipped to detect sounds within the approximate ranges of 20 to 2000 hertz.[49] Generally, the ear is divided into three anatomical structures: the outer ear, the middle ear and the inner ear. The outer ear consists, primarily, of the *pinna* and the ear canal. The *pinna* is the externally visible ear, consisting of cartilage and tissue, and helps to shape incoming airborne vibrations so as to imprint a directionality on them. This information is funneled into the ear canal. The middle ear consists of the ear drum, which is a tympanic membrane whose vibrations are communicated to the *ossicles*, which are three small bones (the *malleus*, *incus* and *stapes*) forming a chain to the inner ear. The inner ear is divided into two parts: the *cochlea*, which pertains to hearing, and the semicircular canals, which help to maintain balance; we will address the former apropos our subject. The *cochlea* is a snail shell-like bone

47   Webb, *The Freemason's Monitor*, Salem: Cushing & Appleton, 1818, pp. 54-55
48   "Quick Statistics About Hearing", *National Institute on Deafness and Other Communication Disorders*, 2016, retrieved at: nidcd.nih.gov
49   Elert (editor), "Frequency Range of Human Hearing", *Physics Factbook*, retrieved at: hypertextbook.com

containing fluid and hair cells which transduce vibratory information into electrical signals which are then sent to the *thalamus* and distributed to the cerebral cortex for final processing.[50] Due to the fact that ears are only necessary because there are sounds (though the inverse argument could also be made!), we must necessarily address the nature and properties of sound.

Physically, sound is described as a "mechanical radiant energy that is transmitted by longitudinal pressure waves in a material medium (such as air) and is the objective cause of hearing."[51] It could further be stated that a sound is a vibration which disturbs an equilibrium and propagates through an elastic medium such plasma, gas, liquid or a solid object – thus satisfying all four states of matter, which directly correspond to the ancient Empedoclean elements: fire, air, water and earth, respectively, despite their not being recognized as such by the modern scientific community. A sound does not need to be perceived by a subject in order to be classified as a sound, as there are sounds such as those used in sonar devices and ultrasound imaging machines, which are deliberately attuned to be emitted and received by a unit specifically calibrated for its pitch, and is then converted into a sonogram, or visible representation of sonic data. Additionally, some inaudible sounds, such as the seismic activity produced by earthquakes or the passing of a large truck, may be "heard" through the body. This sort of tactile perception of sound has been reported to aid some deaf people in their spatial orientation.[52] Of speech, sound and hearing, Albert Pike, rather poetically, said…

> *Even the pulsations of the air, once set in motion by the human voice, cease not to exist with the sounds to which they gave rise. Their quickly-attenuated force soon becomes inaudible to human ears. But the waves of air thus raised perambulate the surface of earth and ocean, and in less than twenty hours, every atom of the atmosphere takes up the altered movement due to that infinitesimal portion of primitive motion which has been conveyed to it through countless channels, and which must continue to influence its path throughout its future existence.[53]*

50   "How We Hear", *American Speech-Language-Hearing Association*, retrieved at: asha.org

51   Entry: "Sound"; *Webster's Collegiate Dictionary*, retrieved at: merriam-webster.com

52   "Deaf Culture and Communication: A Basic Guide", *Victorian Deaf Society*, 2010, pdf retrieved at: expression.com.au

53   Pike, *Morals and Dogma of the Ancient and Accepted Scottish Rite of Freemasonry*, Supreme Council of the Southern Jurisdiction, A.A.S.R., U.S.A., 1871, p. 128

Pike's model of travelling sound waves can be seen as being contingent on the principles of classical Newtonian mechanics, in that he is highlighting the causal relationship occurring among "every atom of the atmosphere". Physically, this may be visualized as being similar to the action which occurs between billiard balls on a "break" in pool; but, unlike the billiard balls which ultimately succumb to sliding friction and rolling resistance, Pike's initial sound "must continue to influence its path throughout its future existence", implying that this sound wave continues not only beyond the point of human audibility but must necessarily forever change the course of all matter in the atmosphere – within twenty hours. This may be this case if there were no reflection or absorption, both of which halt sound propagation, but it is likely that the sound would dissipate before causally affecting every atom in the entirety of the Earth's atmosphere.

Obviously, spoken words are sounds; and sounds are things heard. Words are sounds which represent concepts and are meant to be communicated between a speaker and a hearer. In this very basic context, it may be said that a speaker outwardly utilizes words as meaningful units of language to create larger, more complex conceptual structures which are then decoded by a hearer and inwardly understood as a similar structure. Spoken words *create* images in the mind of the hearer. An example (the reader is asked to imagine that the following is being spoken and heard, as opposed to read):

> *You find yourself standing on a long, rolling expanse of grass. There are black and white cows slowly grazing in the meadow. Some of the cows are close to you, many more are far away – but they seem to go on forever. The pale blue sky is mottled with fluffy, white cumulus clouds and you can smell the greenness of the grass and surrounding foliage. Your feet sink a little into the rich damp earth and you are completely present. Neither your body nor your mind are in need of anything. You begin to hear a sound, not unlike a far-off jet airplane breaking the sound barrier. The low grumble gets louder and you look in the direction from which you think it may be coming. You see what looks like a second Sun in the sky. You're not accustomed to seeing two Suns and this confuses you. The second Sun gets louder and closer until you can see that it is followed by a long, blazing trail of white light. Just then, you hear a roar so loud*

*that it defies comparison to anything in your life experience…
it leaves your ears ringing in a high-pitched whine… but the
ringing quickly fades, giving way to a quiet stillness… it is in
this cocoon of inner silence, that you realize the second Sun is
actually some kind of comet or asteroid (you've never known
the difference) that has just violently penetrated the Earth's
atmosphere… you notice that the cows have begun to run…
you don't have to think too hard to realize the futility of trying
to run… and, through a soft smile, you say aloud, "those silly
cows," and chuckle a little to yourself…*

The vignette above has, hopefully, conveyed an inner picture to the reader/hearer, and will suffice as an example of the creative power of words – words as spoken symbols representing concepts which are communicated to the hearer. Notice how the senses were utilized in creating this scene in the mind; are not these same senses responsible for creating our inner representation of the external world? Can one experience be said to be more real than the other? If so, in what way? It is not the object of the present work to answer these questions for the individual; it is merely to provide fodder for further contemplation, specifically on how our senses and the creative word relate to our very experience of reality. It has long been known that, on the figurative and speculative level, the refinement of one's senses allow one to penetrate deeper into life's Mysteries – to comprehend the veiled language set in otherwise inextricable parables, fables, allegories and myths – the cryptic nature of which is alluded to in the following passage from the Gospel of Matthew…

*Who hath ears to hear, let him hear. And the disciples came,
and said unto him, Why speakest thou unto them in parables?
He answered and said unto them, Because it is given unto you
to know the mysteries of the kingdom of heaven, but to them
it is not given. For whosoever hath, to him shall be given, and
he shall have more abundance: but whosoever hath not, from
him shall be taken away even that he hath. Therefore speak I to
them in parables: because they seeing see not; and hearing they
hear not, neither do they understand. And in them is fulfilled
the prophecy of Esaias, which saith, By hearing ye shall hear,
and shall not understand; and seeing ye shall see, and shall*

not perceive: For this people's heart is waxed gross, and their ears are dull of hearing, and their eyes they have closed; lest at any time they should see with their eyes and hear with their ears, and should understand with their heart, and should be converted, and I should heal them. But blessed are your eyes, for they see: and your ears, for they hear.[54]

The Temple of Horus at Edfu, Dunning, 1905

In the 2nd century BCE Edfu texts, which were culled from inscriptions on the Temple of Horus at Edfu, Egypt, we read of "Seven Sages" who "by the word of the creators" were able to "endue with power the substances of the Earth".[55] We also encounter multiple references in biblical scripture attesting to the creative power of the Word of God; in Hebrews, "[…] the worlds were framed by the word of God, so that things which are seen were not made of things which do appear."[56]; again in Psalms, "By the Word of the Lord were the heavens made; and all the host of them by the breath of His mouth […] For He spake, and it was done; He commanded, and it stood fast."[57]; in the Gospel of John, "In the beginning was the

---

54 *The Holy Bible*, KJV, Matthew 13:9-16

55 Reymond, *The Mythical Origin of the Egyptian Temple*, Manchester University Press, 1969, pp. 25, 41 and 289

56 *The Holy Bible*, KJV, Hebrews 11:3

57 *The Holy Bible*, KJV, Psalms 33:6-9

Word, and the Word was with God, and the Word was God,"[58] and many other passages pertaining to the creative fiat embodied by the Word. This may cause one to ponder the relationship between a fictional tale and the apparently real narrative of both human history and our personal lives – this may thus be a clue to the creative power of sound, hearing and the Word. There is narrative transmitted in oral tradition among the Aymara people – the ancient indigenous inhabitants of the Pre-Columbian archeological site Tiwanaku in Bolivia – that the stones which compose their massive megalithic structures "came down of their own accord, or at the sound of a trumpet, from the mountain quarries and took up their proper positions at the site."[59] It is important to remember, however, that sound and vibration may be both creative and destructive.

The destructive power of sound and vibration may be most graphically expressed in two ways: resonance disasters and earthquakes. In physics, some systems – such as buildings, bridges, wineglasses and molecules, for example – have been determined to consist of a resonant frequency.[60] A resonant frequency is described as "a natural frequency of vibration determined by the physical parameters of the vibrating object."[61] Vibrating physical objects contain a set of normal modes – like the harmonic overtone series in music – at which they will sympathetically vibrate, allowing small periodic forces to affect large amplitude oscillations at "relative maximum" resonance. This is what would allow an opera singer to break a champagne glass from afar, to use a popular model of this phenomenon. Though there are no reliably documented cases of this feat having occurred, the mathematics does work out and it appears to be possible, providing the singer could exceed 100db at the precise resonant frequency of the glass for a sustained interval.[62] When designing physical objects such as airplanes and trains, engineers must consider the resonant frequencies of all the oscillating components, ensuring that none match, which could lead to a phenomenon known as *resonance disaster* – during which, systems may be literally rattled to pieces. Ancient stonemasons, such as the architects and builders of Ollantaytambo, Sacsayhuamán and Machu Picchu in Peru and the Osireion at Abydos, Egypt, appeared to have grasped the concept of the potentially devastating power of vibrational waves by

---

58   *The Holy Bible*, KJV, John 1:1

59   Osborne, *Indians of the Andes: Aymaras and Quechuas*, Routledge, 1962, p. 64

60   Resnick & Halliday, *Physics* (3rd ed.), John Wiley & Sons, 1977, p. 324

61   Nave, "Resonance", *Sound*, retrieved at: hyperphysics.phy-astr.gsu.edu

62   Shrock, "Fact or Fiction: An Opera Singer's Piercing Voice can Shatter Glass?", *Scientific American*, 2007, retrieved at: scientificamerican.com

erecting structures which utilized rounded corners, tightly interlocking shapes and irregular polygonal stones, each dressed to fit their neighbor, often within a razorblade's breadth. The foresight and ingenuity of these ancient architects in creating seismically stable structures helped to enable their creations, particularly those in Peru, to survive multiple devastating earthquakes. One of the most notable instances of the destructive power of sound may be found in the biblical account of the Battle of Jericho, at which the Israelites blew trumpets while marching around the city, ostensibly causing the walls of which to crumble from the destructive blare.

Then the Lord said to Joshua, See, I have delivered Jericho into your hands, along with its king and its fighting men. March around the city once with all the armed men. Do this for six days. Have seven priests carry trumpets of rams' horns in front of the ark. On the seventh day, march around the city seven times, with the priests blowing the trumpets. When you hear them sound a long blast on the trumpets, have the whole army give a loud shout; then the wall of the city will collapse and the army will go up, everyone straight in. [63]

The sense of hearing is said to be highly esteemed among Masons, since it is by hearing that we receive the word of the degree. The transmission of the word is highly ritualized and, at first, given in a jumbled lettered or syllabled form, in order to highlight the necessity of securing it from the profane, thus further illustrating its importance. Words, as we have illustrated, have been said to carry creative and other wondrous powers. The phenomenon of "magic words", though they may seem at first cartoonish, has had a rich and developed history in occultism and, especially, the medieval grimoire tradition. Words and phrases such as *Hocus Pocus* (either from the Latin: *hax pax max Deus adimax*, or a corruption of passage in the Latin Mass: *hoc est corpus*; meaning "this is my Body")[64], *Abracadabra* (either from the Aramaic meaning: "I create like the word" (ארבדכ ארבא), or from the Basilidean Gnostic *Abraxas*)[65], *Open Sesame* (from the Arabic: سمسم اي افتح ; a word used by Ali Baba in the English translation of

---

63   *The Holy Bible*, KJV, Joshua 6:2–5

64   Entry: "Hocus Pocus", *Compact Oxford English Dictionary*, retrieved at: askoxford. com

65   Entry: "Abracadabra", *Oxford English Dictionary*, Oxford University Press, 2009

the *One Thousand and One (Arabian) Nights*)[66] and *Alakazam* (a possible Anglicization of the Arabic *Al Qasam*, meaning "an oath")[67] are so commonly employed we tend not to think of their occult origins. It is also interesting that many of what we recognize as "magic words" seem to be of Arabic origin; this seems to further advance the possibility of linking their original employment to the medieval grimoire tradition. Like much of the alchemical literature of the time, many of these volumes of magical ritual and talismanic composition, such as the wildly influential astral magic grimoire *Picatrix*, entered the milieu of the then-burgeoning occultism of Europe in the Middle Ages. Similarly, incantations (from the Latin: *incantare*, "to bewitch, charm, cast a spell upon, chant magic over")[68], which may be spoken, chanted or sung, are words or phrases used in ritualistic situations and are similar to spells or charms in that they are intended to set a particular, causal magical current in motion.[69] We will further address the power of words in the sections on grammar and rhetoric in Chapter VII, and that of hearing and sound in their musical application in Chapter VIII. The next sense that we encounter in the lecture is seeing, or vision, of which Preston wrote…

> *Seeing is that sense by which we distinguish objects, and are enabled in an instant of time, without change of place or situation, to view armies in battle-array, figures of the most stately structures, and all the agreeable variety displayed in the landscape of Nature. By this sense we find our way in the pathless ocean, traverse the globe of earth, determine its figure and dimensions, and delineate any region or quarter of it. By it we measure the planetary orbs, and make new discoveries in the sphere of the fixed stars. Nay more, by it we perceive the tempers and dispositions, the passions and affections, of our fellow creatures, when they wish most to conceal them; so that though the tongue may be taught to lie and dissemble, the countenance will display the hypocrisy to the discerning eye. In fine, the rays of light which administer to this sense,*

66   *Sesame: Origin, History, Etymology and Mythology*, 2015, pdf retrieved at: MDidea.com

67   Mingren, "Say the Magic Word: The Origins of Abracadabra and Other Magical Mutterings", *Ancient Origins*, 2017, retrieved at: ancient-origins.net

68   Entry: "Incantation"; *Online Etymological Dictionary*, retrieved at etymonline.com

69   Cushman, *Princeton Encyclopedia of Poetry and Poetics*, Fourth Edition, Princeton University Press, 2012, p. 681

are the most astonishing parts of the inanimate creation, and render the eye, with all its appurtenances, a peculiar object of admiration. Of all the faculties, sight is the noblest. The structure of the eye evinces the admirable contrivance of nature for performing its various external and internal motions; and the variety that is displayed in the eyes of different animals, suited to their several ways of life, clearly demonstrates this organ to be the master-piece of nature's works.[70]

The sense of sight, or vision, is the ability of an organism to perceive the spectrum of visible light as emitted by, or reflected off of objects in space. Everywhere light is distributed is capable of being seen by an eye, which is the organ that has evolved to perceive it. The visual system in human beings and many other mammals consists, primarily, of the cornea, lens, retina, the optic nerve and the visual cortex. Light enters the cornea and is focused by the lens and projected onto the retina. The retina transduces this information into neuronal signals which are then transmitted to the visual cortex via the optic nerve.[71] The segment of the electromagnetic spectrum visible to human beings typically spans between about 400 nanometers and 700 nanometers (0.00000040 to 0.00000070 meters)[72] and is bordered by the infrared, which has longer wavelengths, and the ultraviolet, which has shorter wavelengths. Higher frequencies of electromagnetic radiation have shorter wavelengths, whereas lower frequencies have longer; this behavior is contingent on the amount of energy per quantum it carries.

---

70   Webb, *The Freemason's Monitor*, Salem: Cushing & Appleton, 1818, pp. 55-56

71   Tollin, *The Visual System*, 2016, pdf retrieved at: ics.uci.edu

72   Bradt, *Astronomy Methods: A Physical Approach to Astronomical Observations*, Cambridge University Press, 2006, p. 26

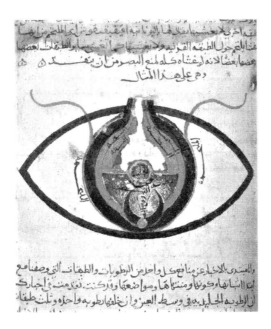

The Anatomy of the Eye, from the Cheshm manuscript, 1200 CE

Just as hearing is predicated on the presence of sound, seeing is predicated on the presence of light. Light is defined as "electromagnetic radiation of any wavelength that travels in a vacuum with a speed of 299,792,458 meters (about 186,000 miles) per second; specifically, such radiation that is visible to the human eye."[73] The word is most commonly used in reference to visible light, which is in reference to the segment of the electromagnetic spectrum perceivable by the human eye.[74] In its broader physical sense, however, light need not be visible, as electromagnetic radiations of other wavelengths, such as gamma rays, x-rays, microwaves and radio waves, are also recognized as forms of light.[75] The Sun is the principal source of light on the planet Earth, though light may also be emitted from other sources, such as fire, electric light and bioluminescence, which is defined as "the emission of light from living organisms (such as fireflies, dinoflagellates, and bacteria) as the result of internal, typically

---

73   Entry: "Light"; *Webster's Collegiate Dictionary*, retrieved at: merriam-webster.com

74   According to the International Lighting Vocabulary, the definition of light is: "Any radiation capable of causing a visual sensation directly." *International Lighting Vocabulary*, Number 17.4. CIE, 4th edition, 1987

75   Kumar, *Comprehensive Physics XII*, Laxmi Publications, 2008, p. 1416

oxidative chemical reactions".[76] All electromagnetic radiation, including visible light, propagates as waves but is locally absorbed as particles called photons, which are the quanta of light; this phenomenon is called wave function collapse and illustrates the wave/particle duality.[77]

The retina of vertebrates, such as human beings, have two type of photoreceptors: rods and cones. Rods allow for vision at low light levels and have comparatively low spatial acuity; cones are active at higher light levels, have greater spatial acuity and allow for color vision.[78] Electromagnetic radiation that is within the range of the visible spectrum stimulates the cone cells in the retina which allows for the perception of color. In 1931, a global commission[79] was convened for the purpose of standardizing the numerical coordinates by which we define and name the colors of the visible spectrum. The colors of the visible light spectrum are as follows: Red (700-635nm), Orange (635-590nm), Yellow (590-560nm), Green (560-520nm), Cyan (520-490nm), Blue (490-450nm) and Violet (450-400nm).[80] Despite this standardization, there remains a wide cultural, historical and linguistic variance in the communication of color, since the pure spectral colors are contiguous. For instance, English natural philosopher Isaac Newton (1642-1726) identified the seven colors as red, orange, yellow, green, blue, indigo and violet; it is thought that what Newton perceived as blue was actually closer to the modern cyan, thus leaving a vacancy between blue and violet which he had designated indigo.[81] White and black are not strictly colors, as colors are defined as having specific wavelength parameters. White contains all wavelengths of visible light and may be thus divided into its constituent colors by being passed through a prism. Black is the absence of all visible light and, consequently, of color.[82] Considering the occult significance and symbolism of color from the perspective of the Western Esoteric Tradition, we will address the following colors in their turn: red, orange, yellow, green, blue (which will be extended to include cyan) and purple (which will cover both indigo and violet); to

76   Entry "Bioluminescence"; *Webster's Collegiate Dictionary*, retrieved at: merriam-webster.com

77   Dyson, "The Collapse of The Wave-Function", *Edge*, 2014, retrieved at: edge.org

78   "Rods and Cones", *Rochester Institute of Technology*, retrieved at: cis.rit.edu

79   The International Commission on Illumination, reference: cie.co.at

80   Bohren, *Fundamentals of Atmospheric Radiation: An Introduction with 400 Problems*, Wiley-VCH, 2006, p. 214.

81   Waldman, *Introduction to Light: The Physics of Light, Vision, and Color*, Mineola: Dover Publications, 2002, p. 193

82   Murmson, "Why Do We Not List Black and White as Colors in Physics?", *Seattle PI*, retrieved at: education.seattlepi.com

these, we will add white and black.

The color red has been culturally associated with sin, guilt, lust, blood and anger. One may be so angry that they are "seeing red" or found guilty after being caught "red-handed". In religious iconography as in popular culture, the devil is often depicted as being red in color, symbolizing his wickedness and evil. In the West, the color red may represent the blood of martyrdom.[83] Psychological studies have shown that men find women in red more attractive[84], which seems to support the evolutionary biology behind the color's association with passion, love and lust – red roses being associated with romance and the "red light district" being a place to find a wanton partner, etc. Many of these symbolic attributions to red (specifically, the high tint of scarlet) are evident in the following passage of scripture relating to the infamous "Whore of Babylon":

> So he carried me away in the spirit into the wilderness: and I saw a woman sit upon a scarlet coloured beast, full of names of blasphemy, having seven heads and ten horns. And the woman was arrayed in purple and scarlet colour, and decked with gold and precious stones and pearls, having a golden cup in her hand full of abominations and filthiness of her fornication: And upon her forehead was a name written, Mystery, Babylon The Great, The Mother Of Harlots And Abominations Of The Earth. And I saw the woman drunken with the blood of the saints, and with the blood of the martyrs of Jesus.[85]

Red is also considered the color of courage and bravery and is a common color used in flags and heraldry, usually for its martial suggestion.[86] In a number of animal species, the color red is associated with dominance signaling and levels of testosterone[87]; this biological function may be the origin of our cultural attribution to the color red as representing anger, aggression and warfare – not to mention its action on bulls. In the mineral kingdom, iron oxide is most commonly responsible for the color red; this

83   Feisner, *Colour* (2nd ed.), London: Laurence King, 2006, p. 127
84   Burriss, "The Uncanny Power of a Red Dress", *Psychology Today*, 2016, retrieved at: psychologytoday.com
85   *The Holy Bible*, KJV, Revelation 17:3-6
86   "Red: Symbolic And Cultural Associations", retrieved at: ucl.ac.uk
87   Little & Hill, "Attribution to Red Suggests Special Role in Dominance Signaling", *Journal of Evolutionary Psychology*, 2007, pp. 161-168

may be observed in the coloration of the Grand Canyon, as well as the planet Mars, both locations being rich in iron oxide. The day associated with the color red is Tuesday (Old English: *Tīwesdæg*), since it is the "day of Tiw", a Germanic war god, who was anciently conflated with Mars (Roman) and Ares (Greek) through religious syncretism. The Empedoclean element associated with Mars is fire, which is further reflected in the zodiacal triplicity[88] of Aries, Leo and Sagittarius. Some herbs and roots associated with Mars are: basil, cayenne, cumin, galangal root, garlic, ginger, pepper and wormwood. Of these herbs and roots, tinctures may be prepared according to the methods of spagyric, or Paracelsian alchemy (see Chapter IX in the section entitled *The Wages of a Fellow Craft* for an outline of this comparatively basic alchemical operation in the vegetable kingdom).

Rosa Rubea, from Donum Dei, 17ᵗʰ century

---

88   In Western Astrology, the ecliptic is divided into three 120° arc segments called trines; each trine represents a classical element: fire, air, earth or water.

In alchemy, *rubedo* (Latin; meaning "redness") is the fourth and final stage in the great work, further signifying the success of an operation.[89] Alchemical symbolism is frequently employed in C.G. Jung's depth psychology and, in that schema, the rubedo stage represents the integration of the ego and the Self.[90] Qabalistically, red is the color corresponding to the *sephirah* of *Geburah* (Hebrew: גבורה; meaning "Severity"). On the *Etz Chaim*, *Geburah* is the fifth *sephirah* and corresponds to the planet Mars, which is the "red planet" (see Appendix B). In magical operations, the consideration of angelic, cosmic, astral, zodiacal, planetary and elemental sympathies is taken into account during the composition of rituals. To this end, the color red is often used to draw subtle martial or *Geburic* sympathies, as red is often used as a color consideration in the choice of altar cover, regalia, paraphernalia, candle color, etc. It is also considered efficacious to utilize the zodiacal sympathies of the constellation Aries (falling between March 20th and April 21st in the tropical system of Western astrology) which is ruled by the planet Mars. Rituals meant to heighten martial qualities are usually composed and/or performed on a Tuesday and during an hour ruled by Mars, such as the hour just after sunrise or the hour beginning three hours after sunset, according to Heinrich Cornelius Agrippa's tables of planetary hours (see Appendix C). Of the planetary hours, which we will be intermittently addressing throughout our study, and their importance in ritualism, Agrippa wrote…

> *[…] the other thing we ought to observe, is about the times of choosing the planetary hours; for almost all Astrologers divide all that space of time from the Sun rising to setting into twelve equall parts, and call them the twelve hours of the day; then the time which followeth from the setting to the rising, in like manner being divided into twelve equall parts, they call the twelve hours of the night, and then distribute each of those hours to every one of the Planets according to the order of their successions, giving always the first hour of the day to the Lord of that day, then to every one by order, even to the end of twenty four hours; and in this distribution the Magicians agree with them […]*[91]

---

89   Mantello & Rigg, *Medieval Latin: An Introduction and Bibliographical Guide*, Catholic University of America Press, 1996, p. 413

90   Euryhaessa, *Running into Myself*, Troubador Publishing, 2010, p. 278

91   Agrippa, *Three Books of Occult Philosophy*, Book II, Part 3, Chapter xxxiv

The color orange is named after the fruit of the same name, which has its etymological root in the Sanskrit *nāraṅga-s*, meaning "orange tree".[92] In the West, the color is associated with amusement, extroversion, energy, danger, taste and aroma. Traditionally, in mythologically-themed paintings, Dionysus (Greek: Διόνυσος, later subsumed by the Roman Bacchus), the god of wine, ecstasy and frenzied ritual, was frequently depicted in orange garb to highlight his attributes; the color has also historically figured prominently in paintings of clowns, jesters and harlequins (particularly in the work of Van Gogh, Renoir, Cezanne and Picasso) in order to accentuate their frenetic energy and amusing qualities. The color orange is, of course, also associated with safety, as any life jacket, buoy and traffic cone will stand in testimony. Since ancient times, artists have devised orange pigments by utilizing the arsenic-containing, highly toxic mineral, orpiment (from the Latin *aurum*; meaning "gold", and *pigmentum*; meaning "pigment"). This mineral, which was an important trade item in the Roman Empire and was used medicinally in China, was of especial interest to alchemists who, due to its coloration, attempted to employ the mineral in their gold-making operations. Orange qabalistically corresponds to the eighth *sephirah* of *Hod* (Hebrew: הוד; meaning "Glory"), which itself corresponds to the planet Mercury, and further to the weekday, Wednesday (Old English: *wodnesdæg* or "Woden's day"; Norse syncretization of the Latin *dies Mercurii* or "day of Mercury").[93] These planetary and qabalistic correspondences reinforce the association between the color orange, mercurial (of Mercury) spirits and the Hermetic Arts, in general. Herbs associated with the planet Mercury are lavender, marjoram, star anise and thyme. Rituals that are intended to summon hermetic and mercurial qualities in the operator often utilize the color orange in regalia and paraphernalia. In order to draw on these subtle influences in the most efficacious way, these operations should utilize as many corresponding elements as possible, such as occurring on a Wednesday in the appropriate planetary hour (see Appendix C), and using tinctures and fumigations corresponding to Mercury. Tarot cards, such as the Magician II (planetarily corresponding to Mercury), the Lovers VI (Gemini is ruled by Mercury) and the Hermit IX (Virgo is ruled by Mercury), which have sympathetic mercurial associations, may also be used in contemplative practices meant to heighten and/or concentrate the influence of the planet.

Yellow, while being a primary color on the classic illustrative color wheel, is a secondary color in the additive RGB model and is made from

92   Entry: "Orange"; *Online Etymological Dictionary*, retrieved at etymonline.com
93   Entry: "Wednesday"; *Online Etymological Dictionary*, retrieved at: etymonline.com

equal parts red and green light. Organic pigments called carotenoids are responsible for the yellowness of bananas, lemons, corn, canaries and egg yolks.[94] Ochre and orpiment pigments were some of the first used in symbolic art produced by human beings and are present at the Lascaux cave in France, which features a seventeen-thousand year old illustration of a horse, rendered in yellow ochre. Yellow ochre pigment was also used very commonly in ancient Egyptian, Roman and Byzantine art.[95] By the Middle Ages, saffron was another popular source of yellow pigment and was employed in medieval manuscripts. In the English-speaking West, the color yellow is most commonly associated with humor, amusement, gentleness and spontaneity – but also with avarice, duplicity and cowardice.[96] The word *yellow* has its etymological root in the Proto-Indo-European base, *ghel*; which is also the root cognate of the words *gold* (gleaming) and *yell* (to cry out).[97] In its association with brightness and brilliance, the color yellow represents the intellect, just as it corresponds to the classical element of air, which also shares a symbolic link with the intellect. Similarly, in Islam, yellow and gold symbolize wisdom. This association with wisdom (Hebrew: חכמה, or *Chokmah*) and the intellect is also reflected in Eastern metaphysics, as the possession of a yellow "aura" is thought to be indicative of one who is an academic or in a scientific profession.[98] Qabalistically, the color yellow is assigned to the sixth *sephirah* of *Tiphareth* (Hebrew: תפארת; meaning "Beauty"); it is the sphere of the Sun and of beauty; and, of course, gold is the metal attributed to the Sun.

Green is a secondary color on the classic illustrative color wheel but it is a primary color on the additive RGB model made from equal parts yellow and cyan-colored light. In the West, the color green is most commonly associated with nature, health, spring, fertility and hope.[99] For instance, a "greenhorn" is one who is new and inexperienced, in the springtime of their life, as it were. Sometimes, however, the color also carries the negative connotations of poor health and envy.[100] When one appears

94   Armstrong & Hearst, *Carotenoids 2: Genetics and molecular biology of carotenoid pigment biosynthesis*, FASEB J. 10 (2), 1996, pp. 228-237

95   Web Exhibits, *Pigments Through the Ages*, "Antiquity", retrieved at: webexhibits.org

96   Heller, *Psychologie de la couleur – effets et symboliques*, Editions Pyramyd, 2000, pp. 69-86

97   Entry: "Yellow", *Webster's New World Dictionary of American English*, Third College Edition, 1988

98   Swami Panchadasi, *The Human Aura: Astral Colors and Thought Forms*, Des Plaines, Illinois: Yogi Publications Society, 1912, p. 33

99   Heller, *Psychologie de la couleur – effets et symboliques*, 2000, pp. 87-104

100   Ibid., pp. 96-97

ill, one is looking a little "green around the gills"; and when jealousy is aroused, one is said to have evoked the "green-eyed monster". Words like *green*, *grass* and *grow* share the same Proto-Indo-European root cognate *grhe*, "to grow".[101] In some Eastern languages, blue and green are not clearly differentiated – in fact, both are considered to be shades of the broader color *qīng*, in Mandarin; *ao* in Japanese; and *thanh* in Vietnamese.[102] Green pigments are almost non-existent in the Neolithic era – as there were only very low-quality examples found, and these made from birch leaves, which produced more of a muted greenish-brown than a true green.[103] Just as iron left to elemental exposure in the open air will begin to corrode and produce a red, flakey outer layer, copper will undergo a series of chemical reactions that result in a pale green patina called *verdigris*[104] – these two phenomena seem to naturally reflect, and likely informed, the martial redness of iron and the venerean greenness of copper. The green in malachite pigments is also caused by its copper carbonate content, thereby strengthening the association with copper and the color green via natural mineral pigmentation. In ancient Egypt, the color green was looked upon favorably as it represented the annual inundation of the Nile and thus fertility, agriculture and regeneration. Consequently, the hieroglyph for the color green was a papyrus shoot. Osiris, the lord of the underworld, was often depicted with green skin to symbolize resurrection, rebirth and regeneration.[105] The Romans were the first to designate the color green an attribute of Venus, due to their viewing her as the goddess of gardens, vegetables and vineyards. Friday, or *Frīġedæġ* (the day of the Germanic goddess Frige), corresponds to the planet Venus, and thereby to the color green.

---

101   Entry: "Green"; *Online Etymological Dictionary*, retrieved at: etymonline.com

102   Kay & Maffi, "Color Appearance and the Emergence and Evolution of Basic Color Lexicons", *American Anthropologist*, March 1999

103   Vachiron, *Couleurs – pigments et teintures dans les mains des peuples*, Seuil, 2005, p. 196

104   Thompson, "Why Does Copper Turn Green?", *Live Science*, 2013, retrieved at: livescience.com

105   de Vries, *Dictionary of Symbols and Imagery*, North-Holland Publishing Company, 1976, pp. 226-228

Mughal painting of al Khidr, "the Green One", ca. 17th-century

Green is the traditionally favored color in Islam, since the robe and banner of Muhammed were green and he had said in the *Hadith* that "water, greenery, and a beautiful face" were universally good.[106] Friday is also the holy day in the Islamic world, as the word *al-jumu`ah* is simultaneously a surah in the Qur'an and means both "Friday" and "day of congregation".[107] We may here make a quick mention of the curious distribution of the three Abrahamic holy days – Friday (Venus) to Islam, Saturday (Saturn) to Judaism, Sunday (Sol) to Christianity – and reflect

106   Lamborn-Wilson, "Cloud Papers for Philip Taafe", *Critical Commentary*, retrieved at: philiptaaffe.info
107   *Qur'an*, Surah 62:1-11

on some of the symbolism and lore surrounding the three faiths; a subject we will pick up again in Chapter VIII, which deals with astronomy. There is an enigmatic figure in the Qur'an known as al-Khidr (Arabic: الخضر), or "the Green One", who was said to have been in possession of great wisdom (Arabic: *Hikmah*, Hebrew: *Chokmah*, both in the second *sephirah*) and mystic knowledge (*Da'ath*, the invisible *sephirah*). Al-Khidr was an important esoteric instructor under whom Musa (Moses) had studied, albeit for a short time, as the Green One's patience was quickly exhausted by the second-guessing of his incredulous pupil.[108]

> *[Moses] said to [al-Khidr], "May I follow you, so that you may teach me some of the guidance you were taught?" He said, "You will not be able to endure with me. And how will you endure what you have no knowledge of?" He said, "You will find me, God willing, patient; and I will not disobey you in any order of yours." He said, "If you follow me, do not ask me about anything, until I myself make mention of it to you." So they set out. Until, when they had boarded the boat, he holed it. He said, "Did you hole it, to drown its passengers? You have done something awful." He said, "Did I not tell you that you will not be able to endure with me?" He said, "Do not rebuke me for forgetting, and do not make my course difficult for me." Then they set out. Until, when they encountered a boy, he killed him. He said, "Did you kill a pure soul, who killed no one? You have done something terrible." He said, "Did I not tell you that you will not be able to endure with me?" He said, "If I ask you about anything after this, then do not keep company with me. You have received excuses from me." So they set out. Until, when they reached the people of a town, they asked them for food, but they refused to offer them hospitality. There they found a wall about to collapse, and he repaired it. He said, "If you wanted, you could have obtained a payment for it." He said, "This is the parting between you and me. I will tell you the interpretation of what you were unable to endure. As for the boat, it belonged to paupers working at sea. I wanted to damage it because there was a king coming after them seizing every boat by force. As for the boy, his parents were believers, and we feared he would overwhelm them with oppression and*

---

108   *Qur'an*, Surah 18:65-82, Al Kahf ("The Cave")

disbelief. So we wanted their Lord to replace him with some-
one better in purity, and closer to mercy. And as for the wall,
it belonged to two orphaned boys in the town. Beneath it was
a treasure that belonged to them. Their father was a righteous
man. Your Lord wanted them to reach their maturity, and
then extract their treasure—as a mercy from your Lord. I did
not do it of my own accord. This is the interpretation of what
you were unable to endure."[109]

The Green One was also regarded as a messenger, mystic initiator and a teacher of esoteric knowledge through his hermeneutical explanations of secret doctrines; these characteristics have reinforced his syncretism with other Hermetic archetypes such as Nabu, Thoth, Hermes, Mercury, Odin, Enoch, Idris and, apropos the Johannine current in Freemasonry[110], Saint John the Baptist.[111] Intriguingly, it has been suggested that al-Khidr was introduced to the West during the Crusades and found his comparative mythological expression as the Green Knight in the Arthurian tale *Sir Gawain and the Green Knight*.[112] He is also given a prestigious position in Sufism, particularly the Sunni tradition. In the Naqshbandi Haqqani Sufi Order, for example, the consensus is that the Green One is still alive and carries on his esoteric transmissions to human beings.[113] Strengthening the Green One's gnostic attributes, he was regarded as one who had received mystic illumination directly from God (Allah) without human mediation or intercession. Paradoxically, but in a common esoterically hermaphrodit-ic motif, al-Khidr is thought to be an Islamization of the female Zoroastri-an rain and fertility goddess, Anahita.[114] Every year, between the 14th and 18th of June, Zoroastrians mainly from Iran and India make a pilgrimage to the *Pir-e Sabz* ("the Green Shrine") in Yazd, Iran where they partake of a sacred feast of wheat, barley and lentil sprouts in honor of greenness

---

109   *Qur'an*, Surah 18:65-82, Al Kahf ("The Cave")

110   Smith, *The Gnostics: History, Tradition, Scriptures, Influence*, Watkins, 2008

111   van Lint, "The Gift of Poetry: Khidr and John the Baptist as Patron Saints of Muslim and Armenian Âšïqs – Ašuls, Redefining Christian Identity", *Cultural Interaction in the Middle East since the Rise of Islam*, Leuven-Paris-Dudley, Peeters, 2005, pp. 335-378

112   Lasater, *Spain to England: A Comparative Study of Arabic, European, and English Literature of the Middle Ages*, University Press of Mississippi, 1974

113   *Naqshbandi: Sufi Way*, retrieved at: naqshbandi.org

114   Babayan, *Mystics, Monarchs and Messiahs: Cultural Landscapes of Early Modern Iran*, Harvard University Center for Middle Eastern Studies, 2002, p. 368

and fertility, the fruits of Anahita.[115] Al-Khidr's conflation with Anahita and with fecundity[116] brings to mind the common correspondences of the Empress III Tarot card. In the Rider-Waite Tarot, the Empress III, who is also associated with fertility, nature and growth, is depicted with a small, heart-shaped shield upon which the planetary glyph for Venus is present, replete with a green field at its center. Qabalistically, green is the color assigned to the seventh *sephirah* on the *Etz Chaim* named *Netzach* (Hebrew: נצח; meaning "Victory"), which is also, unsurprisingly, associated with the planet Venus. These elements may be used in the composition of ritual magic operations and performed on a Friday during a venerean hour such as sunrise, one hour past solar noon (the Sun at its zenith), or three hours past sunset.

It is also worth mentioning the ubiquitous motif of the Green Man in medieval and Renaissance architecture. Term was "Green Man", as pertaining to the mysterious heads or skulls intricately carved into the masonry of European abbeys, cathedrals, churches and chapels, was coined by Lady Raglan in a 1939 issue of *Folklore*.[117] The first known example of a Green Man may be seen at St. Abre, in St. Hilaire-le-grand in Poitiers, France and is circa the 4th or 5th century CE. Some late specimens of these strange and somewhat out-of-place paganistic figures have carved into otherwise Christian architecture as recently as in the 20th century.[118]

Blue is one of the three primary colors in both illustrative color theory (RYB) and in the additive light model (RGB). From ancient Egypt through the Renaissance, lapis lazuli and azurite were the dominant mineral pigments, although vegetable pigments such as *woad* (genus species: *isatis tinctoria*) and, later, indigo (genus species: *indigofera tinctoria*) from America were used. In about 2500 BCE, due to the expense of procuring Afghani lapis lazuli from the caravan routes available to them at that period[119], the ancient Egyptians synthesized their own blue pigment; "Egyptian Blue" was made by combining ground silica, lime, copper and alkali and heating to about 1500°F – a fine example of the early state of Egyptian alchemy.[120] The modern English word *blue* comes to us through the Old French *bleu*

115   Rose, *Zoroastrianism: An Introduction*, India, 2010: I.B. Tauris, p. 123

116   Wheeler, *Moses in the Quran and Islamic Exegesis,* London: Routledge Curzon, 2002, pp. 23-24

117   Raglan, "The Green Man in Church Architecture", *Folklore*, 1939, pp. 45-57

118   Anderson, *Green Man*, Harper Collins, 1990, p. 46

119   Moorey, *Ancient Mesopotamian Materials and Industries: The Archaeological Evidence*, Eisenbrauns, 1999, pp. 86-87

120   Chase, "Egyptian Blue as a Pigment and Ceramic Material", *Science and Archaeology*, MIT Press, 1971

and, earlier, from the old High German *blao*, both meaning "of the color of the clear sky" or "sky-colored".[121] The ancient Egyptians also associated the color blue with the sky and, consequently, with the 11th Dynasty (21st century BCE) sky god, Amun, the patron of Thebes.[122]

> *The Egyptians esteemed blue as a sacred color, and the body of Amun, the principal god of their theogony, was painted light blue, to imitate, as Wilkinson remarks, "his peculiarly exalted and heavenly nature."[123]*

Jupiter-Ammon

In Hellenistic Egypt, Amun was syncretized with Zeus becoming Zeus-Ammon who was, in turn, later subsumed by the Roman Jupiter-Ammon. This jovial correspondence echoes through the Qabalah in the *sephirah* called *Chesed* (Hebrew: חסד; meaning "Mercy") – which is assigned the color blue, in the Queen's Scale; the Tarot card Wheel of Fortune X

121   Entry: "Blue"; *Online Etymological Dictionary*, retrieved at: etymonline.com

122   Heller, *Psychologie de la couleur: effets et symboliques*, Editions Pyramyd, 2000, p. 17

123   Mackey, *An Encyclopedia of Freemasonry and its Kindred Sciences*, Everts & Co., 1884, p. 119

– which represents the planet Jupiter in the accepted Hermetic correspondences; and the weekday Thursday – which comes to us from the Roman *Jovis dies* (Latin, meaning "Jupiter's day") via the Old English *Þūnresdæg* ("Thor's day"; Thor being the Norse syncretization of Jupiter) and the Proto-Germanic *Thonaras daga*.[124] In the early Islamic world, specifically that of Moorish Spain, Jews and Christians were differentiated from their Muslim hosts by blue vestments; green and white being reserved for Muslims only.[125] Since the Middle Ages, blue has been the preferred color for rendering the robes of the Virgin Mary; robes that were previously rendered in black or dark gray. This choice in the Virgin's vestments may be symbolic of her mercy (*Chesed*). The color blue also carries connotations of sadness (colloquially, when one has "the blues") and fidelity ("true blue").

In American Freemasonry, the Regular Craft Lodge is often colloquially referred to as the "Blue Lodge". Mackey, in his Encyclopedia states that blue is "emphatically the color of Masonry".[126] For this designation, several reasons are given; among them, Mackey states…

> *The Hebrew word used on these occasions to designate the color blue is תכלת, tekelet; and this word seems to have a singular reference to the symbolic character of the color, for it is derived from a root signifying perfection; now it is well-known that, among the ancients, initiation into the mysteries and perfection were synonymous terms ; and hence the appropriate color of the greatest of all the systems of initiation may well be designated by a word which also signifies perfection.[127]*

In the composition of ritualism attempting to draw on established correspondences from the greater Western Esoteric Tradition, blue may be used to exemplify the powers of the *sephirah* of *Chesed*, Jupiterian planetary influences, the Wheel of Fortune X Tarot card, and other subtle influences, especially when performed on a Thursday during one of its three jovial hours (see Appendix C).

Purple, which is a combination of the primaries red and blue, is a secondary color in illustrative RYB color theory. Surveys conducted in the Western world find that most people associate the color purple with

124 Entry: "Thursday"; *Online Etymological Dictionary*, retrieved at etymonline.com
125 Varichon, *Couleurs, Pigments et teintures dans les mains des peoples*, Seuil, 2005, p. 175
126 Mackey, *An Encyclopedia of Freemasonry and its Kindred Sciences*, Everts & Co., 1884, p. 119
127 Ibid.

rarity, royalty, magic, mystery and eroticism.[128] The word comes from the Old English *purpul*, itself being an etymological extension of the Greek *porphúra* (Greek: πορφύρα; meaning "purple dye"); *porphúra*, in turn, is presumed to be a cognate of the ancient Semitic name for the murex sea snail (family: *Muricidæ*).[129] This dye is believed to have first been produced in the Phoenician city of Tyre in about 1570 BCE[130]; a location which is of especial interest to Master Masons. Due to its production in the region, the dye was and is still referred to as "Tyrian purple" (Hex triplet: #66023C); although, conversely, it has been suggested that the very name of the Eastern Mediterranean civilization, *Phoenicia*, means "land of purple"[131, 132], leaving us to consider whether the dye was named for the region or vice versa. Tyrian purple is mentioned in both Homer's *Iliad* and Virgil's *Æneid*[133] and the production of the dye was anciently treated by both Vitruvius[134] and Pliny the Elder, who remarked that, "The most favourable season for taking these [shellfish] is after the rising of the Dog-star[135], or else before spring".[136]

---

128   Heller, *Psychologie de la couleur: effets et symboliques*, Editions Pyramyd, 2000, pp. 179-184

129   Entry: "Purple"; *Online Etymological Dictionary*, retrieved at: etymonline.com

130   McGovern, & Michel, "Royal Purple Dye: Tracing the Chemical Origins of the Industry", *Analytical Chemistry*, 1985, p. 57

131   Greek: *phoinike*; entry: "Phoenician"; *Online Etymological Dictionary*, retrieved at: etymonline.com

132   Cunliffe, *Europe between the Oceans: 9000 BC-AD 1000*, New Haven, CT: Yale University Press, 2008, p. 241

133   Ball, *Bright Earth; Art and the Invention of Colour*, University of Chicago Press, 2003, p. 290

134   Vitruvius, *De architectura*, Book VII, Chapter 13

135   Sirius, or Sothis

136   Pliny the Elder, *The Natural History*, Book IX, Chapter 62: *The Natural History of Fishes*, London, UK: Taylor and Francis, Tyrian purple is discussed throughout Chapters 60-65

Bolinus, or Murex Brandaris; the source of Tyrian purple

The dye was procured through the particularly laborious process of collecting the mucous secretions of several species of predatory rock snails (primarily, *Bolinus*, or *Murex brandaris*). Due to the difficulty of its production, the dye was said to have fetched its weight in silver when traded at the ancient Ionian city of Colophon.[137] Consequently, Tyrian Purple – and purple in general – has come to be associated with royalty, social status and the highest echelons of civic and municipal life. Certain Roman magistrates, for example, were among the few permitted to wear the *toga prætexta* and *toga picta*, both of which were produced using the dye; the Hellenic Pharaohs of Ptolemaic Egypt wore robes of Tyrian purple; and King Solomon, when decorating his great Temple at Jerusalem, was said to have brought artisans from Tyre skilled in the art of rendering and applying the dye.[138] Before his crucifixion, Jesus Christ was dressed in purple robes in a deliberate mockery of his claim to being the *Rex Iuda*, or "King of the Jews".[139]

> *And they clothed him with purple, and platted a crown of thorns, and put it about his head, And began to salute him,*

---

137   Theopompus, cited by Athenaeus around 200 BCE, *The Deipnosophists*, Cambridge, MA: Harvard University Press, 1941

138   Varichon, *Couleurs: pigments et teintures dans les mains des peuples*, Seuil, 2005, p. 136

139   *The Holy Bible*, KJV, Mark 15:17 and 20

Hail, King of the Jews! And they smote him on the head with a reed, and did spit upon him, and bowing their knees worshipped him. And when they had mocked him, they took off the purple from him, and put his own clothes on him, and led him out to crucify him.[140]

In the Homeric epics, the *Iliad* and the *Odyssey*, the ancient Greek adjective *porphyreos*, meaning "purple", is used to describe everything from dark clouds and the waves of the "wine-dark sea" to rainbows and spilled blood, of which there is certainly no shortage in the epics.[141] Elsewhere in the *Iliad*, Ajax's belt is said to be purple, as is the tails of the Trojan's warhorses. In the *Odyssey*, the linens on Odysseus' wedding bed are described as being purple, perhaps as an allusion to voluptuousness and eroticism. Later, in the work of the tragedian Aeschylus (525-456 BCE), we learn that, upon the return of her husband Agamemnon from the Trojan war, Clytemnestra welcomed him by decorating their palace with purple rugs. Greek grammarian, Julius Pollux (2nd century CE), attributed the discovery of the color purple to Phoenician god and guardian of Tyre, Melqart (the Punic equivalent to Herakles/Hercules through syncretization), who noticed that his dog's snout was dyed the color after it had partaken of murex shells in a coastal scavenging feast.[142]

Qabalistically, the color purple corresponds to the ninth *sephirah* on the *Etz Chaim*, which is called *Yesod* (Hebrew: יסוד; meaning "Foundation").[143] This *sephirah* is often associated with the sexual and reproductive organs in that it channels the vital, creative forces of the masculine, mercurial energy of *Hod* (Hermes) and unites it with the feminine, venerean energy of *Netzach* (Aphrodite), thereby affecting a synthesis resulting in the divine androgyne (hermaphrodite) – the union of opposites – and channels this into a corporeal form, fit to reside in the kingdom, *Malkuth* (Hebrew: מלכות; meaning "Kingdom"), and on the material plane of *Assiah*, the densest of the four qabalistic worlds. *Yesod* also corresponds to the Moon, in that it is the sphere between the Earth (*Malkuth*) and Mercury (*Hod*), after which the spheres continue to concentrically expand in their

---

140   *The Holy Bible*, KJV, Mark 15:17-20

141   Sampson, "Gladstone as Linguist", *Journal of Literary Semantics*, 2013

142   Grovier, "Tyrian Purple: The Disgusting Origins of the Color Purple", *BBC*, retrieved at: BBC.com

143   Corresponding to purple on the G∴D∴'s Queen Scale representing the Creative World, or *Briah*.

usual Chaldean order: Venus (*Netzach*), Sol (*Tiphareth*), Mars (*Geburah*), Jupiter (*Chesed*) and Saturn (*Binah*). Thus, in the composition of ritualism meant to draw upon the subtle lunar or *Yesodic* energies, the color purple may be used in robes, altar cloth or candles. Rituals meant to sympathize with these influences are most efficacious when performed on a Monday, during a lunar hour and, preferably, in the zodiacal sign of Cancer, which is ruled by the Moon (see Appendix C).[144]

In the Royal Arch Masonry of Mackey's time, the Most Excellent High Priest wears a purple robe, a breastplate (Hebrew: סִימָתָהְוּ סִירוּאָה; *Urim* and *Thummim* meaning "Lights and Perfections") and a mitre.[145] The purple banner of the Hebrew Tribe of Reuben is borne by the Master of the Second Veil in Royal Arch Masonry. In the astrotheological interpretation, the Tribe of Reuben corresponds to the *man* of the *Tetramorph* (a zodiacal sphinx composed of an ox, a lion, an eagle, and a man) and, thereby, represents the zodiacal sign of Aquarius – just as Ephraim represents Taurus, Judah represents Leo, and Dan represents Scorpio.[146] Purple is the symbolic color of the Mark Master degree in Capitular Masonry and, since red and blue tend to make a shade of purple, it is also said to denote the unity between Blue Lodge, or Craft Lodge and the Chapter, or Royal Arch Masonry, who primarily utilize red in their work.[147] In modern American Freemasonry, purple is most often associated with the Grand Lodge of each Masonic Jurisdiction, as the regalia, jewels and aprons worn by the Grand officer's line are typically decorated with purple.

White, being achromatic, reflects all visible wavelengths of light and is perceived when all three types of color-sensing cones are stimulated in nearly equal amounts.[148] In the additive RGB model of color theory, red, green and blue light, when combined, produce white light. The word *white* comes to us from the Old English *hwit*, meaning "bright, radiant; clear, fair" (in Preston-Webb Masonic ritual, "bright", "clear" and "fair" are the dais officer's responses to a favorable ballot) and, more remotely, from the

---

144 See also: *The Key of Solomon the King*, trans. Mathers, Redway, 1889 (Introduction) or its Weiser reprint (2000) for a concordant table of planetary hours with corresponding angelic tables.

145 Mackey, *An Encyclopedia of Freemasonry and its Kindred Sciences*, Everts & Co., 1884, p. 338

146 The Eagle, the Phoenix and the Scorpion have been zodiacally conflated for some time, as all three are associated with the sign of Scorpio; this may be an expression of the sign's three decanic aspects.

147 Mackey, *An Encyclopedia of Freemasonry and its Kindred Sciences*, Everts & Co., 1884, p. 621

148 Wyszecki & Stiles, *Color Science* (2nd ed.), Wiley-Interscience, 1967, p. 506

Proto-Indo-European *kweit*, meaning "white; to shine".[149] Along with charcoal, and red and yellow ochre, white in the form of calcite or chalk was among the first known pigments used in early symbolic art expression. The Paleolithic cave paintings at Lascaux, France depict bulls and other animals on cave walls and are estimated to have been executed in the 18th or 17th centuries BCE.[150] We learn from Pliny the Elder who, in his *Natural History*, informs us that many of the ancient Greek artists used only four colors in their paintings: white, black, red and yellow.[151] Interestingly, these very four colors – the dominant palette from the Paleolithic through the Classical period – were also used by medieval alchemists to describe the stages of the *Magnum Opus*, or "Great Work"; these processes were: *nigredo* (blackness), *albedo* (whiteness), *citrinas* (yellowness) and *rubedo* (redness)…

> *O Turba of Philosophers and disciples, now hast thou spoken about making into white, but it yet remains to treat concerning the reddening! Know, all ye seekers after this Art, that unless ye whiten, ye cannot make red, because the two natures are nothing other than red and white. Whiten, therefore, the red, and redden the white![152]*

These four colors also correspond to those of the horses belonging to the Four Horsemen of the Apocalypse: white to Conquest, red (a fittingly martial color) to War, black to Famine, and "pale" (in the original Koine Greek, this was rendered: *khlōros* (χλωρός), which connotes a sickly, or pallid yellow) to Death…

> *And I saw when the Lamb opened one of the seals, and I heard, as it were the noise of thunder, one of the four beasts saying, Come and see. And I saw, and behold a white horse: and he that sat on him had a bow; and a crown was given unto him: and he went forth conquering, and to conquer. And when he had opened the second seal, I heard the second beast say, Come and see. And there went out another horse that was red: and power was given to him that sat thereon to take peace from*

149   Entry: "White"; *Online Etymological Dictionary*, retrieved at etymonline.com

150   Pastoureau, *Le Petit Livre des Couleurs*, Contemporary French Fiction, 2004, p. 47

151   Gage, *Color and Culture*, University of California Press, 1993, p. 29

152   *Turba Philosophorum*, 12th century, trans. Waite

the earth, and that they should kill one another: and there was given unto him a great sword. And when he had opened the third seal, I heard the third beast say, Come and see. And I beheld, and lo a black horse; and he that sat on him had a pair of balances in his hand. And I heard a voice in the midst of the four beasts say, A measure of wheat for a penny, and three measures of barley for a penny; and see thou hurt not the oil and the wine. And when he had opened the fourth seal, I heard the voice of the fourth beast say, Come and see. And I looked, and behold a pale horse: and his name that sat on him was Death, and Hell followed with him. And power was given unto them over the fourth part of the earth, to kill with sword, and with hunger, and with death, and with the beasts of the earth.[153]

The Four Horsemen of the Apocalypse, von Cornelius, 1845

The ancient Romans used two words to describe whiteness; the most common was *albus*, which was used to describe whiteness generally; the other was *candidus*, which denoted very bright, true white. For instance, when a Roman citizen desired to hold a civic or political position, he brightened his toga with chalk – this was called a *toga candida* and it is the origin of the English word *candidate*. Of white, Mackey states: "It is to be found in all the ancient mysteries, where it constituted, as it does in Masonry, the investiture of the candidate."[154] The words *candle* and *candid* are cognates of the Latin *candidus*, which stems from the Proto-Indo-European root *kand*, meaning "to shine".[155] The Roman priestesses of Vesta, goddess of the hearth and home, were robed in white linen as a symbol of their purity and chastity.[156] White, however, may also have less-than-entirely-wholesome connotations, such as the standards in dream interpretation and art criticism that white horses are symbolic presentiments of death.[157]

In 1666, Isaac Newton demonstrated that white light, when passed through a prism, is differentiated into the spectrum of visible color through the process of refraction. This same phenomenon is qabalistically reflected in the *Etz Chaim*, through which the symbolic white light of *Kether* is sephirothically distributed into its component hues. In the cosmology of Hermetic Qabalah, the pre-manifested nature of deity, designated the *Aur Ain Soph* (Hebrew: אור אין סוף; meaning "Limitless Light"), begins the first process of condensation, *ex nihilo*, in the *sephirah* of *Kether*, whose color is white. From this extremely rarified state in the qabalistic world of *Atziluth* (Hebrew: אֲצִילוּת), the emanation of deity descends through the *sephiroth*, increasing in density, until it finally arrives at the *sephirah* of *Malkuth*, in the world of *Assiah* (Hebrew: עֲשִׂיָּה), and is manifested (see Appendix B).[158, 159]

In nearly every culture, white has long been associated with innocence and purity[160]; this association is carried forward in Freemasonry wherein the white, lambskin apron – which is referred to as "an emblem of innocence"[161] – and gloves denote these virtues. Of the color white, Mackey states:

---

154   Mackey, *An Encyclopedia of Freemasonry and its Kindred Sciences*, Everts & Co., 1884, p. 879

155   Entry: "Candle"; *Online Etymological Dictionary*, retrieved at etymonline.com

156   Varichon, *Couleurs – pigments et teintures dans les mains des peuples*, Seuil, 2005, p. 16

157   Zuffi, *Color in Art*, Abrams, 2012, p. 254

158   Fortune, *The Mystical Qabalah*, London: Society of Inner Light, 1935, pp. 34-38

159   See Mathers' brilliant Introduction (pp. 3-32) to *Kabbalah Denudata*, his 1887 translation of selected books from *Sepher Zohar* (first published by Moses De León (13th century, Spain), and pseudepigraphically attributed to Shimon Bar Yochai (2nd century)) – I know of no better general primer on the subject of Hermetic Qabalah.

160   Heller, *Psychologie de la couleur – effets et symboliques*, Editions Pyramyd, 2000

161   *Duncan's Masonic Ritual and Monitor* (1866), New York: Crown Publishers, 1986, p. 39

In Speculative Masonry, white is the symbol of purity. This symbolism commences at the earliest point of initiation, when the white apron is presented to the candidate as a symbol of purity of life and rectitude of conduct. Wherever in any of the subsequent initiations this color appears, it is always to be interpreted as symbolizing the same idea.[162]

As white may be said to represent light – black oppositely represents darkness. Because of the extreme contrast between the values of black and white, these two colors have, since time immemorial, been symbolically employed to represent all manner of other dichotomies, such as good and evil, day and night, etc.[163] Like white, black is an achromatic color, having no hue. The English word *black* and its immediate predecessors, the Old English *blæc* and the Old High German *blach* (both meaning "absolutely dark, the color of soot or coal"), come to us from the Proto-Indo-European root *bhleg* (meaning "to burn, gleam, shine, flash").[164] In ancient Rome, there were two words for black: *ater*, which denoted a flat black, and *niger*, denoting a more luminous or glossy black. In time, *ater* fell out of regular usage and gradually disappeared, while *niger* is survived by its cognates, now found in the Romance languages (*negru*, *negro*, *noir*, *nero*, etc). The word *ater* survives as the root of the English words "atrocious" and "atrocity" – both stemming from the Latin intermediary *atrox*, meaning "fierce, savage, cruel".[165]

Idiomatically, black carries largely negative connotations and may allude to rejection and exclusion, as in the event of one being "blackballed" or "blacklisted"; rebellion or nonconformity, as in reference to the "black sheep" of the family; threats, extortion or bribery, as in "blackmail"; strategic misinformation and the sewing of confusion, as in "black propaganda", etc. In alchemical vernacular and symbolism, black may be used to represent the stages of *nigredo* or putrefaction, and is associated with the *caput mortuum*, or "dead head", which is the spent and useless byproduct of an operation such as sublimation – though, there is also a later violet artist's pigment by the same name and in reference to iron oxidation and

---

162   Mackey, *An Encyclopedia of Freemasonry and its Kindred Sciences*, Everts & Co., 1884, p. 879

163   Heller, *Psychologie de la couleur – effets et symboliques*, Editions Pyramyd, 2000, pp. 105-127

164   Entry: "Black"; *Online Etymological Dictionary*, retrieved at: etymonline.com

165   Entry: "Atrocious"; *Online Etymological Dictionary*, retrieved at: etymonline.com

its uselessness in further stages.[166] Theologically, black has been associated with Satan, the "Prince of Darkness"[167] – the phrase being an English translation of the Latin *princeps tenebrarum*, which had appeared in the 4th century *Acts of Pilate*. The color black also conveys cosmogonical connotations[168] such as the primordial chaos of pre-Creation – that period described in the opening verses of the *Holy Bible*, preceding the *Fiat Lux*, when the firmament was but a still and barren plain, devoid of the lights of her planets and stars – a period which has been rendered rather beautifully in "contemporary language" scripture as...

> *Earth was a soup of nothingness, a bottomless emptiness, an inky blackness. God's spirit brooded like a bird above the watery abyss.*[169]

The ancient Egyptians regarded black as being representative of the black jackal Anubis, psychopompic guide to the Duat[170], and of fertility, due to rich, black silt left behind by the inundation of the Nile River.[171] In the ancient Egyptian tongue, the name for their land was *Kemet*, which meant "black country"; this was likely in reference to the blackness of the fertile soil within the Nile floodplain.[172] The word *Kemet* was also said, by the famous British Egyptologist E.A. Wallis Budge, to have been the etymological root of the word "chemistry" – the progression running as follows: *kmt* (ancient Egyptian), *kmỉ* (Demotic), *kẽme* (Coptic), *al-kīmiya* (Arabic), *alchimia* (medieval Latin), *alchemy (English), chemistry* (first known usage in the late 16th century).[173] The ancient Greeks also thought the color black to be fittingly symbolic of the underworld, which was separated from the world of the living by the black waters of the river Acheron; and, in the deepest recesses of the underworld, sat Hades on his ebony

---

166   Eastaugh, *Pigment Compendium: A Dictionary of Historical Pigments*, Butterworth-Heinemann, 2004, p. 81

167   Milton, *Paradise Lost*, 1667

168   Zuffi, *Color in Art*, Abrams, 2012, pp. 268-269

169   Peterson (trans.), *The Message: The Bible in Contemporary Language*, 1993-2002, Genesis 1:2

170   Hart, *A Dictionary of Egyptian Gods and Goddesses*, London: Routledge & Kegan Paul, 1986, p. 22

171   Freeman, *The Legacy of Ancient Egypt*, New York: Facts on File, 1997, p. 91

172   Entry: "Egypt"; *Online Etymological Dictionary*, retrieved at etymonline.com

173   Budge, as quoted in Suppan, "The Origin of the Word Chemistry", *The National Druggist*, 1919, retrieved at: todayinsci.com

throne. Roman magistrates of the 2nd century took to wearing the black *toga pulla* to funeral ceremonies – a custom continuing today, as black is considered the color of mourning in the West.

In astronomy, a subject with which we will be dealing more thoroughly in Chapter VIII, the phenomenon of black holes is described as being "a celestial object that has a gravitational field so strong that light cannot escape it and that is believed to be created especially in the collapse of a very massive star".[174] Just as the color black, in general, is caused by the complete, or near-complete, absorption of light radiation, black holes are "black" because they do not allow for the emission of light. The night sky appears to be black because, when the Earth is not in the direct sight of solar radiation, there is an absence of Rayleigh scattering – which causes the daytime sky to appear blue – in our atmosphere.[175]

In the Queen's color scale of Hermetic Qabalah as well as in the qabalistic world of *Briah*, the color black corresponds to the third *sephirah* on the *Etz Chaim*, which is called *Binah* (Hebrew: בינה; meaning "Understanding"). *Binah*, the topmost *sephirah* on the Pillar of Severity (corresponding to *Boaz* on the porch of K∴S∴T∴), represents the celestial sphere of Saturn (Hebrew: *Shabtai*). Also, in Judaism, the *Shabbat* (the Sabbath) is observed from Friday evening at sunset to Saturday evening – Saturday being, of course, "Saturn's Day" and corresponding to the seventh day of Creation – that of rest and repose.[176] The classical element associated with *Binah* is water, which is evocative of the still, black waters of the aforementioned primordial firmament. *Binah* is further associated with the *Aima Elohim* ("Divine Mother") who is in turn reflected in her tripartite manifestations: *Ama*, the dark sterile mother; *Aima*, the bright fertile mother; and *Marah*, the great sea – this is, of course, reminiscent of the triune nature of the Greek goddess Hecate, who is at once the virgin, the mother and the crone. In a psycho-mythological sense, *Binah* may be thought of as the Saturnal Mother – perhaps archetypally expressed as Jung's "Negative Mother" – who, like the titan Saturn, devours her offspring (the seven lower *sephiroth*) as they ascend and their emanations are reabsorbed into her *sephirah*. This is analogous to the absorption of all colors in the color black.

In Binah is a thick darkness which yet veileth the Divine

174   Entry: "Black Hole"; *Webster's Collegiate Dictionary*, retrieved at: merriam-webster.com

175   Nave, "Blue Sky", retrieved at: hyperphysics.phy-astr.gsu.edu

176   ben Asher (trans.), *Shulchan Aruch, Orach Chayim*, 293:2

Glory in which all colours are hidden, wherein is mystery and depth and silence, and yet, it is the habitation of the Supernal Light.[177]

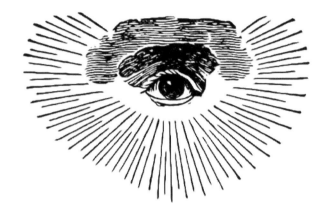

The Eye of Providence

Thus, radiant light is manifested in the visible spectrum and made perceivable through hue, value, tone and saturation. But what of that occult Light which is said to be the protean substance of all Creation, simultaneously preceding manifestation in the phenomenal world and permeating it as the *anima mundi*, or soul of the world?[178] The diaphanous *æther* pervading all forms? That ghostly substance that is, at once, the *azoth* of the alchemists; the *arche* of the Presocratics; the spirit-fire of the Zoroastrians? It is Light: the radiating force that traces its cosmogonical origin to the Grand Pronunciation of the *Fiat Lux* and, in the beginning, is first seen to be "good" by the All-Seeing Eye of Providence – by the Holy Eye of the omnivoyant Grand Architect of the Universe. As Freemasons, we are first acquainted with this concept at the culmination of our Obligation, when we are asked: "Being in a condition of darkness, what do you most desire?" after which the Worshipful Master proceeds to recite a particularly poignant passage from the Volume of Sacred Law. This creative aspect of light is perhaps best represented in Western occultism in the concept of the Astral Light.

---

177   Regardie, *The Complete Golden Dawn System of Magic*, Falcon, 1984, p. 33
178   Edge, *The Astral Light*, Point Loma Publications, 1975, pdf retrieved online

Light, that creative agent, the vibrations of which are the movement and life of all things; light, latent in the universal ether, radiating about absorbing centres, which, being saturated thereby, project movement and life in their turn, so forming creative currents; light, astralized in the stars, animalized in animals, humanized in human beings; light, which vegetates all plants, glistens in metals, produces all forms of Nature and equilibrates all by the laws of universal sympathy--this is the light which exhibits the phenomena of magnetism, divined by Paracelsus, which tinctures the blood, being released from the air as it is inhaled and discharged by the hermetic bellows of the lungs.[179]

In his introduction to Éliphas Lévi's *History of Magic*, Freemason and Golden Dawn initiate, Arthur Edward Waite (1857-1942) summarized the Astral Light as a "universal plastic mediator, a common receptacle for vibrations of movement and images of form; it may be called the Imagination of Nature."[180] This seems to be the common understanding of the term, from the perspective of most 19th century occultists and forward into our day. Less commonly, the term is applied to the cosmic rays emitted from stars, specifically; this, of course being the basis of astral and talismanic magic, such as that prescribed in the *Picatrix* (غاية الحكيم *Ghāyat al-Ḥakīm*, 10th-11th century), and usually accomplished by the concentration of decanic and quinantic light. The "Imagination of Nature" clause in the above definition is particularly interesting, in that its capitalization implies a deific source. The word *imagination* is defined as "the act or power of forming a mental image of something not present to the senses or never before wholly perceived in reality"[181]; a definition which certainly squares with notions of the astral plane and the objects thereupon. In this sense, the Astral Light, or "plastic mediator", may be seen as the diaphanous substance which gives a sort of metaphysical, or plasmic form to consciousness as it is outwardly projected onto the plane. These astral impressions can be made either individually or collectively. The product of collective projections of consciousness into this ethereal, malleable substance would in-

---

179   Lévi, *The History of Magic* (2nd ed.), Rider & Son, 1922, p. 340-341
180   Ibid., p. xii
181   Entry: "Imagination", *Merriam-Webster Dictionary*, retrieved at: merriam-webster. com

clude examples such as the "astral temple", a group spatial creation wherein to meet and perform ritual, and the egregore, an autonomous psychic entity, or thoughtform, created by the projections of a group into the æther, just as two coherent laser beams of artificial light are focused and diffracted such as to produce a holographic image.[182]

Operating within similar theoretical parameters as that of the Astral Light, the *body of light* is another common feature in Western occultism. Originating in the Gnostic literature of the 1st century CE, the body of light is a creation of the adept composed of his or her subtle astral and etheric energy. In some traditions, this body is said to be capable of surviving the corporeal death of the physical body. The light body also aids in the etherealization of the physical body during terrestrial life. Through this process of gradual dematerialization, the adept is said to be made capable of transitioning wholly into his or her body of light at will or the time of physical death – as some believe may have been the case in the lives of Ezekiel and Enoch, and also in the Ascensions of Jesus Christ, his mother Mary, and the prophet Muhammed[183] These "subtle vehicles", as they are sometimes called, have also been organized to theoretically correspond to certain *sephiroth*, or "emanations", on the *Etz Chaim*, in their density (see Appendix B).[184] The infamous British occultist, Aleister Crowley (1875-1947), taught that the astral body could be formed through the Assumption of God Forms, among other practices…

> One passes through the veil of the exterior world (which, as in Yoga, but in another sense, becomes "unreal" by comparison as one passes beyond) one creates a subtle body (instrument is a better term) called the body of Light; this one develops and controls; it gains new powers as one progresses, usually by means of what is called "initiation:" finally, one carries on almost one's whole life in this Body of Light, and achieves in its own way the mastery of the Universe.[185]

---

182   "What is a Hologram?", *Holocenter*, New York City, retrieved at: holocenter.org

183   Stavish, *The Body of Light in the Western Esoteric Tradition*, 1997, retrieved at: hermetic.com

184   Samael Aun Weor, *Types of Spiritual Schools*, retrieved at: gnosticteachings.org

185   Crowley, *Magick Without Tears*, New Falcon Press, 1991, p. 81

It is by seeing that we perceive the sign, hence this sense is said to be highly esteemed among Masons. We are also informed that the candidate's sense of sight was at first deprived so "[…] that [his] heart should be taught to conceive, before [his] eyes beheld, the beauties of Masonry." Throughout his initiatory journey, the Mason asks for and incrementally receives "light", "more light", and "further light". Light has a two-fold meaning in Masonic ritual – taken literally, it refers to the actual light of the Sun, the Three Lesser Lights and the Three Greater Lights; figuratively, it is generally considered to be a symbol for the light of reason – intellectual light. But, as we have illustrated, light may also be considered in its metaphysical, mythological and cosmogonical forms from the wider perspective of the Western Esoteric Tradition. In the sequence of the Fellow Craft lecture, the next perception we encounter is that of touch, or feeling…

Feeling is that sense by which we distinguish the different qualities of bodies: such as, heat and cold, hardness and softness, roughness and smoothness, figure, solidity, motion, and extension. [186]

It is by feeling that we communicate the grip "[…] whereby one Mason may know another in the dark as well as in the light."[187] Feeling, or somatosensation ("a collective term for the sensations of touch, temperature, body position, and pain recognized through neural receptors in the skin and certain internal organs. Thus, it includes processes such as mechanoreception")[188] is the tactile interface between the human mind and its physical surroundings and is governed by the largest sensory network in the human body. It is the sense by which we perceive the shape, texture and other qualities of external objects. Touch (sense) has been defined as the ability "to bring a bodily part into contact with especially so as to perceive through the tactile sense : handle or feel gently usually with the intent to understand or appreciate [… and as] the special sense by which pressure or traction exerted on the skin or mucous membrane is perceived".[189] Mechanically, the sense of touch is governed by four sets of mechanoreceptors: Merkel cells, which respond to low

---

186   Webb, *The Freemason's Monitor*, Salem: Cushing & Appleton, 1818, p. 56
187   *Duncan's Masonic Ritual and Monitor* (1866), New York: Crown Publishers, 1986, p. 74
188   Entry: "Somatosensation", retrieved at: biology-online.org
189   Entry: "Touch"; *Webster's Collegiate Dictionary*, retrieved at: merriam-webster.com

vibrations (5-15 Hz) and are effective in discerning shapes and edges; tactile corpuscles, responding to moderate vibrations (10-50 Hz) which allow for such functions as reading Braille and other similarly fine operations; Lamellar corpuscles, which respond to quicker action potentials (250 Hz) and allow for the discernment of soft versus hard, etc.; and bulbous corpuscles, which respond to lower vibrations and allow for the perception of skin slippage, or stretching.[190] Neurologically, the somatosensory system consists of the mechanoreceptors and afferent neurons which conduct information to the central nervous system, up the spine and to the thalamus, where it is further processed in a similar manner to the previously discussed sensory data.[191]

Feeling, or touch, is the sense by which an individual delineates where subject ends and object begins. That is to say that, without the sense of touch, the human mind would neither be able to control nor orient the body in space. Without a sense of the physical awareness of one's person, one's very notion of what it is to *be* would be dramatically altered. While the superficial contemplation of this scenario may inspire euphoric and blissful ideas as to the gnostic sense of oneness suggested by this state, its deficits would become terrifyingly apparent within a matter of minutes, once the subject came to the rather practical realization that such mundane concerns as eating, drinking and relieving oneself were no longer to be performed at one's liberty. For without the sense of feeling, one would be reduced to a silently screaming prisoner of consciousness. And while the dissolution of subject and object, *in the intellectual and spiritual domains*, is perhaps the central reward of gnosis, the physical sense of feeling, conversely, serves to underscore the emphasis on cultivating a developed sense of Self in addition to a creative and participatory expression of the personal will – both of which being fundamental to the philosophy and practices of the Western Esoteric Tradition. In the Fellow Craft lecture, we next encounter the sense of smelling, or olfaction.

> *Smelling enables us to distinguish odours, which convey different impressions to the mind. Animal and vegetable bodies, and indeed most other bodies, continually send forth effluvia of vast subtlety, as well in the state of life and growth, as in the state of fermentation and putrefaction. The volatile*

---

190   Purves, *Neuroscience*, Fifth Edition, Sunderland, MA: Sinauer Associates, Inc., 2012, pp. 202-203

191   Saladin, *Anatomy and Physiology*, 3rd ed., McGraw-Hill, 2004

particles probably repel each other, and scatter themselves in the air, till they meet with other bodies to which they bear a chemical affinity, with which they unite, and form new concretes. These effluvia being drawn into the nostrils along with the air, are the means by which all bodies are smelled. Hence it is evident, that there is a manifest appearance of design in the great Creator's having planted the organ of smell in the inside of that canal, through which the air continually passes in respiration.[192]

The sense of smell, or olfaction, is activated when aroma compounds (odorants) dissolve in nasal mucous and attach themselves to receptors in the superior nasal concha.[193] This information is then transduced and conducted to areas of the brain known to be primarily responsible for identification, memory and emotion.[194] Olfactory information is stored in long-term memory centers in the brain and is especially tied to the limbic system and, thereby, to "emotional memory"[195]; hence the common belief that smell is the strongest sense. After the reptilian brain, which consists of the brainstem and cerebellum, the limbic system, consisting of the hippocampus, amygdala and hypothalamus, is the most ancient component of the brain; it links us with the remotest periods of our development as a species and, thereby, to the vestigial remnants of our primal consciousness. By extrapolation, it would not be much of a leap to posit that much of what we think of as the collective unconscious, as hypothesized by the analytic psychologist C.G. Jung (1875-1961), may reside in this region. The sense of smell, being especially tied to the limbic system, may therefore be a useful tool in accessing and integrating the universal, archetypal forces therein – perhaps aided by the use of incenses and fumigations composed of planetary herbs which appropriately-correspond to the archetypal forces in question.

The sense of smell is especially important to human beings and other vertebrates in that it aids in the detection of hazards, of pheromones, of

192 Webb, *The Freemason's Monitor*, Salem: Cushing & Appleton, 1818, p. 56

193 de March, Ryu, Sicard, Moon & Golebiowski, "Structure–odour Relationships Reviewed in the Postgenomic Era", *Flavour and Fragrance Journal*, 2015, pp. 342-361

194 Schacter, Gilbert & Wegner, "Sensation and Perception", *Psychology*, Worth Publishers, 2011, pp. 166-171

195 Hamann, "Cognitive and Neural Mechanisms of Emotional Memory", *Trends in Cognitive Sciences*, 2001, pp. 394-400

potential foods and is believed to play an important role in incest avoidance.[196] Interestingly, a neural convergence of olfactory and auditory signals has been documented resulting in the composite sense of "smound"[197], thereby buttressing the argument for synesthesia, which is the automatic or involuntary amalgamation of sensory or cognitive information. It has been recently proposed that olfactory receptor molecules recognize specific features of an odorant molecule and that these characteristics are encoded into the information processed in the brain, producing an effect unique to the odorant.[198] Similarly, the Roman epicurean and atomist philosopher, Lucretius, once posited that it was the shape and size of odor "atoms" which allowed one from the next to be perceived as unique.[199] This observation seems to have been influenced by the concept of the Platonic Solids (the five regular, convex polyhedral introduced by Plato in his *Timaeus*) [200] and their applications.

The production and use of incenses and aromatic oils, both appealing to the sense of smell, have had a very long and developed history in religious, ceremonial, magical and ritualistic practices spanning several millennia. The word *incense* is a cognate of the Late Latin *incensum*, meaning "that which is burnt". [201] Resin-based incenses have been found in ancient Egyptian tombs, with burners found dating from the 5th Dynasty (2500 BCE), and are believed to have been used for both ceremonial and practical reasons, such as masking offensive odors.[202] The Egyptian and Babylonian varieties of incense in North Africa and the Near East were survived by the *bakhoor* (بخور) of the Arabs and the *ketoret* (טְקֹרֶת) of the Jews. The *ketoret* is said to be the incense prescribed by YHVH (Hebrew: יהוה) to be used in King Solomon's Temple and, of its composition and origin, we read…

196   Weisfeld, Czilli, Phillips, Gall & Lichtman, "Possible Olfaction-based Mechanisms in Human Kin Recognition and Inbreeding Avoidance", *Journal of Experimental Child Psychology*, 2003, pp. 279-295

197   Peeples, "Making Scents of Sounds", *Scientific American*, 2010, retrieved at: scientificamerican.com

198   Buck, "A Novel Multigene Family May Encode Odorant Receptors: a molecular basis for odor recognition", *US National Library of Medicine*, retrieved at: ncbi.nlm.nih.gov

199   Holtsmark, *Lucretius, the Biochemistry of Olfaction, and Scientific Discovery*, 1979, retrieved at: academia.edu

200   Zeyl, "Plato's Timaeus", *The Stanford Encyclopedia of Philosophy*, retrieved at: plato.stanford.edu

201   Entry: "Incense"; *Online Etymological Dictionary*, retrieved at etymonline.com

202   Nielsen, *Incense in Ancient Israel*, Brill, 1986, p. 3

*And the L*ORD *said unto Moses, Take unto thee sweet spices,*
stacte, and onycha, and galbanum; these sweet spices with pure
frankincense: of each shall there be a like weight; And you shall
make it a perfume, a confection after the art of the apothecary,
tempered together, pure and holy.[203]

Looking further into the ingredients of the incense to be burned in
the Temple, we first encounter the rather vague "sweet spices", which have
been presumed to include mastic, cassia, cinnamon and saffron, among
other contenders.[204] *Stacte*, though unspecified, is likely a gum resin, such
as myrrh or *storax*.[205] *Galbanum* is the gum resin produced by a Persian
umbelliferous plant from the *genus Ferula*, typically found in the moun-
tainous regions of Northern Iran. Anciently, frankincense was a relatively
common import from the land of Sheba (modern-day Marib, Yemen).[206]
The Hebrew name for frankincense, *levonah* (Arabic cognate: *luban*), is
derived from the pale whiteness of the substance; the word shares a consonantal spelling with *levanah*, which is used in reference to the whiteness
of the Moon. But it is the identity of the elusive ingredient, *onycha*, that
has been debated by scholars for centuries and may be of particular interest
to Freemasons. A recent study has linked this controversial component
of the Temple incense with the murex snail – this is the same Eastern
Mediterranean shellfish from which Tyrian Purple dye is procured, which
strengthens the legendary Tyrian presence (that of King Hiram and the
quasi-scriptural Hiram Abiff) at the building of the first Temple. The
Greek loan word, *onycha* (meaning "fingernail"), is thought to be in reference to the shape of the vacated murex shells. [207]

203   *The Holy Bible*, KJV, Exodus 30:34-35

204   Babylonian Talmud, *Kareithoth*, 6b

205   "Stacte", Monographs, *Making Incense*, retrieved at: making-incense.com

206   Bower, *An Universal History, from the Earliest Account of Time to the Present;*
Compiled from Original Authors and Illustrated with Maps, Cuts, Notes, Chronological and
other Tables (part i), London: Symon, Osborne, Wood & Crokatt, 1734-1747, p. 257

207   Bijayalakshmi, et al, "Volatile and bioactive compounds in opercula from Muricidae
molluscs supports their use in ceremonial incense and traditional medicines", *Nature*,
2017, retrieved at: nature.com

The Altar of Incense, Altdorfer, 1530

Incense is also employed in several systems of modern ceremonial magic, wherein it is sometimes used as a medium to give form to the entities of evocation.

> *Into this Fire he casts the Incense, symbolical of prayer, the gross vehicle or image of his aspiration. [...] Our prayer is the expression of the lower aspiring to the higher; it is without the clear vision of the higher, it does not understand what the higher wants. And, however sweet may be its smell, it is always cloudy. In this smoke illusions arise. We sought the light, and behold the Temple is darkened! In the darkness this smoke seems to take strange shapes, and we may hear the crying of beasts. The thicker the smoke, the darker grows the Universe. We gasp and tremble, beholding what foul and unsubstantial things we have evoked! Yet we cannot do without the Incense! Unless our aspiration took form it could not influence form. This also is the mystery of incarnation. [...] In the burning up of these things arise in our imagination those terrifying or alluring phantasms which throng the "Astral Plane." This smoke represents the "Astral Plane," which lies between the material and the spiritual.[208]*

---

208   Crowley, *Magick: Book IV*, "Chapter XVI: The Magick Fire; With Considerations of the Thurible, the Charcoal, and the Incense", York Beach, ME: Weiser, pp. 113-114

Though incense is not typically burned in the Lodge room, the pot of incense has been adopted as a Masonic symbol, present in the lecture of the third degree of Master Mason. It is therein used to symbolize prayers rising from the heart of the individual, like the fragrant smoke emitted from the censer, to his Creator in Heaven.[209] This raising up of prayers, like incense unto the Most High, is also recorded in Psalms: "Let my prayer be directed as incense in thy sight: the lifting up of my hands, as evening sacrifice".[210] In more recent times, the use of incense among Freemasons in the Lodge room has increased; some Lodges – particularly those operating under the auspices of the Masonic Restoration Foundation[211], or those identifying as "Traditional Observance" – may even install a Thuriber among their officers, whose duty it is to circumambulate the Lodge room with a thurible, or censer, before the opening in order to consecration the space.

In addition to incense preparations, aromatic and anointing oils have long been employed in magical and ceremonial operations and ritualism. One of the more popularly referenced is the holy anointing oil (Hebrew: שמן המשחה) of the *Tanakh*, of which we read in Exodus…

> *Take thou also unto thee principal spices, of pure myrrh five hundred shekels, and of sweet cinnamon half so much, even two hundred and fifty shekels, and of sweet calamus two hundred and fifty shekels, And of cassia five hundred shekels, after the shekel of the sanctuary, and of oil olive an hin, And thou shalt make it an oil of holy ointment, an ointment compound after the art of the apothecary: it shall be an holy anointing oil.[212]*

This oil was used in the ordination of the High Priest and in the consecration of the articles of the Tabernacle and, later, the Temple.[213] In 1897, Freemason, Rosicrucian and founding member of the Hermetic Order of the Golden Dawn, Samuel Liddell MacGregor Mathers completed the first English translation of the *Book of Abramelin* (1608), a medieval

---

209   Mackey, *An Encyclopedia of Freemasonry and its Kindred Sciences*, Everts & Co., 1884, p. 362

210   *The Holy Bible*, KJV, Psalm 141

211   Hammer, "Eight Steps to Excellence: The Observant Lodge", *Masonic Restoration Foundation*, retrieved at: masonicrestorationfoundation.org

212   *The Holy Bible*, KJV, Exodus 30:23-25

213   Ibid.

grimoire and narrative surrounding a quasi-historical Egyptian magus named Abra-Melin. The publication of this volume ignited an interest in the anointing oil in the Victorian magical societies of the time and has since been a mainstay in modern ceremonial magic. The work contained a recipe for the anointing oil, based on the formula in Exodus, to be used in the corresponding magical operation, the purpose of which being to obtain "knowledge and conversation" with one's guardian angel.[214] Regarding the oil's composition, the myrrh, cinnamon, cassia and olive oil are uncontested; the ingredient "sweet calamus", however, has been the subject of some debate. The biblical formula refers to an aromatic cane grass called "kaneh bosem", which was procured along spice trade routes.[215] Commentators have conjectured as to the identity of this plant as being: *Cymbopogon*[216], calamus[217] and cannabis[218]; but galangal appears to be the most widely used in modern ceremonial magic circles, which is likely due to this being designated by Mathers' translation.[219]

As with any ceremonial preparation, such as the consecration of talismans and amulets, incenses and oils are produced and utilized in accordance with very deliberate correspondences – it is in this way that these preparations partake of the Hermetic resonance of the macrocosm (influences of the celestial sphere) in the microcosm (operations in the terrestrial sphere). Care and consideration is then given to utilize zodiacal and planetary correspondences (see Appendix C) in order to strengthen the cosmic sympathies involved; this is equally important in the preparation as it is in the use, since alchemical and apothecarial operations have a hermetic effect on the operator. The patterning of operations performed in the terrestrial sphere on those configurations and cycles occurring in the celestial is a ubiquitous motif in Hermetic literature and is a central feature of magic, astrology, alchemy, Freemasonry and all arts collected under the banner of Western Esotericism. In support of this ancient Hermetic sentiment, we

214   Mathers (trans.), *The Book of the Sacred Magic of Abramelin the Mage*, Dover, 1975

215   Botterweck, Ringgren & Fabry, *Theological Dictionary of the Old Testament*, Eerdmans Publishing, 2004, p. 68

216   Kaplan, *The Living Torah*, New York, 1981, p. 442

217   Abraham von Worms, *Die egyptischen großen Offenbarungen, in sich begreifend die aufgefundenen Geheimnisbücher Mosis; oder des Juden Abraham von Worms Buch der wahren Praktik in der uralten göttlichen Magie und erstaunlichen Dingen, wie sie durch die heilige Kabbala und durch Elohym mitgetheilt worden. Sammt der Geister – und Wunder-Herrschaft, welche Moses in der Wüste aus dem feurigen Busch erlernet, alle Verborgenheiten der Kabbala umfassend*, Köln, 1725

218   Benet, *Early Diffusion and Folk Uses of Hemp*, 1967, pdf retrieved online

219   Mathers (trans.), *The Book of the Sacred Magic of Abramelin the Mage*, Dover, 1975

read in Pico's *Oration on the Dignity of Man* of the sympathetic relationship between the earthly and heavenly "commonwealth[s]"...

> *[...] the magic of Zoroaster is nothing else than that science of divine things in which the kings of the Persians had their sons educated to that they might learn to rule their commonwealth on the pattern of the commonwealth of the universe.*[220]

Since ancient times, organic matter in the vegetable kingdom such as herbs, flowers, resins, etc., have been believed to be ruled by particular planets, stars, constellations and other celestial bodies and phenomena. While it is outside the scope of the present work to enumerate these correspondences in explicit detail, the reader interested in referencing this information is first directed to the work of Paracelsus[221] and Agrippa[222], both of whom had dealt with this topic extensively in their Hermetic, magical and alchemical work and had done much to codify these correspondences as they are recognized in the Western Esoteric Tradition.[223]

The last of the five human senses referenced in the lecture is that of tasting, or gustation.

> *Tasting enables us to make a proper distinction in the choice of our food. The organ of this sense guards the entrance of the alimentary canal, as that of smell guards the entrance of the canal for respiration. From the situation of these organs, it is plain that they were intended by Nature to enable us to distinguish wholesome food from that which is nauseous. Every thing that enters into the stomach must undergo the scrutiny of Tasting, and by it we are capable of discerning the changes which the same body undergoes in the different compositions of art, cookery, chemistry, pharmacy, &c.*[224]

---

220   Pico della Mirandola, *De hominis dignitate* (English: *Oration on the Dignity of Man*), 1486

221   Waite (ed.), *The Hermetic and Alchemical Writings of Paracelsus*, Chicago: de Laurence, Scott & Co., *1910*

222   *Three Books of Occult Philosophy*, Llewelyn, 1992

223   For a reputable modern reference work on the subject, the reader is directed to the excellent *Cunningham's Encyclopedia of Magical Herbs* (Llewelyn, 1985) by Scott Cunningham.

224   Webb, *The Freemason's Monitor*, Salem: Cushing & Appleton, 1818, pp. 56-57

Tasting, or gustation, may be considered a sub-sense of the olfactory system, as both gustation and olfaction work in concert to produce the sense of tasting, whereas smelling is the comparatively more autonomous sense of the two.[225] The mechanical and neural physiological action of gustation follows roughly the same processes of reception and transduction which we have already covered, particularly as it pertains to olfaction, so it is unnecessary to address this process in detail here. Regarding this sense vis-à-vis the Western Esoteric Tradition, we will presently address the communal, or sacramental meal in the Roman *collegia*, the ancient Mysteries (using Mithraism as our exemplar) and in Freemasonry.

The ancient Roman *collegia*, which we had previously discussed in some detail in Chapter I, were bodies assembled for legal representation, guild solidarity, communal burial funding and socialization. However, communal feasting was also a central component to the collegiate experience. There were detailed banqueting and festal regulations in the *lex collegii* of many of the societies, some clauses pertaining to the *magister's* responsibility to provide "good wine", bread, sardines, a place setting, warm water and dinnerware, as was the case in the *cultores Dianae et Antinoi*.[226] It is interesting to note that nearly half the contents of the *lex* documents of many *collegia* were devoted to regulations pertaining to communal feasts.

The Tauroctony, a bas-relief commonly found in mithraea

225   Shepherd, *Neurogastronomy: How the Brain Creates Flavor and Why it Matters*, Columbia University Press, 2013

226   Donahue, "Toward a Typology of Roman Public Feasting", *American Journal of Philology*, 2003, p. 105

Along with the conferral of seven initiatory grades (which we will further address in Chapter VIII in the section on Astronomy), the communal feast was a central component of the rites associated with Mithraism, a Mystery cult, especially popular with Roman legionaries from the 1st through 4th centuries CE. The cult's assemblies were held in subterranean grottoes called *mithraea*, in which their rites and feasts took place. The archeological record clearly illustrates the presence of cutlery, utensils, miscellaneous dinnerware and food residue such as animal bones and fruit and vegetable refuse. Interestingly, an inordinately high concentration of cherry pits have been found at many sites, which have been used to help confirm a mid-summer (late June/early July) date for their feasts.[227] This hypothesis is supported by the *Virunum Album*[228], which records a Mithraic feast date as having occurred on June 26th, 184 CE – comfortably within the vicinity of the summer solstice and very near, as we shall see, the Feast of Saint John the Baptist (June 24th). The indisputable presence of solar and astrological symbolism in other aspects of the cult's rites and proceedings all but precludes the possibility of the summer solstice being chosen at random. Most mithraea were equipped with stone benches for dining on either side of the grottoes and there were separate, above ground dining compartments called *triclinia*.[229]

Occurring more or less simultaneously with the ritual feasts of the Roman Mithraic Mysteries, the Agape (ἀγάπη) feast, or Lovefeast, was an important sacramental and communal banquet in the early Christian religion. Originally, the Eucharist (a central Christian sacramental rite) was a component of the greater Agape feast but by 250 CE the two had become separate functions.[230] The Eucharistic course of the Agape consisted of wine and unleavened bread.[231, 232] Other courses were likely seasonal and brought in by the congregants. The feast is mentioned in the New Testament...

227   Clauss, *The Roman Cult of Mithras*, Routledge, 2001, p.115

228   Piccotinni, "Mithrastempel in Virunum", *Aus Forschung und Kunst* 28, Verlag des Geschichtsvereins für Kärnten, Klagenfurt, 1994, p. 55

229   Clauss, *The Roman Cult of Mithras*, Routledge, 2001, p.43

230   Walls & Collins, *Roman but Not Catholic: What Remains at Stake 500 Years after the Reformation*, Baker Academic, 2010, p. 169

231   Welker, *What Happens in Holy Communion?*, Wm. B. Eerdmans Publishing Company, 2000, pp. 75-76

232   For the entheobotanical interpretation of sacramental or Eucharistic feasts, in general, the reader is directed to the work of R. Gordon Wasson, John M. Allegro and Carl A.P. Ruck; for their significance in Freemasonry, see the work of P.D. Newman and Chris Bennett.

These are spots in your feasts of charity, when they feast with you, feeding themselves without fear: clouds they are without water, carried about of winds; trees whose fruit withereth, without fruit, twice dead, plucked up by the roots.[233]

As we had examined in Chapter I, which dealt with the operative and speculative denominations of Freemasonry and their possible tributaries, there is evidence that many of the collegiate customs, such as communal dining, were carried forward by the medieval craft guilds and on into the present-day Craft. Since at least the Middle Ages, ritual feasts have found expression in operative Masonic culture and the tradition has continued into the speculative Craft, popularly taking form as the feasts of the Saints John – that of Saint John the Baptist on June 24th and Saint John the Evangelist on December 27th. For instance, the Feast of Saint John the Baptist is documented to have occurred among the Masons at work on the Cologne Cathedral (Cathedral of Saint Peter) at North-Rhine-Westphalia, Germany.[234] It should also be noted that the Feast days of the Saints John, due to their proximity to the summer (Saint John the Baptist) and winter (Saint John the Evangelist) solstices, have been said to be recuperative Christianizations of pagan solstitial celebrations.[235]

In speculative Freemasonry, the Feasts of the Saints John, while still regularly celebrated to this day, have also been utilized for the installation of officers, as there are records of the Grand Lodge of Ireland installing their incoming Grand Master on June 24th, 1725[236]; installations held by the Freemason's Lodge in the City of York, England on December 27th, 172[237]; as well as the installation of the Grand Master of the Antient Grand Lodge of England in London in the same year.[238] Though communal dining in Freemasonry is certainly an established tradition, there is a burgeoning tendency to its revival in the modern speculative Craft; this is particularly evident in the restorative or "traditional observance" Lodge models, in which ritualized communal feasts are regularly organized;

233   *The Holy Bible*, KJV, Jude 1:12

234   Speth, *Quatuor Coronati Antigrapha*, vol I, part 3, p. xiii

235   Wilson, *The Celebration of the Feast of Saint John the Baptist*, AMAC, retrieved at: amac.us

236   Mackey, *The History of Freemasonry*, Masonic History Co., 1906, Volume Four, Chapter XXXIX, pp. 1043-1078

237   Blackburn, *A Short History of the Grand Lodge of Ireland*, 2011, pdf retrieved online

238   Bywater, *Notes on Laurence Dermott G.S. and his Work*, London, 1884, pp. 23 and 30

these have been called Festive Boards, Harmony Boards and, less-commonly, Agape Feasts.[239] The focus of these events is on quality in food, decorum, formality and presentation. If this alarming trend continues, the ubiquitous presence in our Lodges of pizza, pancakes and soggy, canned green beans – those hallowed staples of the Masonic dining experience – may become a thing of the past.

THE NUMBER FIVE

At the end of Chapter IV, we touched on the applicable and symbolic import of the number three. The numbers three, five and seven being particularly pertinent to the subject of this volume, we will now turn our attention to the number five. We will examine this number at first in general, and then particularly as it pertains to Freemasonry and Western Esotericism. Beginning with the basics, we find that the number five is a prime number, a Fibonacci number and is the only prime that is the product of two consecutive primes (two and three). Five is classified as a Fermat integer, which means that its polygonal form as a pentagon, or its unicursal form as a pentagram, may be constructed with a square and straightedge. Five is also the length of the hypotenuse of the smallest Pythagorean triangle constructed with whole-numbers (*cathetus* one = 3, *cathetus* two = 4, hypotenuse = 5). There are a total of five Platonic solids, one of which (the dodecahedron) is made up of twelve regular pentagons.[240]

Examining the symbolic import of the number five from the perspective of the Abrahamic faiths, we observe that, in Judaism, it is the number of books in the *Torah*: Genesis, Exodus, Leviticus, Number and Deuteronomy, which are collectively referred to as the *Pentateuch* (Greek; meaning "five containers").[241] In Christianity, the number five figures most prominently as representing the Five Holy Wounds which Jesus Christ was said to have suffered during the Crucifixion: the scourging at the pillar, the crown of thorns, the nail punctures in his hands, in his feet, and the lance wound in his side. Renaissance-era, Christian occultists, such as Athanasius Kircher (1602-1680 CE) also made reference to the

---

239   Mackey, *An Encyclopedia of Freemasonry and Its Kindred Sciences*, Everts & Co. 1884, pp. 41-42

240   Bunch, *The Kingdom of Infinite Number*, W. H. Freeman & Co., 2000, p. 61

241   Entry: "Torah"; *Encyclopedia Britannica*, retrieved at: britannica.com

Pentagrammaton in relation to Jesus, which we will discuss in further detail below. In Islam, five may represent the Five Pillars of Islam (Arabic: أركان الإسلام, *arkān al-Islām*), which were originally summarized in the *Hadith* of Gabriel[242] and include: *Shahadah*, a sincere profession of faith; *Salat*, the performance of five ritual prayers per day; *Zakat*, paying alms to the poor and needy; *Sawm*, fasting during Ramadan; and *Hajj*, a pilgrimage to Mecca.[243]

In the West, the concept of five elements is attributed to Aristotle (384-322 BCE) who added the element *æther* (Greek: αἰθήρ), or quintessence, which was thought to permeate the Universe above the terrestrial sphere[244], to the four classical elements previously established by the Presocratic philosopher, Empedocles (494-434 BCE), as the four "roots" (Greek: ῥιζώματα, *rhizōmata*; viz; fire, air, water and earth). The five elements are associated with the Platonic solids in Plato's *Timaeus* (360 BCE) wherein the smallest particle (the "atom") of each element is assigned to a geometrical solid: fire to the tetrahedron, air to the octahedron, water to the icosahedron, earth to the cube, and æther to the dodecahedron.[245] We find this five-fold distinction of the elements resurfacing in medieval alchemy, particularly in the work of Geber (جابر بن حيان, Abū Mūsā Jābir ibn Hayyān, 721-815 CE)[246], and again in 19th and 20th century ceremonial magic (the elemental pentagram of the Hermetic Order of the Golden Dawn, for instance) and neo-paganism (Wicca, etc.).

A Pythagorean hugieia pentagram and signet ring

242   Entry: "Pillars of Islam", *Oxford Centre for Islamic Studies*, United Kingdom: Oxford University, retrieved at: oxcis.ac.uk

243   Kamal-ud Din, *Five Pillars of Islam*, Nabu Press, 2010

244   Smoot III, *Aristotle's Physics*, 2016, retrieved at: lbl.gov

245   Plato, *Timaeus*, 360 BCE, 53c

246   Norris, *The Mineral Exhalation Theory of Metallogenesis in Pre-Modern Mineral Science*, Ambix, 2006, pp. 43-65

The pentagram (from the Greek: πεντάγραμμον), which is a five-pointed, unicursal star, can be traced back to Assyro-Babylonian cuneiform tablets, where it was used as a logogram representing the word *ub* (meaning "small room, cavity, hole") and was also employed as a talismanic charm, similar to the Greek "evil eye" or an apotropaic horseshoe, securing thresholds from the entry of evil spirits.[247] The Neoplatonists in the first few centuries of the Common Era, such as Iamblichus (250-330 CE), have attributed the use of the pentagram to the Pythagoreans[248], who called it ὑγιεία (Greek: *hugieia*; meaning "health").[249] To the ancient Greeks, this figure was sometimes referred to as the "pentalpha", since it consists of *five* letters *alpha* superimposed in equilateral rotations. The pentagram has also been used as a symbol in Christianity, representing the aforementioned Five Wounds of Jesus Christ[250] in addition to the five human senses.[251] Synonymous with the pentagram, the *pentangle* was emblazoned on the shield of Gawain, the hero of the 14th century English epic poem *Sir Gawain and the Green Knight*, wherein references to the its Christian symbolism were reinforced. The anonymous poet attributed the pentangle's invention to King Solomon[252], which may be an allusion to the symbol's magical applications since it is featured in Solomonic grimoires of the period, such as the *Claviculi Salomonis* (15th century). In mid-19th century occultism – particularly that of Éliphas Lévi (1810-1875) – the distinction was made between the upward-pointing pentagram, which symbolized spirit over matter, and the downward-pointing, its antithesis…

> *A reversed pentagram, with two points projecting upwards, is a symbol of evil and attracts sinister forces because it overturns the proper order of things and demonstrates the triumph of matter over spirit. It is the goat of lust attacking the heavens with its horns, a sign execrated by initiates.[253]*

247   Schouten, *The Pentagram as Medical Symbol: An Iconological Study*, Hes & De Graaf, 1968, p. 18

248   Iamblichus, *Life of Pythagoras*, XXXIII

249   Allman, *Greek Geometry From Thales to Euclid*, Dublin University Press, 1889, p.26

250   Ferguson, *Signs & Symbols in Christian Art*, Oxford University Press, 1966, p. 59

251   Child & Colles, *Christian Symbols Ancient and Modern*, New York: Charles Scribner's Sons, 1971

252   Morgan, *The Significance of the Pentangle Symbolism in Sir Gawain and the Green Knight*, The Modern Language Review, 1979, pp. 769-790

253   Lévi, *Dogme et Rituel de la Haute Magie* (English: *Dogma and Ritual of High Magic*), 1854 and 1856

The above entry in Lévi's *Dogma and Ritual of High Magic* is likely the first written instance of the demonization of the inverted pentagram and its association with the goat's head, or the "sigil of Baphomet". Interestingly, the first association of the Templar reliquary head with caprine imagery occurs in the very same work; until this point in the mid-19ᵗʰ century, Baphomet had not been conflated with the Goat of Mendes, of any other goat, as it was largely conjectured to be either a Christian reliquary head, an oracular brazen head, an idol of some sort or, perhaps, an alchemically produced entheogenic tincture.[254] In the system of magic adopted by the Hermetic Order of the Golden Dawn, the pentagram forms a central part of elemental symbolism (one classical element attributed to each point, with "spirit" assigned to the upward-facing point) but is also ritualistically utilized in its ancient apotropaic application. The Lesser Ritual of the Pentagram is an original Golden Dawn Outer Order ritual in which the *Neophyte* (0=0) is instructed and expected to become proficient. The ritual has an invoking and banishing form, depending on which direction (*widdershins* for invoking; *deosil* for banishing) the pentagrams are "drawn" (traced in the air, as if by a white-hot flame, using either the fingers or an *athame*, ceremonial dagger) by the operator and, as it pertains to liminality, concerns the apotropaic *sealing* of the cardinal directions.

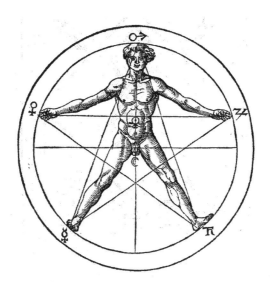

Pentagram from Agrippa's De Occulta Philosophia libri III, 1533

---

254   For a more detailed study of this enigmatic symbol, please see: Lamb, *The Mystery of Baphomet* (2018), which is hosted by phoenixmasonry.org in pdf format.

Perhaps the most common symbolic use of the pentagram, within the context of the greater Western Esoteric Tradition, is its employment as a symbol of the microcosm, man – there are examples of this in the work of Vitruvius, Agrippa, Fludd, and in lesser-known Christian iconography, as we have seen. Conversely, the hexagram represents the macrocosm, the immanent Creator or the Universe itself; thereby making the pentagram a sort of algebraic variable representing the "...so below" term of the Hermetic axiom: "as above, so below", wherein the hexagram would answer for "as above...". This correlation obviously has a lot to do with the pentagram being representative of the number of extremities on the normal human body – two legs, two arms and a head, roughly distributed pentangularly – but, as the pentagram may also be seen to represent the elements, which have been attributed to its points and are the fundamental divisions of the terrestrial sphere, the hexagram represents the seven visible planets of the ancients and, thereby, is a fitting symbol for the celestial sphere. Particularly notable, in this regard, is the Lesser Ritual of the Hexagram, which was an original Golden Dawn ritual given at the grade of *Adeptus Minor* (5=6). Though similar in performance to the Lesser Ritual of the Pentagram, which uses "elemental pentagrams", the Lesser Ritual of the Hexagram uses "planetary hexagrams". Because of their composition and the associations made in the pentagram and hexagram rituals, in most post-Golden Dawn systems of ceremonial magic – as in modern Western Occultism in general – pentagrams refer to elemental operations, whereas hexagrams refer to planetary operations.[255] Qabalistically, this may be visualized as the elements existing in the *sephirah* of *Malkuth* with the six planets – the Moon, Mercury, Venus, Mars, Jupiter and Saturn (by transposing *Binah*'s position for *Da'ath* to complete the final point) – forming a hexagram around the *sephirah* of *Tiphareth*, the central Sun.

A common feature in Masonic Lodge rooms, the Blazing Star is a five-pointed star (geometrically, it is more properly described as a *regular concave decagon*) usually found in the vicinity of the checkered pavement. This symbol has been associated with both the planet Venus and with the binary star system, Sirius A and B.[256] Beginning with the former, we must first note that Venus' apparent path, from the perspective of the Earth, forms a five-petalled rosette against the firmament; this figure is completed over a period of 583.9211 days, which is referred to as Venus' synodic period. This formation was not lost on the astronomers of the

255   Cicero, *Self-Initiation into the Golden Dawn Tradition*, Llewellyn Publications, St. Paul, MN, 1995, P. 689-691

256   Brown, *Stellar Theology and Masonic Astronomy*, 1882, p. 59 (Merchant Books Edition)

ancient world, who long ago conflated the pentagram with the planet Venus. Though not a star at all, Venus was alternately known to the ancients as the "morning star" (*Lucifer*) or the "evening star" (*Vesperugo*); this is due to the fact that the orbit of Venus is concentrically within the Earth's orbit; ergo, Venus is never observed more than 47° from the Sun at its aphelion (the furthest point from the Sun in a planet's orbital pattern).[257] In reference to the fact that Venus appears to accompany the Sun in its rising and setting, the ancients applied the epithets *Phosphoros*, "the bringer of light", and *Hesperos*, "the star of the evening", to the planet.[258]

Other than Venus, Sirius is another contender for the stellar object behind the symbol of the Blazing Star. Sirius (Greek: Σείριος, *Seirios*; meaning: "glowing") is actually a binary system consisting of the stars Sirius *A* and *B*, which are locked in a fifty year inter-orbital cycle.[259] Being the most conspicuous component of the *Canis Major* ("Greater Dog") constellation, Sirius has been colloquially referred to as the "Dog Star" and has, consequently, been the subject of a tremendous body of world-wide stellar lore. Among the most prominent are the Egyptian myths in reference to Sirius' period of heliacal rising which signaled the inundation of the Nile, in the times before the construction of the Aswan dam in Upper Egypt. Due to the agricultural importance of the annual inundation – which replenished the much-needed black silt, making fertile the Nile floodplain – Sirius was allegorized in Egyptian mythology and was particularly made to represent Isis, the consort of Osiris – just as Sirius may be said to be the stellar consort of the constellation Orion, which the Egyptians conflated with Osiris. The Romans referred to these hottest days of summer, when Sirius rose on the horizon, as the *Dies Caniculares* (Latin, meaning "Dog Days"), due to the presence of *Canis Major*.[260] Also pertinent to our study of the number five as it pertains to Sirius, is the cosmology of the Serer people of West Africa. The *Yoonir* is a five-pointed star used in the religious symbolism of the Serer; it is a symbol of their Creation myth and is said to represent the star Sirius.[261] Sirius also figures prominently in the cosmology of the West African Dogon tribe, who apparently had detailed

257   Gaherty, "Cosmic Lights: Bright Venus, Solar Eclipse Dominate Sky This Week", *Space*, 2013, retrieved at: space.com

258   Cain, "Venus: The Morning and Evening Star", *Universe Today*, 2008, retrieved at: universetoday.com

259   Schaaf, *The Brightest Stars*, John Wiley & Sons, 2008, p. 94

260   Holberg, *Sirius: Brightest Diamond in the Night Sky*, Praxis Publishing, 2007, p. 20

261   Madiya, *Tracing Memory: A Glossary of Graphic Signs and Symbols in African Art and Culture*, Mercury series, no. 71. Hull, Québec: Canadian Museum of Civilization, 1996, p. 27

astronomical information regarding both the stars binary composition and their fifty-year orbital cycle[262], although this claim has been contested.[263]

Whether the Blazing Star is a representation of Sirius, of the planet Venus, or of any other star, is ultimately inconsequential as to its symbolic application. In his *Morals and Dogma*, Albert Pike proposed that the Star of Bethlehem, which led the *Magi* (read: Chaldean Astronomers) to the birth of Jesus, and the Blazing Star were one and the same...

> *The Star which guided them is that same Blazing Star, the image whereof we find in all initiations. To the Alchemists it is the sign of the Quintessence; to the Magists, the Grand Arcanum; to the Kabalists, the Sacred Pentagram. The study of this Pentagram could not but lead the Magi to the knowledge of the New Name which was about to raise itself above all names, and cause all creatures capable of adoration to bend the knee.*[264]

Pike's "New Name", mentioned in the passage above, is almost certainly in reference to the *Pentagrammaton* (Greek: πενταγράμματον, or "five-lettered name"), *Yahshuah* (Y-H-Sh-V-H; Hebrew: יהשוה). This name was composed by adding the Hebrew letter *shin* (ש), symbolizing the inner flame, or fire, in the qabalistic tradition[265], to the *Tetragrammaton* (Y-H-V-H; Hebrew: יהוה). In the Renaissance Occultism and Esoteric Christianity of Athanasius Kircher (1602-1680 CE), the five letters of the name were positioned on the points of an upward-facing pentagram, with the added letter, *shin*, inhabiting the top, or "spirit" point of the figure. Though an invention of Kircher, the first printed appearance of the *Yahshuah* pentagram was most likely in de Bry's (1528–1598) *Calendarium Naturale Magicum Perpetuum* (1620).[266] Since the individual letters of the

---

262   Griaule, *Conversations with Ogotemmeli: An Introduction to Dogon Religious Ideas*, International African Institute, 1965

263   van Beek, et al, "Dogon Restudied: A Field Evaluation of the Work of Marcel Griaule", *Current Anthropology*, 1991, pp. 139-167

264   Pike, *Morals and Dogma of the Ancient and Accepted Scottish Rite of Freemasonry*, Supreme Council of the Southern Jurisdiction, A.A.S.R., U.S.A., 1871, p. 842

265   *Sepher Yetzirah*; Hebrew: ריציה רפס

266   While it would be imprudent to go into too much detail here – in a book dealing with the Fellow Craft's work – Master Masons are invited to consider the significance of these "five points" vis-à-vis the pentagram and the symbolism of the number five, in general.

Tetragrammaton each correspond to one of the qabalistic worlds and, thereby, to an Empedoclean element (*yod* to *Atziluth*/fire, first *heh* to *Briah*/water, *vau* to *Yetzirah*/air, second *heh* to *Assiah*/earth), the letter *shin* was thought to represent spirit's descent into matter – just as the Holy Spirit descended into mortal man, producing the Messiah, Jesus. In the 19th century, this concept was reintroduced by Éliphas Lévi and, later in the century, adopted by the Hermetic Order of the Golden Dawn.

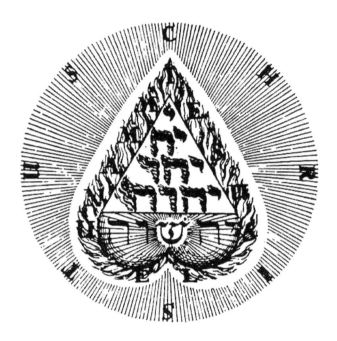

The Pentagrammaton of Jakob Böehme, 17th-century

We will further address the number five in its mathematical context in the section on arithmetic, in addition to the geometrical and Pythagorean significance of the pentagram in the section on geometry, both in Chapter VIII.

CHAPTER VI

∴

THE SEVEN LIBERAL ARTS AND SCIENCES
&
THE NUMBER SEVEN

THE SEVEN LIBERAL ARTS AND SCIENCES

The study of the liberal arts [that valuable branch of educa-tion, which tends so effectually to polish and adorn the mind] is earnestly recommended to your consideration; especially the science of Geometry, which is established as the basis of our Art. [Geometry, or Masonry, originally synonymous terms, is of a divine and moral nature, and enriched with the most useful knowledge: while it proves the wonderful properties of Na-ture, it demonstrates the more important truths of Morality.][1]

The seven liberal arts and sciences comprised the standard aca-demic curriculum in the universities of the late medieval period (12th and 13th centuries CE), with the emphasis being on the development of a classical education. This pedagogical schema, which was taught ex-clusively in Latin, was termed the *artes liberales*, or "free arts", and were undertaken in the pursuit of developing a reference point in the scienc-es with the goal of segueing into the disciplines of philosophy and the-ology. The marriage of religion and reason was the principle aim of the

---

1 Preston (Oliver, commentary), *Illustrations of Masonry*, New York: Masonic Publishing and Manufacturing Co., 1867, p. 39

neo-Aristotelian philosophy of Scholasticism which refined the seven liberal arts, in their medieval form.[2] The *artes liberales* were in contrast to the *artes illiberales*, which were suited more towards trade-oriented vocational ends. The term *free*, in this sense, is in reference to the curriculum's accessibility by those independent pupils who were often of noble birth; whereas the mechanical arts were studied and practiced by the common man for largely economic reasons.[3] The liberal arts were essentially a preparation for one to actively and intelligently take part in civic life; innumerable innovations and contributions to the arts, sciences and Western culture, in general, may be traced to this program. Even to the present day, its sequence – as prescribed on the Winding Staircase in the Fellow Craft lecture (see Appendix D) – stands as an unparalleled curriculum for personal growth and betterment, leading the contemplative Mason to the very pinnacle of the physical sciences and at the doorstep of the metaphysical arts.

The basic concept of a formalized curriculum has its origins in the late Classical/early-Hellenistic period of Greece with the development of a system known as the *enkuklios paideia* ("circular learning"; the origin of the English *encyclopedia*).[4] The *enkuklios paideia* was specifically designed to rear the ideal member of the *polis*, or city-state, through a well-rounded syllabus. This curriculum was relatively broad when compared to later liberal arts programs, in that it included theory and praxis in such diverse disciplines as poetry, mathematics, medicine, gymnastics, wrestling and social etiquette.[5] The impetus for the development of such a program is thought to have stemmed from the Greek's collective desire to cultivate an appreciation for the *kalos kagathos* and a general sense of *arete* in the citizenry. The early-Classical idea of *kalos kagathos* (Greek: καλὸς κἀγαθός; "beautiful and good"), as documented in Herodotus, has been described as "the chivalrous ideal of the complete human personality, harmonious in mind and body, foursquare in battle and speech, song and action".[6] The initially Homeric concept of *arete* (Greek: ἀρετή)[7] was considered the highest virtue and may be generally described as personal excellence and living up to one's fullest potential. The cultivation of *arete* was said to be the

2   Grant, *God and Reason in the Middle Ages*, Cambridge University Press, 2004, p. 159

3   Curtius (Trask trans.), *European Literature in the Latin Middle Ages*, Princeton University Press, 1973, p. 37

4   Doody, "Pliny's 'Natural History: Enkuklios Paideia' and the Ancient Encyclopedia", *Journal of the History of Ideas*, Vol. 70, No. 1, 2009, pp. 1-21

5   Jaeger, Highet (trans.), *Paideia: The Ideals of Greek Culture*, vols. I-III, Oxford University Press, 1945

6   Ibid.

7   Entry: "Arete", Liddell & Scott, *A Greek–English Lexicon*, 9th ed., Oxford, 1940

central driving force in Greek culture; consequently, the importance of the influence of this concept, vis-à-vis the formation of Western Civilization, cannot be overstated.[8]

Though their exact sequence and subject inclusion varied throughout the Classical Roman period[9], the seven liberal arts appeared in something very close to their canonical form in the early 5th century CE, in the work of Martianus Capella (5th century CE; Madaura, Modern-day Algeria).[10] Capella's work, *On the Marriage of Mercury and Philology* (*De nuptiis Philologiae et Mercurii*, 410-420 CE) – which was also called *De septem disciplinis*, or "the seven disciplines" – is a metaphor-laden, prose work describing the allegorical wedding of Mercury, who represents intellectuality and industriousness, and Philologia, who represents the language arts and was immortalized by the Muses, Cardinal Virtues and the Graces.[11] In the narrative, there are seven servant-maidens among the wedding gifts, who are given to Philologia; these maidens are personifications of the seven liberal arts and sciences and are individually introduced as such – much in the manner as they are sequentially introduced in the Masonic Fellow Craft lecture. Interestingly, the eighth book of the *Marriage* describes a geocentric cosmological model in which the Earth, at the center, is orbited by the Moon, Sun, Mars, Jupiter, Saturn and the fixed stars, while Mercury and Venus orbit the Sun in their own epicycles.[12] This may have been Capella's way of correcting for the retrograde motion of these planets since their orbits are concentrically "inside" that of the Earth's. In any case, the observations documented in the astronomical eighth book of the *Marriage* were specifically mentioned and praised by Nicolaus Copernicus (1473-1543 CE) in his *De revolutionibus orbium coelestium* (1543, Nuremberg), the famed astronomer's seminal work on the heliocentric theory.[13] Capella's work, which was a distillation of the preceding Classical Greek and Roman curricula, was widely read, taught and commented upon throughout the Middle Ages and well into the Renaissance.[14]

---

8 Jaeger, Highet (trans.), *Paideia: The Ideals of Greek Culture*, vols. I-III, Oxford University Press, 1945

9 Lausberg, *Handbook of Literary Rhetoric*, Brill, 1998, p. 10

10 Waddell, *The Wandering Scholars* (1927), Dover, 1968, p. 25

11 Stahl, *Martianus Capella and the Seven Liberal Arts*, vol. 1, Columbia University Press, 1992, pp. 21-22

12 Eastwood, *Ordering the Heavens: Roman Astronomy and Cosmology in the Carolingian Renaissance*, Brill, 2007, pp. 238-239

13 McCluskey, *Astronomies and Cultures in Early Medieval Europe*, Cambridge University Press, 1999, p. 159

14 Stahl, *Martianus Capella and the Seven Liberal Arts*, Columbia University Press, 1971, p. 105

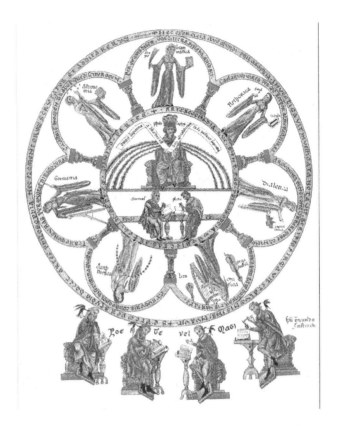

Philosophia et septem artes liberales, from the Hortus deliciarum, ca. 12th century

By pursuing a classical education such as the seven liberal arts and sciences, in the prescribed sequence, one begins from the very basic units of learning – i.e. how to absorb literature and oration, and how to form, write and communicate coherent thoughts – and utilizes these ideas in the further pursuit to the loftiest heights of the physical sciences. But the caveat is that it is only by the laying of a level foundation, built upon "[…] those universal principles which are the condition of the possibility of the existence of anything and everything"[15] that one may erect a sound edifice of substance and learning. This metaphorical edifice, whose ashlars represent the practical and theoretical knowledge gleaned from a thorough study of the arts and sciences, is only then capable of effectively housing the loftier subjects of philosophy and theology which, being metaphysical in essence,

15   Tubbs, *Philosophy and Modern Liberal Arts Education*, Palgrave Macmillan, 2014, p. 1

constitute the apex of human wisdom. For if the final step on the Winding Staircase represents astronomy – which we now call astrophysics, the apex of the physical sciences – then what lays beyond must be *meta*-physical, or *beyond* physical. But the pursuit of this knowledge must begin with first principles.

> *Let no man deceive himself. If any man among you seemeth to be wise in this world, let him become a fool, that he may be wise.*[16]

In Western thought, we find the concept of first principles spanning as far back as the Socratic Paradox: *I know that I know nothing* ("[ἒν οἶδα ὅτι] οὐδὲν οἶδα"), and later during the Renaissance in Descartes' epistemology. To this end, the curricular sequence of the *septivium* (Latin; "seven ways") was devised; this was further divided into the *trivium* and the *quadrivium*.[17]

> *These seven heads were supposed to include universal knowledge. He who was master of these was thought to have no need of a preceptor to explain any books or to solve any questions which lay within the compass of human reason, the knowledge of the trivium having furnished him with the key to all language, and that of the quadrivium having opened to him the secret laws of nature.*[18]

The *trivium* (Latin; "three ways"), also known as the *artes sermocinales* (language arts), consisted of grammar, rhetoric and logic, or dialectic. These three subjects were considered the preliminary education necessary to move on to the loftier subjects dealt with in the *quadrivium*, hence the English word *trivia*.[19] This is not to imply that the subjects enumerated in the trivium were at all *trivial*, in the modern sense, for these were the very building blocks with which the student laid a foundation of future knowledge. Mastery of the subjects within the purview of the

16 *The Holy Bible*, KJV, Corinthians 3:18
17 Castle, *Ancient Education and Today*, 1969, p. 59
18 Enfield, *History of Philosophy*, vol. II, Baynes & Priestly, 1819, p. 337
19 Entry: "Trivia", Ayto, *Dictionary of Word Origins*, University of Texas Press, 1990, p. 542

trivium equipped the student with the skills necessary for effectively digesting literature, a capacity for critical thought, the ability to persuade through discourse, the ability to recognize and circumvent logical fallacies, and the ability to compose compelling arguments and hypotheses. These were indispensable skills for those wishing to move on to the mathematical and physical sciences. A relative succinct definition of the scope of the trivium was posited by Sister Miriam Joseph as follows…

> *Grammar is the art of inventing symbols and combining them to express thought; logic is the art of thinking; and rhetoric is the art of communicating thought from one mind to another, the adaptation of language to circumstance.*[20]

The *quadrivium* (Latin; "four ways"), or *artes physicæ* ("physical arts"), consisted of the study of arithmetic, geometry, music and astronomy. The term was said to have been coined by the Roman senator Anicius Manlius Severinus Boëthius (477-524 CE).[21], though the first known appearance of this quartet as a curriculum may be found in the seventh book of Plato's *Republic*, wherein they appear in the sequence: arithmetic, geometry, astronomy and music.[22] Meant to be studied after the completion of the trivium, the quadrivium is a sequentially ordered curriculum dealing abstract, spatial and temporal mathematics. In the quadrivium, we see the development of the student's capacity for abstract thought through number (arithmetic); the application of these principles into three-dimensional space (geometry); the expansion of these same organizational principles in time (music); and their ultimate extrapolation in space-time (astronomy). This fourfold developmental model is similar to that which was represented by the *Tetraktys* of the Pythagoreans, which taught the unfolding of three-dimensional space: the uppermost point having position but no magnitude; the two points beneath it representing a line and, thereby, duality; the next course of three points representing those needed to construct a plane having width and length but no height; and the four points beneath it representing the nodes of the simplest three-dimensional Platonic solid, the tetrahedron. This correlation was not lost on the ancient cult…

---

20   Joseph, *The Trivium: The Liberal Arts of Logic, Grammar, and Rhetoric*, Paul Dry Books, 2002, p. 3

21   Marrou, *Les Arts Libéraux dans l'Antiquité Classique*, Institut d'Études Médiévales, 1969, pp. 18-19

22   Entry: "Quadrivium", Gilman, Peck & Colby (editors), *New International Encyclopedia* (1st ed.), New York: Dodd & Mead, 1905

The Pythagoreans considered all mathematical science to be divided into four parts: one half they marked off as concerned with quantity, the other half with magnitude; and each of these they posited as twofold. A quantity can be considered in regard to its character by itself or in its relation to another quantity, magnitudes as either stationary or in motion. Arithmetic, then, studies quantities as such, music the relations between quantities, geometry magnitude at rest, spherics [astronomy] magnitude inherently moving.[23]

The seven liberal arts and associated planets, Tübingen, ca. 12th century

We will be addressing the component subjects of the trivium and the quadrivium in individual detail in Chapters VII and VIII, respectively. In keeping with the scope of the present work, we will approach these subjects

---

23   Proclus, *A Commentary on the First Book of Euclid's Elements*, Princeton, 1992, pp. 29-30

primarily from the perspective of the Western Esoteric Tradition – that is to say, that while we will be addressing the seven liberal arts and sciences in their practical, historical and philosophical contexts, our primary focus and lenses of interpretation will be those of Hermetic Qabalah, alchemy, astrology, ceremonial magic, classical mythology and the Tarot. Having already addressed the esoteric symbolism of the numbers fifteen (the total amount of steps on the staircase), three (the first course of steps) and five (the second course of steps), we will now address the occult symbolism of the number seven, which is represented by the final course of seven steps.

THE NUMBER SEVEN

Mathematically, the number seven is the fourth odd number, after one, three and five; and the fourth prime number, after two, three and five. The numbers three, five and seven are, therefore, the three lowest numbers to share both distinctions. The heptagon, or seven-sided polygon, is the first of the regular polygons that cannot be constructed with a compasses and straightedge alone. Septenaries – or, groups of seven objects or concepts – permeate world culture and are manifested in such diverse ways as the seven deadly sins, the seven days of the week, the seven wonders of the ancient and modern worlds, the seven diatonic tones in Western musical theory, the seven seas, the Newtonian septenary division of the spectrum of visible light: red, orange, yellow, green, blue, indigo and violet – and, of course, the seven liberal arts and sciences. Popularly, the number seven appears in *Snow White and the Seven Dwarves*, the *Seventh Seal*, the *Magnificent Seven*, *Seven Samurai*, the *Seven Year Itch*, 7-Eleven and 7-Up.

Probably the most culturally significant septenary, in its overall influence, is that of the seven classical planets. In their Chaldean order, the classical planets are: the Moon, Mercury, Venus, the Sun, Mars, Jupiter and Saturn.[24] These are the planets and luminaries that are visible to the naked eye and, therefore, noted by astronomers predating the invention of the telescope. Our word *planet* comes to us from the Greek *planētēs* which has its etymological root in the verb *planasthai*, meaning "to wander"[25]; ergo, we are able to count celestial objects such as the Sun and Moon among

24   Ellis, "On the Origin of the Weeks and Sabbaths", *Popular Science Monthly*, 1895, p. 335

25   Entry: "Planet"; *Online Etymological Dictionary*, retrieved at: etymonline.com

the planets because they, like the five visible planets, appear to move independently from the sphere of the fixed stars – that is to say that, due to the Sun's relative stasis and the Moon's epicyclic orbit, they appear to *wander* about the ecliptic, through the zodiacal constellations. Along with the four elements and the twelve signs of the zodiac, the seven classical planets have formed the basis of mythological narratives, folklore, religious motifs, initiatory systems and magical systems spanning the globe, since time immemorial. The seven classical planets are also the influence behind such fundamentals as the seven days of the week.[26]

> *The sun, the moon, and the five other planets were not only observed to move independently of the 'sphere' of the fixed stars, but independently of each other, in varying periods. As the whole moving heaven of the 'fixed stars' was a solid 'firmament' studded with stars revolving around a pivot, the earth mountain; so, as the system was perfected, other transparent spheres had to be imagined, one for each planet, carrying it around in its due time. The heavenly mountain of the gods is thus either entirely celestial, the exterior of our firmament, and the whole seven successive domed heavens; or it is the central mountain of this lower world. the prop and pole of the heavens, divided into seven stages, one to each planetary sphere.*[27]

As a typological symbolic device, the number seven is prominently employed in Judeo-Christian scripture. The mention of but a few of these biblical septenaries will amply illustrate this observation: the seven days of Creation[28], seven years of famine in Pharaoh's dream[29], the seven-branched candelabrum (*Menorah*; מנורה) in the Tabernacle and the Temple[30], the Wall of Jericho fell after seven priests blew seven trumpets for seven days[31], the seven pillars of the House of Wisdom[32], the seven demons exorcised from Mary Magdelene[33] and, basically, the entirety of the Book of

26   Richards, *Mapping Time, the Calendar and History*, Oxford University Press, 1999, p. 269

27   Lethaby, *Architecture, Mysticism and Myth*, 1892, p. 124, retrieved at: sacred-texts.com

28   *The Holy Bible*, KJV, Genesis 1

29   *The Holy Bible*, KJV, Genesis 41

30   *The Holy Bible*, KJV, Exodus 25

31   *The Holy Bible*, KJV, Joshua 6:8

32   *The Holy Bible*, KJV, Proverbs 9:1

33   *The Holy Bible*, KJV, Luke 8:2

Revelation with its seven churches, seven seals, seven angels, seven trumpets, seven heads, seven stars, etc.[34] The number is also common in Islam, viz; the seven heavens, the seven hells, seven circumambulations of the Kaaba, the seven sins from the Muhammadian *Hadith*, etc.

Qabalistically, the number seven could either be indicative of *Netzach*, the seventh *sephirah*, or to the gematriac value of the Hebrew letter *zayin* (ז) and its corresponding path on the *Etz Chaim* (see Appendix B). Beginning with the former, the *sephirah* of *Netzach* is associated with feminine mythological archetypes such as Inanna (Sumerian), Ishtar (Akkadian), Astarte (Phoenician), Aphrodite (Greek), Venus (Roman), Frigga (Norse), etc. As such, the Sumerian poem, *The Descent of Inanna* (1900-1600 BCE), specifically addresses the septenary significance of the goddess. Inanna descends through the seven gates of the underworld to visit Ereshkigal, queen of the underworld, and the goddess's older sister, whose husband, Gugulanna, has recently died. Neti, Ereshkigal's hermetic messenger and *psychompompos*, is instructed to guide Inanna, requiring her to remove one of her royal garments at each of the seven gates in her descent. Inanna is sequentially stripped of her turban, scepter, beads, golden ring and all articles of clothing. She is then brought before the throne of her older sister, who was apparently not very happy to receive her.

> *The annuna, the judges of the underworld, surrounded her. They passed judgment against her. Then Ereshkigal fastened on Inanna the eye of death. She spoke against her the word of wrath. She uttered against her the cry of guilt. She struck her. Inanna was turned into a corpse. A piece of rotting meat. And was hung from a hook on the wall.*[35]

---

34   *The Holy Bible*, KJV, Revelation   ·

35   Wolkstein, Kramer & Noah, *Inanna: Queen of Heaven and Earth: Her Stories and Hymns from Sumer*, Harper & Row Publishers, 1983, p. 59

Fragment of a stone plaque from the temple of Inanna at Nippur, ca. 2500 BC

Inanna's descent has been variously interpreted. Famed folklorist and comparative mythologist, Joseph Campbell (1904-1987), sees the myth as being representative of the sense of vulnerability one experiences when confronting the shadowy aspects of oneself while summoning one's strengths from the depths of their psyche.[36] In the French play *Salome* (1891), written by the poet and playwright Oscar Wilde (1854-1900), we find the first appearance of the "Dance of the Seven Veils". Apparently, the dance – an early striptease – was Wilde's prescient and insightful commentary on Inanna's descent and its psychological subtext. Bentley states that, "[...] Wilde assigned this symbolic descent to the underworld of the

36   Campbell, *The Hero with a Thousand Faces*, Bollingen Foundation, 1949, pp. 88-90

unconscious, a ceremony that equates stripping naked to being in a state of truth, the ultimate unveiling, to Salome." [37]

A more recent interpretation of Inanna's descent posits that the myth is an allegorical account of Venus' three day long disappearance during a 2nd millennium BCE meteor shower. In this fascinating celestial interpretation, Inanna represents the planet Venus, naturally, who was obscured in her appearance as the morning (Latin: *Lucifer*) and/or evening (Latin: *Vesperugo*) star. Ereshkigal's husband, Gugulanna, who is conflated with the Bull of the Heavens, was slain by Gilgamesh – a facet of the myth which has been conjectured to represent the Taurian precessional age – a 2,160-year period on the Bronze Age when the vernal equinox was hosted by the constellation Taurus, the Bull. Mercury, Jupiter and the waxing crescent Moon are also personified in this brilliant planetary interpretation of the myth.[38] Along similar lines, her descent may be viewed as being a metaphysical allegory, specifically in terms of spirit's descent into matter by passing through the seven "gates" of the planetary spheres – which may also be read as a qabalistic descent through the *sephirah* of the *Etz Chaim*, eventually arriving at *Malkuth*, the earthly sphere. This is a variation on similar themes found in various Western initiatory systems such as Mithraism.[39] It is certainly possible for elements of this Sumerian myth to have entered – albeit, in a somewhat jumbled form – into the Judaic mytho-cultural transmission, perhaps being communicated to the Jews during the Babylonian Captivity. This is further made plausible owing to the frequency of other repurposed Mesopotamian mythological narratives finding expression in the Abrahamic corpus, such as the Deluge, the Creation in Isaiah, the Garden of Eden and the Tower of Babel.

The number seven, as we had briefly mentioned, is also the gematriac value of the Hebrew letter *zayin*, which means "sword" (Hebrew: זין). *Zayin* corresponds to path seventeen on the *Etz Chaim*, which spans from *Binah* to *Tiphareth* (see Appendix B). Ergo, the path of *zayin* may be said to represent the alchemical transmutation of the base metal, lead, which is associated with *Binah*'s Saturn, to the philosophical gold of *Tiphareth*. This path also corresponds to the zodiacal sign of Gemini and, thereby, to the Tarot card the Lovers VI, which depicts the Archangel Raphael (Hebrew: לאפר). In the Rider-Waite Tarot, Raphael, whose name means "God heals", appears to be presiding over the union of this Edenic couple – representing the melding of the twins (Hermes and Aphrodite, or their corresponding

---

37 Bentley, *Sisters of Salome*, University of Nebraska Press, 2005, pp. 30-36

38 Hostetter, *Star Trek to Hawa-i'i*, Diamond Press, 1991, p. 53

39 Clauss, *The Roman Cult of Mithras*, Routledge, 2001, p.132-133

sephiroth, *Hod* and *Netzach*) into their hermaphroditic union, the *Rebus*. This becomes more obvious when we consider that Gemini is ruled by Mercury, the universal solvent. This is the alkahest, the *Azoth*, the *Menstruum Universalis*, for which the mercurial *caduceus* is a symbol – that which makes all transmutation possible.[40]

In 17th century Valentinian alchemy, seven alchemical processes were delineated: calcination, dissolution, separation, conjunction, fermentation (and its sub-process, putrefaction), distillation and coagulation. These processes, which are the stages of the *Magnum Opus*, or "Great Work", were seven in number; however, other systems document anywhere from four to twelve separate stages.[41] To briefly enumerate these processes, in simple terms, the process of calcination involves heating a substance in a crucible until the substance is burned to white ash. The root of the word is the Latin *calx*, which means "chalk" or "limestone". The ash is then dissolved in a water or acid bath, rendering the *sal salis*, or the "salt of the salt"; this is the process of dissolution. Separation is the process of mechanical filtration, settling or agitation, as the case may be. Conjunction is performed by fixing the substance yielded from separation with a temporary mediator, such as an acid or other catalyst, in order to further transform the matter. The process of fermentation involves the cultivation of bacteria in organic solutions which have been allowed to putrefy. Distillation involves the boiling and condensation of the fermented matter, thus increasing its concentration. The final process of the seven is coagulation, which concerns precipitation and sublimation of the distilled matter. These processes are graphically documented in Basil Valentine's *Azoth of the Philosophers* (1613 CE).[42] These processes have, of course, been famously interpreted by C.G. Jung as to their correlative processes in his analytic psychology.[43] While the investigation of alchemical symbolism as it pertains to personal, inner development is of immense value, it is outside of the scope of the present work to address in any meaningful detail – for this perspective, the reader is directed to the work of Jung and his commentators.

40   Valentine, *Azoth of the Philosophers*, 1613 CE

41   Linden, *The Alchemy Reader: From Hermes Trismegistus to Isaac Newton*, Princeton University Press, 2003, p. 17

42   There are also valuable theoretical websites such as: azothalchemy.org and alchemylab.com

43   Jung, *Psychology and Alchemy*, Collected Works vol. 12, Princeton University Press, 1968

From Basil Valentine's Azoth of the Philosophers, 1659

In metallurgical alchemy, we find the planetary attributions of the seven metals of antiquity – lead to Saturn, tin to Jupiter, iron to Mars, copper to Venus, quicksilver to Mercury, silver to the Moon, and gold to the Sun. In another alchemical context, the number seven may be seen to represent Empedocles' four elements – fire, air, water and earth – added to the *tria prima* – salt, sulfur and mercury. This four-by-three, septenary symbolism is also present in the Masonic apron, as it consists of a rectangular (an oblong square, or quadrilateral) apron overlaid with a triangular flap (usually an isosceles), thus having a total of seven angles – four right angles, two acute angles and one obtuse angle. That the triangle of the flap is pointing downward may symbolize spirit's descent into matter, the rectangle. Additionally, if the triangle may be said to represent the triune nature of the Logos, or the Creative Word, viz; grammar, rhetoric and logic (the trivium); and the oblong square symbolizes the four points of numero-physical Law, viz; arithmetic, geometry, music and astronomy (the quadrivium); then the Masonic apron may be interpreted as being a symbolic representation of the seven liberal arts and, thereby, to the sevenfold nature of Creation and its period of seven allegorical days – wherein the Word was made manifest in spacetime.

The Temple of the Seven Spheres, at the Borsippa archeological site in modern-day Iraq, was a 9th century BCE ziggurat whose colloquial name comes from its dedication to the seven visible planets and their veneration as the "seven lights of the Earth" by the Chaldean astronomers. Of this planetary temple, which was destroyed in 484 BCE, Lethaby writes…

> *The order in which the stages encircled one another spreading outwards to the base, represented in correct sequence the orbits of the planets, as was supposed, around the earth. The small orbit of the moon at the top; the sun taking the place of the earth, as it appears to journey through the twelve signs of the year; and Saturn last of all. Generally, however, as in the walls of Ecbatana, the sun and moon lead the planets in the order of the days of the week.*[44]

An inscription at the Temple of the Seven Spheres, ostensibly written by Nebuchadnezzar II, wherein he commented on the restoration process of the temple of Nabu, read…

> *I have completed its magnificence with silver, gold, other metals, stone, enameled bricks, fir and pine. The first which is the house of the earth's base, the most ancient monument of Babylon; I built and finished it. I have highly exalted its head with bricks covered with copper. We say for the other, that is, this edifice, the house of the seven lights of the earth, the most ancient monument of Borsippa. A former king built it, (they reckon 42 ages) but he did not complete its head.*[45]

In addition to representing the number of steps on the third course of the Winding Staircase, the number seven appears in Freemasonry as the number of Masons needed to convene a Lodge of Entered Apprentices

---

44   Lethaby, *Architecture, Mysticism and Myth*, Macmillan & Co., 1892, p. 130
45   As translated in Loftus, *Travel Researches in Chaldea and Susiana*, Carter & Bros., 1857

as well as the aforementioned number of angles on the Masonic apron. Of the number seven and its relationship to Freemasonry, Mackey, in his Encyclopedia states…

> *Seven is a sacred number in Masonic symbolism. It has always been so. In the earliest rituals of the last century it was said that a Lodge required seven to make it perfect; but the only explanation that I can find in any of those rituals of the sacredness of the number is the seven liberal arts and sciences, which, according to the old "Legend of the Craft," were the foundation of Masonry. In modern ritualism the symbolism of seven has been transferred from the first to the second degree, and there it is made to refer only to the seven steps of the Winding Stairs; but the symbolic seven is to be found diffused in a hundred ways over the whole Masonic system.*[46]

---

46   Mackey, *An Encyclopedia of Freemasonry and its Kindred Sciences,* Everts & Co., 1884, p. 708

CHAPTER VII

∴

GRAMMAR, RHETORIC & LOGIC

GRAMMAR

Grammar teaches the proper arrangement of words, according to the idiom or dialect of any particular people; and enables us to speak or write a language with accuracy, agreeably to reason and correct usage.[1]

Grammar (Greek: γράμμα, or *gramma*: meaning "letter") is the set of rules underlying the use of a language. Since the end of the 18th century, grammar has been considered as falling under the broader purview of *linguistics*, which is defined as, "the study of human speech including the units, nature, structure, and modification of language."[2] Grammar does not include more mechanistic concerns such as spelling and punctuation; these are dealt with under the domain of orthography. Native speakers of any language are endowed with the grammar, or rules, of their language – as these are largely acquired without explicit

---

1 Preston (Oliver, commentary), *Illustrations of Masonry*, New York: Masonic Publishing and Manufacturing Co., 1867, p. 47
2 Entry: "Linguistics"; *Webster's Collegiate Dictionary*, retrieved at: merriam-webster.com

instruction.[3] In the West, the earliest known Greek work on the subject is Dionysius Thrax's *Art of Grammar* (Τέχνη Γραμματική) around 100 BCE; Thrax was a student of Aristarchus of Samothrace, having attended his school at Rhodes.[4] Works on Latin grammar began to emerge near the beginning of the first millennium of the Common Era, most notably in the work of Lucius Orbilius Pupillus (114-14 BCE) and Remmius Palaemon (1st century CE).[5] Latin grammar, as taught in the trivium, was largely influenced by the Priscianus Caesariensis' (500 CE) *Institutes of Grammar* – a work produced in the Late Antiquity which had become canonical in the liberal arts programs of the Middle Ages.

The art of grammar is foundational to any further study, as its contingent subjects, such as rhetoric and logic, are predicated on a thorough grasp of its rules. The composition of concise and impactful expressions in letters, words and speech is indispensable if one wishes to participate in either private or public discourse in any meaningful way; for without this primary structural framework, we are left with only incoherent and disjointed concepts existing in a soup of frustration and misunderstanding. In Freemasonry particularly, grammar is the underlying basis of our lectures and ritualism, not to mention grammar's centrality apropos the immense body of supplementary literature which forms such a large part of the individual Mason's search for further Light. There simply is no Freemasonry – in our present understanding of the Craft – in the absence of grammar. But even beyond its application in the speculative Craft, operative stone-masonry itself is predicated on the "grammar" of architecture – lest we forget that the orders of architecture are bound by the rules of harmony, symmetry, ratio and proportion.

As was stated in the Introduction, it is not the purpose of the present work to provide a grammatical re-education from the ground up – if you are reading at this level and can effectively communicate your thoughts into words, then you have evidently grasped at least the basics of English grammar. Our primary concern is to illustrate that the art of grammar can be seen as the underlying cognitive framework governing not only language but also other systems. In this broader sense, we can conceive of a grammar of ethics, a grammar of morals, a grammar of philosophy, etc. Demonstrably, there are also aesthetic sets of rules which govern and differentiate the various domains of human expression: musical composition,

3   O'Grady, Dobrovolsky & Katamba, *Contemporary Linguistics: An Introduction,* Harlow, Essex: Longman, 1996, pp. 4-7

4   Casson, *Libraries in the Ancient World,* Yale University Press, 2001, p. 45

5   Kolendo, "De Q. Remmio Palaemone Grammatico et Agricola", *Meander,* No. 39, 1984, pp. 407-418

architectural orders, literary styles, fashion trends, cinematic and theatrical direction, etc. It is in this spirit that we will endeavor to investigate grammar's role in Freemasonry and the greater Western Esoteric Tradition.

To begin, we will address the concepts which form the vocabulary of the Western Occult Sciences, viz; angelic alphabets, received or prophetic languages, the ciphers of magical secret societies, the grimoire tradition, the Tarot (with its attendant elemental, planetary and zodiacal correspondences) and the hermeneutic methods of Hermetic Qabalah. This is the symbolic language of Western Esotericism. A sound grasp of the rules of this occult vocabulary – which is to say its *grammar* – is essential to the proper application of Hermetic and Qabalistic exegetical methods. For it is by applying and synthesizing these modes of interpretation – as we have intermittently applied throughout the present work – that we may begin to unveil the otherwise cryptic esoterica and occult substratum of systems such as Freemasonry and ceremonial magic. Since we will be dealing with the planetary and zodiacal material in greater detail in the section on astronomy in Chapter VIII, we will presently address the Hebrew alphabet – or, more accurately, *aleph-beth* – and its significance in the Occult Sciences (see Appendix A).

The Hebrew alphabet is a derivative of the earlier Phoenician alphabet, which is an interesting transmission, from the perspective of Masonic legend, since Phoenicians from Tyre were instrumental in the design and construction of King Solomon's Temple. The Paleo-Hebrew variant of the Phoenician alphabet is believed to have emerged around 800 BCE, about one hundred years after Solomon's reign (970-931 BCE).[6] The alphabet consists of twenty-two letters and five additional variant forms, called "finals", to be used at the end of words. In the 2nd century BCE, the letters of the Hebrew alphabet were assigned a numerical value, in imitation of the alpha-numeric isopsephism of the Greeks.[7] In the Hebrew, this numeric assignment to the letters is called *gematria* (Hebrew: גמטריא) – a device we have been intermittently using throughout the present work. The Hebrew alphabet's mystical quality was first and most thoroughly addressed in the *Sepher Yetzirah* (Hebrew: ספר יצירה; meaning "Book of Formation"), an early work of qabalistic cosmology attributed to 1st century Jewish mystic Akiva ben Yosef.[8]

6   Saénz-Badillos, *A History of the Hebrew Language*, Cambridge University Press, 1993, p. 16

7   Sirat, *Ecriture et civilisations*, Paris: Editions du CNRS, 1976

8   Qafih (editor), *Sefer Yetzirah Hashalem* (with Rabbi Saadia Gaon's Commentary), Jerusalem: Harav Moshe Tzuriel, 1972, p. 46

The foundations are the twenty-two letters, three moth-
ers, seven double, and twelve single letters. Three mothers,
namely A, M, SH, these are Air, Water, and Fire: Mute as
Water, Hissing as Fire, and Air of a spiritual type, is as the
tongue of a balance standing erect between them pointing out
the equilibrium which exists.[9]

The first documented example of the attribution of the twenty-two letters of the Hebrew alphabet to the twenty-two cards in the Major Arcana of the Tarot was in an essay by the Comte de Mellet which was included in volume XIII of Court de Gébelin's *Le Monde primitif, analysé et comparé avec le monde moderne* (1781). In the 19th century, French occultist, Éliphas Lévi published his attributions in his *Dogme et Rituel de la Haute Magie* (English: *Dogma and Ritual of High Magic*, published in two volumes in 1854 and 1856), although these were presented in a different sequence than those used by most occultists today. There is some debate as to whether Lévi jumbled the attribution of the Hebrew alphabet to the Tarot intentionally, as a blind, in order to preserve the integrity of this occult transmission from *profani* or, perhaps, to stay within the bounds of an Obligation. Lévi places the unnumbered Fool card between Judgement XX and the World XXI, whereas the standard order places the Fool 0 before the Magician I and assigns it the letter *aleph*. The attribution of the four classical elements, the seven classical planets, the twelve zodiacal signs and the twenty-two paths of the *Etz Chaim* to the Hebrew alphabet to the Major Arcana of the Tarot was introduced (or reintroduced) to the greater Western Esoteric Tradition by cipher manuscripts which were found by Freemason William Wynn Westcott (1848-1925) among the papers of the recently deceased Freemason and occultist, Kenneth Mackenzie (1833-1886).[10] Again, an understanding of these Victorian era magical correspondences is crucial to the development of an occult grammar – in addition to the wealth of antecedent information available in the grimoire tradition, which we shall address presently (see Appendix A).

---

9   Westcott (trans.), *Sepher Yetzirah*, Chapter II, verse 1, London: The Theosophical Publishing Society, 1887

10   Kunst, *The Complete Golden Dawn Cipher Manuscript*, Holmes Publishing, 1996, pp. 11-15

The Wheel of Fortune, from Lévi's La Clef Des Grands Mystères, 1861

The word *grimoire* is cognate to the word *grammar* as both are et-ymologically linked via the French *grammaire*, meaning "incantation" or "grammar".[11] The term once referred to any book written in Latin but, by the 18th century, it had become specifically associated with books on magic, as grimoires were thought of as "grammars" of magical operations. Like any other grammar, which may be defined as "the principles or rules of an art, science, or technique, [e.g.] 'a grammar of the theater' also: a set of such principles or rules"[12], magical grimoires contained the principles or rules of the Hermetic Arts of magic, alchemy and astrology. Similar to a textbook,

11   Entry: "Grimoire"; *Online Etymological Dictionary*, retrieved at: etymonline.com

12   Entry: "Grammar"; *Webster's Collegiate Dictionary*, retrieved at: merriam-webster.com

grimoires instructed the operator on the proper construction of talismans and amulets, according to planetary, zodiacal and stellar correspondences; the ritualized performance of spells and divinations; the manufacture of tinctures, potions and fumigations; the conjuration, invocation and exorcism of preternatural entities such as angels, dæmons and djinn.[13]

The grimoire tradition has its origin in the 5th and 4th centuries BCE in ancient Mesopotamia. Magical formulae and incantations have been found inscribed on cuneiform tablets uncovered during excavations at the site of the ancient Sumerian (and later, Babylonian) city of Uruk, near Samawah, Al-Muthannā, in modern day Iraq. In Hellenistic Egypt, books on magic flourished under the patronage of the legendary Hermes Trismegistus, who was a conflation of the Egyptian Thoth and the Greek Hermes. Hermes Trismegistus' associations with magic, astrology, alchemy and writing provided the perfect persona for authors of pseudepigrapha to exploit, thus providing an authoritative buoyancy to their work which would be lacking if attributed to an anonymous or unknown author. Certain sects of early Christians, such as the Gnostics, have been known to use tables derived from astrological and angelic apocrypha, such the Book of Enoch, in the creation of magical talismans and amulets, thus effectively making a grimoire of this non-canonical (except for its inclusion in the Ethiopic Bible) piece of biblical scripture.[14] Certainly, the astrological passages in Enoch (himself counted as a Hermetic avatar), colloquially known as "The Astronomical Book" (2nd century BCE)[15], would have lent themselves to astral magical operations, but perhaps no other persona in Abrahamic literature is as inextricably associated with the grimoire tradition than King Solomon himself.

---

13   Davis, *Grimoires: A History of Magic Books*, Oxford University Press, 2009

14   Thomas & Pavitt, *The Book of Talismans, Amulets and Zodiacal Gems*, Rider & Son, 1922, pp. 76-85

15   Martinez & Tigchelaar (eds.), *The Dead Sea Scrolls: Study Edition*, Brill/Eerdmans, 1997, pp. 430-443

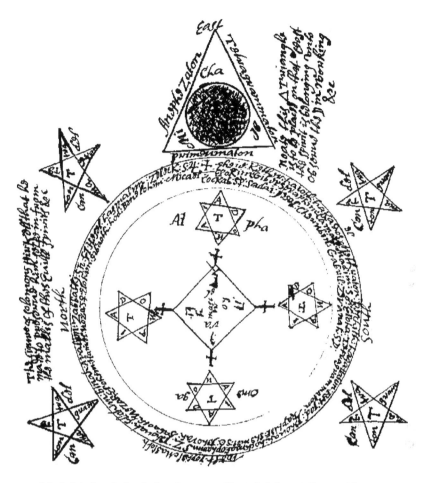

Magical circle and triangle, from Lemegeton Clavicula Salomonis Rex, ca. 17ᵗʰ century

In addition to King Solomon's apparent magical and astrological associations regarding the conjuration of the seventy-two (the number of 5° quinances of the ecliptic) dæmons or djinn in the Qur'an and the *One-Thousand and One* (*Arabian*) *Nights*, the King's persona was, like Hermes Trismegistus', utilized by magicians who authored pseudepigraphic grimoires spanning from about the early first millennium CE until the Late Middle Ages. Among the grimoires attributed of Solomonic magic, *The Testament of Solomon*, *The Key of Solomon*, and *The Lesser Key of Solomon* are the most frequently referenced. *The Testament of Solomon* is a Greek composite text consisting of fragments of 1ˢᵗ millennium CE magical texts which were compiled into a comprehensible grimoire likely some-time during the medieval period. The grimoire contains a syncretization of Judaic, Christian, astrological and mythological themes interwoven with tales of Solomon's magic operations. The zodiacal decans are represented as dæmons, as are the stars of the Pleiades, who are referred to as the "seven demon-sisters". A female dæmon named Obizuth is also encountered by Solomon; having no limbs and a head of disheveled hair, she has been likened to the gorgon, Medusa, who was slain by Perseus (Greek: Περσεύς; meaning "Persian"[16] and perhaps alluding to a euhemeristic Zoroastrian magus) in Greek mythology.[17, 18] One of many such grimoires attributed to King Solomon, *The Key of Solomon* (Latin: *Clavicula Salomonis*, Hebrew: חתפמ המלש) was probably composed during the Italian Renaissance, no earlier than the 14th century, despite pretending to be of a more ancient Jewish (qabalistic) or Arabic (alchemical) origin.[19] The operator is termed an "exorcist" throughout and the magical operations are designated "experiments". Many of the sigils and seals used to summon or restrain the spirits, or dæmons, incorporate the *Transitus Fluvii* occult alphabet, which was used by Agrippa in this *Three Books of Occult Philosophy*.[20] *The Lesser Key of Solomon* (also known as the *Lemegeton*) is a 17th century grimoire, influenced by the *Clavicula Salomonis*, and is principally concerned with demonology and göetic magic. The *Lesser Key* is divided into five books: the *Ars göetia*, *Ars theurgia-goetia*, *Ars paulina*, *Ars almadel*, and *Ars notoria*. The first of the books is the *Ars göetia*, which contains operations for the evocation ("calling out") of the seventy-two dæmons. King Solomon is said to have evoked these dæmons and confined them in a brass vessel sealed with magical symbols. The *Ars göetia* proceeds to hierarchically rank the dæmons – a slight rearrangement of Weyer's *Pseudomonarchia daemonum* (1563) – and provides the seals to which they are obliged to pay allegiance, thus giving the operator the power to command them.[21] In the Hermetic circles of the Renaissance, *göetia* was sometimes contrasted against *magia* and *theurgia*; of this contrast, Agrippa states...

---

16   Herodotus, vii. 61 & 150

17   Conybeare, "The Testament of Solomon", *The Jewish Quarterly Review*, Vol. 11, No. 1, 1898, p. 30

18   Schwarz, "Reconsidering the Testament of Solomon", *Journal for the Study of the Pseudepigrapha*, 2007, pp. 203-237

19   Waite, *The Book of Black Magic and of Pacts*, Chicago: de Laurence, 1910, p. 70

20   Gettings, *Dictionary of Occult, Hermetic and Alchemical Sigils*, Routledge & Kegan Paul, 1981

21   *Lemegeton Clavicula Salomonis: The Lesser Key of Solomon, Detailing the Ceremonial Art of Commanding Spirits Both Good and Evil*, Peterson (ed.), Weiser, 2001, pp. xi-xvii

Now the parts of ceremonial magic are goetia and theurgia.
Goetia is unfortunate, by the commerces of unclean spirits
made up of the rites of wicked curiosities, unawful charms, and
deprecations, and is abandoned and execrated by all laws.[22]

The *Ars göetia* appears to contain material that had previously appeared in Johann Weyer's *De praestigiis daemonum* (1563), the *Heptameron*
of pseudo-Pietro d'Abano, the *Calendarium naturale magicum perpetuum*
(1620) and, of course, Agrippa's *Three Books of Occult Philosophy*.[23, 24] The
second book, *Ars theurgia göetia*, derives primarily from the *Steganographia*
(1499) of Johannes Trithemius (1462 – 1516); it describes the "Dukes"
and "Emperors" who are tied to the four cardinal points and the eleven
"Wandering Princes", each of whom rule a certain number of spirits. The
third book, *Ars paulina* is also derived from the *Steganographia* and the
Heptameron but, as the name suggests, is purported to be derived from
Paul the Apostle. It contains horary and zodiacal magical material in the
form of twenty-four angels – one for each hour of the day – and details the
three-hundred-sixty spirits of the zodiac (one per degree of the ecliptic),
which may be related to the *Monomoiria* of Hellenistic astrology.[25] The
Ars almadel, the fourth book, is presumed by Weyer to be of Arabic origin. From the modern researcher's perspective, however, this is a somewhat
redundant observation, as we know that much of what has come to be
known as the grimoire tradition had been under Arabic custodianship at
some point in its transmission; this is particularly apparent in the case of
the *Picatrix*, which was so influential to Trithemius, Agrippa, Paracelsus,
Bruno, etc. and subsequently to nearly every succeeding grimoire. The *Ars
almadel* instructs the operator (magician) in the construction of wax tablets
which are inscribed with specific signs meant to facilitate angelic contact.[26]
The fifth book of *The Lesser Key of Solomon* is the *Ars notoria*; the book
was mentioned by mathematician and astrologer Michael Scotus (1175 –
1232) in the 13th century, thereby making it the oldest of the five. The book

---

22   Agrippa, *Three Books of Occult Philosophy*, Book III, Ch. LXV
23   Skinner & Rankine (Eds.), *The Goetia of Dr Rudd*, Golden Hoard Press, 2007, pp.
31-43
24   Waite, *The Book of Ceremonial Magic*, Part I, Chapter III, section 2: "The Lesser Key
of Solomon", London, 1913
25   Jones, "Astronomical Papyri from Oxyrhynchus", Volumes I & II, *American
Philosophical Society*, 1999, pp. 11, 284-289
26   Skinner & Rankine (Eds.), *The Goetia of Dr Rudd*, Golden Hoard Press, 2007, pp.
59-60

contains prayers which are intended to grant the magician eidetic memory, which is similar to photographic or iconic memory[27], thereby enabling the him to acquire instantaneous learning.[28]

> *And Solomon inherited David. He said, "O people, we have been taught the language of birds, and we have been given from all things. Indeed, this is evident bounty." And gathered for Solomon were his soldiers of the jinn and men and birds, and they were [marching] in rows.*[29]

Having illustrated the occult significance of grammar vis-à-vis the grimoire tradition, we will address the "language of the birds" (sometimes called the *langue verte*, or "green language"), which is somewhat of a general term to describe a number of occult tongues such as the Adamic, Enochian and Angelic languages. In *The Conference of the Birds* (Persian: منطق الطیر, *Maqāmāt-ut-Ṭuyūr)*, a mystical poem and masterpiece of Persian literature composed by the Sufi poet Farid ud-Din Attar in 1177CE, "thirty or forty" birds are deliberating who will be their sovereign. The hoopoe bird, wisest among them, suggests that they cross the dreaded "seven valleys" in order that they might find the *Simorgh* (Persian: *Si* – "thirty", *morgh* – "birds") who they ask to govern them.

> *If Simorgh unveils its face to you, you will find*
> *that all the birds, be they thirty or forty or more,*
> *are but the shadows cast by that unveiling.*
> *What shadow is ever separated from its maker?*
> *Do you see?*
> *The shadow and its maker are one and the same,*
> *so get over surfaces and delve into mysteries.*[30]

---

27   Coon, *Psychology: A Modular Approach to Mind and Behavior*, Cengage Learning, 2005, p. 310

28   Butler, *Ritual Magic*, part II, chapter 1, "The Solomonic Cycle", 1949, pp. 47-99

29   *Qur'an*, Surah An-Naml; Ayat: 27:16-17

30   Attar, *The Conference of the Birds*, ed. and trans. by Sholeh Wolpé, W. W. Norton & Co, 2017

The talk of shadows and their separation from their cause may be seen as a commentary on the sign surviving that which it once signified, as was discussed in Chapter V in the section on the five human senses. There is also the hint of a Neoplatonic influence in the allusion to Plato's cave allegory, as the metaphoric use of the shadow would have been *de rigueur* in Islamic and Sufic philosophy at this time, contributed by the medieval Neoplatonists, al-Farabi (ابو نصر محمد بن محمد فارابي, 872-950 CE) and Avicenna (ابن سینا, *Ibn Sina*, 980-1037 CE). The above passage also suggests a survival of the central property of the state of gnosis in which the differentiation between subject (in this case, the "thirty birds") and object (Simorgh) becomes blurred or disintegrates altogether, wherein unity with the godhead is achieved. Wolpé, in his commentary on the poem, suggested that the birds "[...] eventually come to understand that the majesty of that Beloved is like the sun that can be seen reflected in a mirror. Yet, whoever looks into that mirror will also behold his or her own image".[31] This language of the birds, imbued with wisdom (*Chokmah*) and understanding (*Binah*) but inaccessible to most, was that which Sulaiman (King Solomon) and Dawud (David) were said to have been taught in Surah 27 of the Qur'an.

In any thorough study of occult grammar, one cannot help but encounter an enigmatic 16th century language and script which has come to be known as *Enochian*. This language was first recorded in the journals of Anglo-Welsh mathematician and occult philosopher, John Dee (1527-1609), and his colleague, Edward Kelley (1555-1598)[32], who referred to it as "angelical" or "celestial" speech; the pair never themselves referred to the language as "Enochian". The pair claimed that the language was transmitted to them by Enochian angels during their magical investigations and scrying sessions beginning in 1583 CE. They believed the language to be of antediluvian origin; in fact, Dee believed it to be the language used by God in the act of Creation. Adam lost the Angelical language after the Fall and substituted it with a sort of proto-Hebrew based on his recollection of Angelical. Inexplicably, the patriarch, Enoch, was said to be in possession of it, but it was again lost during the Deluge.[33] The semantics of the language, as well as its syntax and grammar, are very much like

31 Attar, *The Conference of the Birds*, edited and translated by Sholeh Wolpé, W. W. Norton & Co, 2017

32 Dee, *The Private Diary of Dr. John Dee*, London: The Camden Society, 1842, retrieved at: gutenberg.org

33 Sloane MSS 3188, 3189 and 3191, and Cotton Appendix XLVI, British Library, London

English[34], and its corresponding script – which, like Hebrew, is written right-to-left – has been noted to be very similar to one found in Pantheus' *Voarchadumia Contra Alchimiam* (1550), which was among the volumes in Dee's extensive personal library. Critics have noted that these observations undermine Dee's and Kelley's claims that the language was preternaturally "revealed".[35] Whether angelically transmitted or merely glossolalia contrived by Dee and Kelley, the Enochian script and language are still utilized in systems of adept magic.

Heinrich Cornelius Agrippa catalogued several other "magical alphabets" in the third book of his *Three Books of Occult Philosophy*; three of the most notable being the *Transitus Fluvii*, the Celestial and the Malachim. As the Angelic alphabet was transmitted to Enoch, and the Hebrew to Moses, the *Transitus Fluvii* alphabet was said to be revealed to Abraham. The name – "crossing the waters" – is in reference to the Jews crossing of the Euphrates after the Babylonian Captivity, on their way to build the second Temple at Jerusalem. In addition to its appearance in Agrippa's work, the alphabet is also described a decade earlier in Abraham de Balmis' *Peculium Abrae. Grammatica hebraea una cum latino, Venetiis* (1523). The Celestial alphabet is not to be confused with Dee's and Kelley's Enochian, which is sometimes referred to under the same name. The Malachim alphabet was created by Agrippa, specifically for this *Three Books*. These three alphabets are quite similar in that they are clearly influenced by Hebrew and Greek, each has twenty-two letters, and they are written right to left, horizontally. These scripts were devised for angelic communication and for use in magical operations and correspondence.[36]

34   Laycock & DuQuette (eds.), *The Complete Enochian Dictionary: A Dictionary of the Angelic Language As Revealed to Dr. John Dee and Edward Kelley*, Weiser, 2001, p. 43

35   Laycock, "Enochian: Angelic Language or Mortal Folly?", *The Complete Enochian Dictionary*, London: Askin, 1978, p.33

36   Agrippa, *Three Books of Occult Philosophy* (*De occulta philosophia*), Book III, chap. 29, 1531

Magical alphabets, from Agrippa's De occulta philosophia, Book III, 1531

The subject of grammar may also inspire us to consider the various ciphers which have been employed in the Western Esoteric Tradition. Johannes Trithemius' *Steganographia* (1499), probably the most developed book on the subject, was ostensibly presented as a magical grimoire; the publication of a decryption key to the work in 1606, however, had revealed the work to be largely concerned with cryptography.[37] Trithemius, being obviously enamored with the subject, saw cryptography as a "secular consequent of the ability of a soul specially empowered by God to reach, by magical means, from earth to Heaven."[38] The cipher manuscripts which yielded the fodder for the formation of the Hermetic Order of the Golden Dawn were rendered in a Trithemian cipher alphabet – their author, Kenneth Mackenzie, being a specialist in cryptography.[39] In Freemasonry, the most popularly employed cipher is known as the Pigpen cipher; in fact, it has been referred to as the "Masonic cipher" or the "Freemason's cipher" due to its extensive use by the Craft in the 18th century in correspondence between Lodges and in safeguarding their histories, records and rites.[40]

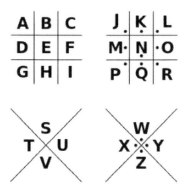

The Pigpen Cipher

It is a simple substitution wherein letters are exchanged for their corresponding graphical symbols assigned according to a geometric key or grid.[41] To explain in slightly greater detail, the letters of the Latin alphabet are distributed across two, nine-cell lattices and two saltires, thus providing a total of twenty-six vacancies; the shape of the vacancy is drawn as a

37   Reeds, "Solved: The Ciphers in Book III of Trithemius's Steganographia", *Cryptologia*, 22 (4), 1998, pp. 191-317

38   Entry: "Trithemius, Johannes", Brann, *Dictionary of Gnosis & Western Esotericism*, ed. Wouter J. Hanegraff, Brill, 2006, pp. 1135-1139

39   Küntz (editor), *The Complete Golden Dawn Cipher Manuscript*, Holmes Publishing, 1996, p. 12

40   Barker, (ed.), *The History of Codes and Ciphers in the United States Prior to World War I*, Aegean Park Press, 1978

41   Wrixon, *Codes, Ciphers, and other Cryptic & Clandestine Communication*, Black Dog & Leventhal Publishers, 1998, p. 27

substitute for its inhabitant letter. The Pigpen, or Freemason's cipher is a variation on its predecessor known as the Rosicrucian cipher which consisted of one, nine-celled lattice, each cell of which contained three letters of the Latin alphabet which were, in turn, represented by the inscription of a dot at the position of its corresponding letter within the cell.[42] Both the Pigpen and the Rosicrucian ciphers are variants on a qabalistic cipher known as *AIQ BKR*.

The exegetical methods of Qabalah are divided into three parts: *gematria*, *notariqon* and *temurah*. Gematria, as we have intermittently discussed in the present volume, is an alphanumeric system, wherein a numerical value is assigned to each letter of the Hebrew alphabet; words having the same numerical value are believed to have an occult resonance (see Appendix A).[43] Notariqon is the process of treating a given word as an acronym, then using each letter as the first letter of a word in a phrase or sentence; this process is believed to further elucidate the esoteric import of the "mother" word.[44] We are presently concerned with the latter of the three, temurah, which means "permutation" or "substitution". The *AIQ BKR* cipher, also known as the "Qabalah of Nine Chambers", is a form of temurah consisting of a nine-celled lattice into which the twenty-two letters and the five finals are distributed in groups of three per cell. Like its Rosicrucian successor, up to three dots are used in each cell in order to signify a certain letter.[45]

300	30	3	200	20	2	100	10	1
ש	ל	ג	ר	כ	ב	ק	י	א
600	60	6	500	50	5	400	40	4
ם	ס	ו	ך	נ	ה	ת	מ	ד
900	90	9	800	80	8	700	70	7
ץ	צ	ט	ף	פ	ח	ן	ע	ז

The AIQ BKR Cipher

42   Pratt, *Secret and Urgent: The story of codes and ciphers*, Aegean Park Press, 1939, pp. 142-143

43   Schechter & Levias, Entry: "Gematria"; *The Jewish Encyclopedia*, Volume 5. Funk & Wagnalls Co., 1904, p. 589

44   Entry: "Notariqon"; *The Dictionary of Jewish usage: a guide to the use of Jewish terms*, Steinmetz, 2005

45   *Kabbalah Denudata: The Kabbalah Unveiled* (selected books of the Zohar, זֹהַר), Mathers (translation and commentary), Redway, 1887

As we have illustrated, the grammar of the Western Esoteric Tradition is comprised of a complex body of correspondences involving angelic alphabets, received or prophetic languages, the ciphers of magical secret societies, the grimoire tradition, the Tarot (with its attendant elemental, planetary and zodiacal correspondences) and the hermeneutic methods of Hermetic Qabalah. Armed with a theoretical knowledge of these interpretive tools – and having reached a level of proficiency in their practical application – the Freemason and/or Western occultist may investigate the otherwise concealed aspects of ritualistic, symbolic and allegorical systems such as Freemasonry and ceremonial magic. For it is by peering beyond the veil of the superficial, outer layer of said systems that we gain access to their hidden, inner Light.

RHETORIC

Rhetoric teaches us to speak copiously and fluently on any subject, not merely with propriety, but with all the advantages of force and elegance; wisely contriving to captivate the hearer by strength of argument and beauty of expression, whether it be to entreat or exhort, to admonish or applaud.[46]

Rhetoric is the theory and practice of persuasion in spoken and written discourse[47]; by it, one may influence or motivate one's listener or reader. The art of rhetoric is formal as well as functional, in that the structure and sequence of the speech or text should comprise a suitable vehicle for the substance of a central argument or proposition. Though there exist Mesopotamian[48] and Egyptian[49] works on the subject, rhetoric had been formally taught and practiced from the time of the ancient Greeks until the middle of the 19th century and was considered an indispensable

---

46   Preston (Oliver, commentary), *Illustrations of Masonry*, New York: Masonic Publishing and Manufacturing Co., 1867, p. 47

47   Corbett, *Classical Rhetoric for the Modern Student*, Oxford University Press, 1990, p. 1

48   Lipson & Binkley (eds.), "The Rhetoric of Origins and the Other: Reading the Ancient Figure of Enheduanna", *Rhetoric before and beyond the Greeks*, State University of New York Press, 2004, pp. 47-64

49   David, "Ancient Egyptian Rhetoric in the Old and Middle Kingdoms", *Rhetorica*, 2002, pp. 213-233

component in the curricula and training of orators, councilors, statesmen, lawyers, historians and poets.[50] In more recent times, the domain of rhetoric has been expanded to include journalism, digital media, advertising and creative fiction.[51]

In ancient Greece, as today, rhetoric was used to sway political opinion and, consequently, public oration on matters political was a common practice in the polis as well as its courts and assemblies. The Sophists (600 BCE) were the first to codify and instruct others in the art of rhetoric and were very active in the political sphere; they also made their services available, for a fee, to those who were unskilled in the art but found themselves in need of representation. Perhaps the most notable pre-Socratic Sophist, Gorgias (483-375 BCE) was keen to widen the field of rhetorical discourse, applying it to the Homeric epics in an effort to prove the innocence of Helen of Troy, as a challenge to himself, in true Sophistic rhetorical style.[52] Plato was critical of the Sophists, particularly Gorgias, who he argued were doing a deliberate disservice to truth in the practice of their deceptive oratorical gymnastics – hence the negative connotation of the word *sophistry*, which is defined as "subtly deceptive reasoning or argumentation".[53] Aristotle tried to resuscitate the reputation of the art of rhetoric – which had suffered abuse by the Sophists and Plato – by narrowing its focus and classifying various genres of rhetoric: deliberative (political), forensic (judicial) and epideictic (ceremonial).

Three distinctions were made regarding the forms of rhetorical oration, these are known as the modes of persuasion, or the rhetorical appeals: *ethos* (ἦθος), *pathos* (πάθος) and *logos* (Λόγος), as found in Aristotle's *Rhetoric* (4th century BCE). Ethos referred to how authoritatively the orator displayed mastery of the subject at hand. This was achieved by being fluent in the technical vernacular of the subject and involved a demonstration that the orator was indeed qualified in the given field. Ethos is practiced today in the form of the presenter's professional and academic credentials, as well as in the citation of the source documents of other authorities. Pathos involved appealing to the emotions of the audience. The words *sympathy*, *empathy* and *pathetic* are derived from pathos. Pathos was best achieved by inspiring an emotional resonance with the audience through

50   Conley, *Rhetoric in the European Tradition*, University of Chicago, 1991

51   Nelson, Megill, & McCloskey, *The Rhetoric of Human Sciences: Language and Argument in Scholarship and Public Affairs*, University of Wisconsin Press, 1987

52   Sprague (ed.), *The Older Sophists: A Complete Translations by Several Hands of the Fragments in Die Fragmente Der Vorsokratiker*, University of South Carolina Press, 1972, pp. 50-54

53   Entry: "Sophistry"; *Webster's Collegiate Dictionary*, retrieved at: merriam-webster.com

value judgements and conveying a sense of justice – such as arguing that a certain perspective or position *feels* right. In some cases, pathos is achieved by appealing to the imagination, hopes and fears of the audience – and, at times, the worst-case scenario of holding a position contrary to that which is being promoted by the orator; the latter method being particularly evident in modern political discourse, as mainstream media outlets frequently utilize this strategy. Logos, from whence we get the word *logic*, is the appeal to reason in which facts and figures are used to support the orator's thesis. However, unsupported, miscontextualized or falsified data may be presented in an effort to confuse or mislead the audience.[54] We will further address logic, or dialectic, in the next section of the present Chapter.

Under the custodianship of the Roman Empire, the art of rhetoric was reorganized and repurposed. Being a highly valued aspect of civic life, several notable rhetoricians were produced in the Empire, Cicero (106-43 BCE) being the best known and most referenced. The *Rhetorica ad Herennium* (late-80's BCE), which was attributed to Cicero but may have come from an anonymous source, was used extensively throughout the Middle Ages and the Renaissance; it is, in fact, widely referenced to the present day.[55] The Roman orator and rhetorician, Quintilian (35-100 CE), codified the five canons of oration in his *Institutio Oratoria* (95 CE); these were: invention (*inventio*), arrangement (*dispositio*), style (*elocutio*), memory (*memoria*), and delivery (*actio*). Invention pertains to the formulation of a thesis or argument; arrangement is concerned with the sequencing of the argument; style deals with the idiom and tone; memory refers to the process by which the orator digests and recalls the information; and delivery is concerned with pacing, dynamics, gesticulation and the overall *presence* transmitted by the orator. Freemasons will immediately note that several of these canons – particularly those of memory and delivery – are necessary components of successful and impactful ritualism.

The art of memorization (*ars memoriæ*) has its origin in the pre-literate cultures spanning the globe and is made evident by documented prehistoric oral traditions.[56] Tribal lore, myth and familial genealogies have been transmitted orally since time immemorial, thus necessitating memrization.[57] Though it is impossible to discern, from the modern perspective,

54   Aristotle, "Rhetoric"; *Stanford Encyclopedia of Philosophy*, retrieved at: plato.stanford. edu

55   Manuwald, *Cicero: Philippics 3–9*, vol. 2, De Gruyter, 2007, p. 129

56   Vansina, *Oral Tradition as History*, University of Wisconsin Press, 1985

57   Ki-Zerbo, "Methodology and African Prehistory", *UNESCO International Scientific Committee for the Drafting of a General History of Africa*, James Currey Publishers, 1990, pp. 54-61

precisely which mnemonic methods were in use in prehistory, the general consensus is that these were accomplished via memorization techniques such as repetition, metering and balladry. For our purposes, and so as to not to go unnecessarily deep into the anthropological aspects of the matter, we will confine our study of memorization to Western antiquity, the classical period, the Middle Ages and the Renaissance – the contributing cultural forces to Freemasonry and the Western Esoteric Tradition.

In the West, the Homeric epics comprise the most significant example of the ancient oral tradition, as the transmission of this poetic corpus required the memorization of extrememly long passages.[58] Clearly, due to the presence of a measurable dactylic hexametric form, metering was utilized as a mnemonic aid. In late-20th century studies, researchers have detected a mnemonic method at play in the oral transmission of the epics which undermines the previous notion that the epics were learned by the common techniques of rote memorization, or repitition. This method has been referred to as "oral-formulaic composition" and it involves the use of modular phrases and formulas such as *eos rhododaktylos* ("rosy fingered dawn") and *oinops pontos* ("winedark sea"), along with many other epithets, which are copiously employed throughout the work.[59] Since the discovery of this pattern in Homer, oral-formulaic composition has been detected in Serbian and Yugoslavian poetry, Japanese poetry and the Old English epic, *Beowulf*.[60] Recently, the theory has also been controversially applied to some parts of the Qur'an.[61]

The poet, Simonedes of Ceos (500 BCE), was credited with the codification of the art of memorization, even by his ancient contemporaries. The *Dialexis* (400 BCE), a fragment attributed to Simonedes, contains a section on memorization which features a synoptic overview of the classical features associated with the art.[62] Simonedes was the first to propose the "method of *loci*" (plural of the Latin *locus* for "place"), in which the spatial memory is engaged through visualization in the process of recall. The method of *loci* is still widely used and has been elaborated on to include imaginary locations such as one's home, memory palaces, roads and cities.[63]

58   Gagarin, *Signs of Orality*, Brill Academic, 1999, pp. 163-164

59   Lord, *The Singer of Tales*, Cambridge: Harvard University Press, 1960, p. 4

60   Dundes, *Fables of the Ancients? Folklore in the Qur'an*, Rowman & Littlefield, 2003, p.17

61   Bannister, *An Oral-Formulaic Study of the Qur'an*, Lanham, Maryland: Lexington Books, 2014

62   Yates, *The Art of Memory*, University of Chicago Press, 1966, pp. 27-30

63   Bremer, *The Manual - A Guide to the Ultimate Study Method (USM)*, Cambridge, United Kingdom: Fons Sapientiae Publishing, 2011

Cicero recounts Simonedes' process in his *De Oratore*...

> *He inferred that persons desiring to train this faculty (of memory) must select places and form mental images of the things they wish to remember and store those images in the places, so that the order of the places will preserve the order of the things, and the images of the things will denote the things themselves, and we shall employ the places and the images respectively as a wax writing-tablet and the letters written upon it.*[64]

Metrodorus of Scepsis (145-70 BCE), who was renowned for his personal memory as well as his many contributions to the art, was frequently referenced in classical antiquity by Cicero, Quintilian and Pliny the Elder[65], as the art of memorization was extensively treated in the aforemention rhetorical works: *Rhetorica ad Herennium* (anon.), Cicero's *De Oratore* and Quintilian's *Institutio Oratoria*. These volumes greatly contributed to later advancements in the art, forming some of the principal reference works in the Middle Ages and the Renaissance. In his *Institutio*, Quintilian makes a particularly interesting reference to Metrodorus' unusual method of *loci*, when he states that the latter used the 360° of the ecliptic – that is to say, the sphere of the fixed stars along which the zodiacal constellations progress – as the *locus* of his memory palace.

> *Images are as words by which we note the things we have to learn, so that as Cicero says, 'we use places as wax and images as letters'. [...] which makes me wonder all the more how Metrodorus can have found three hundred and sixty places in the twelve signs through which the sun moves. It was doubtless the vanity and boastfulness of a man glorying in a memory stronger by art than by nature.*[66]

As we have previously discussed, the ecliptic may be divided into not only the signs of the zodiac (30° arc segments, of which there are twelve) but may also be further subdivided into the decans (10° arc segments, of which there are thirty-six) and the quinances (5° arc segments, of which there are seventy-two), thereby providing Metrodorus with an expansive

---

64   Cicero, *De Oratore*, II:lxxxvi, Sutton (trans.)

65   Yates, *The Art of Memory*, University of Chicago, 1966, pp 39-42

66   Quintilian, *Institutio oratoria*, XI, ii, 17-22, Butler (trans.)

and well-ordered "filing cabinet" of images to which he could associate articles to be memorized. This particular method was to be recycled much later by the Florentine Neoplatonists – most notably, Giordano Bruno. Bruno (1548-1600 CE) was a defrocked Dominican friar, Hermetic philosopher and Renaissance magician especially known for his cosmological theories which included the idea of an infinite universe that could, as a consequence of being infinite, have no center – a particularly heretical idea in his time.[67] Apart from his cosmological work, Bruno wrote exstensively on magical memorization, taking many cues from classical sources. Basing his work on both the zodiacal model of Metrodorus and the concentric spheres of Ramon Llull (1232-1315 CE), Bruno wrote the *Ars memoriae* in 1582. In the work, expounds on Hermetic techniques to create a microcosmos within the mind, populated by the astral symbolism and decan images common to Renaissance magic and influenced by the Arabic grimoires, such as the *Picatrix*.[68] In his *De Umbris Idearum* (1582), Bruno synthesized the Neoplatonic spherical model of the cosmos – a model based on the Chaldean order of the planets being nested in concentric spheres, from the innermost planets to the outermost (the Moon, Mercury, Venus, the Sun, Mars, Jupiter, Saturn) – with the sphere of the fixed stars, which constituted the signs of the zodiac and their corresponding decans and quinances, enclosing the planetary spheres. This schema afforded Bruno with an unprecedented amount of *loci* into which he could fit his assignments of magical memorabilia. It is the method of *loci* which may provide the Freemason with a unique insight and opportunity, particularly since the Lodge room is said to be a microcosmic model of the World.[69]

---

67   Gatti, *Giordano Bruno and Renaissance Science: Broken Lives and Organizational Power*, Cornell University Press, 2002

68   Greer, *Ars Memorativa: An Introduction to the Hermetic Art of Memory*, retrieved at: synaptic.ch

69   Mackey, *The Symbolism of Freemasonry*, Clark & Maynard, 1882, "Chapter XIII: The Form of the Lodge"

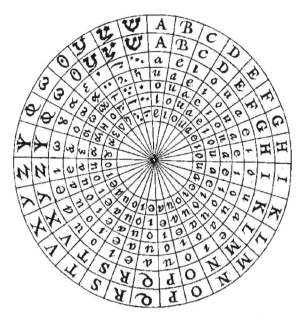

Yates' reconstruction of Bruno's memory wheel from his De Umbris Idearum, 1582

Memorization is central to the Masonic initiatory experience. In the catechisms of Masonic ritual, for example, the candidate is required to minutely recount his movements about the Lodge room and the events which took place at each position or station, thereby proving proficiency in his work and his digestion of the material. As in the Ancient Mysteries, he must recount things seen, said and heard. During segments of the degree ritual, the candidate is hoodwinked (blindfolded), which necessarily brings him in contact with the visual imagination. As he moves about the Lodge room, in this *condition of darkness*, a spatial definition begins to form in his mind – he is surveying the ground plan of a mental Lodge room which he is to build throughout his Masonic career, demarcating its perimeter, identifying objects in his imagination corresponding to those in the three-dimensional world. This spatial orientation is further reinforced by the frequent references to the East, South, West, North, Northeast Corner, West Gate, etc. Using this mnemonic methodology, the candidate is able to recall the sequence of events in the ritual, either for his proficiency examination or to take part in the ritual as an officer. Not only may the Freemason use this schema as a way to memorize – and, thereby, *internalize* – the material of Masonic ritual, but he may also use this microcosmic mental model of the Lodge room as the *locus* for all manner of Hermetic correspondences. The Lodge room, and the body of symbols contained within it, is a vast depository for articles of memory. Since the Lodge room is a microcosmic model of the World, the candidate's construction of its corresponding mental model is, by extension, a step toward the construction of its hermetic mirror in his mind – in the manner of Bruno's Neoplatonic and astral *loci* – which will one day culminate in the raising of the Temple within.

In addition to the canon of *memoria* (memory) from Quintilian's *Institutio*, *actio* (delivery) is also central to the impactful performance and transmission of the material. The canon of delivery speaks to how the piece is conveyed. An emphasis on this canon is integral to the delivery of the material in a way that is impactful for the audience. The best orators are able to emote the material by carefully sculpting their performance with suitable tone, inflection, dynamics, accurate pronunciation and meaningful pauses for emphasis, in addition to gesticulation and other non-verbal modes of communication.

> *Before you can persuade a man into any opinion, he must first be convinced that you believe it yourself. This he can never be, unless the tones of voice in which you speak come from the heart, accompanied by corresponding looks, and gestures, which naturally result from a man who speaks in earnest.*[70]

The efficacy of Masonic ritual is contingent upon this concern, as is the transformational impact on the candidate – to this end, all the best ritualists display a certain level of proficiency in the canon of *actio*. This is not merely confined to the performance of the ritual of the degrees; for example, at times, the Chaplin of the Masonic Lodge is asked to offer an impromptu prayer to the Grand Architect of the Universe, in which case he should be ever-prepared to eloquently and comfortably deliver a suitable offering. Like the Homeric epics, the language of Freemasonry is somewhat modular; meaning there are certain recurring phrases and formulas regularly peppering the work, a mnemonic device known as oral-formulaic composition. The Chaplin should be familiar with the general tenor and literary devices at play in Masonic ritual if he is to offer an extemporaneous invocation, dedication or prayer. In some Lodges and Jurisdictions, we find the office of Orator, whose duties entail the reading of research and education pieces, in addition to being responsible for the presentation of educational material by others. The Orator, as the title implies, should also be conversant in the rhetorical canons.

---

70   Thomas Sheridan, *British Education*, Routledge/Thoemmes Press, 1756

Freemasonry has been popularly described as "a peculiar system of morality, veiled in allegory and illustrated by symbols".[71] The entirety of Freemasonry's teachings are contained in its ritual and symbolism, and these teachings are layered – concealed by symbolic language. The use of metaphor and allegory in Masonic ritual is part of the way the Hidden Mysteries of Freemasonry are transmitted. Their use engages the mind and imagination of the candidate in a way that explicit literalism cannot. The Mason is tacitly charged to seek further Light in the work of the Craft, to labor in its figurative quarries in an ongoing search for deeper meaning and personal applicability. To this end, rhetorical devices such as metaphor and allegory are liberally employed throughout the work of the Lodge. Metaphor is defined as, "a figure of speech in which a word or phrase literally denoting one kind of object or idea is used in place of another to suggest a likeness or analogy between them"[72] The Lost Word is probably the prime metaphorical example in Masonic ritual. Of the Word, Mackey states…

> *No matter what was the Word, no matter how it was lost, nor why a substitute was provided, nor when nor where it was recovered. These are all points of subsidiary importance, necessary, it is true, for knowing the legendary history, but not necessary for understanding the symbolism. The only term of the myth that is to be regarded in the study of its interpretation, is the abstract idea of a word lost and afterward recovered.*[73]

The Lost Word is a metaphor for the *quest* for further Light. In order for this to be an effective device in Masonic ritual, *the Word must remain lost*; for in the absence of this Mystery there can be no quest, hence the substitute Word and the search for the True Word. Obviously, the Freemason is not in search of an actual word – he is forever in search of the Light and Truth for which the Word is but a metaphor. The quest for the Lost Word is analogous to the idea of the *journey* being the true object, as opposed to the *destination*, which is merely a device to demarcate a segment on an individual's path of introspection and gradual attainment of personal gnosis. Being that the present volume is an extended commentary on the Fellow Craft lecture and, as such, may be read by those who have are not

---

71   *First Degree Lecture*, pub. Lewis, London, 1801

72   Entry: "Metaphor"; *Webster's Collegiate Dictionary*, retrieved at: merriam-webster.com

73   Mackey, *An Encyclopedia of Freemasonry and its Kindred Sciences*, Everts & Co., 1884; Entry: 'Lost Word'

yet Master Masons, it would be imprudent to go too much deeper into this metaphor, as it is largely confined to the Master Mason degree ritual.

Allegory is defined as, "the expression by means of symbolic fictional figures and actions of truths or generalizations about human existence".[74] The central allegory in Masonic ritual is also confined to the third degree ceremony. Those who have attained the Sublime Degree of Master Mason can attest to the efficacy of this allegorical device. Suffice it to say that the rhetorical devices of metaphor and allegory play a significant role in the Masonic initiatory experience.

LOGIC

Logic teaches us to guide our reason discretionally in the general knowledge of things, and direct our inquiries after truth. It consists of a regular train of argument, whence we infer, deduce, and conclude, according to certain premises laid down, admitted, or granted; and in it are employed the faculties of conceiving, judging, reasoning, and disposing; which are naturally led on from one gradation to another, till the point in question is finally determined.[75]

Logic (Greek: Λόγος) is defined as "a science that deals with the principles and criteria of validity of inference and demonstration: the science of the formal principles of reasoning".[76] As such, logic may refer to the branch of philosophy which distinguishes the quality of a thought, argument or proposition by inductive and deductive reasoning, or to any system of reasoning or inference which is uninfluenced by whim or emotion. The etymological root of the word is the Greek *logos*, meaning "reason, idea, word".[77] Historically, logic has been considered to fall under the broader subjects of philosophy and mathematics; however, it has recently been

74   Entry: "Allegory"; *Webster's Collegiate Dictionary*, retrieved at: merriam-webster.com
75   Preston (Oliver, commentary), *Illustrations of Masonry*, New York: Masonic Publishing and Manufacturing Co., 1867, p. 47
76   Entry: "Logic"; *Webster's Collegiate Dictionary*, retrieved at: merriam-webster.com
77   Entry: "Logic"; *Online Etymological Dictionary*, retrieved at etymonline.com

studied in the context of the fields associated with cognitive science, such as psychology, linguistics, computer science and artificial intelligence.[78] Logic's scope of inquiry includes the form, classification and validity of arguments, inference through deduction and induction, the formulation of proofs, the identification of paradoxes and fallacies, and the study of syntax and semantics.

Inquiry into formal logic begins with Aristotle, who referred to the science as *analytics*. In many ways, every development in the science since his time may be seen as an expansion on the basic principles raised by the ancient Greek philosopher.[79] In 40 BCE, Andronicus of Rhodes, leader of the Peripatetic school at the time, compiled Aristotle's six works on logic (*Categories, On Interpretation, Prior Analytics, Posterior Analytics, Topics* and *Sophistical Refutations*) into a volume called the *Organon* (Greek: Ὄργανον; meaning "instrument, tool, organ"). Aristotle is credited with the introduction of the concepts of *terms* and *propositions*, as well as the development of the *syllogism* (Greek: συλλογισμός; meaning "inference" or "conclusion").[80] In his *Prior Analytics*, Aristotle defines a syllogism as "a discourse in which certain (specific) things having been supposed, something different from the things supposed results of necessity because these things are so."[81] A categorical syllogism consists of a general statement (also called the *major premise*) and a specific statement (also called the *minor premise*) which are combined producing a conclusion. These arguments often occur in three-line form. For example:

All Shriners are Masons.
Brother AB is a Shriner.
Therefore, Brother AB is a Mason.

The preceding example consists of three categorical propositions (two premises and a conclusion) and three categorical terms (*Shriner, Mason, Brother AB*).[82] It is expressed in a formal deductive argument, reasoning from the general to the specific. This is the classic form of the Aristotelian syllogism. A syllogism may also be expressed, graphically, in the form of

---

78   Thagard, "Cognitive Science", *The Stanford Encyclopedia of Philosophy* (Zalta ed.), 2008

79   Aristotle, "Posterior Analytics", Mckeon (ed.), *The Basic Works*, Modern Library, 2001

80   Lear, *Aristotle and Logical Theory*, Cambridge University Press, 1986, p. 34

81   Aristotle, *Prior Analytics*, 24b18–2

82   Entries: "Categorical Proposition", "Categorical Syllogism" and "Categorical Term"; retrieved at: philosophypages.com

a Venn diagram, and the conclusion of this form of argument may be visually proved by such a construction.[83] Operations such as the syllogism, and geometrical figures such as the Venn diagram, display an obvious concordance with mathematical operations and proofs; the ancients realized this, as we find mathematical and geometrical language being applied to problems in the logical domain, as well as the use of logical concepts being used to elucidate problems in mathematics and geometry.[84]

In the medieval sequence of the seven liberal arts and sciences, logic was sometimes supplanted by dialectic (Greek: διαλεκτική). Dialectic is defined as "discussion and reasoning by dialogue as a method of intellectual investigation specifically: the Socratic techniques of exposing false beliefs and eliciting truth [...] the Platonic [...] investigation of the eternal ideas".[85] In true dialectical discourse, a rhetorical device such as *pathos* (emotional appeal), as well as other subjective arguments, are excluded from consideration, as the focus is on the attempt to establish truth from sound reasoning. Classically, dialectic consists of a proposition (thesis) and a counter-proposition (antithesis); each position is argued in the form of a dialogue, which produces possible outcomes such as: the refutation of the proposition or counter-proposition, or a combination of both propositions resulting in a synthesis.[86] Two of the most popular forms of dialectic are the Socratic Method and the Hegelian Dialectic.

---

83 *Introduction to Logic Venn Diagrams Categorical Syllogisms*, 2018, retrieved at: philosophy.lander.edu

84 Barnes, *The Cambridge Companion to Aristotle*, Cambridge University Press, 1995, p. 27

85 Entry: "Dialectic"; *Webster's Collegiate Dictionary*, retrieved at: merriam-webster.com

86 Ayer & O'Grady, *A Dictionary of Philosophical Quotations*, Oxford, UK: Blackwell Publishers, 1992, p. 484

Marble bust of Socrates, ca. 1ˢᵗ century

Beginning with the former, the Socratic Method is based on an argumentative dialogue in which a statement or a belief is challenged by a series of clarifying questions meant to expose any inherent ambiguities or contradictions. The central technique of the Socratic Method is known as *eclenchus*, a Latinization of the Ancient Greek: ἔλεγχος; meaning "argument of disproof or refutation [...] scrutiny".[87] This method was first introduced by Plato in his *Theaetetus* (369 BCE) and was primarily employed as a method of hypothesis elimination. In some ways, the Socratic Method was in response to what Socrates saw as a particularly manipulative and deceitful brand of sophistry, popular in his time. The Socratic Method has been said to consist of five steps: the interlocutor asserts a thesis; Socrates detects falsehood and targets for refutation; Socrates secures the interlocutor's agreement to further premises; Socrates argues and the interlocutor agrees that these premises support an antithesis; Socrates summarily explains how the original thesis was false.[88] The validity of the Socratic Method, or *eclenchus*, continues to be a subject of debate among modern scholars and logicians, with some finding it to be merely a way to negate false claims without necessarily leading to truth.[89]

Despite bearing his name, the Hegelian Dialectic was never formally

87   Liddell, Scott & Jones, *Greek-English Lexicon*, 9th Edition, retrieved at: stephanus. tlg.uci.edu

88   Vlastos, "The Socratic Elenchus", *Oxford Studies in Ancient Philosophy I*, Oxford University Press, 1983, pp. 27-58

89   Klagge & Smith (eds.), *Methods of Interpreting Plato and his Dialogues*, Oxford: Clarendon Press, 1992, p. 280

used by Georg Wilhelm Friedrich Hegel (1770-1831), rather it was an observation made by the German philosopher, Heinrich Moritz Chalybäus (1796-1862) in his *Historische Entwicklung der spekulativen Philosophie von Kant bis Hegel* (1837). Chalybäus formulated his dialectic method as consisting of three parts: thesis, antithesis and synthesis (German: *an sich, fuer sich* and *an sich und fuer sich*). He framed this as representing a problem, a reaction and a solution; a thesis (problem) gives rise to an antithesis (reaction), which negates or contradicts the thesis, and the resultant dissonance is resolved by a synthesis (solution). The model was popularized by the German idealist, Johann Gottlieb Fichte (1762-1814), who attributed it to Kant through Hegel.[90] While Hegel was not known to have specifically used Chalybäus' dialectical formula, he did employ a similarly tripartite dialectic comprising the terms: *abstract, negative* and *concrete*.[91] Hegel's own critique of the Hegelian Dialectic is that it does nothing to explain why a thesis requires an antithesis – a critique which could not be levelled at Hegel's terms, since the abstract implies an ambiguity in the original thesis that necessitates further processing and mediation through the negative term (trial and error), thereby producing the rectified concrete.[92] Obviously, a thorough treatment of even this particular aspect of logic would require – nay! has required – many volumes to begin to elucidate; suffice it to say that dialectical methods such as the Socratic Method and the Hegelian Dialectic have had a substantial impact on argumentation.

Qabalistically, there is a synthetic dynamic similar to that of the Hegelian Dialectic at play in the diagram of the *Etz Chaim* (see Appendix B). Like the thesis and antithesis, the Pillars of Mercy and Severity represent polarization – the Pillar of Mercy denotes positivity, activity and masculinity; and that of Severity denotes negativity, passivity and femininity. The Middle Pillar represents the synthesis of these dichotomies; it is the reconciling vertical axis of celestial ascent which bisects the horizontal axis of all apparent terrestrial contradictions. As we discussed in Chapter II, the Pillars of Mercy and Severity are also representative of the pillars on the porch of K∴S∴T∴ – *Jachin* and *Boaz* – Jachin denoting "establishment" and the positive polarity in the South, and Boaz signifying "strength" and the negative polarity in the North. One might say that the candidate, when passing between these pillars and gaining entry to the Temple, represents the synthesis of the two extremes – the rectified human being who has

---

90   Fox, *The Accessible Hegel*, Prometheus Books, 2005, p. 43
91   Lincoln, *Hegelian Dialectical Analysis of U.S. Voting Laws*, 42 U. Dayton L. Rev. 87, 2017
92   Hegel, *Werke*, Glockner (ed.), XIX, 610

reconciled the apparent contradictions of his mind (*psyche*), body (*soma*) and spirit (*pneuma*). These pillars – whether interpreted as those of the Temple, those of the *Etz Chaim*, or as symbols of polarization in general – are present on several cards in the Tarot deck. In the symbolism of the Tarot, these pillars also represent polarity, and their inherent dissonance implies an eventual resolution or synthesis. The symbolic implication is that they must be brought into focus until they have become one synthesized pillar, having the full breadth and scope of meaning – not merely two representations of oversimplified extremes. Just as the best characters in literature and the cinema are never wholly good or bad – they are never so simplistic and one-dimensional. The most developed and complex characters reflect the histrionic range of human emotion, characteristics and experience. At times, they are in need of equalization, just as humans strive to find balance, equilibrium – the pillars symbolize this polar dialectic and its resultant synthesis.

In this age of widespread and deliberate deception, manipulation and sophistry in mainstream and social media platforms, it would behoove us all, in our study of logic, to become conversant with a few of the more common fallacies one is likely to encounter on any given day. Armed with this information, one would be better enabled to detect the presence of falsehood, ambiguity or outright contradiction in modern argumentation and persuasion. Fallacies are generally considered to be divided into two types: *formal* and *informal*.[93] A formal fallacy is proved invalid by inherent flaws in its structure – its conclusion does not follow its premises. An informal fallacy arises from errors in reasoning, though the argument may be structurally sound.[94] Fallacies may be, and often are, deliberately employed as rhetorical devices in order to sway opinion rather than to arrive at something resembling the truth through the rigorous application of the principles of sound reasoning. The same fallacies may also be unconsciously employed when they are regurgitated in conversation by those who may have a less-than-critical approach to discourse. We will now address a few of the most common logical fallacies, which one would do well to attempt to recognize in one's everyday life.[95, 96, 97]

93   Madsen, *How to Win Every Argument: The Use and Abuse of Logic*, A&C Black, 2006, p. 46

94   "Informal Fallacies", Northern Kentucky University, retrieved at: nku.edu

95   *Logical Fallacies*, Purdue University, retrieved at: owl.purdue.edu

96   *Drake's List of the Most Common Logical Fallacies*, University of Idaho, retrieved at: uidaho.edu

97   Wilson, "Formal Fallacy", Robert (ed.), *The Cambridge Dictionary of Philosophy* (2nd ed.), Cambridge University Press, 1999, pp. 316-317

The Slippery Slope: "If we slow down on bringing in new candidates, our Lodge membership will decline and we will have to surrender our Charter." This fallacy states that if event A happens then, inevitably, events B, C, D, etc. will follow, leading all the way to event Z, being the worst possible outcome. So, A is being unreasonably equated with Z, despite the fact that there are many intervening steps between the two. In our example, the Brother may not see that, by focusing on the individual attention to fewer candidates, member retention could actually increase; potentially forming a stronger core of dedicated and invested members. Instead, he unjustifiably equates a smaller number of initiations per year with surrendering the Lodge's Charter.

Post Hoc Ergo Propter Hoc: "The education program last month was weak; that's why we had poor attendance at this month's Stated Communication." This fallacy states that, since event B occurred after event A, then event A must have been the cause of event B. There are several missing variables in this equation. Any number of unspecified things may have been the actual cause of event B. In our example, the poor attendance at the Stated Communication may have been caused by the weather, or competing events with another Lodge or an appendant body, for instance.

The Genetic Fallacy: "We are receiving visiting Brethren from a French Lodge this month – they must be atheists." This fallacy states that the origins of a person or thing must necessarily determine its character or worth. The conclusion does not follow the premise. In our example, the Brother is erroneously concluding that since some French Freemasons are atheists, all of them must be. His belief stems from the fact that, in 1877, the Grand Orient de France removed the requirement for a belief in a Supreme Being, beginning an ongoing schism with the United Grand Lodge of England. The Grande Loge Nationale Française, however, is in fact recognized by the U.G.L.E., hence it is highly likely that these visiting French Brethren are not atheists.

The Circular Argument: "Our Senior Deacon has a great memory because he did well memorizing the Middle Chamber lecture." In this fallacy, the argument is restated rather than proved. In our example, the conclusion (that the Senior Deacon has a great memory) and the evidence (that he did well memorizing a lecture) are the same idea. The premise *is* the conclusion, with both appearing in the absence of support.

Either/Or: "We can either keep serving pancakes or completely discontinue our Saturday breakfast program." This fallacy is based on an oversimplification, wherein two possible outcomes are proposed as the only options, precluding the possibility of a synthesis or an outcome based on alternate premises. In our example, the Brother, in an obvious effort to support his preference for retaining the pancake breakfast, posits that the only other option would be to end the breakfast program altogether when, clearly, there are other alternatives.

Ad Hominem: "Our Junior Warden voted no to host the Rainbow Girls Assembly at our Temple – he's mean to little girls!" This sort of fallacy is an attack on a person's character, not the content or validity or their argument. This is very commonly employed as a rhetorical device in the political arena, usually delivered with a healthy dose of *pathos.* In our example, the accuser jumps to the conclusion that the Junior Warden chose to vote down hosting the Rainbow Girls event because he dislikes little girls when, in actuality, there is no evidence inherent in the claim to support this conclusion. Perhaps the Junior Warden is privy to information regarding the presence of black mold in the dining hall and is protecting the girls – we simply have no idea until we hear his reasoning and would be wise to refrain from judgement until we do.

The Red Herring: Brother A says, "We need new officer's jewels and aprons." Brother B asks, "But if we were to get new jewels and aprons, how will we participate in the DeMolay bicycle program?" The Red Herring fallacy centers around a mid-argument diversion to a subject the person redirecting the argument can better respond. By doing so, Brother A's proposal is avoided and supplanted. In our example, Brother B aims to dismiss the proposal to get new aprons and jewels while simultaneously advancing his preferred proposal of participating in the bicycle program. No evidence is given that one option precludes the other.

The Straw Man: "Doing away with our hardcopy Trestleboard mailers will destroy the tradition and culture of our Lodge!" This fallacy involves the oversimplification of the original viewpoint and the highlighting of the worst possible outcome. In our example, the speaker equates the digitizing of the monthly Trestleboard with the destruction of the Lodge's tradition and culture – as if the maintenance of said tradition and culture is entirely contingent upon the mailing of a hardcopy Trestleboard. There are many available solutions to this problem that are apparently eluding the speaker, who prefers to overdramatize the issue.

Moral Equivalence: "The Worshipful Master of my Lodge is literally Hitler." In this fallacy, minor misdeeds (whether perceived or real) are equated with major atrocities, suggesting an equal level of iniquity. In our example, the speaker has obviously had less-than-harmonious dealings with the Worshipful Master of his Lodge. While this may or may not be the objective reality of the situation, the W.M. is certainly not Adolf Hitler, nor is he anywhere near the same level of heinousness.

And so, we come to the close of our overview of the subjects treated within the purview of the trivium: viz; grammar, rhetoric and logic (or, dialectic). As we have stated, these three subjects comprised the preliminary education which was necessary for the student of the *artes liberales* to move on to the subjects dealt with in the quadrivium: viz; arithmetic, geometry, music and astronomy. The trivial subjects formed the very foundation upon which the student could begin to raise their personal temple – a temple dedicated to knowledge (*Da'ath*), wisdom (*Chokmah*) and understanding (*Binah*). The subjects of the trivium prepared the student to effectively digest literature, to clearly and succinctly record their own thoughts in letters, to compose sound arguments, to deliver persuasive and impactful discourse, to think critically, and to recognize and circumvent logical fallacies in the work of others, as well as their own. Though any one of these three subjects alone could comprise a lifetime's work, after having become conversant with the trivium, the student could then consider themselves to be adequately prepared to move on to the mathematical and physical sciences which comprise the quadrivium.

CHAPTER VIII

∴

ARITHMETIC,
GEOMETRY,
MUSIC
&
ASTRONOMY

ARITHMETIC

Arithmetic teaches the powers and properties of numbers; which is variously effected by letters, tables, figures, and instruments. By this art reasons and demonstrations are given for finding out any certain number, whose relation or affinity to others is already known.[1]

Arithmetic (Greek: ἀριθμός; *arithmos* meaning "number" and *téchne* meaning "art") has been defined as "a branch of mathematics that deals usually with the non-negative real numbers including sometimes the transfinite cardinals and with the application of the operations of addition, subtraction, multiplication, and division to them".[2] This science is the central component of what is now technically referred to as *number theory* – a term which has largely supplanted *arithmetic* since the

---

1 Preston (Oliver, commentary), *Illustrations of Masonry*, New York: Masonic Publishing and Manufacturing Co., 1867, pp. 47-48
2 Entry: "Arithmetic"; *Webster's Collegiate Dictionary*, retrieved at: merriam-webster.com

early 20th century.[3] Number theory is the branch of pure (abstract) mathematics devoted to the study of integers (non-fractional numbers), of which Carl Friedrich Gauss (1777-1855) commented "[…m]athematics is the queen of the sciences – and number theory is the queen of mathematics."[4] Though, traditionally, the four operations of arithmetic are: addition (+), subtraction (−), multiplication (×) and division (÷), these are sometimes augmented by percentage manipulations, exponentiation and logarithmic functions.

There are very few artifacts which may be seen to definitively indicate the practice of arithmetical operations in prehistory; the most notable of these being the *Ishango* bone (dated from 20000-18000 BCE), which was discovered in central Africa. The artifact is a length of the fibula bone of a baboon and was apparently used as a tally stick, replete with a sharp piece of quartz affixed to one end, presumably for the purpose of engraving. The *Ishango* bone has been interpreted to show remedial operations of addition and subtraction; though this observation has been contested.[5] By the dawn of the 2nd millennium BCE, we find definitive written evidence of arithmetical operations and, by 1850 BCE, a fully developed system appearing in ancient Mesopotamia. A short time later, we begin to see evidence of an algorithm for multiplication as well as the use of unit fractions in the *Rhind Mathematical Papyrus* dating from 1650 BCE, in Ancient Egypt.[6] The numerical glyphs of the Mesopotamians and Egyptians are, like the later system of Roman numerals, clearly descended from simple tally marks, such as those used for counting. Because all of these systems initially lacked positional notation (a place-value concept, such as the one's, ten's and hundred's place in the decimal system), complex operations had to be calculated using counting boards (precursor to the abacus; a stone or wood surface with bead or pebble markers) and, later, the widespread use of *abaci*.

Some relatively common number systems possessing a positional notation include the decimal (base 10), duodecimal (base 12), vigesimal (base 20) and the sexagesimal (base 60) system. The decimal system was widely used by ancient cultures such as the Greek, Roman, Brahmin and Hebrew; probably having its origins in the method of counting using the fingers and thumbs on both hands. Certain West African and Indian cultures are

3   Davenport, *The Higher Arithmetic: An Introduction to the Theory of Numbers* (7th ed.), Cambridge University Press, Cambridge, 1999

4   Long, *Elementary Introduction to Number Theory* (2nd ed.). Lexington, VA: D.C. Heath and Company, 1972, p. 1

5   Rudman, *How Mathematics Happened: The First 50,000 Years*, Prometheus Books, 2007, p. 64

6   Entry: "Arithmetic", *New World Encyclopedia*, retrieved at: newworldencyclopedia.org

known to have used a duodecimal system; it has been attributed to a method of counting the phalanges (three per finger) on one hand using the thumb as a place marker.[7] The vigesimal system was most notably used by pre-Columbian Mesoamerican cultures, such as the Mayan and Aztec civilizations; the base 20 system forms the numerical foundation of the Mayan Long Count Calendar, which gives a creation date of 4 *Ahaw*, 8 *Kumk'u* (August 11th, 3114 BCE)[8] and was recently misinterpreted to indicate a global cataclysm on December 21st, 2012, which merely signaled the end of a regular cycle known as a *b'ak'tun*. The sexagesimal system, though not commonly used in computational or logical applications, is perhaps the most important of these systems, as it is central to understanding and communicating our experience in and of the cosmos, in the broadest sense. The sexagesimal number system, which was developed by the Sumerians in the 3rd millennium BCE, is the base system of such fundamental concepts as degrees, planar angles, hours, minutes and seconds; it is used to quantify our spatial and temporal orientation; it forms the quantitative basis of the method by which organize and navigate our experiences in space-time. The Sumerians understood one annual solar circuit to be approximately 360 days, rounding down very slightly. This observation led to their seeing each day as one *degree* of that cycle. Ecliptically, one degree of the Sun's apparent path around the Earth is divided into 60 arcminutes, and one arcminute is divided into 60 arcseconds – which is the method by which we describe the location of celestial objects and events in modern astrophysics.[9] Temporally, one hour is divided into 60 minutes, and one minute is divided into 60 seconds – which are minute subdivisions of the Earth's rotation and revolution.[10] Geometrically, there are a total of 360° (six 60° arc segments) in a circle – which is how we quantify the angles of any given polygon.[11] The operative and speculative denominations of Masonry have also made much use of the sexagesimal system, as they both utilize the system of degrees based upon the divisions of a 360° circle, as established by the Sumerians. Correspondingly, many aspects of the Western Esoteric Tradition are arranged according to the sexagesimal system, such as those

7   Pittman, "Origin of Mesopotamian Duodecimal and Sexagesimal Counting Systems", *Philippine Journal of Linguistics*, 1997, p. 97

8   Rice, *Maya Calendar Origins: Monuments, Mythistory, and the Materialization of Time*, University of Texas Press, 2007

9   Hermans-Killams, *Cosmic Reference Guide: Angular Measurements*, retrieved at caltech.edu

10   Coolman, "Keeping Time: Why 60 Minutes?", *Live Science*, 2014, retrieved at: livescience.com

11   Entry: "Degree"; *Math Open Reference*, retrieved at mathopenref.com

which are dependent upon the Hermetic Arts of astrology and talismanic magic. Of particular significance are those talismans and amulets devised by the Basilidean Gnostics, who utilized the name of *Abrasax* (Greek: ΑΒΡΑΣΑΞ), or *Abraxas*, which totals to the more diurnally accurate 365 in the Greek numerological system known as isopsephy. We will further address this system and its association with Mesopotamian astronomy in the section on astronomy in the current Chapter.

Engraved Abrasax amulets - in Greek isopsephy, ΑΒΡΑΣΑΞ totals to 365

In the second half of the 6th century BCE, arithmetic was combined with three other quantitative mathematical sciences, into what was collectively known to the Pythagoreans as the *mathemata*; these arts included arithmetic, geometry, harmonics (music) and astronomy, and corresponded to the later quadrivium.[12] In the Pythagorean context, arithmetic (as well as the other subjects within the scope of *mathemata*) overlapped with philosophy and mysticism, often being couched in metaphysical terms. In the Hellenistic Period, it wasn't until the work of Euclid (4th century BCE) that we see mathematics as being divorced from its mystical interpretations and treated as a discrete physical science. Slightly later, in his *Introduction to Arithmetic*, Nichomachus of Gerasa (60-120 CE) reintroduced mystical, Pythagorean perspectives to arithmetical operations by using the language of philosophy rather than that of formal equations.[13] The work also leans heavily on the Platonic idea of number existing in corporeal realms or abstract planes – which is not quite as mystical as it sounds, since

---

12   Sider & Obbink, *Doctrine and Doxography: Studies on Heraclitus and Pythagoras*, De Gruyter, 2013, p. 42

13   Nicomachus of Gerasa, *Introduction to Arithmetic*, D'Ooge (trans.) University of Michigan Studies, London: Macmillan, 1926

pure mathematics deals only with abstractions, as opposed to its applied forms in physics and engineering.[14] The philosophical and mystical approaches to the mathematical sciences, though never entirely disappearing, were to resurface yet again in the Renaissance.

In the Renaissance fusion of mathematics and logic, a system of the symbolic application of numerical operations emerged known as *mathesis* (Greek: μάθησις; meaning "science" or "learning"). In the work of Giordano Bruno, this took the form of a quasi-Pythagorean interpretation of symbol sets. The Florentine Neoplatonists, in general, approached number with "Pythagorean intentions", as noted by Yates.[15] Theirs was a more qualitative approach to number rather than merely quantitative. In considering the deeper symbolic meaning of number rather than the strictly numeric value, we again find ourselves to be in the presence of the operative and speculative dynamic, except this time within the world of mathematics. This is a reflection of the Hermetic relationship between the microcosm and the macrocosm. This Neopythagorean methodology utilized the glyphs, terms and operations of mathematics but also retained the accompanying Hermetic belief that these glyphs, terms and operations were mirrored by operations within the *pneuma*, *psyche* and *soma* of the mathematician. It is worth the risk of being redundant to state again here that this is the essence of the Hermetic Arts – that operations in the microcosm resonate with operations in the macrocosm, and vice versa. In the present study, we are not as concerned with formal mathematical operations as we are with the numinous product of those operations and their symbolic import vis-à-vis Western Esotericism.

In the 17th century, Descartes and Leibniz developed their mathesistic languages in what was termed a *mathesis universalis*, in an effort to develop a more mathematically formal language.[16] In the 20th century, Michel Foucault (1926-1984) was to refer to *mathesis* as "the science of establishing a systematic order for things".[17] To some extent, these developments marked a continuation of the Pythagorean melding of mathematics and philosophy; they also helped cement the modern multidisciplinary codification of formal *logic* by using the *grammar* of *arithmetic*, thereby applying a *quadrivial* theoretical approach to a *trivial* subject.

Arithmancy (Greek: ἀριθμομαντεία; meaning "divination by num-

14   Entry: "Arithmetic"; *New World Encyclopedia*, retrieved at: newworldencyclopedia.org

15   Yates, *Giordano Bruno and the Hermetic Tradition*, University of Chicago Press, 1964, p. 297

16   See: Descartes' *Rules for the Direction of the Mind* (1628) and Leibniz' incomplete treatise *Mathesis Universalis* (1695)

17   Horrocks, *Introducing Foucault*, Totem Books, 1997, p. 69

bers") is a broad term encompassing all methods of numerological divination, specifically those which assign numerical values to letters and words. Two of the most common forms of arithmancy are the ancient Greek *isopsephy* and the Hebrew *gematria*. Isopsephy (Greek: ἴσος meaning "equal" and ψῆφος meaning "pebble") is the ancient Greek practice of enumerating the values of letters or words, reducing them to a single number.[18] Literally, the term means "equal pebbles" which is in reference to the ancient Greek practice of arranging pebbles for the purpose of illustrating arithmetical and geometrical patterns and operations; two words with equal numerical values (pebbles) were believed to have a metaphorical resonance.[19] Before the adoption of Arabic numerals in the 8th century, numerals were expressed alphabetically, as in early Hebrew. Through the multipurposing of the alphabet for arithmetical operations, the Greeks discerned numbers in words and consequently began to write with this numerical dimension in mind. This illustrates a deliberately employed numerical interpretive layer being encrypted in the text. As we have previously discussed and applied throughout the present volume, gematria is an alphanumeric system wherein a numerical value is assigned to each letter of the Hebrew alphabet (see Appendix A); words having the same numerical value are believed to have an occult resonance.[20] A famous example of a cryptic numerological code, which utilizes both Greek isopsephy and Hebrew gematria, may be found in Revelation 13:18, which reads:

> *Here is wisdom. Let him that hath understanding count the number of the beast: for it is the number of a man; and his number is Six hundred threescore and six.*[21]

In this passage, the reader possessing "understanding" (*Binah*), in his search for the "wisdom" (*Chokmah*) hidden therein, is encouraged to "count the number [...] of a man" in order to reveal the identity of the beast. The word "count" (Greek: ψηφισάτω, *psephisato*) has the same root as isopsephy (*psephos*, meaning "pebble"), as a further hint to the reader to apply this numerological method. The Greek name and title, *Neron Kaiser*, when

18   Ash & Lougovaya, *The Art of Isopsephism in the Greco-Roman World in Ägytische Magie und ihre Umwelt*, Jördens (ed.), Wiesbaden: Harrassowitz, 2015, p. 82-98

19   Ifrah, *The Universal History of Numbers: From Prehistory to the Invention of the Computer*, 1998, p. 256

20   Schechter & Levias, Entry: "Gematria"; *The Jewish Encyclopedia*, Volume 5. Funk & Wagnalls Co., 1904, p. 589

21   *The Holy Bible*, KJV, Revelation 13:18

transliterated in Hebrew renders רסק ןורנ (*NRVN QSR*), whose gematriac value is 666. Thereby, we find that "the beast" is quite likely Nero Caesar – a view supported by Preterist theologians and modern biblical scholars.[22, 23] The reign of Roman emperor, Nero Claudius Caesar Augustus Germanicus (37-68 CE), was widely considered to be one of corruption, tyranny and extravagance.[24] To say that he was less-than-universally appreciated in the Empire would be a gross understatement. He died by suicide in 68 CE, after learning he had been tried *in absentia* and condemned to death as an enemy of the Empire. It was not wise to openly criticize the emperor, regardless of public opinion; consequently, some of the critique levelled at Nero was veiled in isopsephy.

> *The Roman historian Suetonius wrote about the days of Emperor Nero and how he was strangely patient with the* "curses and abuses of the people" *and* "lenient towards those who assailed him with gibes and lampoons." *One example Suetonius gave is of a posted and/or circulated saying that condemned Nero for murdering his mother:* "A calculation new. Nero his mother slew." *(Suetonius,* Life of Nero, *39:1-2). In Greek isopsephy, the numerical value of Nero is 1,005, and the numerical value of the statement that he killed his own mother is also equal to 1,005. Thus, we have a "calculation", an equation in the saying and therefore, the man Nero is propagated to be equivalent to unthinkable murder. This evidence shows that isopsephy was well known by the populace in the mid-first century.*[25]

As we have amply illustrated in the foregoing, the numbers three, five and seven figure prominently in the ritual and symbolism of Freemasonry, as they are the number of steps per course on the Winding Staircase as it appears in the Fellow Craft lecture (see Appendix D). Three, five and seven are also the numbers of Masons needed to open a Lodge of Master Masons, Fellow Crafts and Entered Apprentices, respectively. It is the purpose

22   Cory, *The Book of Revelation*, Collegeville, Minn.: Liturgical Press, 2006

23   Hillers, "13, 18 and a scroll from Murabba'at", *Bulletin of the American Schools of Oriental Research*, 170 (170): 65, 1963

24   Patrick, "Nero's *Luxuria*, in Tacitus and in the Octavia", *The Classical Quarterly*, 2000, pp. 494-515

25   Campbell, *Days of Restoration: A Commentary on the Book of Revelation*, 2019, Crestespace, redaction retrieved at: daysofrestoration.com

of the present section on arithmetic to illustrate how this first science of the quadrivium may be used to uncover the occult implications of these numbers. This, we will support by utilizing the methodology of Hermetic Qabalah and its associated body of correspondences (see Appendix A). We will begin with a theoretical example and then apply these methods to the numbers three, five and seven.

In occult numerology, there is an arithmetical process referred to as "theosophical addition" by which a multi-digit number may be reduced to a single digit. For example, the number 123 becomes 6 (1 + 2 + 3 = 6); and the number 456 becomes 6 (4 + 5 + 6 = 15; 1 + 5 = 6). In the syncretized system Hermetic Qabalah, theosophical addition is often used in conjunction with standard qabalistic gematria. For example, the gematriac value for the word *Tiphareth* (תראפת) is 1081 – this is quite an unwieldy number, yielding relatively few possibilities for contemplating qabalistic resonance with other Hebrew words and their gematriac values. However, through the application of theosophical addition, this number may be reduced to the number 10 (1 + 0 + 8 + 1 = 10), and further to the number one (1 + 0 = 1). Contemplating the import presented by the products of this operation, we find we have produced the numbers of the tenth *sephirah*, *Malkuth*, and the first *sephirah*, *Kether*. These two *sephiroth* delineate the extremes of the Middle Pillar, at the very center of which lays *Tiphareth*. We have thus generated a simple qabalistic proof as to the centrality of *Tiphareth*, which also speaks of the *sephirah*'s intercessional character between the abode of God (*Kether*) and that of man (*Malkuth*), and also the role of the Microsopropus (*Zeir Anpin*) as inhabiting the intermediate region between the Macroprosopus (*Arich Anpin*) and the Bride of the Microprosopus (*Shekinah*).[26]

---

26   See: Mathers' Introduction to *Kabbalah Denudata*, Redway, 1887

The Fool and the Hermit, Tarot de Marseilles

Furthermore, by having reduced the total gematriac value of *Ti-phareth* to the digits 10 and 1, we have also produced the values of the Hebrew letters *yod* (י, 10) and *aleph* (א, 1). In the established tradition of Hermetic Qabalah (see Appendix A), *yod* is said to mean "hand" or "open hand" and is attributed to the Hermit IX Tarot card; *aleph* is said to mean "ox" and is attributed to the Fool 0 card (see Appendix A). Using this data for further qabalistic elucidation on the word *Tiphareth*, we find that the Fool 0 card adds a dimension of creativity and improvisation to the sphere – this is the spirit of creativity and improvisation which is needed to compose and perform ceremonial magic rituals when the initiate reaches the *Adepti* grades in the Golden Dawn system, for example. The grade *Adeptus Minor* 5=6 is especially associated with the *sephirah Tiphareth*, and is followed by *Adeptus Major* 6=5, *Adeptus Exemptus* 7=4 of the Inner Order (*Roseae Rubeae et Aureae Crucis*) which also concern practical ceremonial magic. The letter *aleph* also connotes the limitless force of the ox empowering this expression of the magical will. In the present context, the Hermit IX card may be seen to represent the introspection and honest self-reflection necessary at the critical initiatory juncture in *Tiphareth* – a time when one has pierced the Veil of *Paroketh*, a quite liminal initiatory stage, indeed and is poised to encounter the "Dweller on the Threshold"[27], a mysterious figure embodied by the Hermit, a personification of Jung's "wise old man" archetype. The open hand of *yod* may be thought of as being indicative of this reception – note that the very word *Qabalah* means "Reception" – and the bestowal of the fruits of the theoretical learning grades having left the

---

27   See: Edward Bulwer Lytton's *Zanoni* (1842), Book IV of which is entitled "The Dweller on the Threshold" – probably the first public introduction of this oft-referenced occult term.

initiate qualified to pass, as an adept, into the sphere of *Tiphareth*.

Having addressed the numbers three, five and seven, particularly in relation to their being the number of steps on the three courses comprising the Winding Staircase, we will now provide a qabalistic proof – utilizing the interpretive methods of gematria and theosophical addition. With their application, we find that the Staircase may be placed within the greater schema of the *Etz Chaim* (see Appendix B). We begin by calculating the gematriac value of each of the *sephiroth*; these are as follows:

Sephirah	Hebrew	Gematria
Kether	כתר	620
Chokmah	חכמה	73
Binah	בינה	67
Chesed	חסד	72
Geburah	גבורה	216
Tiphareth	תפארת	1081
Netzach	נצח	148
Hod	הוד	15
Yesod	יסוד	79
Malkuth	מלכות	496

When these values are distributed as to their corresponding Pillar (viz; *Binah*, *Geburah* and *Hod* to the Pillar of Severity; *Chokmah*, *Chesed* and *Netzach* to the Pillar of Mercy; and *Kether*, *Tiphareth*, *Yesod* and *Malkuth* to the Middle Pillar), they produce the following totals per Pillar:

Pillar of Severity	300
Pillar of Mercy	293
Middle Pillar	1780

By the application of theosophical addition, we may reduce the above figures to a single digit; the operation is as follows:

Pillar of Severity	$3 + 0 + 0 = 3$
Pillar of Mercy	$2 + 9 + 3 = 14; 1 + 4 = 5$
Middle Pillar	$1 + 7 + 8 + 0 = 16; 1 + 6 = 7$

Thereby, we produce the number 3 from the Pillar of Severity; 5 from the Pillar of Mercy; and 7 from the Middle Pillar. This qabalistic proof, which uses the gematriac values of the pillars, and their further reduction by the operation of theosophical addition, effectively places the course of three, five and seven steps into the general schema of the *Etz Chaim*.

It is by the application of proofs such as these that one utilizes the theoretical aspects of Western Esotericism in order to gain deeper insight into the correspondences and resonances which occur between seemingly disparate systems. In the present example, we have attempted to illustrate the synergistic relationship between the Masonic Winding Staircase and the qabalistic *Etz Chaim*, in an effort to corroborate both systems and, thereby, unveil the otherwise occulted aspects of each. When applied more broadly, semiotic practices such as these afford the occultist opportunities to actively engage in *meaning-making*. Meaning-making is a constructivist psychotherapeutic model which has been described as "the process of how persons construe, understand, or make sense of life events, relationships, and the self"[28] and also as a method of "retaining, reaffirming, revising, or replacing elements of their orienting system to develop more nuanced, complex and useful systems".[29] By means of an esoteric praxis, one may develop one's imaginative sense and impression of the World; the composition of a personal mythology; an appreciation of the allegorical, metaphorical and symbolic in life's narratives, objects and events; a sense of active participation in the construction of one's reality; and a truly magical application of the Will.

---

28   Ignelzi, *Meaning-making in the learning and teaching process*, New Directions for Teaching and Learning, 2000, p. 5

29   Gillies, Neimeyer & Milman, "The meaning of loss codebook: construction of a system for analyzing meanings made in bereavement", *Death Studies*, 2014, p. 208

GEOMETRY

Geometry treats of the powers and properties of magnitudes in general, where length, breadth, and thickness, are considered. By this science, the architect is enabled to construct his plans; the general, to arrange his soldiers; the engineer, to mark out ground for encampments; the geographer, to give us the dimensions of the world, delineate the extent of seas, and specify the divisions of empires, kingdoms, and provinces; and by it, also, the astronomer is enabled to make his observations, and fix the durations of times and seasons, years and cycles. In short, Geometry is the foundation of architecture, and the root of the mathematics.[30]

Geometry (Greek: γεωμετρία; from *geo* meaning "earth" and *metron* meaning "measurement") is defined as "a branch of mathematics that deals with the measurement, properties, and relationships of points, lines, angles, surfaces, and solids".[31] The origins of this science may be traced to several disparate early cultures in an effort to quantify lengths, areas and volumes.[32] Specifically, the recorded history of geometrical works dealing with the science's application in astronomy, surveying and construction begins in Mesopotamia and Egypt in the 2nd millennium BCE.[33] That the word *geometry* literally means "earth measurement" is indicative of its origin in these first applications – specifically in regard to astronomical observation, since it is only by segmenting the ecliptic into its current sexagesimal divisions that the Sumerians arrived at the concept of a circle having 360°. Some authors, however, have attributed the impetus for the development of the science to surveying land and delineating agricultural tracts.

---

30   Preston (Oliver, commentary), *Illustrations of Masonry*, New York: Masonic Publishing and Manufacturing Co., 1867, p. 48

31   Entry: "Geometry"; *Webster's Collegiate Dictionary*, retrieved at: merriam-webster.com

32   De Risi, *Mathematizing Space: The Objects of Geometry from Antiquity to the Early Modern Age*, Birkhäuser, 2015, p. 1

33   Neugebauer, *The Exact Sciences in Antiquity* (2 ed.), Chap. IV "Egyptian Mathematics and Astronomy", Dover Publications, 1969, pp. 71-96

Where was Geometry first founded?

    At Alexandria in Egypt.

Why there?

> *The River Nile having overflowed its banks, caused the inhabitants to retire into the interior part of the country; when the waters had subsided, they returned to their native homes, but the fury of the waves having washed away most of their landmarks, caused many disputes amongst them, which often terminated in war. At length, hearing there was a Lodge of Masons held at Alexandria, in Egypt, over which Euclid presided, they therefore went and laid their complaints before him; he, with the assistance of his Wardens and Brethren, gathered together the scattered fragments of Geometry, and brought them into a regular system, by which means he taught them how to ascertain their different tracks [sic] of land, which put an end to their disputes, and terminated their wars.*[34]

The conclusion above is somewhat problematic, however, since the measurement of the terrestrial sphere of the Earth could only be established vis-à-vis its relationship to the celestial sphere of the Heavens – otherwise, the product will always reflect a 1:1 ratio; this is the equivalent of measuring a ruler with the very same ruler. This would necessarily mean that astronomical observation has primacy over geometry, surveying, navigation and all other arts dependent upon this science, leading one to reflect on the second subject of the Fellow Craft lecture, which pertains to the two Brazen Pillars of the Masonic Lodge – one with the terrestrial, the other with the celestial sphere atop the capital (see Chapter II), further supporting Oliver's claim that "[t]hey are the noblest instruments for giving the most distinct idea of any problem or proposition, as well as for enabling us to solve it".[35] The Hermetic relationship between the microcosm and the macrocosm is reinforced in this view, in that our very sense

---

34   Finch, *Masonic Treatise with an Elucidation on the Religious and Moral Beauties of Freemasonry*, Fellow Craft Degree, Chapter II, 1802, reprint of 1956 edition

35   Preston (Oliver, commentary), *Illustrations of Masonry*, New York: Masonic Publishing and Manufacturing Co., 1867, p. 49

of directionality and orientation (a word whose very etymology directs us to the East[36]) is based upon the Earth's position in relation to other celestial bodies – for, how would the ancients, in the absence of the magnetic compass (which, due to *magnetic declination*, does not accurately reflect true, geographic North)[37], delineate something even as fundamental as the four cardinal points without reference to the Sun's equinoctial and solstitial stations and the geographical extrapolation of these constants? Ergo, one may argue in support of both the astronomical and proto-hermetic roots of geometry, since its basic angular principles are contingent on the position of the Earth (the microcosm) in relation to the canopy of stellar objects (the macrocosm) – a dynamic symbolized by the Brazen Pillars.

As we had briefly discussed in the arithmetic section of the present Chapter, the sexagesimal number system is central to understanding and communicating our experience in and of the cosmos and, thereby, the geography of the Earth. This system was first conceptualized by the ancient Sumerians who observed the length of the solar year and thereby quantified the 360° of the ecliptic – yielding very close to one degree per day. This astronomical orientation provided mankind with the first practical frame of reference by which he could describe the position of celestial and, consequently, terrestrial objects in space (we will further address this concept, apropos its applications in *time* and *space-time*, further on in this Chapter, in the sections on music and astronomy, respectively). This model was subsequently applied to our planar angles, hours, minutes, seconds, and forms the very foundation upon which geometrical theory was erected. For it was only by establishing the 360° of a circle that we have recourse to this system which enables us to describe, say, the 60° angles of an equilateral triangle, the 120° angles of a hexagon, and the 90° angle of a square, or "the fourth part of a circle".

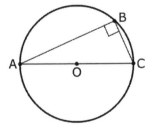

Thales's theorem

36   Entry: "Orientation"; *Online Etymological Dictionary*, retrieved at etymonline.com
37   "Declination", *National Centers for Environmental Information*, retrieved at: ngdc.noaa.gov

Continuing our historical overview, we next encounter the work of Thales of Miletus. The first of the pre-Socratic philosophers in the 7ᵗʰ century BCE, Thales is credited with using geometrical formulæ to discern the height of the pyramids and the distance of ships from the shoreline; he also used geometrical principles in deductive reasoning. A geometrical proof for the latter application was described in the third book of Euclid's *Elements* (the 31ˢᵗ Proposition), wherein it is stated that the diameter of a circle (*A-C*) always subtends a right angle to any point (*B*) on the perimeter of a circle.[38] This may also be described using the Masonic *Point Within A Circle* diagram, wherein a diametric line is drawn through the center point and another point is drawn on the perimeter; if a line is drawn from the two extremities of the diametric line to the point on the perimeter, then a right angle will always be produced. Conversely, in order to find the point within the center of the circle, if a right angle whose vertex is on the perimeter is described; the *catheti* (legs) of the right angle will always bisect at the diameter. Since the diameter always passes through the center of a circle, two diametric lines must be described, and their intersection will always be the point within the center of the circle. A point has been described as "[a] precise location or place on a plane"[39], and "a primitive notion upon which the geometry is built, meaning that a point cannot be defined in terms of previously defined objects"[40], reinforcing the primacy of this geometrical concept and causing us to reflect on what this "Point" may symbolize in the context of the Point Within A Circle diagram. In Masonic ritual, we are informed that…

> *[…] the point represent[s] an individual brother, the circle the boundary-line of his conduct beyond which he is never to suffer his prejudices or passions to betray him. This circle is embodied by two perpendicular parallel lines, representing St. John the Baptist and St. John the Evangelist; and upon the top rest the Holy Scriptures. In going round this circle, we necessarily touch upon these two lines, as well upon the Holy Scriptures, and while a Mason keeps himself circumscribed within their precepts it is impossible that he should materially err.[41]*

---

38   See: "Thales's Theorem"; Boyer, *A History of Mathematics* (2ⁿᵈ ed), New York: Wiley, 1989, p. 43

39   Entry: "Point"; *Math Open Reference*, mathopenref.com

40   *Manuel S. Enverga University Foundation*, retrieved at: coursehero.com

41   *Duncan's Masonic Ritual and Monitor* (1866), New York: Crown Publishers, 1986, p. 53-54

The Holy Saints John and the Point Within a Circle

Looking at this diagram from the perspective of Thales Theorem, we find that the Saints John (denoted *B* and *E*) represent the extremities of the diametric line through the center point; the Volume of Sacred Law (*VSL*) is on the upper perimeter of the circle; if a line were drawn from each of the Saints John, then their vertex would always form a square. There is a mention in the above passage regarding "going round this circle", seeming to cryptically indicate that any point on the perimeter of the circle will always yield a right angle, if the extremities of its *catheti* are tied to the points *B* and *E* of the Saints John, to whom the Lodge is dedicated. From this perspective, the diagram seems to be emphasizing, in geometrical symbolism, that Freemasons ("the point represent[s] an individual broth-er")[42] are advised to "act upon the square" throughout their entire sphere of influence, a domain indicated by the circle. When viewed in this way, the Point Within A Circle diagram becomes a rather intriguing speculative

---

42   *Duncan's Masonic Ritual and Monitor* (1866), New York: Crown Publishers, 1986, p. 53

symbol, the esoteric meaning of which is made accessible by applying the interpretive lens of operative geometry.

Chronologically, after Thales' advancements in the science of geometry, we encounter Pythagoras of Samos (Greek: Πυθαγόρας; 570-495 BCE) in the 6th century BCE. An eminent philosopher, mathematician and mystic, Pythagoras exerted a heavy influence on all Greek philosophy which was to follow, including that of Plato and Aristotle. He is, in fact, credited with giving philosophy its name[43], by calling himself a "lover of wisdom" (Greek: *philo* meaning "loving" and *Sophia* meaning "knowledge, wisdom").[44] He was the founder of the school of Pythagoreanism at Crotona – which, from the modern perspective, is seen as being akin to the ancient Mystery cults[45] – and is credited with the discovery of the Pythagorean Theorem. Some of the major concepts associated with Pythagoreanism are the doctrine of reincarnation known as *metempsychosis*, or the "transmigration of souls"[46], the *musica universalis*, or "harmony of the spheres"[47], which we will address in the next section of the present Chapter, and, of course, Pythagoras' metaphysics and number theory. There is much debate, however, as to Pythagoras' discovery of many of the concepts and doctrines attributed to him, as many of these were extant in and before his time, such as the 3:4:5 triangle.[48]

Much has been written about Pythagoras, particularly in the domain of Masonic literature; for, it has even been said of "our ancient friend and Brother Pythagoras" that he had "traveled in Egypt, Asia and Africa, and who was initiated into various orders of priesthood and raised to the sublime degree of Master Mason".[49] While claims of Pythagoras' involvement in Masonry, or the implication that there was, at some point, an active current of Pythagoreanism in the early Craft, are untenable – there is certainly something to be said for the symbolic transmission of concepts and ideas believed to have emanated from this seminal "lover of wisdom". In light

---

43   De Vogel, *Pythagoras and Early Pythagoreanism*, Van Gorcum & Co., 1966, pp. 97-102

44   Entry: "Philosophy"; *Online Etymological Dictionary*, retrieved at: etymonline.com

45   Entry: "Pythagoreanism"; *Encyclopedia Britannica*, retrieved at britannica.com

46   Entry: "Metempsychosis"; *Oxford University Reference*, oxfordreference.com

47   Calter, *Pythagoras and the Music of the Spheres*, Dartmouth College, 1998, retrieved at: dartmouth.edu

48   "In geometry, the Pythagoreans cannot be credited with any proofs in the Euclidean sense." Thesleff, Entry: "Pythagoreanism"; *Encyclopedia Britannica*, retrieved at: britannica.com

49   Stewart, *Symbolic Teaching or Masonry and its Message*, Stewart & Kidd Co., 1917, p. 5

of his treatment of subjects such as philosophy, religious mysticism and geometry, it is no mystery why Pythagoras would be venerated by Freemasons, since these subjects are squarely within the purview of the Craft. Of the philosopher, Mackey somewhat more reasonably states that...

> *He travelled through Egypt, Chaldea, and Asia Minor, and is said to have submitted to the initiations in those countries for the purpose of acquiring knowledge. On his return to Europe, he established his celebrated school at Crotona, much resembling that subsequently adopted by the Freemasons.*[50]

References to Pythagoras and his school have a long and developed history in the supplementary literature in and of Freemasonry, as illustrated an excerpt from what appears to be a species of Masonic catechism found in the *Leland Manuscript*. The manuscript, which is of unknown date, was discovered by celebrated antiquarian John Leland; it was first printed in 1753 in *The Gentleman's Magazine* in London. It is said that the metaphysician, John Locke (1632-1704), believed the following passage to be a cryptic allusion to the philosopher[51]:

> *How comede ytt [Freemasonry] jm Engelonde? Peter Gower, a Grecian, journeyeded for kunnynge yn Egypte and in Syria, and yn everyche londe whereat the Venetians hadde plaunted-de Maconrye, and wynnynge entraunce yn al Lodges of Maconnes, he lerned muche, and retournedde and worked yn Grecia Magna wachsynge and becommynge a myghtye wysacre and gratelyche renowned, and here he framed a grate Lodge at Groton, and maked many Maconnes, some whereoffe dyd journeye yn Fraunce, and maked manye Maconnes wherefromme, yn process of tyme, the arte passed yn Engelonde.*[52]

Note, in the passage above, the names rendered here as "Peter Gower", "Venetians" and "Groton"; these appear to be the thinly veiled

50   Entry: "Pythagoras"; Mackey, *An Encyclopedia of Freemasonry and its Kindred Sciences*, Everts & Co., 1884

51   Walker, *Francis Bacon and the 1753 Leland Manuscript*, 2010, retrieved at: sirbacon. org

52   As cited in Mackey, *An Encyclopedia of Freemasonry and its Kindred Sciences*, Everts & Co., 1884; Entry: "Pythagoras"

corruptions of *Pythagoras*, *Phoenicians* and *Crotona*, respectively. Though there are many more biographical and Masonic anecdotes dealing with Pythagoras, we will circumscribe our present study to only address a few of the salient points associated with his teachings and thought surrounding geometry. To this end, we will examine three important geometrical symbols utilized in what may be termed the Pythagorean's *meta-geometrical* philosophy: the *Tetraktys*, the Pythagorean Theorem, and the *pentalpha*.

The *Tetraktys* (Greek: τετρακτύς) is a figure consisting of ten regularly spaced points, arranged in an upward pointing equilateral triangle, thereby rendering four rows of one, two, three and four points, descending from the top. Collectively, the figure represents the number ten, which is the fourth *triangular number* after one, three and six.[53] In the Pythagoreans' speculative interpretation, the single point at the top represented the *monad*, denoting the unity and totality of all things, as well as the immanence of the Supreme Being; the next tier of two points represented the *dyad*, denoting the concept of "otherness" and of the polarity of all binary opposites, such as masculine/feminine, active/passive, etc. – this is much in the same sense that the Brazen Pillars of K∴S∴T∴ and the qabalistic pillars of Mercy and Severity are symbolically understood; the tier of three points represented the *triad*, which was a Pythagorean symbol for harmony because it was thought to resolve the dissonance produced by the *dyad*; lastly, the lowest tier of four points represented the *tetrad*, symbolic of the four classical elements, the four cardinal directions and, thereby, the World.

Thus, to the Pythagoreans, the *Tetraktys* was a cosmogonical model in that it geometrically illustrated the very act Creation; yet it could also be seen as a useful ontological model in that it symbolizes the most general metaphysical ideas about the nature of being. This view of the *Tetraktys* is akin to the cosmogonical and ontological interpretations of the later *Etz Chaim* of qabalism, as the acts of *creation* and *being* can be symbolically expressed in both systems. The 20th century British occultist, Dion Fortune, was to make a similar observation in her classic *Mystical Qabalah*: "The point is assigned to Kether; the line to Chokmah; the two-dimensional plane to Binah; consequently, the three-dimensional solid naturally falls to Chesed."[54] We will presently endeavor to explain these interpretations, in geometrical terms.

---

53   Entry: "Triangular Number"; *Wolfram Math World*, retrieved at: mathworld.wolfram.com

54   Fortune, *The Mystical Qabalah*, London: Society of Inner Light, 1935

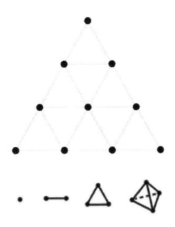

The Tetraktys and its geometrical implications

The *Tetraktys* embodies the point, the line, the plane and the solid. The top row of the *Tetraktys* depicts one single point, which is described as "that which has no part"[55], having no dimension, only position, and is the primary geometrical abstraction. The second row depicts two points, suggesting a line, which is described as a "breadthless length [which] lies equally with respect to the points on itself."[56] The next row of the model depicts three points, because three points, when triangularly connected, form the most basic plane. A plane is described in Euclid as "a flat, two-dimensional surface".[57] In the final row of the *Tetraktys*, there are four points, which are the necessary elements to construct the most basic solid, the *tetrahedron* (Greek: τετράεδρον; meaning "four faces"). Thus the *Tetraktys* geometrically symbolizes the abstract point of pre-existence, since a point is literally *no-thing* – it merely defines a theoretical position in space; the point *moves* and becomes a line, which has but one dimension; the points are then triangulated, a process which yields a superficies, or a two-dimensional plane; the fourth point is then added, yielding a tetrahedronal shape in three-dimensions. The *Tetraktys* illustrated such sublime truths to the Pythagoreans that they deemed it "holy" and were said to have taken their oaths upon it.[58]

55   *Euclid's Elements – All thirteen books in one volume*, Heath (trans.), Green Lion Press, 2017

56   Ibid.

57   Ibid.

58   Entry: "Tetraktys"; Mackey, *An Encyclopedia of Freemasonry and its Kindred Sciences*, Everts & Co., 1884

Bless us, divine number, thou who generated gods and men! O holy, holy Tetractys, thou that containest the root and source of the eternally flowing creation! For the divine number begins with the profound, pure unity until it comes to the holy four; then it begets the mother of all, the all-comprising, all-bounding, the first-born, the never-swerving, the never-tiring holy ten, the keyholder of all.[59]

The Pythagorean Theorem states that the square of the *hypotenuse* (the longest side, opposite the right angle) of a right triangle is equal to the sum of the squares of the other two *catheti* (legs). The theorem is most popularly expressed in the mathematical equation: $a^2 + b^2 = c^2$, where a and b represent the length of the *catheti* subtending at the vertex of ninety degrees, while c represents the length of the *hypotenuse*. Though the discovery of the theorem has been popularly attributed to Pythagoras, its true origin remains obscure.

[T]he Greek literature which we possess belonging to the first five centuries after Pythagoras contains no statement specifying this or any other particular great geometric discovery to him.[60]

The oldest extant example alluding to knowledge of the theorem is found in the form of an ancient Babylonian artifact known as *Plimpton 322*. Written in cuneiform script impressed on a clay tablet, *Plimpton 322* dates from 1790-1750 BCE and contains a list of several Pythagorean triples.[61] Though he almost certainly did not discover the theorem, we can say with a good deal of certainty that Pythagoras was familiar with it.[62] It is said that, upon the realization of the theorem's implications (an event which had apparently inspired a great deal excitement in the philosopher), Pythagoras cried "Eureka!" (Greek: Εύρηκα; meaning

59   Dantzig, *Number: The Language of Science*, Macmillan, 1930, p. 42

60   Heath (trans.), *The Thirteen Books of Euclid's Elements*, Dover, 1925, pp. 351-352

61   Friberg, "Methods and traditions of Babylonian mathematics: Plimpton 322, Pythagorean triples, and the Babylonian triangle parameter equations", *Historia Mathematica*, 1981, pp. 277-318

62   Hawking, *God Created the Integers: The Mathematical Breakthroughs that Changed History*, Philadelphia: Running Press Book Publishers. 2005, p. 12

"I have found it!")[63] and sacrificed a *hecatomb* (one-hundred ox-en).[64] This reads as hyperbole, however, as this would have been quite an unusual act from one who was ostensibly vegetarian.

From Higgins' Hermetic Masonry, 1916

Special right triangles like the Pythagorean theorem were known to have been used in ancient Egypt [65] and that triangles having a ratio of 3:4:5, particularly, were used by a certain class of Egyptian builder known as *Harpedonaptae*.[66] The *Harpedonaptae*, literally "rope stretchers", were a skilled class of astro-geometers who were called in to survey and delineate the foundations of buildings according to terrestrial and celestial coordinates defined by the architect; this was done in order to ensure that they were laid *square* and cardinally oriented. Egyptian architects were aware of the fact that a triangle having a ratio of 3:4:5, with five units being the length of the *hypotenuse*, always yielded a perfect square at the vertex of the *catheti* of three and four units. To this end, the *Harpedonaptae* fashioned ropes which were knotted or otherwise marked with, for example, twelve unit measures (3 + 4 + 5 = 12) or any other multiple of the 3:4:5 ratio. This marked rope was then used to establish a perpendicular extending off of

63   Entry: "Eureka"; *Online Etymological Dictionary*, retrieved at: etymonline.com

64   Doesburg, *Revised Freemasonry Illustrated: A Complete Exposition of the First Three Masonic Degrees*, Chicago: Cook, 1922, p. 310

65   Cooke, *The History of Mathematics: A Brief Course* (2nd ed.), John Wiley & Sons, 2011, pp. 237-238

66   Plutarch, *Moralia* Vol. V, "On Isis and Osiris", Loeb Classic Library, 1936, p. 135

the astro-geometrically defined main axis. Here we see the construction of the aforementioned Cartesian coordinates x (main axis) and y (perpendicular), with the z (vertical) coordinate being established later, by means of a plumb line, thereby establishing the three dimensions of length, width and height. The Greek essayist, Plutarch (46-120 CE; Greek: Πλούταρχος), after commenting on the Egyptian's veneration for the 3:4:5 triangle, likens the three sides to the Egyptian trinity: Isis (*a*, base), Osiris (*b*, vertical) and Horus (*c*, *hypotenuse*).

> *One might conjecture that the Egyptians hold in high honour the most beautiful of the triangles, since they liken the nature of the Universe most closely to it, as Plato in the Republic seems to have made use of it in formulating his figure of marriage. This triangle has its upright of three units, its base of four, and its hypotenuse of five, whose power is equal to that of the other two sides. The upright, therefore, may be likened to the male, the base to the female, and the hypotenuse to the child of both, and so Osiris may be regarded as the origin, Isis as the recipient, and Horus as perfected result.*[67]

Echoing this ancient sentiment, Mackey, in his *Encyclopedia*, had written the following of the right-angled triangle...

> *The right-angled triangle is another form of this figure which is deserving of attention. Among the Egyptians, it was the symbol of universal nature; the base representing Osiris, or the male principle; the perpendicular, Isis, or the female principle; and the hypotenuse, Horus, their son, or the product of the male and female principle. This symbol was received by Pythagoras from the Egyptians during his long sojourn in that country, and with it he also learned the peculiar property it possessed, namely, that the sum of the squares of the two shorter sides is equal to the square of the longest side–symbolically expressed by the formula, that the product of Osiris and Isis is Horus. This figure has been adopted in the Third Degree of Freemasonry, and will be there recognized as the Forty-seventh Problem of Euclid.*[68]

---

67 Plutarch, *Moralia* Vol. V, "On Isis and Osiris", Loeb Classic Library, 1936, p. 135
68 Entry: "Triangle"; Mackey, *An Encyclopedia of Freemasonry and its Kindred Sciences*, Everts & Co., 1884

The numbers three, four and five are the smallest integers with which the unit relationship of a Pythagorean triangle may be expressed; these are followed multiples such as: 6:8:10, 9:12:15, 12:16:20, etc., and "Pythagorean triples" such as 5:12:13, 8:15:17, 7:24:25, etc., all of which satisfy $a^2 + b^2 = c^2$.[69] Taken collectively or individually, the numbers three, four and five afford us some interesting interpretive possibilities worthy of our contemplation. Having already addressed the symbolism of the numbers three and five in considerable detail, we will here examine the esoteric significance of these three numbers as a whole, beginning with a thought-provoking qabalistic exegesis...

> *"Moses in Hebrew is spelled with the three letters Mem (40) that means water, Shin (300) that means fire, and Heh (5) that means the breath of life," explained Isaac. "Moses, the Hebrew deliverer, has a Gematria of 345. Now, Moses (345) is a reflection of I AM THAT I AM (543). [Hebrew:* רֶשֲׁא הֶיְהֶא *הֶיְהֶא; Ehyeh Asher Ehyeh] Furthermore, if you take the two numbers 345/543 and add them together 345 + 543, you get 888, the number of the Christian Messiah, Yeshua or Joshua."[70]*

There are several other ways one could hermeneutically interpret the numbers three, four and five using the various occult methodologies. For example, the addition of three, four and five produces twelve (3 + 4 + 5 = 12), which is, of course, the number of zodiacal signs. By the further application of theosophical addition, twelve reduces to three (1 + 2 = 3), reflecting the aforementioned Egyptian trinity: Isis, Osiris and Horus. Three plus four equals seven (3 + 4 = 7), representing the seven classical planets (the planetary *heptagram* of the Chaldeans), leaving us with the number five, representing man (the microcosmic *pentagram*), which could be seen to represent man's hermetic resonance with the planetary spheres. Qabalistically, the numbers three, four and five correspond to the *sephiroth* of *Binah*, *Chesed* and *Geburah*, which form a right-angled triangle on the *Etz Chaim* (see Appendix B). Furthermore, the magic squares of Saturn (9 cells), Jupiter (16 cells) and Mars (25 cells) – which correspond to the three aforemention *sephiroth*, respectively – *have the same number of cells as the three squares of the sides of the Pythagorean triangle* ($3^2 = 9$; $4^2 = 16$; $5^2 = 25$). The gematriac values three, four and five correspond to the Hebrew let-

69   Knotts, *Pythagorean Right-Angled Triangles*, retrieved at: maths.surrey.ac.uk

70   Wigowsky, *God in Three Persons: A Spiritual Odyssey*, Infinity Publishing, 2007, Chapter 888

ters *gimel, daleth* and *heh*, which are attributed to paths on the *Etz Chaim* creating another right-angled triangle. The Tarot cards corresponding to the paths of these letters are: the High Priestess II, the Empress III and the Emperor IV, representing the Moon, Venus and Mars, whose *sephiroth* (*Yesod, Netzach* and *Geburah*) form yet another right-angled triangle on the *Etz Chaim*. In addition to the Hebrew words for *Moses* and *I AM THAT I AM*, the Hebrew words meaning "Egyptian" (ירצמה) and "pomegranate" (סינמרה) also have gematriac values of 345 — offering further correspondences for our contemplation, in terms of the Trinity of Osiris, Isis and Horus, their aforementioned relationship to the 3:4:5 triangle, and the Greek agrotheological Mysteries featuring the pomegranate. Many other qabalistic, zodiacal, planetary, elemental and tarotic "proofs" could be applied to this short series to great effect. As we have hopefully illustrated throughout this work, the occultist is only limited in the practice of *meaning-making* by the scope of their imagination and their fluency in the *grammar* of the Western Esoteric Tradition (see Appendix A).

The Pythagorean Theorem is venerated by Freemasons under the name of one of its many proofs, the 47th Problem of Euclid.[71] This symbol is addressed in the lecture of the Master Mason degree, where it is said to teach Masons to be "general lovers of the arts and sciences"[72], and it is sometimes featured in Masonic jewelry. It is important to note that there are no extraneous symbols used in the Craft — as we have seen in our analysis of the 47th Problem of Euclid. Every symbol employed in Masonic ritual should be seen as a prompt — or perhaps a *clue* — which the individual Mason would do well to investigate beyond its superficial reading. Each of these symbols, the exoteric interpretations of which are given during the lectures, represent a wealth of *wisdom* and *understanding* awaiting those who are prepared to penetrate their Mysteries by the application of occult exegetical and interpretative methods.

Though we have addressed the pentagram in significant detail in our study of the symbolism of the number five in Chapter V, we will now address this symbol purely in its Pythagorean context. As we had discussed, Neoplatonists such as Iamblichus (250-330 CE) have commented on the symbolic use of the pentagram by the Pythagoreans.[73] There are several reasons why the Pythagoreans may have adopted the symbol, ranging from the mythological, the planetary and, of course, the geometrical. Beginning

---

71 Euclid, *Elements*, Book I, Proposition 47

72 Doesburg, *Revised Freemasonry Illustrated: A Complete Exposition of the First Three Masonic Degrees*, Chicago: Cook, 1922, p. 310

73 Iamblichus, *Life of Pythagoras*, XXXIII

with the former, we find that, generally, the ancient Greeks referred to this figure as the pentalpha, since they imagined it to consist of five of their letters alpha superimposed in rotations; the Pythagoreans, however, specifically referred to it as *hugieia* (Greek: ὑγιεία; meaning "health") and ascribed the letters of the word to the points of the pentalpha, clockwise from the top point: U-G-I-EI-A[74] In Greek Mythology, Hygeia was the goddess of health, cleanliness and sanitation; she was the sister of Panacea (Greek: Πανάκεια), whose name has entered the English vocabulary and has come to mean "a remedy for all ills or difficulties".[75] Appropriately, the two sisters were fathered by Asclepius (Greek: Ἀσκληπιός), son of Apollo and god of medicine and the healing arts. Because of these associations, ὑγιεία is a common inscription appearing on Græco-Egyptian magical amulets from the Ptolemaic era – an era we know to have seen the presence of a reemerging (Neo)Pythagoreanism.[76]

Pythagoras is credited with the identification of Venus as being the morning and evening star, which may have reinforced the Pythagorean adoption of the pentagram as a symbol of their order.[77] The epithets, "morning" and "evening star" are in reference to Venus' accompanying of the Sun in its rising and setting, since the planet is never further than 47° from the Sun at its aphelion.[78] In ancient Greece, the terms *Phosphoros*, "the bringer of light", and *Hesperos*, "the star of the evening" were used to describe this aspect of the planet Venus.[79] As we had briefly discussed in Chapter V, another notable phenomenon, in terms of Venus' pentagrammic symbolism, is the planet's synodic orbit (583.9211 days). Venus' apparent path over this period, from the perspective of the Earth, forms a five-petalled rosette against the firmament – a formation which was apparently observed by the astronomers of the ancient world, who long ago conflated the pentagram with the planet Venus.

---

74   Allman, *Greek Geometry From Thales to Euclid,* Dublin University Press, 1889, p.26

75   Entry: "Panacea"; *Webster's Collegiate Dictionary*, retrieved at: merriam-webster.com

76   Bonner, *Studies in Magical Amulets, chiefly Graeco-Egyptian*, Ann Arbor, University of Michigan Press, 1950

77   Weisstein, "Pythagoras of Samos", *Wolfram Research*, 2007, retrieved at: scienceworld. wolfram.com

78   Gaherty, "Cosmic Lights: Bright Venus, Solar Eclipse Dominate Sky This Week", *Space*, 2013, retrieved at: space.com

79   Cain, "Venus: The Morning and Evening Star", *Universe Today*, 2008, retrieved at: universetoday.com

The pentagrammic rosette created by Venus' synodic orbit

Perhaps the main reason for the Pythagorean's adoption of the pentagram as a symbol in their order was due to the discovery of its hidden mathematical properties. Ancient Greek mathematicians and geometers discerned what is now referred to as the "golden ratio" as a frequently occurring phenomenon in their work; particularly as the ratio pertains to the line divisions of pentagrams and pentagons.[80] The golden ratio is defined as "a special number found by dividing a line into two parts so that the longer part divided by the smaller part is also equal to the whole length divided by the longer part."[81] The late 5th century Pythagorean philosopher, Hippasus of Metapontum (530-450 BCE), who was the founder of a Pythagorean sect called the *Mathematici* (Greek: μαθηματικοί) near Crotona, is credited with the discovery that the golden ratio was neither an integer of a fraction – thereby introducing the concept of irrational numbers. Being an irrational number, the golden ratio is inexpressible as a fraction and possesses an interminable decimal expanse; ergo, it is often rounded to 1.618 and is symbolized by the 21st letter of the Greek alphabet, *phi* (φ). The first documented definition of the golden ratio is found in Euclid's *Elements*, which contains several propositions and proofs of the ratio.[82]

The golden ratio has influenced the work of countless artists and

80   Livio, *The Golden Ratio: The Story of Phi, the World's Most Astonishing Number*, New York City: Broadway Books, 2003, pp. 4-8

81   Hom, "What is the Golden Ratio?", *Live Science*, 2013, retrieved at: livescience.com

82   Hemenway, *Divine Proportion: Phi In Art, Nature, and Science*, New York: Sterling, 2005, pp. 20-21

scientists over the course of many centuries; it may be detected in the architecture of structures such as the Pyramid of Cheops at Giza[83] and the Parthenon at Athens.[84] In addition to its veneration by the ancients, we see its influence in the work of luminaries such as Leonardo of Pisa (1170-1250 CE; a.k.a. Fibonacci), who discerned it in the sequence of rabbit reproduction; Leonardo Da Vinci (1452-1519 CE), who called it the *sectio aurea* (Latin; meaning "the golden section") and used it to achieve balance and pleasing proportions in his *Last Supper*, *Vitruvian Man* and *Mona Lisa*; Johannes Kepler (1571-1630 CE), who fused it with the Pythagorean Theorem and employed both in the formula for *Kepler's Triangle*; and twentieth century architects and artists such as Le Corbusier (1887-1965 CE) and Salvador Dali (1904-1989 CE).[85] The golden ratio has been a mainstay of mathematical and geometrical inquiry, leading to innovations in various domains such as the visual arts, music, architecture and design aesthetics. Let us also not forget that the golden ratio is a ubiquitous ratio found in the works of nature, with such diverse examples being flower petals, seed heads, pinecones, tree branches, sea shells, spiral galaxies, hurricanes, fingers and even in the structure of our very DNA.[86]

It is not inconceivable to propose that Pythagoras – who we know to have observed and identified the planet Venus – calculated the planet's synodic orbit, and its resultant pentagrammic rosette, and perhaps thereby discovered the golden ratio in the geometric extrapolations of his findings. In a similar spirit of speculation, we will conclude our study of Pythagoras' pentagram with a passage from eminent Scottish Rite Freemason, Albert Pike who, in his *Morals and Dogma*, proposed an interesting, though achronological, astrotheological interpretation of the pentalpha:

> [T]he mysterious Pentalpha of Pythagoras [...] is indissolubly connected with the number seven. Christ fed His disciples and the multitude with five loaves and two fishes, and of the fragments there remained twelve, that is, five and seven, baskets full. Again He fed them with seven loaves and a few little fishes, and there remained seven baskets full. The five apparently small planets, Mercury,

83   Herz-Fischler, *The Shape of the Great Pyramid*, Wilfrid Laurier University Press, 2000

84   Borg, "The Parthenon and the Golden Ratio", *Discovering Design*, 2014, retrieved at: blogs.lt.vt.edu

85   Hom, "What is the Golden Ratio?", *Live Science*, 2013, retrieved at livescience.com

86   Liu, "Is the Golden Ratio a Universal Constant for Self-Replication?", *National Center for Biotechnology Information*, 2018, retrieved at: ncbi.nlm.nih.gov

Venus, Mars, Jupiter, and Saturn, with the two greater ones,
the Sun and Moon, constituted the seven celestial spheres.[87]

At the close of the 4th century BCE, a new paradigm in mathematical rigor was introduced in the form of Euclid's *Elements* (Greek: Στοιχεῖα), which addressed problems of plane and solid geometry. In the thirteen books of this most influential mathematical treatise[88], the earliest example of the axiomatic method is employed; this consists of *definition*, *axiom*, *theorem* and *proof* – which are still the standards of modern rigorous mathematics and logic – and are generally rendered by his detailing the steps of compasses and straightedge constructions. In many ways, the books of the *Elements* comprise a compilation of previously established propositions, formulæ and constructions, with books I and II being a distillation of Pythagoras, book III of Hippocrates of Chios (470-410 BCE), book V of Eudoxus (408-355 BCE) and the remaining books from other Greek mathematicians.[89] While much of the material was extant and established by Euclid's time, many of the proofs were his own and, perhaps more significantly, it was in the *Elements* that we first see the system codified into a logical framework, rendered solely as abstractions, with the advancement of ten axioms, or postulates, and several hundred theorems which were proved by means of deductive logic.[90] The *Elements* would go on to influence innumerous mathematicians and philosophers such as Copernicus, Kepler, Galileo, Newton, Hobbes, Spinoza and other such luminaries, and is second only to the *Holy Bible* in its number of printed editions since 1482 CE.[91] Out of the many proofs given in the *Elements*, the 47th Problem of Euclid[92] is perhaps the most important from the perspective of Freemasonry, since it appears in the Master Mason degree lecture and in Masonic jewelry (usually on Past Master's jewels). It is important, however, to recognize the distinction between the Pythagorean Theorem and the 47th Problem (more accurately, *Proposition*) of Euclid – the former is a *theorem*, the latter is a *proof*, in that it utilizes a deductive process in order to establish the validity of the theorem.

---

87   Pike, *Morals and Dogma of the Ancient and Accepted Scottish Rite of Freemasonry*, Supreme Council of the Southern Jurisdiction, A.A.S.R., U.S.A., 1871, p. 29

88   Boyer, *A History of Mathematics* (2nd ed), New York: Wiley, 1989, p. 119

89   Ball, *A Short Account of the History of Mathematics* (4th ed.), Dover Publications, 1908, p. 54

90   Entry: "Geometry"; *Encyclopædia Britannica*, retrieved at: britannica.com

91   Boyer, *A History of Mathematics* (2nd ed), New York: Wiley, 1989, p. 100

92   Euclid, *Elements*, Book I, Proposition 47

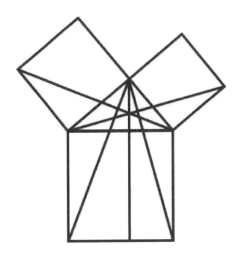

The 47th Proposition of Euclid

Moving on, chronologically, from Euclid, we encounter the work of Archimedes of Syracuse (287-212 BCE), who was a Greek mathematician, engineer and astronomer, considered by some to be the greatest mathematician of antiquity.[93] He is most notably credited with the aptly named *Archimedes' Principle*, which is a method of determining the volume of an irregularly shaped object.[94] Archimedes' discovery of this principle is said to have begun when, one day, Hiero II, king of Syracuse, supplied a quantity of gold to be fashioned by a smith into a votive crown for the temple. The King suspected the goldsmith of using less than the given amount in the casting of the crown. He then tasked Archimedes to devise a formula to confirm or deny his suspicions. Puzzled at first, Archimedes drew a full bath and found that, as he entered the tub, an amount of water, equal to his own volume, was displaced onto the floor – thus giving him the idea to use this method in determining the volume of the votive crown. He is said to have jumped out of the tub and ran naked through town shouting, like Pythagoras before him, "Eureka!"[95] Another rather amusing anecdote regarding the death of Archimides is recounted by Valerius Maximus, who wrote that, one day, while Archimedes was working out a problem in the

93   Hawking, *God Created the Integers: The Mathematical Breakthroughs that Changed History*, Running Press, 2007, p. 12

94   *Incompressibility of Water*, Harvard University, retrieved at: scictr.fas.harvard.edu

95   Vitruvius, *De Architectura*, Book IX, 9-12

sand, a hostile Roman soldier came upon him; and just before dying at the hands of the soldier, Archimedes somewhat tersely admonished him, saying "Μὴ μου τοὺς κύκλους τάραττε!" (Greek; meaning "Do not disturb my circles!").[96]

During the Middle Ages, advancements made in mathematical arts and sciences, such as geometry and algebra (Arabic: *al-jabr*), were largely under the custodianship of the Islamic world. During the 9th and 10th centuries, particularly, we see the synthesis of Greek and Indian mathematics occurring in Arabia (the Middle East, Persia and North Africa), which resulted in an unprecedented period of development. These included the development of the place value of decimal fractions, the algorithm (Arabic: *al-kwārizmī*) and the first formal systemization of algebra, which is defined as "a generalization of arithmetic in which letters representing numbers are combined according to the rules of arithmetic"[97] and was consequently employed in geometrical proofs. The Islamic transmission of these developments proved to be crucial to European scientific advancements in the 10th through 12th centuries.[98] Along with advancements in the mathematical sciences, it is via these same, largely Moorish, routes of transmission that esoteric currents such as alchemy (Arabic: *al-kīmiyā*) and astral magic enter Europe. This is the route by which we first encounter alchemical concepts such as the elixir (Arabic: *al-iksīr*) and the philosopher's stone (Arabic: *ḥajar al-falāsifah*) in the West, beginning with Latin translations of Arabic alchemical codices, such as Robert of Chester's *De compositione alchemæ* in 1144 CE, and eventually leading to the first indigenously European codices, such as Micheal Scot's *Ars alchemia* in 1225 CE.[99] As we had previously discussed, the transmission of astral magical operations, such as talisman and amulet construction, come to Europe largely via Arabic texts such as *Picatrix* (Arabic: *Ghāyat al-Ḥakīm*, 10th or 11th century), which was perhaps the single largest influence on Agrippa, forming the theoretical basis of his *De occulta philosophia* (1531), and eventually feeding into the current of Renaissance Occultism begun by the Florentine Neoplatonists.

---

96   Valerius Maximus, *Memorable Doings and Sayings*, 1st century CE; as cited in *The Death of Archimedes*, retrieved at: nyu.edu

97   Entry: "Algebra"; *Webster's Collegiate Dictionary*, retrieved at: merriam-webster.com

98   Sertima & Van, *Golden age of the Moor*, Volume 11, Transaction Publishers, 1992, p. 394

99   Entry: "Islamic Alchemy"; retrieved at: encyclopedia.com

René Descartes

Last in the sequence of our present historical overview of geometry (which will not be extended to include 19th and 20th century developments, as our focus is on the tributaries to early Freemasonry), we will briefly address the work of René Descartes (1596-1650 CE). A French philosopher and mathematician, Descartes' major contribution to geometry was the application of algebra and the designation of spatial coordinates coupled into a system known as analytic, or Cartesian geometry. He systemized algebraic notation by assigning a, b and c to "knowns", and x, y and z to "unknowns", as well as pioneering the use of a superscript to notate an exponent (e.g. x^2).[100] His analytic geometry is widely used in physics, engineering, aviation and astro-physics, and is fundamental to most modern forms of geometry. The Cartesian coordinates are employed both on the Euclidean plane (two dimensions) and in Euclidean space (three

---

100   Descartes, *Discourse de la Méthode*, Jan Maire, 1637, appended book: *La Géométrie*, book I, p. 299

dimensions). He assigned the spatial coordinates: x (the *abscissa*), y (the *ordinate*) and z (the *applicate*) to Euclidean space; the x axis representing a line going from side-to-side, the y axis representing a line from front-to-back, and the z axis representing a line running up-and-down, with all three axes meeting together at a point called the *origin*, as we had previously discussed in Chapter IV.

The cube, which symbolizes materiality, may be seen as a representation of the space created by the aforementioned Cartesian coordinates: x (side-to-side), y (front-to-back) & z (up-and-down) – rendering the cube a microcosm of the physical world. When the fourth dimension of time is added to this spatial schema, we are able to locate ourselves, and other points, in the continuum of space and time. In the *Sepher Yetzirah* (Hebrew: ספר יצירה; meaning "Book of Formation"), the oldest known qabalistic text, dating to sometime between the 2nd century BCE and the 2nd century CE[101], the six directions are said to have been "sealed" by Yah, the "Lord of Hosts", thus describing a cubic spatial model at least a millennium before Descartes. After having created the four elements, Yah is said to have...

> [...] *selected three letters from the simple ones, and sealed them as forming his great Name, I H V and he sealed the universe in six directions. Five. - He looked above, and sealed the height, with I H V. Six. - He looked below, and sealed the deep, with I V H. Seven. - He looked forward, and sealed the East, with H I V. Eight. - He looked backward, and sealed the West, with V H I. Nine. - He looked to the right, and sealed the South, with V I H. Ten. - He looked to the left, and sealed the North, with H V I.[102]*

This yetziric spatial model was illustrated and expanded upon by prominent 20th century American occultist, Paul Foster Case (1884-1954), in his *Tarot: A Key to the Wisdom of the Ages* (Macoy Publishing, 1947). Case, a member of the post-Golden Dawn order *Alpha et Omega* and founder of the Builders of the Adytum (B.O.T.A.), associates the twenty-two letters of the Hebrew alphabet with the center point, the three Cartesian axes, the six sides of the hexahedron and the twelve edges of the solid (1 + 3 + 6 + 12 = 22). To these twenty-two positions, he further assigns the cardinal and ordinal directions in addition to the Tarot keys of the Major Arcana

---

101   Reitzenstein, *Poimandres*, Leipzig, 1904

102   Westcott (trans.), *Sepher Yetzirah*, The Theosophical Publishing Society, 1887, Chapter I, v. 11

as well as other standard Hermetic correspondences (see Appendix A). Of this model, which he had denominated the "Cube of Space", Case said "In the study of the Qabalah, there is no more important glyph than the Cube of Space, with perhaps the exception of the Tree of Life."[103]

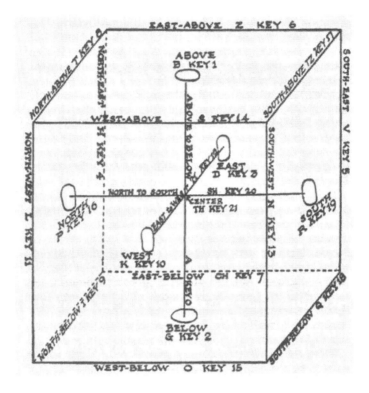

The Cube of Space from Paul Foster Case's Tarot: Key to the Wisdom of the Ages, 1947

In the interest of hermetically mirroring operations performed in the macrocosm with those performed in the microcosm, and the value of cultivating such sympathetic resonances, the reader is encouraged to perform a few basic compasses and straightedge constructions. The Freemason or esotericist who wishes to hermetically internalize these constructions may envision the process as a ritualistic and/or creative exercise, with the goal of bringing about organized states both in the external world – represented by the operative geometrical constructions on paper – as well as within the inner world of the speculative geometer desiring to affect analogous

103   As quoted in: Townley, *The Cube of Space: Container of Creation*, Archive Press, 1993

changes on the mental (the psychic, *mercurial* modality), spiritual (the pneumatic, *sulfuric* modality) and corporeal (the somatic, *saline* modality) planes. Particular attention should be paid to the following definitions and propositions as they are described in Euclid's *Elements*:

Book I, Definition 15:

A circle is a plane figure contained by one line such that all the straight lines falling upon it from one point among those lying within the figure equal one another.

Book I, Definition 16:

And the point is called the center of the circle.

Book I, Proposition 1:

To construct an equilateral triangle on a given finite straight line.

Let AB be the given finite straight line. It is required to construct an equilateral triangle on the straight line AB. Describe the circle BCD with center A and radius AB. Again describe the circle ACE with center B and radius BA. Join the straight lines CA and CB from the point C at which the circles cut one another to the points A and B. Now, since the point A is the center of the circle CDB, therefore AC equals AB. Again, since the point B is the center of the circle CAE,

therefore BC equals BA. But AC was proved equal to AB, therefore each of the straight lines AC and BC equals AB. And things which equal the same thing also equal one another, therefore AC also equals BC. Therefore the three straight lines AC, AB, and BC equal one another. Therefore the triangle ABC is equilateral, and it has been constructed on the given finite straight line AB.

Book I, Proposition 46:

To describe a square on a given straight line.

Let AB be the given straight line. It is required to describe a square on the straight line AB. Draw AC at right angles to the straight line AB from the point A on it. Make AD equal to AB. Draw DE through the point D parallel to AB, and draw BE through the point B parallel to AD. Then ADEB is a parallelogram. Therefore AB equals DE, and AD equals BE. But AB equals AD, therefore the four straight lines BA, AD, DE, and EB equal one another. Therefore the parallelogram ADEB is equilateral. I say next that it is also right-angled. Since the straight line AD falls upon the parallels AB and DE, therefore the sum of the angles BAD and ADE equals two right angles. But the angle BAD is right, therefore the angle ADE is also right. And in parallelogrammic areas the opposite sides and angles equal one another, therefore each of the opposite angles ABE and BED is also right. Therefore ADEB is right-angled. And it was also proved equilateral. Therefore it is a square, and it is described on the straight line AB.

Book IV, Proposition 11

To inscribe an equilateral and equiangular pentagon in a given circle.

Let ABCDE be the given circle. It is required to inscribe an equilateral and equiangular pentagon in the circle ABCDE. Set out the isosceles triangle FGH having each of the angles at G and H double the angle at F. Inscribe in the circle ABCDE the triangle ACD equiangular with the triangle FGH, so that the angles CAD, ACD, and CDA equal the angles at F, G, and H respectively. Therefore each of the angles ACD and CDA is also double the angle CAD. Now bisect the angles ACD and CDA respectively by the straight lines CE and DB, and join AB, BC, DE, and EA. Then, since each of the angles

ACD and CDA is double the angle CAD, and they are bisected by the straight lines CE and DB, therefore the five angles DAC, ACE, ECD, CDB, and BDA equal one another. But equal angles stand on equal circumferences, therefore the five circumferences AB, BC, CD, DE, and EA equal one another. But straight lines that cut off equal circumferences are equal, therefore the five straight lines AB, BC, CD, DE, and EA equal one another. Therefore the pentagon ABCDE is equilateral. I say next that it is also equiangular. For, since the circumference AB equals the circumference DE, add BCD to each, therefore the whole circumference ABCD equals the whole circumference EDCB. And the angle AED stands on the circumference ABCD, and the angle BAE on the circumference EDCB, therefore the angle BAE also equals the angle AED. For the same reason each of the angles ABC, BCD, and CDE also equals each of the angles BAE and AED, therefore the pentagon ABCDE is equiangular. But it was also proved equilateral, therefore an equilateral and equiangular pentagon has been inscribed in the given circle.

Book IV, Proposition 15

To inscribe an equilateral and equiangular hexagon in a given circle.

Let ABCDEF be the given circle. It is required to inscribe an equilateral and equiangular hexagon in the circle ABCDEF. Draw the diameter AD of the circle ABCDEF. Take the center G of the circle. Describe the circle EGCH with center D and radius DG. Join EG and CG and carry them through to the points B and F. Join AB, BC, CD, DE, EF, and FA. I say that the hexagon ABCDEF is equilateral and equiangular. For, since the point G is the center of the circle ABCDEF, GE equals GD. Again, since the point D is the center of the circle GCH, DE equals DG. But GE was proved equal to GD, therefore GE also equals ED. Therefore the triangle EGD is equilateral, and therefore its three angles EGD, GDE, and DEG equal one another, inasmuch as, in isosceles triangles, the angles at the base equal one another. And the sum of the three angles of the triangle equals two right angles, therefore the angle EGD is one-third of two right angles. Similarly, the angle DGC can also be proved to be one third of two right angles. And, since the straight line CG stand-ing on EB makes the sum of the adjacent angles EGC and CGB equal to two right angles, therefore the remaining angle CGB is also one-third of two right angles. Therefore the angles EGD, DGC, and CGB equal one another, so that the angles vertical to them, the an-gles BGA, AGF, and FGE, are equal. Therefore the six angles EGD, DGC, CGB, BGA, AGF, and FGE equal one another. But equal angles stand on equal circumferences, therefore the six circumferences AB, BC, CD, DE, EF, and FA equal one another. And straight lines that cut off equal circumferences are equal, therefore the six straight lines equal one another. Therefore the hexagon ABCDEF is equilat-eral. I say next that it is also equiangular. For, since the circumference FA equals the circumference ED, add the circumference ABCD to each, therefore the whole FABCD equals the whole EDCBA. And the angle FED stands on the circumference FABCD, and the angle AFE on the circumference EDCBA, therefore the angle AFE equals the angle DEF. Similarly it can be proved that the remaining an-gles of the hexagon ABCDEF are also severally equal to each of the angles AFE and FED, therefore the hexagon ABCDEF is equian-gular. But it was also proved equilateral, and it has been inscribed in the circle ABCDEF. Therefore an equilateral and equiangular hexagon has been inscribed in the given circle.

After becoming familiar with the basic constructions of planar, or two-dimensional geometry, we turn our attention to the Platonic solids, which are five regular, convex polyhedra, with regular polygonal faces meeting in the same number at each vertex, in three-dimensional space. There are precisely five solids which satisfy the above criteria, they are: the *tetrahedron*, the *hexahedron*, the *octahedron*, the *dodecahedron* and the *icosahedron*. The Greek Neoplatonist, Proclus (412-485 CE), credits their discovery to the Pythagoreans sometime before 450 BCE, although there is evidence that the Egyptians identified at least three of the five regu-lar, convex polyhedra.[104] Although Theaetetus of Athens (417-369 BCE), a contemporary of both Socrates and Plato and, like Plato, a student of mathematician, Theodorus of Cyrene, has been credited with the first for-mal proof of the five regular, convex polyhedra[105], Plato most popularly described the Platonic solids in intuitive and philosophical terms, theo-rizing that these were the literal building blocks of phenomenal reality. In

104   "The Platonic Solids", *University of Illinois*, retrieved at: uiuc.edu

105   Allman, *Greek Geometry from Thales to Euclid*, Hodges, Figgis & Co., 1889, p. 206

this supposition, Plato's conceptualization of the solids may be said to be somewhat built upon notions in circulation among pre-Socratic philosophers such as Empedocles (494-434 BCE), who posited that the *arche* (the primordial element or principle underlying and permeating the universe) was not a single element but a combination of earth, water, air and fire, and Atomist philosophers such as Democritus (460-370 BCE) and Leucippus (5th century), who posited that the universe was composed of indivisible, microscopic units they called "atoms". Similarly, in his *Timaeus* (360 BCE), Plato attributed each of the five solids to one of the classical elements (earth, air, water and fire, plus *æther*); the tetrahedron being associated with fire; the hexahedron (cube) with earth; the octahedron with air; the dodecahedron with æther; and the icosahedron with water, thus implying their status as the primal units of matter.[106, 107] In what may be seen as a nod to Pythagoras' meta-arithmetical numerology applied to astrology, Plato's association of the dodecahedron with æther is apparently based on the twelve faces of the dodecahedron corresponding to the twelve signs of the zodiac, as the philosopher somewhat cryptically wrote that "[...] god used [it] for arranging the constellations on the whole heaven."[108] At the dawn of the 3rd century BCE, Euclid devoted the entirety of the XIIIth and last book of his *Elements* to the mathematical description and construction of the Platonic solids, arguing in Proposition 18 the impossibility of a sixth convex, regular polyhedron.[109]

106   Plato, *Timaeus*, 360 BCE, 55c4-6

107   Zeyl & Sattler, *Stanford Encyclopedia of Philosophy*, Entry: "Plato's *Timaeus*", 2017, retrieved at: standford.edu

108   Plato, *Timaeus*, 360 BCE, 55

109   Euclid, *Elements*, Book XIII, Propositions 13-18, 300 BCE

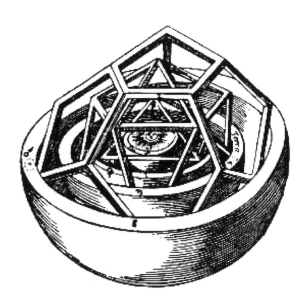

Kepler's polyhedral cosmology in the Mysterium Cosmographicum, 1596

In his first major astronomical work, the *Mysterium Cosmographi-cum* (Tübingen, 1596 CE)[110], 16th century German astronomer, astrologer and mathematician, Johannes Kepler (1571-1630 CE), argued that the distances between the planets Mercury, Venus, Earth, Mars, Jupiter and Saturn could be described using the Platonic solids. In this cosmological schema – which was based on the Copernican, heliocentric model – the convex, regular polyhedra were concentrically enclosed within the sphere of Saturn and were explained as being indicative of the handiwork of God, who Kepler imagined to be a Geometrician. The *Mysterium Cosmograph-icum* marked the first attempt since Copernicus to prove the theory of heliocentrism.[111]

110   The actual title of which is the unwieldy *Prodromus dissertationum cosmographicarum, continens mysterium cosmographicum, de admirabili proportione orbium coelestium, de que causis coelorum numeri, magnitudinis, motuumque periodicorum genuinis & proprijs, demonstratum per quinque regularia corpora geometrica* (English: *Forerunner of the Cosmological Essays, Which Contains the Secret of the Universe; on the Marvelous Proportion of the Celestial Spheres, and on the True and Particular Causes of the Number, Magnitude, and Periodic Motions of the Heavens; Established by Means of the Five Regular Geometric Solids*).

111   Voelkel, *Classics of Astronomy by Johannes Kepler*, 2010, retrieved at: chapin.williams. edu

Anyone with the least knowledge of geometry [...] would im-
mediately recall the five regular solids with the ratio of circum-
scribed orbs to the inscribed ones, and there would immediate-
ly appear before his eyes the Euclidean [...] proposition [...]
where it is proved that there cannot be, or be imagined, more
regular solids than five [...] As a memorial of the event [Ke-
pler's discovery] I present you with this idea, just as it occurred,
in the words conceived at that very moment: The Earth is the
circle which is the measure of all. About it circumscribe a do-
decahedron. The circle enclosing this will be Mars. About Mars
circumscribe a tetrahedron. The circle enclosing this will be
Jupiter. About Jupiter circumscribe a cube. The circle enclosing
this will be Saturn. Now in the Earth inscribe an icosahedron.
The circle inscribed in this will be Venus. In Venus inscribe an
octahedron. The circle inscribed in this will be Mercury. Here
you have the reason for the number of the planets.[112]

Using Kepler's cosmological model of the solar system as an interpretive key, we find that the Platonic solids may be attributed to the several
paths which are distributed between the *sephiroth* on the *Etz Chaim* (see
Appendix B), thereby providing us with further Hermetic and qabalistic insight due to their correspondences – elemental, planetary, zodiacal,
mythological, tarotic and so forth. As we have illustrated throughout the
present work, the diagram of the *Etz Chaim* is but a linear reworking of
the concentric planetary spheres devised in the first few centuries of the
Common Era by the ancient Hermeticists and Neoplatonists. In their
geocentric cosmological model – and, consequently, that of the Qabalists
– the planets are sequenced in their typical Ptolemaic, or Chaldean order,
viz; the Moon, Mercury, Venus, the Sun, Mars, Jupiter, Saturn and, finally,
the firmament, or sphere of the fixed stars and the constellations of the
zodiac; each of these spheres being nested within the other with the Earth
at the center, enveloped by the lunar sphere, which is itself enveloped by
the mercurial sphere, etc. However, in Kepler's *Mysterium Cosmographicum*,
we are dealing with the newly (re)discovered[113], Copernican, heliocentric

112   Kepler, *Mysterium Cosmographicum*, 1596

113   An observation first attributed to Aristarchus in Archimedes's *The Sand Reckoner*.
Dreyer, *A History of Astronomy from Thales to Kepler*, Dover Publications, 1953, pp. 135-
148

model – *not the geocentric, Ptolemaic or Chaldean models, upon which the Etz Chaim was constructed* – and, thereby, the Earth and Sun are transposed, leaving the Earth inhabiting the position of the sixth *sephirah, Tiphareth*, and the Sun situated in *Malkuth*, the tenth *sephirah*. With this transposition, we find the planets in their true, heliocentric order on the *Etz Chaim*. This transposition constitutes a step towards a rectified heliocentric Qabalah, for those who are wishing to investigate this rewarding alternate magical paradigm. Of course, there is the problem of *Yesod* and maintaining twenty-two attributable paths for the Hebrew alphabet and other correspondences, but these are relatively easy to solve – their solution being outside of the scope of the present work. Modifications such as this, along with sidereally accurate astrological adjustments to the largely cardinal and tropical system currently in use by the vast majority of Western occultists, allow the practitioner to work within the system of astronomically accurate cosmic sympathies, while taking stellar displacement due to axial precession into account.

The Copernicus Planishere, from Cellarius's Harmonia Macrocosmica, 1660

Beginning with the octahedron, we find this solid representing the 27th path, which runs between the *sephiroth, Hod* and *Netzach*, just as it runs between Mercury and Venus – the planets respectively corresponding to *Hod* and *Netzach* – in Kepler's model. In the standard correspondences established in the cipher manuscripts which lead to the foundation of the Hermetic Order of the Golden Dawn (see Appendix A)[114], the Tarot card assigned to this path is the Tower XVI. This Tarot card represents transformation and may be interpreted to imply the necessity of a mediating, or rather, synthesizing force between two poles. Interestingly, the 27th path connects the sphere of Hermes (*Hod*) with that of Aphrodite (*Netzach*), whose synthesis is the hermaphrodite or *Rebis*, a synthesis and union of opposites, as depicted in alchemical codices wherein it represents the end product of the *magnum opus*.[115] The octahedron, representing air in the Platonic correspondence, may be seen to represent the action of the intellect in this operation, as the element air is associated with this process. The Hebrew letter *peh*, meaning "mouth", is assigned to this path as well; which may be interpreted as representing the *Logos* (Greek: λόγος; from λέγω, meaning "I say"), simultaneously extrapolated to mean both "word" and "reason", thereby strengthening the aforementioned association of the intellect in the process of transformation. Furthermore, the gematriac value of *peh* is eighty, which reduces to eight by Theosophical addition (8 + 0 = 8), thus illustrating its connection with the octahedron, which has eight sides, and the eighth *sephirah, Hod*. (see Appendix A).

The next Platonic solid we encounter is the icosahedron, which Kepler inscribed between the spheres of Venus and the Earth. The icosahedron is qabalistically represented by the 24th path, which connects the *sephiroth Netzach* (representing Venus) and *Tiphareth* (which houses the Earth, in the heliocentric model). The Tarot assigned to this path is Death XIII, to which the zodiacal sign of Scorpio – a water sign – is attributed in the established Hermetic correspondences. In his *Timaeus*, Plato attributed the element of water to the icosahedron, thus reinforcing the watery nature of this path. The Hebrew letter associated with the twenty-fourth path is *nun*, which means "fish", further elucidating the concept of life, or consciousness, within the waters. As we had previously discussed, words sharing a gematriac value are believed to have an occult resonance, from the qabalistic perspective. The gematriac value of the word *Netzach* is 128;

---

114   Küntz (editor), *The Complete Golden Dawn Cipher Manuscript*, Holmes Publishing, 1996, pp. 59 and 116

115   e.g., Valentine, *Azoth of the Philosophers*, 1613, and Nollius, *Theoria Philosophae Hermeticae*, 1617

this value is also shared by the Hebrew words סילמגה, meaning "camel"; לחנמ, meaning "river"; and יעובמ, meaning "spring". The words for river and spring are obviously aquatic; but the camel also affords us a unique insight, in that it may be seen to represent the inverse of the fish – as the fish lives within the water, the store of water lives within the camel. Thus, we have constructed several qabalistic "proofs" verifying Plato's intuition as to the watery nature of the icosahedron.

The dodecahedron, which Kepler inscribed between the Earth and Mars, is associated with the 22nd path on the *Etz Chaim*, spanning from *Tiphareth* to *Geburah*. The Tarot card attributed to this path is Justice XI, which represents balance and equilibrium. Just as Mercury and Venus may be said to be a matched pair of opposing forces brought into a unity by the path which spans their *sephiroth*, so may the Earth and Mars be viewed. For the Earth represents the fertile mother and receptive femininity, while her antithesis, Mars, represents the active, fiery violence associated with the god of war. These forces – like those of Mercury and Venus – may be brought into a state of equilibrium and balance, as suggested by Justice's scales as well as by the symbol of Libra, the zodiacal sign associated with this path.

Between the spheres of Mars and Jupiter, Kepler inscribed the tetrahedron. The reader will recall that Plato associated the tetrahedron with the classical element of fire, which figures quite prominently in our hermeneutic of this particular solid. From the perspective of classical Greek mythology, we find the archetypal presence of the Olympians, Ares (Latin: Mars) and Zeus (Latin: Jupiter) in these planets; Ares, being the son of Zeus, was subordinate to him. Being the god of war and of military valor, Ares' qualities were considered necessary – yet, he was treated ambivalently by the votary and populace, and was despised by his father, Zeus, who recognized his tendency to pervert his archetypal characteristics into arbitrary violence and cruelty. For, in the Vth book of the *Iliad*, Zeus addresses Ares thus…

> *Most hateful to me art thou of all gods that hold Olympus, for ever is strife dear to thee and wars and fightings. Thou hast the unbearable, unyielding spirit of thy mother, even of Hera; her can I scarce control by my words. Wherefore it is by her promptings, meseems, that thou sufferest thus. Howbeit I will no longer endure that thou shouldest be in pain, for thou art mine offspring, and it was to me that thy mother bare thee; but wert thou born of any other god, thus pestilent*

as thou art, then long ere this hadst thou been lower than the sons of heaven.[116]

Qabalistically, Mars and Jupiter correspond to the *sephiroth*, *Geburah* and *Chesed*, respectively; and the path on the *Etz Chaim* between these two *sephiroth* is nineteen, which is associated with the Strength VIII Tarot card. The zodiacal sign of Leo, which is a fire sign, is also attributed to this path, as is the Hebrew letter *teth*, meaning "serpent". Bearing these standard correspondences in the highly syncretized system of Hermetic Qabalah in mind, we find that the 19th path, and the sephirothic conjunction it represents, communicates the sublimation of the fiery, warlike agency of *Geburah* into the kingly righteousness of *Chesed* – a process perhaps best symbolized by the serpent; as the serpent may be interpreted to represent the wisdom necessary to transmute the raw and potentially destructive martial power of *Geburah* into a dynamic force, wielded with the jupiterian agency of *Chesed*. Thus, as in the symbolism surrounding the *demiurgos* Ialdabaoth and the Mithraic Leontocephaline, serpentine wisdom feeds the regal lion, whose creative dominion is inscribed within the circumference of his will.

Lastly in the Keplerian planetary distribution of the five Platonic solids, we encounter the hexahedron, or cube, which is inscribed between the spheres of Jupiter and Saturn. At this planetary junction, we may note that, as the sphere of Saturn concentrically encapsulates the inner planets circumscribed by its orbit, it was Saturn (Greek: Κρόνος; Cronus), the titanic father of the gods in classical mythology, who ostensibly swallowed Jupiter and the rest of his offspring whole.[117] The cube also affords us valuable symbolism for our contemplation, in that it represents materiality and, when unfolded into a two-dimensional, planar diagram, it becomes a cross – itself a symbol of the material world, or the Earth. This may be part of the reason why Plato attributed the hexahedron to the classical element of earth in his *Timaeus*.

Qabalistically, Jupiter and Saturn correspond to the *sephiroth*, *Chesed* and *Binah*, respectively, and only an invisible path runs between them; this invisible path, however, is the only leg of the "Lightning Flash" that does not follow an established sephirothic path. This path has no number or Tarotic attribution – however, there are two qabalistic touchstones corresponding to this gulf-like region of the *Etz Chaim*; the first is the "hidden" *sephirah*, Da'ath (Hebrew: דעת; meaning "Knowledge"), and the

---

116   Homer, *Iliad*, Book V, v. 890-897
117   Hesiod, *Theogony*, 7th century BCE, 453-467

second is referred to as the "Abyss" – both denoting the only passage by which one may access *Atziluth* (Hebrew: אֲצִילוּת), the qabbalistic "World of Emanation". *Da'ath* may be seen as the guardian, or gatekeeper, of the Divine Light of the three supernal *sephiroth*: *Binah*, *Chokmah* and *Kether*. The Abyss is an imaginary line which separates the three supernals from the lower *sephiroth*. It is a principal aim of the Practical Qabalah to attain this *atziluthic* state – in the gnosis of an unmediated apprehension of the supernal emanations – but it does not come without experiencing the perils of crossing the Abyss.

> *The Paths pursued by the Emanations in these successive over-flowings is represented upon the Tree of Life by a Lightning Flash, or in some diagrams by a Flaming Sword. It will be observed by reference to diagram I that the Lightning Flash must proceed from Kether outwards and downwards to the right to reach Chokmah, and then turns on a level course to the left and proceeds an equal distance beyond Kether upon that side, and there establishes Binah. The result is a triangular figure upon the glyph, and it is called the Triangle of the Three Supernals, or the First Trinity and is separated from the rest of the Sephiroth by the Abyss, which normal human conscious-ness cannot cross.*[118]

And so, we have traced the art and science of geometry from its origins in astronomy and "earth measurement", to its handling by Thales, Pythagoras, Euclid, the Islamic world of the Middle Ages and, finally, Decartes. Originally synonomous with Masonry[119], we must admit geometry's centrality to the Craft. For, when we consider the square's relationship to the compasses – the both of which may be operatively used in architecture as well as purely speculative geometry – a number of juxtapositions arise, inspiring our imaginations and meriting our deepest contemplation; such as the masculinity denoted by the square and the femininity of the circle described by the compasses; as well as the materiality expressed by the square vis-à-vis the spirituality of the infinite circle, having neither beginning nor end. We have considered the sympathetic resonance occurring between the microcosm and the

118   Fortune, *The Mystical Qabalah*, London: Society of Inner Light, 1935, p. 27

119   Preston (Oliver, commentary), *Illustrations of Masonry*, New York: Masonic Publishing and Manufacturing Co., 1867, p. 39

microcosm, which is to be gained by the ritualistic performance of compasses and straightedge constructions. We have also addressed the fundamental significance of the Platonic solids, as well as their association with the qabalistic *Etz Chaim*, via Kepler's cosmological model. It is fitting to close this section with a particularly pertinent passage from Preston...

> *The study of the liberal arts [that valuable branch of education, which tends so effectually to polish and adorn the mind] is earnestly recommended to your consideration; especially the science of Geometry, which is established as the basis of our Art. [Geometry, or Masonry, originally synonymous terms, is of a divine and moral nature, and enriched with the most useful knowledge...][120]*

MUSIC

> *Music teaches the art of forming concords, so as to compose delightful harmony, by a proportional arrangement of acute, grave, and mixed sounds. This art, by a series of experiments, is reduced to a science, with respect to tones and the intervals of sound only. It inquires into the nature of concords and discords, and enables us to find out the proportion between them by numbers.[121]*

In this section we will discuss the various attempts which have been made toward arriving at an all-encompassing definition of music – a more difficult task than one might initially surmise – as well as some of the philosophical problems arising from such an endeavor. We will address music's use in ceremony and ritual, thereby hinting at the very origin of this art and science. We will also investigate the mechanism by which music transmits emotional and conceptual data through cultural conditioning, melodic figuration, tonal coloration and the dynamics of rhythm. From there, we will trace the history and development of the art through the currents of philosophy and the Western Esoteric Tradition, beginning

120   Preston (Oliver, commentary), *Illustrations of Masonry*, New York: Masonic Publishing and Manufacturing Co., 1867, p. 39
121   Ibid., p. 48

with its first notation on a 3,500 year old cuneiform tablet in Babylonia; to music's Hermetic association with Thoth in ancient Egypt; its connection to the Orphic Mysteries; the codification of its ratios and proportions by Pythagoras; the architectural correspondences to melody, harmony and rhythm; music's uncharacteristically myopic handling by Plato and Aristotle; the evolution of music in the Roman Empire and during the medieval period; the resurgence of music's Neo-Orphic virtues in the work of Florentine Neoplatonist, Marsilio Ficino; the Renaissance-era *musica universalis* of Johannes Kepler, Robert Fludd and Athanasius Kircher; and finally, to music's handling among philosophers, Rosicrucians and Freemasons in the Modern Era.

It has been said that "architecture is to space what music is to time"[122]; a particularly astute observation when we consider that music has been defined as "the science or art of ordering tones or sounds in succession, in combination, and in temporal relationships to produce a composition having unity and continuity"[123]; a definition which accords with the analogous spatial considerations of architecture, particularly in the Vitruvian sense of the craft. Many of the terms in the above definition – "ordering", "succession", "temporal" and "continuity" – imply sequencing or, in some way, describe the arrangement of events in time; specifically, tonal elements organized such as to happen in a regular chronological sequence. As we have previously stated, the order of the subjects of the quadrivium may similarly be seen as detailing a sequential evolution, that of number: *arithmetic* studies pure number in abstract operations; *geometry*, number in multi-dimensional space; *music*, number in time; and *astronomy*, number in space-time. This sequence prompts us to again consider the *Tetraktys* of the Pythagoreans, with its ten dots arranged such as to represent a *point*, a *line*, a *superficies* and a *solid*, and to contemplate how this arrangement may relate to the sequence of the quadrivium. However, this temporal aspect of music, while certainly in keeping with the trajectory of our quadrivial study, is but one air in a symphony of elements comprising the collected oeuvre that is music. In order to collate these elements into a coherent picture, we must first define the terms of our inquiry and recognize some of the philosophical pitfalls which lay in wait at its boundaries.

The early-to-mid 20th century modernist composer, Edgard Varèse,

---

122   von Schelling, who attributed it to Goethe who, in turn, attributed it to Novalis, along with the saying: "architecture is frozen music"

123   Entry: "Music", *Webster's Collegiate Dictionary*, retrieved at: merriam-webster.com

once famously defined music as "organized sound".[124] While this is a sufficiently broad definition, certainly flexible enough to encompass all forms of musical expression – the obvious deficiency is that it does little to restrict sounds such as speech, birdsong and industrial noise that, while being organized, are not properly classifiable as being music.[125] Perhaps due this broadened categorical inclusivity, avant-garde idioms such as "sound art", "*musique concrète*", "soundscapes", "tape music", "sound collage" and "noise music" have recently become appreciable as music to some Western ears. In some cases, standard musical notation has been eschewed altogether in favor of "graphic scores" – such as those employed in the work of Krysztof Penderecki, Anthony Braxton, Brian Eno and John Zorn – wherein elements such as pitch and duration are communicated via shapes, colors and other extra-musical symbols. These new forms and media have introduced certain philosophical problems into the modern musical critique, similar to those raised in the art world by Marcel Duchamp's readymade sculpture, *Fountain* (1917) – which was, literally, a standard-issue porcelain urinal, submitted by the artist for an exhibition of the Society of Independent Artists in New York – which had not only caused an initial commotion but, consequently, set a challenging new precedent in the field.[126]

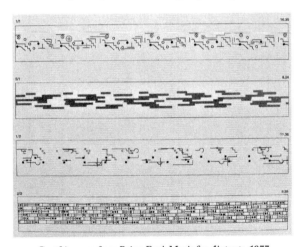

Graphic scores from Brian Eno's Music for Airports, 1977

124   Goldman, "Varèse: Ionisation; Density 21.5; Intégrales; Octandre; Hyperprism; Poème Electronique. Instrumentalists, cond. Robert Craft. Columbia MS 6146 (stereo)", *Musical Quarterly*, vol. 47, no. 1, 1961, pp. 133-34

125   Kania, "The Philosophy of Music", *Stanford Encyclopedia of Philosophy*, 2007, retrieved at: stanford.edu

126   Hicks, *Explaining Postmodernism: Skepticism and Socialism from Rousseau to Foucault*, Tempe, AZ: Scholargy Press, 2004, p. 196

One of the most striking musical statements, blurring the parameters of what may be classified as such, was made by American composer John Cage (1912-1992) who, in 1952, composed the infamous *4'33"*. The piece was composed such as to bracket off a dedicated period of time – precisely, four minutes and thirty-three seconds (or 273 seconds, which may be a cryptomusicological pun on -273°C being very close to absolute zero) – with the prescribed intention that all ambient noise, no matter how seemingly insignificant, was a part of the piece and was to be appreciated as *music*. At the four minute and thirty-four second mark, those same sounds were to be relieved of their duties as "tones" in the composition, and were once again free to dissolve into the anonymity of ambient noise. That the sounds during the four minute and thirty-three second interval are to be deemed music, in a mutual agreement between the composer and his audience, seems to inarguably place the work within the confines of music proper. Cage's *4'33"* may be performed by anyone, anywhere at any time, providing one has a stopwatch in order to delineate the length of the performance. Simply listen to the ambient noise during the interval of the piece as if it were music; one may consider this performance as a type of meditation or, rather, a contemplative exercise. The acclimation of a culture to find certain noises appreciable as music, while restricting other sounds, is a dynamic and malleable condition – a condition which is solely subject to the cultural evolution of the people. Again, Varèse addressed this issue by stating that "to stubbornly conditioned ears, anything new in music has always been called noise".[127]

> *The border between music and noise is always culturally defined—which implies that, even within a single society, this border does not always pass through the same place; in short, there is rarely a consensus [...] By all accounts there is no single and intercultural universal concept defining what music might be.*[128]

The musical tumult of the 20th century notwithstanding, the definition of music seems to have always been in flux. Since time immemorial, what certain cultures classify as music, others have perceived as

---

127   Varèse, as quoted in Chou Wen-chung, "The Liberation of Sound", *Perspectives of New Music*, vol. 5, no. 1, 1966, pp. 11-19

128   Nattiez, *Music and Discourse: Toward a Semiology of Music*, Princeton University Press, 1990, p. 48 and 55

undifferentiated and inseparable components of ritual and ceremony. This is evidenced by the fact that the languages of some cultures, such as that of many African and North American indigenous peoples – cultures with a discernible musical expression, from the Western perspective – contain no word which could be accurately translated as "music"; their understanding of the art being so holistically braided into broader cultural activities as to render the usage of the word pointless and devoid of context.[129] It would seem that music has only recently emerged as an independent activity, to be appreciated *for its own sake* in special settings such as concert halls or in the form of recordings played on personal devices. Yet even these settings may be seen as ritualistic, or perceived as being components of a greater social or cultural system of behaviors. For example, a couple participating in the activities of courtship may attend a musical performance in a concert hall and, as the concert itself is subordinate to the greater courtship ritual, the element of musical appreciation may be seen as being encapsulated by the broader category of reproductive behavior. Similarly, music played on the radio or other device may be appreciated less as a standalone experience of active listening than as an ambient backdrop for, say, love-making or dishwashing – activities which may then be said to relegate the experience of music to the status of passive accompaniment in a ritualized event. While this subordination of music may not *always* be the case, it is certainly *sometimes* the case, again blurring the boundaries of definition. There seems to be no discernible point at which the action of musical appreciation becomes enveloped and/or eclipsed by a broader pattern of ritual behavior. Is music inextricably bound to these patterns, in the ever-increasing convolution of their cycles and epicycles, at all times?

Bearing these defining and disqualifying elements in mind, the author advances the following definition for the reader's consideration: "Music is the deliberate human manipulation of audible media, rendered in a temporal sequence, which has been composed or improvised to be independently appreciated as such, or experienced as a component of a broader ritualistic structure". This definition seems expansive enough to catch all of the necessary elements, including forms which are dependent on broader social and cultural activities, while simultaneously precluding organized sounds produced in the absence of musical intention. The deficiency in this, or any definition with which the author is familiar, seems to be that it doesn't sufficiently address the communicative power of music, which is a quality so central to the art. This is the great mystery of music – we simply

---

129   Nettl, "The Art of Combining Tones: The Music Concept", *The Study of Ethnomusicology* (2nd ed.), University of Illinois Press, 2005, pp. 26-37

have not been able to accurately qualify or quantify exactly how moods, emotions, scenarios, and even fairly developed narratives are transmitted through this medium. Of course, we know that major keys are generally "happy" sounding, and minor keys register as sounding vaguely "sad", but this doesn't explain why they are perceived as such. Is it as simple as a flatted third? The prevailing theory is that we, as listeners, have been culturally conditioned by the context in which these harmonic colorations have been presented[130]; this theory seems to support music's station as being nested within broader social contexts. In the West, we are acclimated to the idea that Mendelssohn's "Wedding March" and "Happy Birthday", for example, are meant to inspire optimism, joy and celebration; whereas Chopin's "Funeral March" and the "Song of the Volga Boatmen" instantly evoke mourning, weariness and toil.[131] While cultural conditioning may account for some of music's hidden emotional and conceptual payload, would it be irrational to propose that the very set of aesthetics by which we interpret other domains may be useful in understanding this emotional encryption in sound? Evaluative criteria such as proportion, ratio and symmetry are primary concerns in the domain of architecture, for example, and after having established music's geometrically appreciable relationship to that art – *architecture is to space as music is to time* – we may be able to repurpose that critical methodology to decipher its analogue in the air pressure waves which communicate music to our ears. In the end, the very rules by which master architects, such as Vitruvius, judged the quality of the constructions of his day may be a useful key – a sort of Rosetta Stone – by which we may decode these enigmatic messages in sound.

In common Western parlance, music is popularly recognized as consisting of *songs* and *tunes*; songs being vocalized and lyrical, tunes being played and instrumental – most songs have a tune (i.e., a melody), and any tune may be set to lyrics. In its basic form, music may be said to consist of three major component parts: melody, harmony and rhythm. The melody is the linear expression of a sequence of tones, a tonal phrase, it is the part of a tune or song that you would whistle or hum, and is the part that is most often described as being "catchy". Harmony is the structure which supports the tune, providing tonal coloration and context while utilizing tension and resolution to propel the melody forward in time. Rhythm is the pulse of the piece, usually represented by a regular pattern, which sub-

130 Willimek, "Why do Minor Chords Sound Sad? The Theory of Musical Equilibration and the Emotions of Chords", *Journal of Psychology & Psychotherapy*, 2014, p. 139

131 Williamson, "Why do Songs in a Minor Key Sound Sad?", *The Science of Music Series*, 2013, retrieved at: nme.com

divides a period of time in intervals of duration and silence. The rhythm generally dictates the genre of the piece, as the application of rhythmic idioms – such as bossa nova, swing, calypso, mazurka and waltz – render the music identifiable as such.

This tripartite division of music may be seen as being akin to others that we have addressed in our study, such as the three philosophical principles of alchemy, with melody corresponding to *mercury* or spirit; harmony to *sulfur* or mind; and rhythm to *salt* or body. Taking these principles in their turn, we find that mercury, being fluvial, corresponds to the melodic element of music because both elements share a flowing linearity while partaking of the universal spirit of their respective domains. Sulfur, which represents the soul or psyche, corresponds to the complexity and supportive coloration of harmony, which provides context for the melody. Just as the psyche may said to be in service of the spirit of the organism, harmony is analogously in service of melody. The philosophical principle of salt represents form and physical organization, thereby corresponding to the earthiness of rhythm. For rhythm, upon which both melody and harmony depend, materializes the watery, mercurial nature of melody and the fiery, sulfuric nature of harmony, temporally rooting them in the earth; the physicality of dance being the most obvious example of this telluric correspondence.

As we have discussed throughout the present volume, the numbers three, seven and twelve inhabit particularly significant roles in the occult numerology of the Western Esoteric Tradition: three symbolizing the Trinity, the philosophical principles (the *tria prima*) and the tripartite nature of man; seven symbolizing the planets and their corresponding mythological archetypes; and twelve symbolizing the signs of the zodiac and their myriad cultural manifestations. As we shall see, the numbers three, seven and twelve are also fundamental in the context of music and its theoretical substratum. In Western music theory, a triad consists of three notes: a tonic, a third and a fifth, either played simultaneously or written on music manuscript paper to be played as such. A triad is built by "stacking" three alternating notes of a (usually diatonic) scale. Utilizing the *solfège* major scale (*do, re, mi, fa, sol, la, ti*), for example, a triad built upon the first degree (1) of the scale would consist of *do, mi* and *sol*, and would form a major triad (I); a triad built on the second degree (2) would consist of *re, fa* and *la*, and would form a minor triad (II); and so on.[132] The *diatonic* scale is *heptatonic*, meaning it consists of seven tones. In the *solfège* system, the major form of the scale consists of the seven familiar syllables:

132   Pen, *Introduction to Music*, New York: McGraw-Hill, 1992, p. 81

do, re, mi, fa, sol, la, ti (representing the scale degrees 1, 2, 3, 4, 5, 6 and 7, with no accidentals, of any theoretical key). The major heptatonic scale (step pattern: W-W-H-W-W-W-H) is the basis of Western music theory, as its notation, scalar and chordal, is based upon the scale's intervallic relationships.[133] There are a total of twelve tones in Western music; this is known as the *chromatic* scale. The chromatic scale consists of all the notes in the diatonic scale, but also its five possible accidentals (which, incidentally, form the standard *pentatonic* scale), totaling to twelve tones. The twelve notes in Western music are: C, C sharp (D flat), D, D sharp (E flat), E, F, F sharp (G flat), G, G sharp (A flat), A, A sharp (B flat) and B.

C major chord – three notes

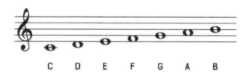

C diatonic, or major scale – seven notes

Chromatic scale – twelve notes

In the *Sepher Yetzirah* (Hebrew: ספר יצירה; meaning "Book of Formation"), a foundational qabalistic document from the 2nd century[134], we learn that "[...] from the Spirit [God]

133   Clough, "Aspects of Diatonic Sets", *Journal of Music Theory*, Vol. 23, 1979, pp. 45–61
134   Singer et al. (eds.), Entry: "Sepher Yetzirah", *The Jewish Encyclopedia*, New York: Funk & Wagnalls, 1901-1906

made Air and formed for speech twenty-two letters, three of which are mothers, Aleph, Mem, Shin, seven are double, Beth, Gimel, Daleth, Kaph, Peh, Resh, Thav, and twelve are single, Heh, Vav, Zain, Cheth, Teth, Yod, Lamed, Nun, Samech, Ayin, Tzaddi, Qoph, but the spirit is first among these."[135] The three mother letters have elemental correspondences (*aleph* to air, *mem* to water, *shin* to fire), the seven double letters have planetary correspondences (*beth* to Mercury, *gimel* to the Moon, *daleth* to Venus, *kaph* to Jupiter, *peh* to Mars, *resh* to the Sun, *tau* to Saturn), and the twelve single letters have zodiacal correspondences (*heh* to Aries, *vau* to Taurus, *zayin* to Gemini, *cheth* to Cancer, *teth* to Leo, *yod* to Virgo, *lamed* to Libra, *nun* to Scorpio, *samekh* to Sagittarius, *ayin* to Capricorn, *tzaddi* to Aquarius, *qoph* to Pisces). These may also be attributed to the three aforementioned foundations of Western music theory: the *triad*, which consists of three tones; the *heptatonic* (diatonic) scale, which consists of seven tones; and the *chromatic* scale, which consists of twelve tones. Just as a triad consists of three tones stacked vertically (the *tonic*, *third* and *fifth*), so too do the elements of water, air and fire vertically rarefy. The seven planets have been variously attributed to the seven tones of the diatonic scale with little uniformity, although we find an early source for their attribution in the work of Roman statesman and historian, Cassius Dio (185-235 CE), who wrote in his *Roman History*:

> *The custom, however, of referring the days to the seven stars called planets was instituted by the Egyptians, but is now found among all mankind, though its adoption has been comparatively recent; at any rate the ancient Greeks never understood it, so far as I am aware. But since it is now quite the fashion with mankind generally and even with the Romans themselves, I wish to write briefly of it, telling how and in what way it has been so arranged. I have heard two explanations, which are not difficult of comprehension, it is true, though they involve certain theories. For if you apply the so-called "principle of the tetrachord" (which is believed to constitute the basis of music) to these stars, by which the whole universe of heaven is divided into regular intervals, in the order in which each of them revolves, and beginning at the outer orbit assigned to Saturn, then omitting the next two name the lord of the fourth, and after this passing over two others reach*

---

135   Westcott (trans.), *Sepher Yetzirah*, Theosophical Publishing Society, 1893

the seventh, and you then go back and repeat the process with the orbits and their presiding divinities in this same manner, assigning them to the several days, you will find all the days to be in a kind of musical connection with the arrangement of the heavens. This is one of the explanations given; the other is as follows. If you begin at the first hour to count the hours of the day and of the night, assigning the first to Saturn, the next to Jupiter, the third to Mars, the fourth to the Sun, the fifth to Venus, the sixth to Mercury, and the seventh to the Moon, according to the order of the cycles which the Egyptians observe, and if you repeat the process, you will find that the first hour of the following day comes to the Sun. And if you carry on the operation throughout the next twenty-four hours in the same manner as with the others, you will dedicate the first hour of the third day to the Moon, and if you proceed similarly through the rest, each day will receive its appropriate god. This, then, is the tradition.[136]

The attribution of the twelve signs of the zodiac to the twelve chromatic tones of Western music is similarly varied from source to source, with no authority forming an inarguably seamless fit. It may be that, in time, the three horizontal paths (14, 19 and 27), the seven vertical paths (13, 16, 18, 21, 23, 25 and 32) and the twelve diagonal paths (11, 12, 15, 17, 20, 22, 24, 26, 28, 30, 29 and 31) on the *Etz Chaim* may somehow be made to accommodate the twelve tones in a contiguous and pleasing way but, as yet, this seems to be a largely subjective, though potentially rewarding endeavor (see Appendix B).

It is also worth noting, apropos the steps on the Winding Staircase, that the numbers three, five and seven, when taken together, also form a crucial component of modern Western harmony. Seventh chords are the next most logical harmonic extension after the triad; they consist of a third (3), a fifth (5) and a seventh (7) built upon a tonic (1). Seventh chords differ from triads in that they feature the addition of the seventh interval; this destabilizes the otherwise consonant triad, introducing a dissonance which provides a sense of motion toward resolution. Seventh chords are another excellent example of cultural acclimation in music, in that it wasn't until after the *bebop* era in jazz composition (1940's, U.S.A.) – which was initially

---

[136]   Cassius Dio, *Roman History*, Book XXXVII, sec. 18-19, Loeb Classical Library edition, 1914, retrieved at: uchicago.edu

met with great derision[137] – until this chord family was widely accepted. Today, seventh chords are commonly encountered in popular music, without upsetting the sensibilities of your average listener. Without getting too deep into the minutiæ of Western music theory, we will address how these criteria apply to the interpretation of musical compositions later in the present section – but, first, we will place the art and appreciation of music in a historical context, particularly as it pertains to the West's mythological, theological, philosophical and esoteric currents.

The earliest known empirical evidence of instrumental music-making was discovered in a 1995 archeological dig near Cerkno, Slovenia. The *Divje Babe* bone flute, or the "Neanderthal flute", to which it is sometimes referred, is a cave bear femur bone flute, featuring regularly-spaced keys, and is estimated to date from the Late Pleistocene Epoch, and to be at least 41,000 years old.[138] Other specimens of wind, percussion and stringed instruments have been found in China and the Indus Valley dating to as early as 7th and 8th millennia BCE. The earliest extant piece of notated music is the anonymous *Hurrian Hymn to Nikkal*, dating to approximately 1400 BCE.[139] This artifact features a primitive form of musical notation inscribed in cuneiform script on a clay tablet. The artifact includes lyrics dedicated to Nikkal, the Canaanite, and later Phoenician goddess of orchards or fruit, along with instructions for both vocal and *sammûm* (nine-stringed lyre) accompaniment.[140]

In ancient Egypt, the god Thoth was credited with the invention of both music and magic. Thoth (Ancient Egyptian: *ḏḥwtj*, or *Tahuti*, meaning "He is like the Ibis") was alternately depicted as a man with the head of an ibis, or as a baboon, in his more ancient lunar form. This zoomorphic conflation may have had something to do with the ancient Egyptian's viewing the beak of the ibis as being representative of the crescent moon.[141] His worship was centered at Hermopolis ("City of Hermes"), the name of which location betrays Thoth's association and eventual syncretization with the Greek god, Hermes, during Egypt's Ptolemaic

137   Porter, *Dizzy Atmosphere: The Challenge of Bebop*, 1999, pdf retrieved at: amherst.edu

138   Omerzel-Terlep, "Koščene piščali: pričetek slovenske, evropske in svetovne instrumentalne glasbene zgodovine (English: Bone flutes: Beginning of the history of the instrumental music in Slovenia, Europe, and world)", *Etnolog*, 2013, p. 292

139   Stolba, *The Development of Western Music: A History*, Brown & Benchmark Publishers, 1995, p. 2

140   West, "The Babylonian Musical Notation and the Hurrian Melodic Texts", *Music and Letters 75*, no. 2, 1994, pp. 161-79

141   Wilkinson, *The Complete Gods and Goddesses of Ancient Egypt*, Thames & Hudson, 2003, p. 217

Kingdom. Like Hermes and the Roman Mercury, Thoth was an ever-present persona in Egyptian mythology, having fulfilled some of the same archetypal roles which were to be later occupied and subsumed by Greek and Roman gods.[142] His being credited with the invention of the arts of magic, astrology and alchemy, puts Thoth squarely within the vicinity of the Hermetic Arts, which we have been discussing vis-à-vis the broader category of Western Esotericism. Beyond these arts, Thoth was also said to have invented music, geometry, mathematics, writing, surveying and botany. In a manner similar to that of the children of Lamech, who were said to have hidden the records of the civilizing arts inside two pillars of stone and of bronze[143], Thoth (in the form of the euhemerized Hermes Trismegistus) was said to have hidden the collected arts and sciences in such a way as to prevent them from being destroyed by the conflagrations of fire and the inundations of water.[144]

| Clio | Thalia | Erato | Euterpe | Polyhymnia | Calliope | Terpsichore | Urania | Melpomene |

The Nine Muses

The English word *music* comes from the Greek *mousikē* (*technē*), meaning "(art) of the Muses".[145] In classical Greek mythology, the Muses (Greek: Μοῦσαι) were the goddesses of creative inspiration, as the knowledge underlying all poetry, lyrics, music and the myths themselves was attributed to them. In English, the term is sometimes used in reference to one who inspires an artist, writer or musician. By most accounts, including those of Homer and Hesiod, the Muses are said to be nine in number: *Cleio, Euterpê, Thaleia, Melpomenê, Terpsichorê, Erato, Polymnia, Urania* and

142   Budge, *Gods of the Egyptians* Vol. 1, Dover Publications, 1969, p. 403

143   Anonymous, *Mason's Constitutions*, 1701, reprinted in Hughan's *Masonic Sketches and Reprints*, Masonic Publishing, 1871, pdf retrieved online, p. 174

144   Elshamy, "Our Roots in the Great Pyramid", *Ancient Egypt: The Primal Age of Divine Revelation*, 2019, pp. 180-182

145   Entry: "Music"; *Online Etymology Dictionary*, retrieved at: etymonline.com

Calliopê.[146] According to Hesiod's account, the Muses were the nine daughters of Zeus and Titan goddess *Mnemosyne* (the female personification of *memory*)[147], an association which may allude to the function of the mnemonic art in Epic poetry transmission, involving the modular structure of oral-formulaic composition, as we had discussed in the section on rhetoric in the preceding Chapter. The Muses were also periodically referred to as the *Pegasides*, a name stemming from a myth involving the winged horse, Pegasus, who, stamping his hooves into the ground at Helicon, caused four sacred springs to issue forth, from which the Muses were born.[148] Sometime during Hellenistic period (321-31 BCE), the nine Muses were each officially assigned their corresponding domain of the arts; history to Cleio, lyric poetry and flutes to Euterpê, pastoral poetry and comedy to Thaleia, tragedy to Melpomenê, dance to Terpsichorê, love poetry to Erato, sacred poetry to Polymnia, astronomy to Urania, and epic poetry to Calliopê. Due to the Muses mastery of metrical speech, and the orderliness it communicates, both Plato and the Pythagoreans viewed philosophy as a sub-category of *mousike*.[149] Hence we get an idea of the length of the ancient's reverence for the organizational principles underlying music; principles expressed in stone as well as sound; principles they saw as being naturally intrinsic to reality.

Perhaps no figure in classical mythology is more closely associated with the art of music than the Greek hero, Orpheus (Greek: Ὀρφεύς), whom Pindar had called "the father of songs".[150] This is made particularly apparent, even in the modern era, by the wealth of European concert music (a term employed, as opposed to the more common *classical music*, in order to differentiate it from the musical traditions of other cultures, such as Indian or Vietnamese classical music, which would normally be qualified as such) directly inspired by the Orphic cycle, such as Monteverdi's *L'Orfeo* (1607), Haydn's *L'anima del filosofo, ossia Orfeo ed Euridice* (1791), Liszt's *Orpheus* (1854), Stravinsky's *Orpheus* (1948), and many others. Not to mention the preponderance of theaters and concert halls, named in reference to Orpheus, in cities across the United States, such as the Orpheum Theaters in New York City, Boston, Memphis, San Francisco, Los Angeles and Phoenix, to name but a few; and also New Haven, Connecticut's Lyric Hall, which is in reference to his instrument, the lyre. Orpheus' influence

146   Diodorus Siculus, *The Library of History*, 4.7.1-2, 1st century BCE
147   Hesiod, *Theogony*, 52-53, 8-7th century BCE
148   Propertius, *Poems*, 1st century BCE, 3.1.19
149   Strabo, *Geographica*, 10.3.10, 1st century BCE
150   Pindar, *Pythian Odes*, 5th century BCE, 4.4.315

was not restricted to the domain of music, however, as allusions to his myth may be found in all manner of poetry, prose, theater and the cinema.

> *Orpheus with his lute made trees, And the mountain tops that freeze, Bow themselves, when he did sing; To his music, plants and flowers Ever sprung; as sun and showers There had made a lasting spring. Every thing that heard him play, Even the billows of the sea, Hung their heads, and then lay by. In sweet music is such art, Killing care and grief of heart Fall asleep, or hearing, die.[151]*

Though he is absent from the Homeric epics and Hesiod's *Theogony*, Orpheus is mentioned in a fragment as early as the 6th century BCE, wherein he is referred to as "Orpheus, famous of name" (Greek: *onomaklyton Orphēn*).[152] The son of the Muse, Calliopê, and the Thracian king Oeagrus, Orpheus acquired his lyre as a gift from the god, Apollo.[153] The instrument was said to have been invented by Hermes, which supports the musical transmission of Thoth, as Hermes had subsumed the role and attributes of his Egyptian predecessor. With this instrument, Orpheus was said to be able to charm both man and beast, using it, along with his singing, to mesmerize the Styxian ferryman, Charon, the three-headed dog, Cerebus, and even Hades himself, in order to gain entry to the underworld to retrieve his ill-fated bride, Eurydice. This rare chthonic access was beautifully recounted in Milton: "Or bid the soul of Orpheus sing Such notes as, warbled to the string, Drew iron tears down Pluto's cheek."[154] Not only was this unfortunate and tragic hero to lose Eurydice in the couple's attempted ascent, but he was soon to be torn to pieces by the Mænads of Dionysus who, in the ecstatic throes of a Bacchic orgy, took offense to his preferring the worship of his lyric patron, Apollo.[155] After his dismemberment and decapitation, Orpheus' head and lyre were thrown into the sea, whereby they floated to the island of Lesbos. An oracle was established on the island at which his decapitated head prophesized for some time, becoming very popular until, rivaling the Delphic oracle of Apollo, it was

---

151   Shakespeare, *Henry VIII*, 1623

152   Ibycus, *Fragments 17*, 6th century, cited in: Lee, *Virgil as Orpheus: A Study of the Georgics*, University of New York Press, Albany, 1996, p. 3

153   Hoopes & Evslin, *The Greek Gods*, Scholastic, 1995, p. 77

154   Milton, *Il Penseroso*, 1631, I.105

155   Wilson, *Encyclopedia of Ancient Greece*, Routledge, 2013, p. 702

silenced by the Sun god.[156] This is the first of many oracular heads which were to come, such as that of Odin, Bran the Blessed, the brazen heads said to be in the possession of Albertus Magnus, Catherine de Medici, William of Paris and Roger Bacon[157] and, of course, the mysterious Baphomet head (*capud LVIII M*) of the Knights Templar.[158] The Muses, in the manner of Isis retrieving the remains of Osiris, gathered up the scattered limbs of Orpheus, burying them. His lyre was placed in the celestial sphere, whereupon it is known as the constellation Lyra, by these nine sisters, one of whom being the hero's very mother, Calliopê.

Orpheus and his Lyre

156   Philostratus, *Life of Apollonius of Tyana*, 3rd century CE, IV.14

157   Bartlett, *King Solomon's Goat*, Everett Print, 1918, pp. 84-85

158   Lamb, "The Mystery of Baphomet", *Knight Templar Magazine*, August (pp. 23-29) and September (pp. 21-27), 2018

As early as the ancient Greek and into the Hellenistic period, a particular mythological cycle taken from the Orphic theogonies[159] was utilized as an allegorical narrative in a Mystery religion bearing the name *Orphism* (Greek: Ὀρφικά). The theogonies, as well as the *Orphic Hymns* (which we will discuss further in the next section), were ostensibly composed by Orpheus himself, in his poetic aspect. The myth, of which there were several variations, involved the birth, death and resurrection of Zagreus (Greek: Ζαγρεύς), the first metemphsychotic incarnation of Dionysus.[160] Zagreus-Dionysus is said to be the son of Zeus (sometimes said to be in the euhemeric form of a Cretan king, or in that of a serpent) and Persephone. Hera, the wife of Zeus, is naturally rather upset by this and enlists the help of the Titans in her infanticidal plan. The Titans use toys and mirrors to lure the young Zagreus into their clutches, after which they dismember (an event known as the *sparagmos*, which was apparently central to the corresponding initiatory rites), boil and consume him.[161] Athena, goddess of wisdom and daughter of Zeus, manages to save the victim's heart and informs her father who, in a fit of rage, reduces the guilty Titans to cinders by the use of his mighty lightning bolt.

In what may very possibly be a mytho-alchemical allegory, the ashes and soot of the incinerated Titans are collected and put aside; from these, the incorruptible soul of Zagreus is later to be extracted. Exploring this idea further, we note that Zagreus is a Dionysian avatar and, as such, is associated with wine. Wine (and its further distillation, brandy[162]) was known to have been used as a universal plant mercury (the "spirit" or alcohol) by medieval alchemists to leech out the "soul" (the essential oils, or the "sulfur" principle) of plant matter in *spagyric*, or Vegetable Kingdom alchemical operations.[163] From a Paracelsian alchemical perspective, one may interpret this myth as allegorizing the process by which the sulfur

---

159   The *Protogonos* and *Eudemian* theogonies, both 5th century BCE, and the *Rhapsodian* theogony, Hellenistic period

160   Gantz, *Early Greek Myth: A Guide to Literary and Artistic Sources*, Johns Hopkins University Press, 1996, p. 118

161   Diodorus Siculus, *The Library of History*, Vol. 2, Loeb Classic Library Edition, 1935, 3.62.6

162   The word *brandy* comes from the Dutch *brandewijn*, meaning "burnt wine" – which is in reference to the distillation process.

163   Quincy, *The American Medical Lexicon: On the Plan of Quincy's Lexicon Physico-medicum, with Many Retrenchments, Additions, and Improvements; Comprising an Explanation of the Etymology and Signification of the Terms Used in Anatomy, Physiology, Surgery, Materia Medica, Chemistry, and the Practice of Physic. Compiled from the Most Approved Authorities*, T & J Swords, 1811, Entry: "Alchemy"

(the Zagrean "psychic" principle) is to be extracted by being immersed in the universal plant mercury (the Dionysian "pnuematic" principle), and that the calcified salt (the Titanic "somatic" principle) is to be added to complete the completed Orphic tincture containing all three philosophical principles in their spagryrically perfected forms.

According to Orphic doctrine, the Zagrean matter represented the soul of man, which is to be separated from the Titanic ashes of material bondage.[164] At the dawn of the Common Era, we begin to encounter a very similar motif surfacing among the disparate cults of early Christianity, particularly in the cosmology of the Gnostic sects, who viewed the material nature of man to be the product of an evil creator deity, the *Demiourgos* (Greek: δημιουργός). This prison of matter, into which man's descent was allegorized by the Fall of Man[165], was only to be overcome by the attainment of *gnosis* – a personal communion with the Godhead resulting in liberation from the fetters of materiality and the return of his "divine spark" to the Monad, from whence it was issued – to be achieved by the practice of a rigid asceticism.[166]

At the conclusion of the Orphic theogonic cycle, Zagreus' limbs are collected and reassembled by Demeter (Attic: Δημήτηρ), goddess of the harvest and mother of Persephone; his resurrection occurring after the restoration of his heart.[167] Thereby, the initiate of the Orphic Mysteries was imparted with the knowledge of the immortality and incorruptibility of the human soul. In a manner very similar to the chthonic instructions given to the dead in the Egyptian *Book of the Dead*[168], the initiate was also prepared with certain "passes" by which he would appease the guardians of the underworld. In one such passage, the recently deceased, on their arrival to Hades, was to communicate the words: "I am a son of Earth and starry sky. I am parched with thirst and am dying; but quickly grant me cold water from the Lake of Memory to drink." For it was believed that, by drinking from the pool of *Mnemosyne* ("Memory"), as opposed to that of *Lethe* ("Forgetfulness"), the earthly life would be seamlessly joined with

---

164   Nilsson, "Early Orphism and Kindred Religious Movements", *The Harvard Theological Review*, Vol. 28, No. 3, 1935, pp. 181-230

165   Zandee, "Gnostic Ideas on the Fall and Salvation", *NVMEN: International Review for the History of Religions*, Vol. 11, Brill, 1964, pp. 13-74

166   Rudolph, *Gnosis: The Nature and History of Gnosticism*, A&C Black, 2001, p. 2

167   Diodorus Siculus, *The Library of History*, Vol. 2, Loeb Classic Library Edition, 1935, 3.62.6

168   Taylor (Ed.), "Journey through the Afterlife", *Ancient Egyptian Book of the Dead*, British Museum Press, London, 2010, pp. 135-137

the afterlife, thus perpetuating an unbroken cycle of metempsychosis.[169]

The similarities to Egyptian funerary rites and initiatory systems do not end there, however, as the general outline of the Zagrean mythos has long been compared to the Osirian cycle, wherein we encounter a similar sequence of events: the god's murder and dismemberment by his brother, Set; the disappearance of his remains; the discovery and restoration of his limbs by his sister-wife, Isis; and his subsequent resurrection.[170] The arc of this narrative – involving a murder and interment (*pastos*), disappearance (*aphanism*), search, discovery (*enuresis*) and eventual resurrection (*autopsy*) – is a ubiquitous theme found in the initiatory systems of many Mystery religions since time immemorial – Freemasonry included.

> *In the Ancient Mysteries, there was always a legend of the death or disappearance of some hero god, and the subsequent discovery of the body and its resurrection. The concealment of this body by those who had slain it, was called the aphanism [meaning] to conceal. As these Mysteries may be considered as a type of Masonry, as some suppose, and as, according to others, both the Mysteries and Masonry are derived from one common and ancient type [...]*[171]

---

169   Graf & Johnston, *Ritual Texts for the Afterlife: Orpheus and the Bacchic Gold Tablets*, Routledge, 2007, pp. 4-5

170   Rutherford (ed.), *Greco-Egyptian Interactions: Literature, Translation, and Culture, 500 BC-AD 300*, Oxford University Press, Feb 19, 2016, pp. 69-70

171   Entry: "Aphanism"; Mackey, *An Encyclopedia of Freemasonry and its Kindred Sciences*, Everts & Co., 1884

Death XIII, Tarot de Marseilles

A non-linear distillation of this body of Orphic and Osirian symbolism may be found depicted on the Death XIII Tarot card, particularly
as these symbols are arranged in the *Tarot de Marseilles*. Thereupon, we
find the skeletal form of Death personified, wielding the scythe in the
harvest of human life. In a rather gruesome display, decapitated heads and
dismembered limbs are shown strewn across the field, where they await
collection. This card is attributed to the zodiacal sign of Scorpio, which
hosted the autumnal equinox during the 2,160-year period known as the
Taurian precessional age – an age whose inauguration coincided with the
commencement of the Masonic *Anno Lucis* (4000 BCE). Annually, the
autumnal equinox introduces autumn and the harvest, and was thereby
held sacred to the agrotheological cults of both Demeter (grains) and Dionysus (grapes). Similarly, Osiris was associated with vegetation, regeneration and the annual inundation of the Nile, which dictated the agricultural
cycle of the region. The Death XIII card also corresponds to the Hebrew

letter *nun* (meaning: "fish"). In Egyptian cosmology, *Nun*, whose name means "primeval waters", is the oldest of the deities and was believed to be responsible for the annual inundation, with which the regeneration of the vegetative Osiris was associated.[172] These aquatic and piscine attributions resonate with the sign of Scorpio – a water sign – which leads us back to the Death XIII Tarot (see Appendix A).

In further support of the Orphic influence on Freemasonry, we may note that, of the many mythological allusions to be found in the symbolism, furniture, regalia and ritual corpus of the Masonic Lodge[173], none are more evocative of the poet-hero Orpheus than the Organist's jewel – the lyre. The emblem is quite fitting, for it is the role of the Lodge Organist to provide a musical accompaniment to the performance of ritual, and to alternately evoke a mood of solemnity or conviviality, as dictated by the phases of labor and refreshment. To this end, he employs both prescribed hymns and improvised interludes, thus acting as an Orphic emissary to the Lodge, on behalf of this eminent hero of myth and Mystery.

> *The Orphics were an ascetic sect; wine, to them, was only a symbol, as, later, in the Christian sacrament. The intoxication that they sought was that of "enthusiasm," of union with the god. They believed themselves, in this way, to acquire mystic knowledge not obtainable by ordinary means. This mystical element entered into Greek philosophy with Pythagoras, who was a reformer of Orphism as Orpheus was a reformer of the religion of Dionysus. From Pythagoras Orphic elements entered into the philosophy of Plato, and from Plato into most later philosophy that was in any degree religious.[174]*

We will presently turn our attention, again, to the Pythagoreans, who believed that music – as well as all other mysteries in the universe – could be interpreted by applying the "language" of number; for, as we have seen, Pythagoras and his followers were wont to communicate their teachings in mathematical and geometrical terms. The *monad* (1) through the *decad* (10), in addition to the aforementioned pentalpha, the 3:4:5 triangle and, of course, the holy *Tetraktys*, were invested with deep meaning,

---

172   Entry: "Nun", *Encyclopedia Britannica*, retrieved at: britannica.com

173   Lamb, *Myth, Magick & Masonry: Occult Perspectives in Freemasonry*, The Laudable Pursuit, 2018, Section III

174   Russel, *History of Western Philosophy*, George Allen and Unwin, 1947, p. 37

symbolically concealing a wealth of knowledge. To the Pythagoreans, each of these mystical figures had an exceedingly wide application, spanning the subjects of the quadrivium and beyond – from the abstract operations of *arithmetic*; the points, lines, surfaces and solids of *geometry*; the fundamental organizational principles of *music* and its physical manifestation, architecture; the celestial harmonies of *astronomy*; as well as a trove of metaphysical applications.

In the domain of music, Pythagoras is believed to have pioneered the art's quantitative study, specifically in terms of experimentation and the application of practical mathematics in an effort to establish a formal theory – truly connecting the art and science of music for the first time in recorded history.[175] The legendary impetus for Pythagoras' study of music and its intervallic relationships was said to have occurred one day as he was passing a blacksmith's workshop, whereupon he had heard four smiths hammering simultaneously and perceived alternating patterns of consonance and dissonance in the resultant tones. Hammers *A* and *B*, when struck together, produced a consonant interval, as did hammers *C* and *A*; however, when hammers *B* and *C* struck simultaneously, they produced a dissonant interval; hammers *D* and *A* seemed to be producing the same tone in different registers. Determined to find out the cause of this phenomenon, Pythagoras weighed the hammers, noting that hammer *A* was 12 pounds, *B* was 9 pounds, *C* was 8 pounds, and *D* was 6 pounds. Armed with this data, Pythagoras was able to deduce the following ratios: *A* and *D* = 2:1, *A* and *B* = 4:3, *A* and *C* = 3:2, *B* and *C* = 9:8, which is an *octave*, a *fourth*, a *fifth* and a *second*, respectively.[176]

175   Vamvacas, *The Founders of Western Thought – The Presocratics*, Springer Science & Business Media, 2009, p. 68

176   Nicomachus, *Enchiridion harmonices*, 2nd century CE, as cited in: Weiss, Piero & Taruskin (eds.), *Music in the Western World: A History in Documents*, 2nd ed., Thomson Schirmer, 1984, p. 3

Pythagoras in Gaffurius' Theorica musicae, 1492

Though this event likely never occurred (it is believed to be based on a Middle Eastern folk tale)[177], it is well established that Pythagoras and his followers measured and documented the length and harmonic subdivisions of the strings of a monochord (a single string instrument with an adjustable bridge) at various tensions, the pitch produced by striking identically shaped receptacles filled with varying amounts of water, and the relative distance between the keys (finger holes) of wind instruments of various lengths and diameters. It was by conducting experiments such as these that Pythagoras was said to have first quantified those most consonant of musical intervals: the *octave* (8:16 or 1:2, *diapason*), the *fifth* (4:6 or 2:3, *diapente*) and the *fourth* (9:12 or 3:4, *diatesseron*).[178]

> *[The Pythagoreans] saw that the [...] ratios of musical scales were expressible in numbers [and that] all things seemed to be modeled on numbers, and numbers seemed to be the first things*

177   Guthrie & Fideler, *The Pythagorean Sourcebook and Library: An Anthology of Ancient Writings which Relate to Pythagoras and Pythagorean Philosophy*, Red Wheel/Weiser, 1987, p.24

178   Bruhn, *The Musical Order of the World: Kepler, Hesse, Hindemith*, Pendragon Press, 2005, p. 66

in the whole of nature, they supposed the elements of number to be the elements of all things, and the whole heaven to be a musical scale and a number.[179]

The *Tetraktys* not only concealed the aforementioned microcosmological journey of a point (having position but no dimension) to a line (having length but no width or height), to a triangular surface (having length and width but no height), to its materialization in the tetrahedron (having length, width and height; the simplest Platonic solid), but was also thought to demonstrate the intervallic relationships in music. The consonant ratios – 1:2 (*octave*), 2:3 (*fifth*) and 3:4 (*fourth*) – use the first four integers, which are representative of the rows of the *Tetraktys*.[180] The Pythagoreans also noted that these integers, when added together, total to ten (1 + 2 + 3 + 4 = 10), the *decad*, which they considered the perfect number.

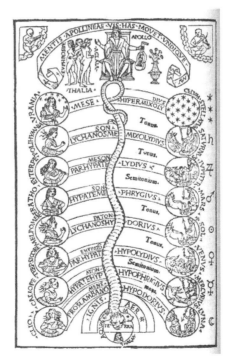

The Muses, modes and celestial spheres in Gafurius' Practica musicae, 1496

179   Aristotle, *Metaphysics*, Book A:5

180   Vamvacas, *The Founders of Western Thought – The Presocratics*, Springer Science & Business Media, 2009, p. 68

After having codified the musical ratios, and recognizing them as being constants in the phenomenal world, Pythagoras and his followers hypothesized that the planets must operate by a set of similar natural laws. In their estimation, the planets' orbits combined to produce pleasing intervals which resulted in a sort of planetary chord – an observation which has since been referred to as the Music of the Spheres.[181] Using the Pythagorean astronomical model, wherein the Sun and the seven classical planets all revolved around a central fire[182], they imagined that the closer planets produced a low tone or drone, whereas those more distant, ostensibly moving faster, produced a higher pitch.[183] This concept met with regular critique throughout the centuries; typical of these is that posed by Pliny the Elder (23-79 CE) in his *Natural History*, which was presented without offering an alternate for, or a refinement on, the Pythagorean model.

> *[…] occasionally Pythagoras draws on the theory of music, and designates the distance between the earth and the moon as a whole tone, between Mercury and Venus the same, between her and the sun a tone and a half, between the sun and Mars a tone, between Mars and Jupiter half a tone, between Jupiter and Saturn half a tone, between Saturn and the zodiac a tone and a half; the seven tones thus producing the so-called diapason, i.e. a universal harmony; in this Saturn moves in the Dorian mode, Jupiter in the Phrygian, and similarly with the other planets – a refinement more entertaining than convincing.[184]*

The concept was also denounced by Aristotle, on a slightly more material basis…

> *From all this it is clear that the theory that the movement of the stars produces a harmony, i.e. that the sounds they make are concordant, in spite of the grace and originality with which it has been stated, is nevertheless untrue. Some thinkers suppose*

181   Pliny the Elder, *Natural History*, pp. 277-278, II.xviii.xx

182   Entry: "Philolaus", *Stanford Encyclopedia of Philosophy*, retrieved at: plato.stanford. edu

183   Calter, *Pythagoras and the Music of the Spheres*, Dartmouth College, 1998, retrieved at: Dartmouth.edu

184   Pliny the Elder, *Natural History*, 1st century CE, II.xviii.xx

that the motion of bodies of that size must produce a noise, since on our earth the motion of bodies far inferior in size and in speed of movement has that effect. Also, when the sun and the moon, they say, and all the stars, so great in number and in size, are moving with so rapid a motion, how should they not produce a sound immensely great? Starting from this argument and from the observation that their speeds, as measured by their distances, are in the same ratios as musical concordances, they assert that the sound given forth by the circular movement of the stars is a harmony.[185]

The Pythagoreans anticipated the argument as to why these tones would be apparently inaudible, as it is raised – though left unresolved – in the above passage from Aristotle. They reasoned that, since the planets have been producing this perpetually droning celestial chord since well before the presence of mankind, humans would have no reference point for the sound and would not be able to distinguish it from what they have come to know as silence.[186] It is akin to asking one to perceive oxygen – which is colorless, odorless and tasteless – as being distinct from nitrogen, argon, carbon dioxide, methane and the other gases that make up the air we breathe. Furthermore, in modern times, we have learned that there actually *is* a discernible pattern in the distances of the planets from the Sun, with each planet being between 1.4 and 1.8 times farther from the Sun than the planet whose orbit is inscribed within its own. The contiguity of this sequence, beyond the orbit of Mars, is contingent on the "Main Asteroid Belt" being considered an orbiting body, as it is likely the remnants of the hypothetical planet, *Phaëton*.[187, 188] The obliterated sphere, Phaëton, was named in reference to the destruction of the son of Phoebus-Apollo, during his ill-fated ride on his father's solar chariot.

185   Aristotle, *On the Heavens*, Stock (trans.), 350 BCE, Book II, Part 9

186   Samuel, "The Music of the Spheres", *Sensory Studies*, retrieved at: sensorystudies.org

187   Jordan, "What is the Pattern to the Distances between each Planet and the Sun?", *Ask an Astronomer*, 2015, retrieved at: cornell.edu

188   McSween, *Meteorites and Their Parent Planets*, Cambridge: Cambridge University Press, 2004

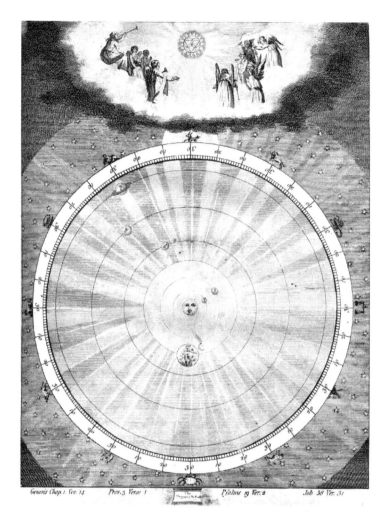

The Harmony of the Worlds, from Sibly's New and Complete Illustration of the Occult Sciences, 1805

At the present time, whether the ratios produced by the relative distances of the planets from one another yields an imperceptible tone, chord or celestial harmony of any kind is still an open debate. However, a recent discovery seems to raise the plausibility of this age-old Pythagorean hypothesis. A certain tone has been measured in the form of pressure waves 30,000 light years wide with an oscillation period of 10 million years (the deepest notes available to human perception have an oscillation period of about one-twentieth of a second). This tone is being emitted from a super-massive black hole in the Perseus galactic cluster, which is 250 million light years away. It is a B flat, fifty-seven octaves lower than middle C, making it the "lowest known note in the universe".[189]

The Pythagoreans were to apply the principles of vibration and of ratio as liberally as they had previously applied the abstract concept of number, in general. In time, vibrations permeated the universe, giving shape and form, not only to sounds produced by instruments and the celestial spheres, but to *everything*. On a metaphysical level, the entire contents of the universe vibrated and were governed by the underlying rules of harmony, which Pythagoras had discovered. This idea was to surface again, 2,500 years later, in a recent candidate for the sought-after unified field theory known as *string theory*. This theory attempts to reconcile quantum mechanics with Einstein's general theory of relativity and posits that sub-atomic particles are actually very small one-dimensional string-like units, whose vibrations correspond to properties such as mass and charge, as opposed to the conventional understanding of their being zero-dimensional point particles.[190]

Naturally, to the Pythagoreans, the idea that music and architecture are structurally and aesthetically bound by the essentially numerical rules of ratio, proportion and symmetry was obvious. They reasoned that the same ratios we find pleasing to the eye, must be pleasing to the ear, and vice-versa, thus aligning music and architecture as kindred arts. This analogy was most directly noted by the Italian Renaissance architect, Leone Battista Alberti (1404-1472 CE), who, adopting the Pythagorean stance on the matter, wrote in support of the architecture-as-frozen-music thesis.

The Rule of these Proportions is best gathered from those Things in which we find Nature herself to be most compleat and admirable; and indeed I am every day more and more convinced of the Truth of Pythagoras' Saying, that Nature is sure to act consistently, and with a constant Analogy in all her Operations: From whence I conclude that the same Numbers, by means of which the Agreement of Sounds affects our Ears with Delight, are the very same which please our Eyes and Mind. We shall therefore borrow all our Rules for the

189   Fabian, as cited in: Overbye, "Music of the Heavens turns out to Sound a lot like B Flat", *The New York Times*, 2003, retrieved at: nytimes.com

190   Entry: "String Theory", *Encyclopedia Britannica*, retrieved at: britannica.com

*Finishing our Proportions, from the Musicians, who are the
greatest Masters of this Sort of Numbers, and from those Things
wherein Nature shows herself most excellent and compleat.*[191]

In classical architecture, columns and their intercolumniations (the
spacing between the columns) were thought of as a rhythmic architectural
element – akin to a note and a rest, in modern musical notation – which
defined the meter, or pulse, of a structure. Various "speeds" were represented
in intercolumniation, such as the *pyncostyle*, representing the fastest beat,
due to its short, *staccato* intercolumniation; *systyle* and *eustyle* colonnades
being considered mid-tempo; *diastyle* and *areaostyle* having a slower, loping
rhythm, used to evoke a dignified, unhurried feel. Harmony was architecturally expressed by stacked arcades, galleries and *triforia*, which formed
vertical "chords". Just as in musical harmony, tensions could be created and
dissonances resolved by the intervallic relationships of these vertical lay-
ers. Melodic content, being linear, was architecturally rendered in flowing
curvature as well as in the straight and true horizontal tones of cornices
and moldings. Even the very earliest post and lintel constructions – in the
stark austerity of their right angles, horizontals and perpendiculars – may
be seen to contain the musical elements of harmony, melody and rhythm
in spatial form.[192]

Strangely, Plato's and Aristotle's contributions to music and its philosophy are negligible, as both were relatively silent on the subject. The
former, while believing that music had an influence on the soul of man,
and consequently on the *polis* peopled by him, viewed the art as being
strictly good or bad for society – "good" music served the state, while "bad"
music deteriorated it.[193] Having digested enough Pythagoreanism to see
music's analogues in astronomy and mathematics, Plato was primarily interested in the harmonic aspect of music and what of the dynamic between
consonance and dissonance might be repurposed in the social architecture
of the ideal city-state. Beyond his civic views on the subject, Plato was
vehemently opposed to innovation and experimentation in music – an odd
position for a philosopher to take – and said so, in no uncertain terms, in
his *Republic*: "For a change to a new type of music is something to beware

---

191   *Alberti, De re aedificatoria (English: Ten Books on Architecture), 1452*

192   Jencks, "Architecture Becomes Music", *The Architectural Review*, 2013, retrieved at:
architectural-review.com

193   Masselis, *Plato, or Music's Important Role in a Political Ideal*, 2017, retrieved at:
francemusique.com

of as a hazard of all our fortunes."[194] He considered instrumental music to be next to valueless and tolerated poetry when set to music, believing the *lógos* ("words") to be the only redeeming quality. Music was, to Plato, a shadowy representation of nature – not an expression of nature-herself – and was therefore looked upon with suspicion. Sadly, this was the great philosopher's view on the arts in general, and we are left to wonder what greatness, insight and innovation could have come about by the application of so penetrating a mind.

Music fares only slightly better in Aristotle, as the philosopher had elevated it – along with poetry, theater, painting and sculpture – to the status of *mimesis* ("imitation"). Aristotle judged the art to be almost as secondary and insignificant as it is considered in Plato's evaluation. In the mimetic arts, the intention of the creator is to be the primary locus of appreciation, while the medium itself – be it stone, pigment, odorants, air pressure waves, etc. – merely serves to give form to the artist's concept.[195] Interestingly, this idea was only to come to its complete conclusion in the *conceptual art* of the 1970's. Defined as "art for which the idea (or concept) behind the work is more important than the finished art object"[196], conceptual art, in its purest and final form, is only completely realized in the disintegration of the art object; that is to say, art produced in the absence of an object perceivable by the senses – a low state of mimesis, indeed. Obviously, we again encounter the long looming "shadow" of Plato's Theory of Forms here, in that the perfect abstract concept loses something of its spirit when communicated via the imperfect concrete simulacrum.

During the Roman Empire, music had culturally submerged once again, as it was largely viewed as being inseparable from its ritualistic and ceremonial contexts. The social structure of the Empire seemed to bleed into the role and production of music, in that works were commissioned in the same manner one would commission a construction project, such as the aqueducts. At its most independently appreciable, music was seen as a reflection of universal organizational principles, such as those found in astronomy and mathematics – this perspective reflecting an obvious Greek inheritance.[197] Apart from the introduction of several types of instruments – such as the Roman *tuba*, the *cornu*, the *tibia*, the *askaules*, and especially

---

194   Plato, *The Republic*, 375 BCE, Book IV, 424c

195   Halliwell, "Inside and Outside the Work of Art", *The Aesthetics of Mimesis: Ancient Texts and Modern Problems*, Princeton University Press, 2002, pp. 152-59

196   Art Terms: "Conceptual Art", Tate Gallery, London, retrieved at: tate.org.uk

197   Entry: "Roman Music", *The New Oxford History of Music*, vol.1: "Ancient and Oriental Music" (Scott), Oxford University Press

the *cithara* (from whence we derive the English "guitar")[198] – the Roman Empire contributed little to the art, which mirrors the critique leveled at the Empire in the domain of architecture; for, as we read in Oliver's commentaries to Preston's *Illustrations...*, it is "[...t]o the Greeks, and not to the Romans, we are indebted for what is great, judicious, and distinct, in architecture."[199]

Between the fall of the Western Roman Empire in the 5th century and the dawn of the Renaissance in the 15th century, music was largely under the custodianship of the Roman Catholic Church. Both liturgical and secular music flourished in the medieval era, however, in the form of early monophonic chant, polyphonic *organum*, liturgical drama, *Ars antiqua*, the music of the troubadours, *Ars nova* and *Ars subtilior*. The earliest known music produced by the Church was monophonic, meaning it consisted of an unaccompanied melodic line, and was set to regional liturgies in celebration of the Mass. In the 11th century, trained vocalists were sent throughout the Holy Roman Empire to teach the standardized vocal accompaniment for the Mass; this would eventually lead to the body of work known as Gregorian chant. Between the 10th and 12th centuries, contrapuntal vocal lines, initially utilizing the aforementioned intervals of perfect *fourths* (3:4), *fifths* (2:3) and *octaves* (1:2), were introduced, resulting in the *organum* styles. Most of this music was composed anonymously, though the German composer, mystic, oracle and polymath, Hildegard von Bingen (1098-1179 CE), certainly stands out during this period, due to her immense talent and productivity.[200] Also around this time, we see the development of liturgical dramas. These consisted of short plays, based on biblical narratives such as the Passion of Christ, or the Easter Pageant, and the Nativity, and included poetic embellishments on liturgical texts, sung to musical accompaniment. The *Ars antiqua* boasted an advanced harmonic approach, exemplified by the Parisian *organum*, and is marked by the first appearance of rhythmic notation in Western music. This movement is especially important to our study because it was directly influenced by gothic cathedral architecture, in terms of its analogous attention to proportion, ratio and texture. Occitan lyric poetry from the South of France was set to music between the 12th and 14th centuries resulting in the body of secular music associated with the troubadours. The main lyrical themes were

198 Marcuse, *Musical Instruments: A Comprehensive Dictionary*, The Norton Library, New York: W. W. Norton & Company, Inc, 1975

199 Preston (Oliver, commentary), *Illustrations of Masonry*, New York: Masonic Publishing and Manufacturing Co., 1867, p. 43

200 Bennett & Hollister, *Medieval Europe: A Short History*, New York: McGraw-Hill, 2001, p. 317

chivalry, ribaldry, courtly love and vulgar satires. The period of troubadour activity was concurrent with the Albigensian Crusade, during which Pope Innocent III launched a campaign to eliminate Catharism in Languedoc.[201] In the early 14th century, an extensive compilation of music and poetry known as the *Roman de Fauvel* was published, marking the beginning of the *Ars nova* movement. The style was characterized by lyrically secular, polyphonic compositions dealing primarily with the abuses of the Roman Catholic Church. Rounding out the medieval era, we encounter the rhythmic complexity of the largely secular *Ars subtilior*. The style is seen as being excessively manneristic, especially by modern scholars, due to its hyper-stylization, extreme syncopation and the inherent, self-consciousness cleverness in composition.[202] From the perspective of popular music in the modern era, one might view the sort of self-indulgent "progressive rock" produced by groups such as Yes, Rush and Kansas in the 1970's as a species of neo-*Ars subtilior*, in that compositions in this style are marked by abrupt and changes in both key and time signature, rather than a more naturalistic harmonic and rhythmic accompaniment in support of the melody, and often sound arbitrary, gratuitous or simply "overwritten".

Marsilio Ficino, engraving by de Boulonois, 1682

201   Lorde, *Music in the Middle Ages*, London: Greenwood Press, 2008

202   Günther, *The Motets of the Manuscripts Chantilly, Musée condé and Modena*, American Institute of Musicology, 1965

Toward the end of the 15th century, Marsilio Ficino (whom we will discuss in greater detail in the following section), one of the most influential figures of the early Italian Renaissance, reignited interest in Orphism by spearheading a return to what was known as the *prisci theologia* ("ancient theology")[203]. The aim of this movement, which proliferated among a small cadre of Florentine Neoplatonists, was to reform Roman Catholicism by fortifying it with aspects gleaned from newly translated documents from the recently fallen Byzantine Empire. These documents included the *Corpus Hermeticum*, the *Chaldean Oracles* and the *Orphic Hymns*, among other source material.[204] Ficino's work at this time was extremely syncretic and, through the cross-fertilization of these various currents of esoterica, he had developed a sort of neo-Orphic, astro-musical therapy. In addition to ritualized performances of the *Orphic Hymns*, which he set to music on a specially made restoration of an Orphic lyre, Ficino was a practitioner of what he termed "natural magic". He believed imbalances in the four temperaments, a proto-psychological system of personality types and their corresponding bodily fluids, could be rectified by the hymns and their astrological correspondences. [205]

The four temperaments: *sanguine, choleric, melancholic* and *phlegmatic*, as described by Hippocrates (460-370 BCE), were representative of the bodily fluids: blood, yellow bile, black bile and phlegm, respectively. These fluids were referred to as the *humors*. This idea was later refined by Galen (129-200 CE) in his *De temperamentis*, wherein he developed the first typology of temperament and collated the humors with the four Empedoclean elements (and their Aristotelian sensible qualities (hot/dry, hot/wet, cold/dry, cold/wet).[206] Though temperament theory has been rejected by modern medical science, the basic concepts have been echoed in the work of Immanuel Kant, Rudolf Steiner and Alfred Adler, wherein it persisted largely as a psychological metaphor.[207] Almost 200 years before Nicholas Culpeper's collation of the humors with astrological influences, Ficino was

203   Yates, *Giordano Bruno and the Hermetic Tradition*, University of Chicago, 1964, pp 14-18

204   Heiser, *Prisci Theologi and the Hermetic Reformation in the Fifteenth Century*, Repristination Press, 2011

205   Crossan, "Marsilio Ficino's Music Theory", *Oglethorpe Journal of Undergraduate Research*, Vol. 6, Issue 2, 2016, retrieved at: digitalcommons.kennesaw.edu

206   Merenda, "Toward a Four-Factor Theory of Temperament and/or Personality", *Journal of Personality Assessment* 51, 1987, pp. 367-374

207   Martindale & Martindale, "Metaphorical equivalence of elements and temperaments: Empirical studies of Bachelard's theory of imagination", *Journal of Personality and Social Psychology* 55 (5), 1988, p. 836

utilizing his musical arrangements of the *Orphic Hymns* in order to draw subtle planetary, stellar and zodiacal sympathies which he believed had an effect on such temperamental imbalances.[208] The ritualized singing and playing of the *Orphic Hymns* was central to Ficino's personal natural magic practice and to his work in the Florentine Platonic Academy – leading Ficino's prize student, Pico della Mirandola, to claim that "nothing is more effective in natural magic than the Hymns of Orpheus."[209]

> *This age, like a golden age, has brought back to light those liberal disciplines that were practically extinguished: grammar, poetry, oratory, painting, sculpture, architecture, music and the ancient singing of songs to the Orphic Lyre.*[210]

Ficino's skill on the lyre was apparently of such sublimity that he was called "Orpheus" by his friends. In testimonial to Ficino's handling of the instrument, his friend and Neoplatonic colleague, the scholar and poet Poliziano (1454-1494 CE), once remarked that "[Marsilio's] lyre [...] far more successful than the lyre of Thracian Orpheus, has brought back from the underworld what is, if I am not mistaken, the true Eurydice, that is Platonic wisdom with its most all-embracing understanding."[211] As the primary scholar charged with reconstructing the transmission of the *prisci theologia*, Ficino believed that Orpheus had learned the secrets of immortality from Hermes Trismegistus – and that both had been living human beings. He believed that Orpheus, in turn, transmitted them to Pythagoras. From Pythagoras, the Mysteries were communicated to Plato and, subsequently, to the Neoplatonic (Plotinus, Porphyry, et al.) and Neopythagorean (Apollonius of Tyana, Moderatus of Gades, et al.) philosophers of the first few centuries CE. The documents left behind by these eminent sages, gathered from the ashes of the medieval world and translated by Ficino on behalf of the court de' Medici, culminated in a new, Renaissance-era emergence of this font of wisdom.

---

208   Culpeper, *An Astrologo-Physical Discourse of the Human Virtues in the Body of Man*, 1653, and *Culpeper's Complete Herbal* (English Physician), London: Peter Cole, 1652; retrieved at: skyscript.co.uk

209   Pico della Mirandola, *Conclusiones XXXI*, no. 2, *Omnia quae extant opera*, Venice, 1557, p. 159

210   Ficino, "Letter to Paul Middelberg", as quoted in: Voss, *Orpheus redivivus: The Musical Magic of Marsilio Ficino*, Brill, 2002, retrieved at: faculty.umb.edu

211   Poliziano, as cited in: Voss, *Orpheus redivivus: The Musical Magic of Marsilio Ficino*, Brill, 2002, retrieved at: faculty.umb.edu

Just about 2,000 years after Pythagoras had quantified the musical ratios and extrapolated this data into a new conception of the cosmos, which he called the "Music of the Spheres", we finally begin to see the resurgence of his ancient *musica universalis* in the Renaissance with the work of Johannes Kepler. The idea of the *musica universalis*, which was anciently taught in the Pythagorean quadrivium[212], had fascinated Kepler, particularly after having failed to have fully resolved his case in the decidedly geometrical cosmology of his *Mysterium Cosmographicum* (1597).[213] In his *Harmonices Mundi* (1619; meaning "Harmony of the Worlds"), Kepler christianized many of the otherwise secular or paganistic ideas found in earlier notions of the *musica universalis*, positing a Christian Creator who expressed Himself in the universal terms of geometry, astronomy and, especially, music.

> *[…T]he magnificent edifice of the harmonic system of the musical scale […] as God, the Creator Himself, has expressed it in harmonizing the heavenly motions […] I grant you that no sounds are given forth, but I affirm […] that the movements of the planets are modulated according to harmonic proportions.[214]*

As in the *Cosmographicum*, his thesis involved proving the necessity of a creative intelligence in the arrangement of the planets, this time emphasizing a harmonic approach as opposed to his previous, largely geometrical interpretive schema. Books I and II essentially restate his ideas concerning the polyhedra and their relationship to the planetary orbits. In Book III of the work, Kepler lays out the general rules of the Western harmony of his time, as well as addressing advancements anciently introduced by the Pythagoreans, while Book IV deals with the theological underpinning of his cosmology. In Book V, Kepler details the relationship between the planetary orbits and their harmonic correlatives, in the astrophysical terminology of his day, along with a brief discussion of astrology. He ends the work with an exposition on how the interval between the orbital velocity at the *perihelion* (closest to the Sun) and the *aphelion* (furthest from the Sun) of each planet corresponds to a consonant musical interval, in addition

212 Voelkel, "The Music of the Heavens: Kepler's Harmonic Astronomy", *Physics Today*, 48(6), 1994, pp. 59-60

213 Caspar, *Kepler*, Dover Publications, 1993, pp. 60-65

214 Kepler, *Harmonices Mundi*, 1619

to other mathematical harmonies produced by these phenomena. Based on the intervals he documented in *Harmonices Mundi*, Kepler was able to organize the planets by "voice type", thus describing a celestial choir composed of one soprano (Mercury), two altos (Venus and Earth), one tenor (Mars) and two bass (Jupiter and Saturn).[215]

> *The heavenly bodies are nothing but a continuous song for several voices (perceived by the intellect, not by the ear); a music which [...] sets landmarks in the immeasurable flow of time. It is therefore, no longer surprising that man, in imitation of his creator, has at last discovered the art of figured song, which was unknown to the ancients. Man wanted to reproduce the continuity of cosmic time [...] to obtain a sample test of the delight of the Divine Creator in His works, and to partake of his joy by making music in the imitation of God.[216]*

Somewhat of a controversy arose during the peak of what has been called the "Rosicrucian Furore" (1618-1622)[217] due to an appendix in Kepler's *Harmonices* which was highly critical of a theory of cosmic harmony recently posited by one Robert Fludd (1574-1637 CE). In his *De Musica Mundana* (1618), Fludd, an English physician, qabalist and Rosicrucian apologist[218], expounded upon the virtues of a Neopythagorean, monochordal model of the universe, which he had partially developed in his earlier *Tomus Primus*[219] of 1617. In the corresponding diagram, illustrating the model, Fludd was to use the established Pythagorean divisions of the monochord – i.e., the octave (*diapason*), the fifth (*diapente*) and the fourth (*diatesseron*) – in the elemental stratification of the sublunary sphere, the planetary spheres and the supernal Heavens beyond the zodiacal firmament.[220] In the sublunary sphere, Fludd stratified the Empedoclean el-

215   Brackenridge, "Kepler, elliptical orbits, and celestial circularity: A study in the persistence of metaphysical commitment part II", *Annals of Science*, 39(3), 1982, p. 265

216   Kepler, *Harmonices Mundi*, 1619, Book V, Ch. 7, as quoted in Koestler (trans.), 1959

217   Yates, *The Rosicrucian Enlightenment*, Routledge, 1972, p. 126-138

218   Huffman, *Robert Fludd and the End of the Renaissance*, Routledge London & New York, 1988

219   The full title being: *Utriusque Cosmi, Maioris scilicet et Minoris, Metaphysica, Physica, Atque Technica Historia*

220   Gozza (ed.), *Number to Sound: The Musical Way to the Scientific Revolution*, Springer, 2013, p. 279

ements from densest to rarest: earth (*Terra*), water (*Aqua*), air (*Aer*) and fire (*Ignie*); the planetary spheres are presented in the geocentric, Ptolemaic order; and the angelic or celestial realm, beyond the firmament, is presented roughly as in the traditional Pseudo-Dionysian arrangement as found in the *Coelesti Hierarchia* (Greek: Περὶ τῆς Οὐρανίας Ἱεραρχίας; 5th century).[221]

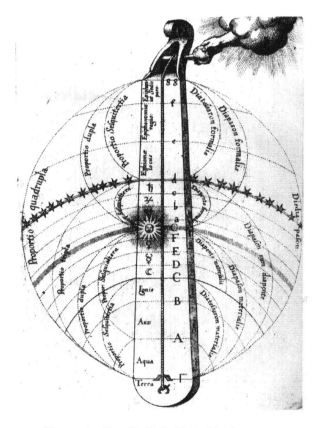

The monochord from Fludd's De Musica Mundana, 1618

Fludd's monochord is divided into two octaves, from G to G, apparently utilizing the diatonic step pattern of the key of C, due to the absence of accidentals. The tonic (Γ, the Greek *gamma*) is shown as representing the Earth, the first octave as representing the Sun (G), and the highest octave as representing Deity (gg), at the nut of the instrument, His hand

221   Hawkins, *Pythagoras, The Music of the Spheres, and the Wolf Interval*, 2012, pdf retrieved at: semanticscholar.org

is manipulating the tuning peg. The sublunary sphere is divided at the interval of a fourth (C); the sphere of the fixed stars is delineated at the interval of a fifth (d). This arrangement accords very nicely with the *Etz Chaim* of the qabalists, in that the "middle G", which may be said to intercede between the heavenly and earthly octaves, corresponds to the Sun, as does the *sephirah Tiphareth*, which intercedes between *Kether* ("Crown") and *Malkuth* ("Kingdom"). The centrality of the letter *G* in this model may also inspire the Freemason to reflect on its prominent placement in American Lodge rooms (see Appendix E). Finally, in Fludd's monochord, we are given planetary attributions to the seven tones of the major diatonic scale in the key of C; these, and their corresponding ecclesiastical modes[222], are as follows:

Tone	Planet	Mode
D	the Moon	Dorian
E	Mercury	Phrygian
F	Venus	Lydian
G	the Sun	Mixolydian
A	Mars	Aeolian
B	Jupiter	Locrian
C	Saturn	Ionian

Kepler, however, was very clear that he viewed Fludd's Hermeticism as a detriment to the study of celestial harmony.[223] He also took offense to Fludd's insistence on using the Ptolemaic planetary order, as opposed to acquiescing to the increasingly popular Copernican heliocentrism[224] which he championed. Fludd's qabalism, however, likely informed his notion of the planetary spheres, apropos the *Etz Chaim*'s geocentric ordering of the *sephiroth*. During the peak years of the Furore, Kepler and Fludd

---

222   The ecclesiastical modes, or church modes, are the modular scales produced by following the step pattern of the parent major scale from each scale degree to its octave.

223   Yates, *The Rosicrucian Enlightenment*, Routledge, 1972, p. 281

224   Copernicus, *De revolutionibus orbium coelestium*, 1543

were to compose a veritable series of replies to one another in what turned out to be a rather contentious affair. In the first of Fludd's replies, entitled *Veritatis Proscenium* (1621), he argued the merits of the Hermetic, or "chymical" approach, specifically the use of the microcosm-macrocosm analogy, in contrast to what he believed to be Kepler's astigmatic, strictly mathematical perspective on the Music of the Spheres.[225] Similarly, Fludd's *Monochordon Mundi Symphoniacum* (1622) was at once a polemic against Kepler's *Mathematice* (1622) and a defense against the initial criticism raised in the *Harmonices*.

Kepler, in turn, had accused Fludd of being a "theosophist" who relied more on Hermetic magic and Böehmian mysticism[226] than the scientific approach that was being taken by more and more natural philosophers in the transitionary period between the Renaissance and the Enlightenment. While his views as a physician were essentially Paracelsian, Fludd differed from the German alchemist in his conception of the *tria prima*; for Paracelsus, these consisted of salt, sulfur and mercury, whereas for Fludd – who was, as a hermeticist, probably under the influence of Ficino's translation of the *Poimandres*[227], in which a Genesis-like cosmogonical account is given – all things were composed of an admixture of the darkness of chaos, the divine light and the waters, or spirit, which contained the four Empedoclean elements in their Aristotelian qualities. Fludd's *tria prima*, though not strictly Paracelsian, was equally as Hermetic, and certainly informed his musical conception, as evidenced in his monochord. As an astronomer, Fludd certainly didn't maintain the same mathematical rigor as that of Kepler, this apparently being the basis of their dichotomous relationship, although both men availed themselves to the *prisci theologia* and the *philosophia perennis*, which they had inherited from the same ancient sources.

---

225   Huffman, *Robert Fludd and the End of the Renaissance*, Routledge, 1988, p. 57

226   Faivre, "Access to Western Esotericism", *SUNY Series in Western Esoteric Traditions*, Albany, NY: State University of New York Press, 1994, p. 19

227   "Poimandres to Hermes Trismegistus", *Corpus Hermeticum*, Book I, verse 4

Frontispiece to Kircher's Musurgia universalis, 1650

In keeping with something akin to the Ficinian lineage and transmission of the *prisca theologia*, Athanasius Kircher (1602-1680 CE) believed that Moses and Hermes Trismegistus were one and the same person, that their transmission followed roughly that as outlined by his Florentine predecessors, and that the Egyptian language was spoken by Adam and Eve. A German Jesuit scholar and polymath, Kircher was also the architect of the *Etz Chaim* in its modern, recognizable form (see Appendix B), having gleaned this information from the *Sepher Yetzirah*. His arrangement of the *sephiroth* has become the standard qabalistic model, generally accepted in all traditions of Western Occultism. More than this, Kircher is perhaps best known for his *Œdipus Ægyptiacus* (1652), in which he claimed to have deciphered hieroglyphics, thus establishing himself as the "founder of Egyptology".[228] While Kircher's translations of hieroglyphics were sometimes laughably erroneous, he did establish a link with the Coptic language, with which he was conversant. Hieroglyphs remained undeciphered until the 19th century with the work of Thomas Young and Jean-François Champollion, both of whom consulted Kircher's *Œdipus Ægyptiacus*. His work was also said to be instrumental in the interpreting of the Rosetta Stone.[229] In his *Musurgia universalis* (1650), Kircher agrees with the central tenets of the Pythagorean *musica universalis* – particularly that of the orbital ratios reflecting a "Music of the Spheres". The book contains plans for a water-powered organ, a *xylorgan* (keyed xylophone), and notations of birdsong, a full three centuries before Messiaen's *Réveil des oiseaux* (1953). Though he provided no design, Kircher discussed the analogy between tone and color and essentially described what would later become the "color organ".[230] Though he is not known to have actually constructed the instrument (thankfully), Kircher designed a *Katzenklavier* ("cat piano"). This hypothetical instrument consists of a number of cats, fixed in a line and organized by pitch, with their tails stretched beneath keys, causing them to yowl when struck.[231] He also outlined various acoustical innovations involving all manner of tubes and horns, such as those described in his *Phonurgia nova* (1673).

French mathematician, philosopher and Jesuit, Louis Bertrand Castel (1688-1757 CE) is best known for his *L'Optique des couleurs* (1740), which was largely a critique of Newton's spectral description of prismatic color – an argument that was later resumed by Goethe (1749-1832), and developed in his *Theory of Colours* (1810). Before his *L'Optique*, however, Castel had developed an instrument known as the ocular harpsichord (French: *Clavecin pour les yeux*, 1725), admittedly taking his cues from a passage from Kircher's aforementioned *Musurgia*. The instrument contained sixty pieces of colored glass, each obscured by a curtain which opened when a key was struck, allowing light to penetrate the glass, creating a neo-Kircherian "optical sound". Castel imagined *color music* to be a universal, paradisiacal

228   Woods, *How the Catholic Church Built Western Civilization*, Regnery Publishing, 2005, p. 109

229   MacDonnell, *Jesuit Geometers*, St Louis: Institute of Jesuit Sources, 1989, p. 12

230   Peel, "The Scale and the Spectrum: A History of Color Music", *Cabinet Magazine*, Issue 22, 2006

231   Kircher, *Musurgia universalis*, 1650, retrieved at: uiowa.edu

language, which even the deaf could enjoy.[232] This concept led to a rich tradition of "color organs", advanced by the visual artists such as Bainbridge Bishop, Alexander Wallace Rimington, Arnaldo Ginna and Vladimir Baranoff Rossiné in the 19th and 20th centuries.

Much in the manner of his eminent predecessors, Castel had a multidisciplinary, polymathic approach to his studies and prescribed to analogical thinking as a way of reconciling concepts in disparate fields.[233] This same sort of cognitive mechanism underlies Hermeticism, sympathetic magic and Freemasonry, in the sense that these analogous relationships are reflected in the Hermetic axiom "That which is below is like that which is above"[234], in the Frazerian *Laws of Similarity* and *Contagion*, and in the Masonic Temple allegory. Whereas analogical thinking is predicated on the transference of meaning from one source (the *analog*) to another (the *target*) in order to penetrate a remote or problematic concept[235], the Hermetic microcosm is understood to sympathetically resonate with its macrocosm in such a way as to provide occult access to the otherwise inaccessible, ultimately resulting in a condition of *gnosis* – the disintegration of the barrier between subject and object, who become one in the act of knowing. More specifically, the very concept of correspondence, which is so central to the Western Esoteric Tradition, is contingent on analogical thinking.[236]

Any study of music, particularly in a Masonic context, would be incomplete without making mention of Wolfgang Amadeus Mozart (1756-1791), one of the most influential composers of the classical era and also a Freemason. Due to the probability that many readers are already familiar with the man and his work, and that his life has been minutely discussed elsewhere, we will limit our study to a few of the more Masonically pertinent articles of interest. Mozart was made a Mason in Zur Wohltätigkeit Lodge at Vienna in 1784.[237] It appears that Mozart was affiliated with the rationalist faction within Austrian Masonry at that time, as opposed to with those of a more mystical and occult inclination. Among the Ma-

---

232   Peel, "The Scale and the Spectrum: A History of Color Music", *Cabinet Magazine*, Issue 22, 2006

233   Richard, *The Art of Making Rain and Fair Weather: The Life and World System of Louis-Bertrand Castel*, Baltimore, Maryland: Johns Hopkins University, 2015, p. 1

234   *Tabula Smaragdina* (*The Emerald Tablet*), 6-8th century, Newton (trans.) in "Keynes MS. 28", Cambridge University

235   Diengott, "Analogy as a Critical Term: A Survey and Some Comments", *Style*, vol. 19, no. 2, 1985, pp. 227-241

236   See also: David, "The Correspondence Theory of Truth", *Stanford Encyclopedia of Philosophy*, 2002, retrieved at: plato.stanford.edu

237   Solomon, *Mozart: A Life*, Harper Collins, 1995, p. 321

sonic rationalists was Mozart's friend Adam Weishaupt, founder of the Bavarian *Illuminati*, who were a humanistic, Enlightenment-focused society influenced by the work of French philosophers, Rousseau and Diderot.[238] In terms of his Masonic compositions, Mozart was certainly more interested in taking a more humanist approach – that of evoking feelings of brotherly love and affection – rather than delving into the cryptic astro-geometrical arcana associated with the *musica universalis*.[239] However, Mozart was known to have written certain symbolic elements, some of Masonic interest, into his compositions, such as the "three knocks" associated with Masonic initiation, which occurs in his opera, the *Magic Flute*.[240] The liberal use of the number three and certain aspects of the set design notwithstanding, the *Magic Flute* has far less to do with Freemasonry than one may be led to believe in consulting the annals of operatic criticism. The symbolism is certainly more in reference to Enlightenment-era thought than it is strictly Masonic, in nature.

Erik Satie, former Chapel Master of the Ordre de la Rose-Croix Catholique, du Temple et du Graal, 1909

In 1892, the French composer, pianist and Rosicrucian, Erik Satie (1866-1925), best known for his *Gymnopédies*, composed a piece for piano

238   Thomson, *The Masonic Thread in Mozart*, London: Lawrence and Wishart, 1977, p. 14

239   Ibid., p. 41

240   Ibid., p. 42

entitled *Trois sonneries de la Rose+Croix* while he was the official composer and Chapel Master of the *Ordre de la Rose-Croix Catholique, du Temple et du Graal*, led by Joséphin Péladan. In what was likely a deliberate nod to the pentalpha of the Pythagoreans, Satie had encrypted the golden ratio in the piece. In 1988, Alan Gillmor of Carleton University (Ontario, Canada) discovered that the ratios of the beat counts in the three movements were close enough to 1.61803... to preclude the possibility of it being accidental. Gillmor was able to corroborate his suspicion by conducting research which suggested that Satie and the composer Claude Debussy had discussed using the golden ratio in their work around the time of the *Sonnories'* composition.[241] Also, the fact that Satie preferred the term *phonometrician* ("one who measures sounds") to the terms *musician* or *composer* seems to support this idea, apropos his conscious adherence to the mathematical principles of ratio, proportion and symmetry which are, as we have seen, so central to the *musica universalis*.[242]

As long as there are sounds to be organized in pleasing, ritualized or otherwise evocative ways, there will be those who will make music of them. Moreover, there will be those who will peer behind the veil of mere entertainment and ambience in an attempt to discover the universal secrets encrypted in music's ratios and proportions. Over several millennia, many penetrating minds have tried to learn to speak in the language of music. This quest has resulted in a variety of music theories spanning many cultures. In the West, we have inherited a well-developed system resting on the triad, the heptatonic scale and the twelve chromatic tones. We have also discerned the elements of melody, harmony and rhythm as forming music's building blocks, and we are again reminded of the elemental correspondences to the three mother letters in Hebrew: *aleph* (air), *mem* (water) and *shin* (fire). *Aleph* represents the flowing melodious *air* (Italian: *aria*; French: *ayre*), which rides upon air pressure waves. *Mem*, like harmony, provides a fluvial buoyancy upon which the air may act and react in waves. *Shin* symbolizes the fiery, spirited rhythm – the *fuoco* – over which the harmony boils like water which, in turn, dissipates into the vaporous air. As we have seen in the work of so many great artists and philosophers, it is by the application of analogical thinking – such as we have employed by using the theory and vernacular of the Hermetic, qabalistic and alchemical philosophies – that we are able to gain occult insight into arts and sciences such as music.

---

241   Gillmor, *Erik Satie*, Twayne Publishers, 1988, pp. 86-88

242   Innes & Shevtsova, *The Cambridge Introduction to Theatre Directing*, Cambridge University Press, 2013, p. 151

ASTRONOMY

Astronomy is that art by which we are taught to read the won-
derful works of the Almighty Creator in those sacred pages,
the celestial hemisphere. Assisted by astronomy, we observe the
motions, measure the distances, comprehend the magnitudes,
and calculate the periods and eclipses, of the heavenly bodies.
By it we learn the use of the globes, the system of the world,
and the primary law of Nature. While we are employed in
the study of this science, we perceive unparalleled instances of
wisdom and goodness, and through the whole of creation trace
the glorious Author by his works.[243]

The reader may have observed that, throughout our study of the quadrivium thus far, each subject has occasioned that we address the subject of
astronomy in order to complete an idea or address the historical impetus
of such an idea. This has been necessary because, not only does astronomy
represent the culmination of the quadrivium, but it is the very bedrock
upon which these studies rest. *Astronomy is, at once, the capstone and the*
foundation of the quadrivium. The sexagesimal system – the very system by
which we measure our seconds, minutes, hours, days, months, years, precessional ages and Great Years – is based on astronomical observation[244]; ergo,
all arithmetical operations of a spatial or temporal nature are in reference
to data gleaned from astronomical observation. Angles and degrees, which
are so central to how we quantify and describe every shape and dimension
of geometry, are in reference to the 360° of the ecliptic, which is the apparent path of the Sun as viewed from the perspective of the Earth. Likewise, the Harmony of the Spheres, which we had amply discussed in the
preceding section, has been an ever-present philosophical problem, linking

243 Preston (Oliver, commentary), *Illustrations of Masonry*, New York: Masonic
Publishing and Manufacturing Co., 1867, p. 48
244 Lombardi, "Why is a minute divided into 60 seconds, an hour into 60
minutes, yet there are only 24 hours in a day?", *Scientific American*, 2007, retrieved at:
scientificamerican.com

the domains of both music and astronomy, for at least two and a half millennia. So symbolically entangled are music and astronomy that one may be reticent to question whether the seven tones of the diatonic scale and the twelve tones of the chromatic scale are but a microcosmic reflection of the seven visible planets and the twelve signs of the zodiac projected onto the collective unconscious of man. In fact, by way of analogical thinking and from the perspective of Hermetic philosophy, they are precisely that. In other words, we can say with certainty that the seven classical planets and the twelve signs of the zodiac, over the course of many millennia, have made a deeply symbolic, though largely unconscious impression on mankind's collective psyche. We may support this conclusion simply by referencing the myriad examples of planetary and zodiacal themes which have provided an allegorical foundation upon which mythological narratives are erected; as well as the presence of astrological symbolism common to art, the cinema, alchemical codices and dreams. The Western mind is absolutely saturated with concepts, images and schemata inherited from ancient cultures such as the Sumerians and the Egyptians, which they had gleaned some five millennia ago from their astronomical observations; and there is no question that this inheritance has colored mankind's creative output at a very base, perhaps subconscious level over such a protracted period.

In addressing the subject of astronomy, we will also be availing ourselves to that of astrology. We will be doing this for two reasons; first, because these arts and sciences were conflated to the point of being essentially indistinguishable, until their gradual separation during the Age of Reason (17th century)[245] and, second, because we are addressing astronomy specifically in the context of the greater Western Esoteric Tradition, of which astrology is a subcategory, thereby meriting our investigation from the Hermetic, Neoplatonic, qabalistic, mythological, magical and Masonic perspectives. With this orientation in mind, we recognize that, while astronomy and astrology both measure and chronicle the movement of celestial bodies, they are differentiated by astrology's accompanying Hermetic belief that these objects, cycles and events have an effect on the observer. Therefore, we must necessarily consider the dynamic between the macrocosm and the microcosm; the manipulation of cosmic sympathies; the astrological principles underlying astral or talismanic magic; horoscopes and stellar divination; terrestrial ritualism meant to mirror celestial events or phenomena; as well as other manifestations of the Hermetic and magical applications of astronomical data.

---

245   Pedersen, *Early Physics and Astronomy: A Historical Introduction* (Rev. ed.), Cambridge University Press, 1993, p. 214

Also pertinent to our study of astronomy are the adjacent anthropological subjects of *astrotheology* and *astromythology*. Taken literally, the word *astrotheology* means "the study of god in the stars" (*astron* "star", *theos* "god", *logia* "study") and is usually applied to the interpretation of theological narratives and symbolism from the perspective of astronomy or astrology. In other words, it recognizes celestial events and phenomena as being the underlying themes upon which certain religious allegories have been erected. For instance, the twelve disciples of Jesus Christ have been interpreted, in an astrotheological context, as the twelve signs of the zodiac through which the Sun moves.[246] Astromythology is essentially the secular version of the same literary mechanism. For instance, the twelve labors of Herakles could be interpreted as an astromythological allegory in which the Sun's apparent path through the twelve signs of the zodiac during one annual circuit is personified in the hero's corresponding labors – Herakles' slaying of the Cretan bull and the Nemean lion, for example, being the Sun's overcoming of the signs of Taurus and Leo, respectively.

We will begin with a cursory overview of the science of astronomy as a whole before developing a historical orientation, meanwhile highlighting those facets of astronomy and astrology which resonate with the Western Esoteric Tradition in general, and Freemasonry in particular. When dealing with proper astrological concerns, we will be primarily referring to the tropical system, as opposed to the sidereal system. Western astrology has predominantly employed the tropical system; ergo, it is practical that, for the present study, we remain consistent with the historical record, as well as with the corresponding theoretical substratum of the various systems within the scope of Western Esotericism. In the interest of clarity on this matter, we will take a moment to differentiate these two systems, as well as briefly address the phenomenon of axial precession, before we begin our historical synopsis of astronomy and astrology.

---

246 See: Stowe, *Stowe's Bible Astrology*, Health Research, 1907 and Murdock (Acharya S.), *The Christ Con: The Greatest Story Ever Sold*, Adventures Unlimited, 1999

Zodiac with 36 decanic arc segments, from Kircher's Œdipus Ægyptiacus, 1652

In both tropical and sidereal astrology, the 360° ecliptic, which is defined as "the imaginary plane containing the Earth's orbit around the sun"[247], is divided into twelve 30° arc segments. Each of these 30° arc segments is represented by one sign of the zodiac. In sidereal astrology, these signs are defined by the position of the fixed stars; whereas, in tropical astrology, they are defined by the event of the vernal (spring) equinox. In the equinoctially fixed arrangement of tropical astrology, the commencement of the zodiacal sign of Aries is concurrent with the vernal equinox. Consequently, the cardinal signs of the zodiac – Aries, Cancer, Libra and Capricorn – inhabit the vernal equinox, summer solstice, autumnal equinox and winter solstice, respectively. This is the current orientation of tropical astrology and is the basis for its corresponding body of symbolism. However, due to a recurring phenomenon called axial precession (the slow wobble of the Earth on its axis; also known as "the precession of the equinoxes")[248], the vernal equinox *actually* occurs in the zodiacal sign of Pisces – this has been the case for approximately the last 2,000 years. Therefore, in our interpretations, we must be mindful to distinguish tropical

247   "The Plane of the Ecliptic", *NASA*, 2008, retrieved at: nasa.gov
248   Stern, "Precession", *NASA*, 2016, retrieved at: nasa.gov

symbolism, which is cardinal (i.e., based on the cardinal signs inhabiting the equinoxes and solstices), from precessional symbolism, which is currently mutable (i.e., based on the mutable quadriplicity inhabiting the equinoxes and solstices).

Every seventy-two years, the equinoctial point *precedes* by about one degree on the ecliptic and, over the course of approximately 2,160 years, passes from the beginning of one 30° sign into the end of its predecessor. Over the course of approximately 25,920 years, the equinoctial point precedes all the way through the 360° of the ecliptic, returning to its theoretical starting point.[249] The last time the Earth had completed one 2,160-year precessional cycle was at the dawn of the common era when the vernal equinoctial point preceded from 1° Aries into 30° Pisces. At that time, we had passed into what is known as the Piscean Age – an age marked by ichthyic symbolism. Signaling the beginning of the Piscean Age, we encounter the first appearance of the ΙΧΘΥΣ (Greek, meaning "fish") acrostic and the *vesica piscis* (Latin, meaning "fish bladder") in Christian iconography. About two millennia earlier, the equinoctial point had preceded from 1° Taurus into 30° Aries, marking the beginning of the Arian Age – an age distinguished by ovine symbolism, such as the Golden Fleece and the *shofar* of Moses. Preceding that was a period known as the Taurian Age, which commenced in the vicinity of 4000 BCE. This age was marked by bovine symbolism such as the golden calf, the minotaur and the Egyptian Hathor.

Gaps in recorded human history before 4000 BCE prevent us from discerning much of the symbolism from earlier precessional ages. However, recent studies have been conducted on and around the Sphinx at Giza, having culminated in such potentially revolutionary theories as the water erosion hypothesis[250] and the Orion correlation theory[251]. Mainstream archeology dates the building of the Sphinx to approximately 2500 BCE, during the reign of the pharaoh Khafre, whom the Sphinx's head is said to represent; however, the new studies have cast doubt on the accepted date. Geologist Robert Schoch and archeoastronomer Robert Bauval have introduced data that could place the Sphinx back to about 10,500 BCE, if

249   Hohenkerk, Yallop, Smith & Sinclair, "Celestial Reference Systems", *Explanatory Supplement to the Astronomical Almanac*, Sausalito: University Science Books, p. 99

250   Schwaller de Lubicz, *Sacred Science: The King of Pharaonic Theocracy*, New York: Inner Traditions International, 1982 – originally entitled: *Le Roi de la Théocratie Pharaonique*, Paris: Flammarion, 1961; and later: Schoch, "Redating the Great Sphinx of Giza", *Circular Times*, 1992, retrieved at: robertschoch.net

251   Bauval & Gilbert, *The Orion Mystery: Unlocking The Secrets of the Pyramids*, London: Heinemann, 1984

not earlier, which would be well within the confines of the Leonine Age – the 2,160 period during which the vernal equinox occurred in the sign of Leo. It has also been suggested that the head of the Sphinx was re-carved during Khafre's reign in the 4th Dynasty and that it had previously been the head of a lion.[252]

As it pertains to the Western Esoteric Tradition, the Taurian Age seems to carry a special significance, as symbolism specific to this period may be discerned in Freemasonry, Rosicrucianism and several occult and magical societies, such as the Hermetic Order of the Golden Dawn. From approximately 4000 to 2000 BCE, the equinoctial and solstitial points were inhabited by the fixed quadriplicity of the zodiac: Taurus, Leo, Scorpio (anciently conflated with the eagle, *Aquila*)[253] and Aquarius. This zodiacal quartet has appeared in theological, magical, mythological and Masonic symbolism for the last 6,000 years, beginning with the *Lamassu* of the ancient Sumerian astronomers. The *Lamassu* were hybridized, zoomorphic sphinxes, commonly consisting of the hooves and tail of a bull, the body of a lion, the wings of an eagle and the head of a man.[254] In the Old Testament, we find the same figures depicted as the *Tetramorph*, or the Four Living Creatures (Hebrew: חַיּוֹת, *hayyoth*) of Ezekiel's Vision.

> *Also out of the midst thereof came the likeness of four living creatures. And this was their appearance; they had the likeness of a man. And every one had four faces, and every one had four wings. And their feet were straight feet; and the sole of their feet was like the sole of a calf's foot: and they sparkled like the colour of burnished brass. And they had the hands of a man under their wings on their four sides; and they four had their faces and their wings. Their wings were joined one to another; they turned not when they went; they went every one straight forward. As for the likeness of their faces, they four had the face of a man, and the face of a lion, on the right side: and they four had the face of an ox on the left side; they four also had the face of an eagle.*[255]

---

252   West, "The Age of the Sphinx", *Timewatch*, BBC Two, 1994

253   Lewis, *The Astrology Book: The Encyclopedia of Heavenly Influences* (2nd ed.), Detroit: Visible Ink Press, 2003, pp. 601-608

254   Kriwaczek, *Babylon: Mesopotamia and the Birth of Civilization*, St. Martin's Griffin, 2012, p. 37

255   *The Holy Bible*, KJV, Ezekiel 1:5-10

The Vision of the Prophet Ezekiel, von Carolsfeld, ca. 19th century

In Christian iconography, the Tetramorph is associated with the four Evangelists: Matthew, Mark, Luke and John. However, they are described in the Book of Revelation in such a way as to barely veil their zodiacal origin.

And round about the throne were four and twenty seats: and upon the seats I saw four and twenty elders sitting, clothed in white raiment; and they had on their heads crowns of gold. And out of the throne proceeded lightnings and thunderings and voices: and there were seven lamps of fire burning before the throne, which are the seven Spirits of God. And before the throne there was a sea of glass like unto crystal: and in the midst of the throne, and round about the throne, were four beasts full of eyes before and behind. And the first beast was like a lion, and the second beast like a calf, and the third beast had a face as a man, and the fourth beast was like a flying eagle.[256]

---

[256] *The Holy Bible*, KJV, Revelation 4:4-7

An astrological interpretation of the above passage yields a model in which we find the four and twenty elders representing the rulers of the twenty-four planetary hours (see Appendix C) experienced in the sublunary sphere, due to the Earth's diurnal/nocturnal rotation; the lamps of fire before the throne representing the seven classical planets; the four beasts representing the fixed signs of the zodiac; and the sea of glass representing the firmament, or the crystalline sphere of the fixed stars, around which the constellations of Taurus, Leo, Scorpio and Aquarius are distributed in cruciform. In this context, the revelatory initiation occurs by the conferral of the planetary grades, whereby the initiate gains access to the *ogdoad*, or the eighth sphere, i.e., the firmament, which lies beyond the sphere of Saturn. Qabalistically, this is the ascent from the earthly *sephirah Malkuth*, through the planetary *sephiroth* of *Yesod* (the Moon), *Hod* (Mercury), *Netzach* (Venus), *Tiphareth* (the Sun), *Geburah* (Mars), *Chesed* (Jupiter), *Binah* (Saturn) and, finally, to *Chokmah* (the sphere of the fixed stars) wherein we encounter the Tetramorph (the fixed signs of the zodiac). Hermetically, we find this very same initiatic ascent in the *Corpus Hermeticum*, whereupon the initiate sheds the particular vice associated with each planetary sphere.

> *Thus a man starts to rise up through the harmony of the cosmos. To the first plane he surrenders the activity of growth and diminution [the Moon]; to the second the means of evil, trickery now being inactive [Mercury]; to the third covetous deceit, now inactive [Venus]; and to the fourth the eminence pertaining to a ruler, being now without avarice [the Sun]; to the fifth impious daring and reckless audacity [Mars]; and to the sixth evil impulses for wealth, all these now being inactive [Jupiter]; and to the seventh plane the falsehood which waits in ambush [Saturn]. Then, stripped of the activities of the cosmos, he enters the substance of the eighth plane [the zodiac].[257]*

The Tetramorph, consisting of the bull, lion, eagle and man, also appears frequently in the symbolism of Freemasonry. The fixed signs of the zodiac are depicted on the banner of Royal Arch, or Capitular Masonry. On the banner, each creature inhabits a square on the heraldic crest, which

257   Salaman et al. (trans.), "Poimandres to Hermes Trismegistus", *The Corpus Hermeticum*, I:25-26. Bracketed commentary is mine. JPL

is flanked by two winged *androsphinxes* representing the solstices. The ox, lion, eagle and man are also depicted on the four veils of the Royal Arch Tabernacle, wherein they are said to represent the four Judaic tribes of Ephraim, Judah, Dan and Reuben, respectively. In the Masonic invitational society, the *Societas Rosicruciana in Civitatibus Foederatis*, the Four Ancients are not only attributed to the four fixed zodiacal signs but also the elements to which they correspond (Taurus/earth, Leo/fire, Scorpio/ water, Aquarius/air). The zodiacal Ancients present the *Zelator* with the elements by which he is tried. Perhaps the most blatant example of Freemasonry's link to the symbolism of the Taurian Age is the *Anno Lucis*. The *Anno Lucis* (Latin, meaning "Year of Light") is a dating system, peculiar to Freemasonry, which is used on cornerstones and in documentation; it adds 4,000 years to the Common Era (6000 BP) and symbolically points to the *Fiat Lux* (Hebrew: יְהִי אוֹר; *The Holy Bible*, KJV, Genesis 1:3). When the *Anno Lucis* is calculated in terms of axial precession, we find that it roughly corresponds to the dawn of the Taurian Age. Just as archeoastronomical motifs in ancient architecture direct the interpreter to a certain epoch, so too does the Masonic *Anno Lucis* direct us to the Taurian Age. The cultivation of this precessional reference point is essential if one wishes to grasp the full scope of Freemasonry's astrological import.[258]

An understanding of both tropical astrology and the phenomenon of axial precession, and how these have culturally shaped man's symbolic language, is central to temporally orienting oneself in order to accurately interpret the esoteric import of all manner of theological, mythological and Masonic symbol sets. This understanding – particularly in the domain of *archeoastronomy*[259] – is also crucial to dating ancient monuments and architecture, as well as to deciphering their symbolism. The ancients tended to use precessionally-specific symbolism in order to refer us to a particular temporal vantage point and, if perceived in the absence of that context, the modern interpreter runs the risk of misunderstanding the intended import of a symbol, thereby lowering its communicative efficacy. A modern example of this ancient practice may be found at the Hoover Dam in Nevada, USA.[260]

In the 1930's, sculptor Oskar J.W. Hansen was commissioned to design and erect a monument commemorating the dedication of the dam.

258 Lamb, *Myth, Magick & Masonry: Occult Perspectives in Freemasonry*, The Laudable Pursuit, 2018, Section II

259 "What is Archeoastronomy?", *The Center for Archeoastronomy*, 2002, retrieved at: umd.edu

260 "The Story of the Hoover Dam", Essays: Artwork, *Bureau of Reclamation*, 2015, retrieved at: usbr.gov

Regarding the scope of the project, Hansen had compared the dam to the Egyptian pyramids – which have, thus far, left ensuing generations with more questions than answers. In light of this inconvenience, the sculptor elected to design a monument that would reflect the characteristics of the men who built it as well as the epoch of its construction. The monument consists of one 142-foot flagpole, flanked by two, 30-foot bronze, winged statues, not unlike the *cherubim* on the mercy seat of the Ark of the Covenant. The base is of black diorite, around which is a terrazzo floor inlaid with a celestial map. This star chart, due to the relative position of celestial bodies on the precessional ecliptic, preserves the very date on which the Hoover Dam was dedicated by President Franklin D. Roosevelt.

> *The designer of the star chart [...] placed the bodies of our solar system in the terrazzo, correct to the minutest fraction of an inch in scale of the design. One versed in the abstruse mathematics of astronomy may calculate the precession of the Pole Star for the next 14,000 years by studying the design of the star chart. Conversely, future generations may look upon this monument and determine – if no other means are available – the exact date on which engineers and craftsmen of our generation completed this giant structure.*[261]

In the design of this monument – and many others, far more ancient, across the globe – the truly universal language of astronomy has been employed. The relatively new field of archeoastronomy utilizes an interdisciplinary approach, involving archeology, anthropology and astronomy, in order to investigate ancient sites with a penetrative power that would be impossible from merely one academic perspective.[262] For it is exactly this sort of approach that would enable those in the future to decipher the code of Hansen's monument. If they were to collate the existing information from a interdisciplinary perspective, the data would coalesce into a coherent picture, thus giving the future observer an idea of who made this, and when. Perhaps data such as this exists at megalithic sites, awaiting the interdisciplinary interpreter, as we speak. Through the application of

---

261   *The Boulder Canyon Project*, United States Bureau of Reclamation, 1948, pp. 115-116

262   Aveni, "Frombork 1992: Where Worlds and Disciplines Collide", *Archaeoastronomy: Supplement to the Journal for the History of Astronomy*, 26 (20), 1995, S74-S79

several interpretive vantage points – as opposed to the comparatively limited scope of one single perspective – one develops a more nuanced and holistic picture of objects, events and phenomena. Hence the emphasis on civilization's polymaths, and the simultaneous application of several interpretive lenses, throughout the present study.

Alcyone, the brightest Pleiadian star, from Hansen's monument, Hoover Dam, 1935

Astronomy (from the Greek: ἀστρονομία, meaning "star arranging")[263] is the study of celestial objects and their movement in space. In modern times, astronomy and astrophysics have become increasingly conflated and the two terms are often used interchangeably.[264] Astronomy has been specifically defined as "[…] the study of the sun, moon, stars, planets, comets, gas, galaxies, gas, dust and other non-Earthly bodies and

263   Entry: "Astronomy", Online *Etymological Dictionary*, retrieved at: etymonline.com
264   Unsöld & Baschek, *The New Cosmos: An Introduction to Astronomy and Astrophysics*, Brewer (trans.), New York: Springer, 2001, pp. 6-9

phenomena."[265] Whereas astrophysics, as the name implies, is primarily concerned with the application the laws and theories of physics to the interpretation of observational data.

Just as Freemasonry is divided into two denominations, so is the science of astronomy divided into the *observational* and *theoretical* denominations. Observational astronomy is concerned with the gathering of data via observation and its use in general understanding, description and prediction[266]; whereas theoretical astronomy, which is more what is meant by the term *astrophysics*, focuses on the development of simulations and the analysis of systems.[267] The quantitative and qualitative tools of theoretical astronomy are mathematics, physics and chemistry, as these domains are essential in the collecting and processing of data gleaned from observation. Observational data is gathered in a variety of ways, such as by telescopes, radio waves, infrared and ultraviolet radiation, and gamma rays. These denominations are complimentary, however, in that the theorists use the data collected by the observers in order to create simulations and analytical models; in turn, these models are further confirmed or contradicted by observation.[268] The synergetic relationship which exists between these two denominations is beneficial, particularly in a field wherein the scientist is only rarely able to observe the completion of an astronomical cycle in the course of one human lifetime, as these cycles may include such phenomena as a protracted orbital period[269] or the "birth" or "death" of a celestial body.

Beyond these denominations, astronomy is further divided into branches, or specialized fields of study; these include: *planetary, stellar, solar* and *galactic astronomy*, *astrometry* and *cosmology*. Planetary astronomy studies the planets in our solar system as well as hypothesizing about hypothetical planets around other stars. Its primary concerns are the growth, evolution and death of such bodies.[270] Stellar astronomy studies the birth, development and death of stars, including nebulae, supernovas and black holes. Particularly attention is paid to the chemical diversity produced by

265   Redd, "What is Astronomy? Definition and History", *Space*, 2017, retrieved at: space.com

266   "Methods of Observational Astronomy", *Introduction to Astronomy*, University of San Diego, 2002, retrieved at: ucsd.edu

267   "Astronomy", *Swinburne Cosmos*, retrieved at: swin.edu.au

268   Redd, "What is Astronomy? Definition and History", *Space*, 2017, retrieved at: space.com

269   The orbital period of Neptune, for example, is 164.8 years, which is well beyond the lifespan of any single human being.

270   "Planetary Astronomy", *National Academies Press*, retrieved at: nap.edu

stellar phenomena, which makes life as we know it possible.[271] Solar astronomy, also known as solar physics, offers a unique opportunity in observational stellar astronomy due to the proximity of this star.[272] This is considered an ancient branch of astronomy, as solar eclipses have been documented in records dating from at least 1300 BCE.[273] Galactic astronomy is the study of the Milky Way galaxy, exclusively, while extragalactic astronomy studies those outside of it. Patterns of distribution, composition and the study of chemical emissions are the focus of galactic astronomy.[274] Along with solar astronomy, astrometry is one of the ancient branches of astronomy. It studies the measurement, relative positions and trajectories of celestial bodies.[275] Cosmology is the study of the universe as a complete system; from its birth and evolution, to its death. Because of the elusive nature of the study, cosmology is largely abstract and theoretical. The subcategories of *cosmogony* (theories regarding the birth or origin of the universe) and *eschatology* (theories regarding death, the end of the world or man's destiny) are also major concerns in philosophy, theology and mythology, where their accompanying mysteries often account for much of the field's esoteric content. While approaching from their own peculiar philosophical perspective, the myriad creation myths and apocalypses found in world mythology and religion attempt to answer the primary cosmogonical and eschatological questions. These most nagging of enigmas have been the subject of both idealistic and materialistic inquiry for millennia. However, as was somewhat frustratingly observed by Edward Bulwer-Lytton (1803-1873), English Rosicrucian interlocutor[276] and author of *Zanoni*…

> [...t]here is no Œdipus to solve the enigma of life. We are – whence came we? We are not, – whither do we go? All things in our existence have their object; existence has none.[277]

271   "Stellar and Planetary Astronomy", *Research School of Astronomy and Astrophysics*, retrieved at: anu.edu.au

272   Mullan, *Physics of the Sun: A First Course*, Taylor & Francis, 2009

273   Littman, Willcox & Espenak, *Totality: Eclipses of the Sun* (2nd ed.), Oxford University Press, 2000

274   Redd, "What is Astronomy? Definition and History", *Space*, 2017, retrieved at: space.com

275   "Astrometry", *The Planetary Society*, 2019, retrieved at: planetary.org

276   Bulwer-Lytton, *Zanoni*, Routledge, 1874, p. xx

277   Bulwer-Lytton, *The Works of Edward Lytton Bulwer, Esq. in Two Volumes*, Vol I, Carey & Hart, 1836, p. 415

Astronomy, as we know it, has its origins in ancient Mesopotamia, among civilizations such as the Sumerians and the Akkadians (and, later, the Assyrians and Babylonians), beginning with the advent of recorded history in the early 4th century until the Fall of Babylon in 539 BCE. The discoveries and methodology established during this period were to inform and influence the development of astronomy in India, China, the Islamic world and the West.[278] The astronomy of these civilizations was inextricably woven into a fabric which also contained their theology, mythology, agricultural cycles and prognostication, thereby making it indistinguishable from what we now think of as astrology. In fact, the art and the science of celestial observation were not completely separated until the Copernican Revolution in the 16th century, with the mathematization of astronomy. As we had briefly discussed in the sections on arithmetic and geometry in the present Chapter, the sexagesimal system, which is central to understanding and communicating our experience in and of the cosmos, was developed in ancient Sumer in the 3rd millennium BCE. This system, which was developed by dividing the plane of the ecliptic into 360° (approximately one degree for each day of a solar year), forms the base numerical system of how we quantify our degrees, planar angles, hours, minutes and seconds, etc.; it is used to quantify our spatial and temporal orientation; it forms the quantitative basis of the method by which organize our experience of space-time.[279] This 360° circle was further subdivided into the 30° zodiacal signs by the Babylonians sometime between 1300-1000 BCE[280], though there are records of constellated groupings of stars spanning as far back as 3000 BCE in the region.[281]

278   Aaboe, "Scientific Astronomy in Antiquity", *Philosophical Transactions of the Royal Society*, 276 (1257), 1974, pp. 21-42

279   Aaboe, "The culture of Babylonia: Babylonian mathematics, astrology, and astronomy." *The Assyrian and Babylonian Empires and other States of the Near East, from the Eighth to the Sixth Centuries B.C.*, Cambridge University Press, 1991

280   Rochberg-Halton, "Stellar Distances in Early Babylonian Astronomy: A New Perspective on the Hilprecht Text (HS 229)", *Journal of Near Eastern Studies*, 1983, pp. 209-221

281   Rogers, "Origins of the Ancient Constellations: I. The Mesopotamian Traditions", *Journal of the British Astronomical Association*, 1998, p. 9

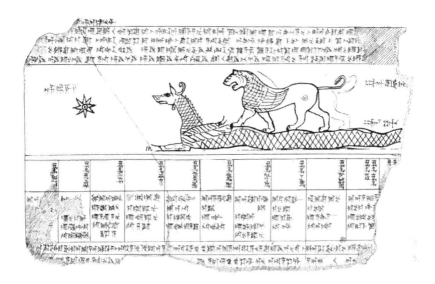

Babylonian text, referencing Sirius, Arcturus (the yoke star), the Pleiades, Orion and Ursa Major, 1200 BCE

Cuneiform tablets dating from the First Babylonian Empire (1830-1531 BCE), such as the *Enûma Anu Enlil* series of artifacts, catalog a variety of celestial and atmospheric phenomena as well as the interpretations of such events. These interpretations, called omens, were an early form of astrological prediction and divination, first appearing in Mesopotamia in the 2nd millennium.[282] Most omens were interpreted in reference to the state and the kingdom, such as those of Esarhaddon (681-669 BC), wherein the king was advised how to avoid the consequences of negative omens. In some cases, a substitute king was installed while the true king went into hiding; when the king was advised by his astronomer that the danger had passed, the substitute king was executed and the king reinstated.[283] From their perspective, there were omens produced by man and omens produced by the gods through the agency of celestial and atmospheric phenomena. Negative omens produced terrestrially were considered circumventable; whereas those produced by the gods, being much more powerful, required a series of rites to be successfully avoided. A text known as the *Omen Com-*

282 Koch-Westenholz, *Mesopotamian Astrology*, Museum Tusculanum Press, 1995, p. 78
283 Entry: "Omen", Beck (ed.), *The Anchor Yale Bible Dictionary*, New Haven: Yale University Press, 2009

pendia, a compilation of omens beginning in the early 2nd millennium, contained rites of aversion known as *nam-bur-bi* (Akkadian, meaning "evil loosening").[284] The *nam-bur-bi* rites constitute early documented examples of truly astral magic, in that they were operations specifically designed to avert or placate stellar and planetary forces.

The discovery of a Late Babylonian *kalendartexte* dating from the 5th century BCE has provided insight on the practice of Babylonian astral medicine. The text, which had belonged to a mašmaššu priest from the City of Uruk named Iqīšâ, described the process by which illnesses that had developed under a particular zodiacal sign might be treated by anointing the afflicted with ointments prepared with materials reflecting the attributes of the sign. These astrological preparations were prescribed for use on particular days, sometimes at certain planetary hours of that day (see Appendix C), and under specific zodiacal influences. Some of these formulas are reminiscent of the weird preparations found in the *Picatrix*, such as eyedrops made from the bile of a kite dried in the shade mixed with fennel juice as a cure for the bites of tarantulas, vipers, wasps and asps; or, for the generation of enmities, the magician is to eat a half ounce of pig brains, black cat bile, fat from a black dog and two grains of sweet myrrh.[285] For example, in the event of illnesses developed under the zodiacal influence of Aries, the *āšipu*, "healer-seer", or the *asû*, "physician", was to anoint the patient with sheep's blood or sheep's fat; for Capricorn, goat's blood or fat; for Cancer, crab's blood; for Taurus, bull's blood or fat; for Leo, lion's blood or fat. Most of the zoomorphic attributions seem to match those with which we are familiar today, however some of the preparations call for unusual ingredients, such as that for Pisces, which called for the head of a dove or the blood of a swallow; Virgo, which called for a raven's head or wing; Aquarius, for the head, wing or blood of an eagle.[286] While these cures initially sound outlandish from our modern perspective, this 2500 year old (at least) practice of curing an ailment contracted under a certain zodiacal influence with a preparation composed of ingredients associated with that influence stands up to the homeopathic law of *similia, similibus, curantur* ("let likes be cured by likes").[287] As we have seen, this idea is, at once, central to Hermeticism, while also upholding the Frazerian

---

284   Hunger & Pingree, *Astral Sciences in Mesopotamia*, Brill, 1999, pp. 1-33

285   *Picatrix*, غاية الحكيم, *Ghāyat al-Ḥakīm*

286   Steele, "Astronomy and culture in Late Babylonian Uruk", *Proceedings of the International Astronomical Union*, 2011, pp. 331–341

287   Whorton, *Nature Cures: The History of Alternative Medicine in America*, New York: Oxford University Press, 2004, pp. 52-54

Law of Similarity (like produces like), a staple in the anthropological study of magic.

Another notable artifact is the *Venus Tablet of Ammisaduqa* (17th century BCE), which documents the heliacal rising and setting of the planet Venus over a twenty-one-year period. This tablet and others in the *Enûma Anu Enlil* series are the earliest examples of documented planetary motion, retrogrades and periodicity, consequently, marking the beginning of planetary theory.[288] Later, in the 7th century BCE, the motions of the Sun, Moon and five visible planets were plotted in a pair of cuneiform tablets known as the *MUL.APIN*.[289] Colloquially, we refer to the ancient sequence of the seven planets (the Moon, Mercury, Venus, the Sun, Mars, Jupiter and Saturn) as being in the Chaldean order[290]; we do this because ancient Babylonian, or Chaldean astronomers ordered them according to the speed of their transit along the ecliptic from the perspective of Earth – the faster the transit, the closer the planet. The Babylonians were responsible for the archetypal model that would follow the planets and their mythological correspondences as they were subsumed by the Egyptian, Greek and Roman panthea. These are as follows:

Planet	*Babylonian*	*Egyptian*	*Greek*	*Roman*
the Moon	Sin	Khonsu	Artemis	Luna
Mercury	Nabu	Thoth	Hermes	Mercury
Venus	Ishtar	Hathor	Aphrodite	Venus
the Sun	Shamash	Ra	Helios	Sol
Mars	Nergal	Her-deshur	Ares	Mars
Jupiter	Marduk	Amun	Zeus	Jupiter
Saturn	Ninurta	Heru-ka-pet	Kronos	Saturn

288   North, *Cosmos: An Illustrated History of Astronomy and Cosmology*, University of Chicago Press, 2008, p. 41

289   Rochberg, "Astronomy and Calendars in Ancient Mesopotamia", *Civilizations of the Ancient Near East*, 2000, p. 1930

290   The word *Chaldean* is defined as "a member of an ancient Semitic people that became dominant in Babylonia […] a person versed in the occult arts." *Merriam-Webster Dictionary*, merriam-webster.com

The archetypal attributes are remarkably consistent throughout the planetary panthea of various cultures. The Babylonian Nabu, for example, is the mercurial deity in the Babylonian pantheon. He is the god of scribes, literacy and wisdom[291], fitting rather nicely with the attributes of the Egyptian Thoth. Nabu, like Thoth-Hermes, is symbolized by the stylus and tablet, which is not unlike the quill and parchment of the Masonic secretary, as they share the same symbolic meaning. Inanna is the Sumerian goddess of love and beauty, later subsumed by the Babylonian Ishtar, who directly corresponds to Aphrodite and Venus, but also to Hathor in her sexual aspect.[292] Nergal, in his fiery aspect, was known as *Lugal-Banda* (meaning: "fighting cock") in reference to the attributes of Ares and Mars, which he embodied in the Late-Babylonian Period. Like the Roman Saturn, Ninurta is the Babylonian god of agriculture, appearing in texts dating as early as the 3rd millennium BCE.[293] This agricultural aspect is shared by Cronus, the saturnian deity of the Greek pantheon, who is frequently depicted holding a scythe, as if in preparation for the grain harvest. The Babylonian Marduk is the king and arbiter of the gods, as is Amun (*Jupiter-Ammon*), Jupiter (*Deus-pater*, or "Zeus-father") and Zeus, the father of the Olympians.

By the dawn of the Egypt's Dynastic Period in the 3rd millennium, the 365-day solar calendar was already in use. The Egyptians had also become conversant with stellar observation by this remote period. The heliacal rising of certain stars, such as *Sopdet* (Greek: *Sothis*, or *Sirius*, Σείριος, meaning: "glowing"), were indicators of the annual inundation of the Nile, which dictated the agricultural cycle in the region.[294] It is also well documented that structures such as the Great Pyramid at Giza and the Temple of Amun-Re at Karnak were astronomically aligned with shocking degrees of accuracy and precision.[295] When surveying the architecture and stone work of this ancient civilization, it is difficult to fathom how this was accomplished with copper chisels, stone hammers and the extant examples of the somewhat primitive implements they purportedly used

---

291   Bertman, *Handbook to Life in Ancient Mesopotamia*, Oxford: Oxford University Press, 2005, p. 122

292   Pinch, *Votive Offerings to Hathor*, Griffith Institute, 1993, p. 138

293   Kasak & Veede, "Understanding Planets in Ancient Mesopotamia", *Folklore: Electronic Journal of Folklore*, Tartu, Estonia: Folk Belief and Media Group of ELM, 2001, pp. 25-26

294   Wilkinson, "Sothis", *The Complete Gods and Goddesses of Ancient Egypt*, London: Thames & Hudson, 2003, pp. 167-168

295   Ionides & Ionides, "Astronomy in Ancient Egypt", *Astronomical Society of the Pacific Leaflets*, Vol. 4, No. 153, 1941

in their astronomical observations. Clement of Alexandria (150-215 CE), in a passage in his *Stromata* regarding the forty-two books of Hermes, described the *horologe* and *palm*, which were two instruments used in ancient Egyptian astronomy.

> For the Egyptians pursue a philosophy of their own. This is principally shown by their sacred ceremonial. For first advances the Singer, bearing some one of the symbols of music. For they say that he must learn two of the books of Hermes, the one of which contains the hymns of the gods, the second the regulations for the king's life. And after the Singer advances the Astrologer, with a horologe in his hand, and a palm, the symbols of astrology. He must have the astrological books of Hermes, which are four in number, always in his mouth. Of these, one is about the order of the fixed stars that are visible, and another about the conjunctions and luminous appearances of the sun and moon; and the rest respecting their risings. Next in order advances the sacred Scribe, with wings on his head, and in his hand a book and rule, in which were writing ink and the reed, with which they write. And he must be acquainted with what are called hieroglyphics, and know about cosmography and geography, the position of the sun and moon, and about the five planets; also the description of Egypt, and the chart of the Nile; and the description of the equipment of the priests and of the places consecrated to them, and about the measures and the things in use in the sacred rites.[296]

According to similar artifacts in the Berlin Museum, the *horolage* consisted of a short handle from which hung a plumb line; and the *palm* was a palm branch with a sight-hole on one end. The *horolage* was held out at arm's length while being viewed through the sight of the *palm* which was held near the eye. It is interesting to imagine how the evolution of these instruments relate to their cousins found in the domains of navigation, surveying and stonemasonry, all of which utilizing the principles of geometry (literally "Earth measurement"), which is itself predicated on astronomical observation. Also noteworthy in the above passage from Clement is the sequence in which these Hermetic books appear in the procession; the singer leads with the "symbols of music" before the astrologer follows

296   Clement of Alexandria, *Stromata*, Book IV, Ch. 4

with the instruments of his art. After this, the scribe who, in the man-ner of the Roman Mercury, is described as having "wings on his head", documents the astronomical data and uses it for the purposes of a sort of sacred cartography – mapping the sacred sites vis-à-vis those in the heavens. This passage illustrates an example of the terrestrial mirroring of celestial objects in what can only be a deliberate attempt to draw upon cos-mic sympathies. But this concept does not find its origin in the forty-two Hermetic books described by Clement.

> *In an astrological document of the third century B.C., in which the priest Petosiris counsels King Nechopso, Hermes already appears as the teacher of all secret wisdom, which, however, can be experienced only in a state of ecstasy. This wisdom ap-pears to the prophet as a "voice" wrapped in a dark garment. As the follower prays, this voice points out to him the paths of the celestial bodies in the universe and reveals to him the wisdom of the cosmos.*[297]

Marie-Louise Von Franz' commentary on a 3rd century BCE, ear-ly-Hellenistic prototype of 1st-3rd century CE, Trismegistic literature[298] seems to betray something akin to a qabalistic cosmology, in that the "paths" demarcated by the celestial bodies are said to reveal the "wisdom of the cosmos", just as the nodal *sephiroth* on the paths of the *Etz Chaim* rep-resent the planets in the Chaldean, or Ptolemaic order, and terminate at the sphere of the fixed stars, *Chokmah*, which means "Wisdom". The con-cept of ascending or descending through the planetary spheres was ubiq-uitous in the theology and cosmology of ancient cultures, as evidenced by the aforementioned *Descent of Inanna*, the Hermetic *Piomandres* and the architecture of the Temple of the Seven Spheres at Borsippa. The general form of this recurring narrative follows that, when descending into mat-ter, the soul of the initiate passes into the Gate of Cancer (the summer solstice) and takes on various negative attributes or vices (e.g., the Seven Deadly Sins) attributed to each of the planets before being fully incarnated on the terrestrial sphere. The metals which are associated with each plan-et (the Moon, silver; Mercury, quicksilver; Venus, copper; the Sun, gold;

---

297   von Franz, *Projection and Re-collection in Jungian Psychology: Reflections of the Soul*, Open Court Publishing, 1980, p. 150

298   Mead (ed. & commentary), "Petosiris and Nechepso", *Thrice-Greatest Hermes*, Vol. 1, 1906, retrieved at: sacred-texts.com

Mars, iron; Jupiter, tin; Saturn, lead) are also symbolic of the matter with which the soul is incarnated in its descent. In the soul's ascent, the material world and its associated vices are gradually shed, until the soul is free to pass through the Gate of Capricorn (the winter solstice). A notable example of this pattern occurs in Porphyry's ancient commentary on the "Cave of the Nymphs" sequence in the thirteenth book of Homer's *Odyssey*.

> *[...A] cavern is an image and symbol of the world [...] there are two extremities in the heavens, viz., the winter tropic, than which nothing is more southern, and the summer tropic, than which nothing is more northern. But the summer tropic is in Cancer, and the winter tropic in Capricorn. And since Cancer is nearest to us, it is very properly attributed to the Moon, which is the nearest of all the heavenly bodies to the earth. But as the southern pole by its great distance is invisible to us, hence Capricorn is attributed to Saturn, the highest and most remote of all the planets. Again, the signs from Cancer to Capricorn are situated in the following order: and the first of these is Leo, which is the house of the Sun; afterwards Virgo, which is the house of Mercury; Libra, the house of Venus; Scorpio, of Mars; Sagittarius, of Jupiter; and Capricorn, of Saturn. But from Capricorn in an inverse order Aquarius is attributed to Saturn; Pisces to Jupiter; Aries to Mars; Taurus to Venus; Gemini to Mercury; and in the last place Cancer to the Moon. Theologists therefore assert, that these two gates are Cancer and Capricorn; but Plato calls them entrances. And of these, theologists say, that Cancer is the gate through which souls descend; but Capricorn that through which they ascend.[299]*

---

[299] Porphyry, *On the Cave of the Nymphs in the Thirteenth Book of the Odyssey* (3rd century CE), Taylor (trans.), London: Watkins, 1917, 10-11

Mithraic Tauroctony, encircled by the zodiacal signs

As we read in the work of Masonic authors such as Mackey, Pike, Haywood, Oliver and many others, there are many elements of Masonic ritual that have a precedent in the rites of ancient Mystery religions. This is a demonstrable fact, notwithstanding the lack of evidence for any kind of unbroken lineage, which is not required to illustrate the point. A suitable example being Ruck's claim that the Scottish *Picti*, through contact with Roman legionaries in the North, communicated the Mithraic Mysteries to the operative guilds who, in turn, communicated them to the modern speculative Craft.[300] This need neither be true, nor otherwise support a claim regarding any other unbroken Mystery transmission in order for there to be an obvious presence of similar symbolic motifs and ritualism between the two systems. For the sake of comparison, the initiatory systems of both Freemasonry and Mithraism included: the display of *sacra* which were specific to each degree or grade; both the Lodge and the Mithraeum being considered microcosmic representations of the universe[301]; that there was an oath or Obligation which bound the candidate to the tenets of the degree of grade; that there were catechisms which accompanied each

---

300   Ruck, Hoffman and Celdran, *Mushrooms, Myths and Mithras*, City Lights, 2011, p. 210

301   Pike, *Morals and Dogma*, L. H. Jenkins Inc., 1947, p. 413

degree or grade[302]; that both Masons and Mithraic initiates were invested with a grip by the *Pater*, their equivalent to the Worshipful Master.[303] Again, this does not prove a direct cultural inheritance between the two systems, but it does speak to the archetypal universality of how initiatory rites manifest, even across expanses of time and distance. Bearing this in mind, it is not unreasonable to interpret the Winding Staircase, particularly the course of seven steps which comprise the seven liberal arts and sciences, in the context of other septenarian ascents, such as that made on the planetary ladder in Mithraic initiation (*Corax*, Mercury; *Nymphus*, Venus; *Miles*, Mars; *Leo*, Jupiter; *Perses*, Moon; *Heliodromus*, Sun; *Pater*, Saturn).[304] The fact is that ascending or descending through seven spheres, up seven stairs, or up seven rungs of a ladder, are all indicative of an initiatory constant, common to many systems.

The *Orphic Hymns*, which we had occasion to mention in the section on music, contained planetary and stellar devotions, in addition to those dedicated to the gods, goddesses and natural forces, many of which Ficino was said to have set to music on his lyre. Before we move on to the application of these hymns in planetary and astral magic, it is in the interest of context that we briefly address how these documents – and others, such as the *Corpus Hermeticum* – came to fuel the current of Renaissance magic which was ignited by the Florentine Neoplatonists.

In 1462 CE, Cosimo di Giovanni de' Medici (1389-1464 CE), the *de facto* ruler of Renaissance-era Florence, Italy, supplied Marsilio Ficino (1433-1499 CE), a scholar under his patronage, with a cache of Hellenistic Greek documents, which he was to translate into Latin.[305] Cosimo de' Medici's vision was to reestablish Plato's Academy in the city and, to that end, he had commissioned a monk named Leonardo da Pistoia to scour the remains of the Byzantine Empire, which had recently fallen to the Ottoman Turks, in an effort to acquire as many of these documents as were extant. The translated works were to be the foundational documents of the Florentine Platonic Academy, an informal philosophical study group, led by Ficino, whose members would include such luminaries of the period as Poliziano, Gentile de' Becchi and the Christian cabalistic philosopher, Pico della Mirandola (1463-1494 CE).[306] However, the writings procured

---

302   Geden, *Select Passages Illustrating Mithraism*, Macmillan, 1925, p. 51
303   Clauss, *The Roman Cult of Mithras*, Routledge, 2001, p. 42
304   Pike, *Morals and Dogma*, L. H. Jenkins Inc., 1947, p. 11
305   Bartlett, *The Civilization of the Italian Renaissance: A Sourcebook*, University of Toronto Press, 2011, p. 98
306   Burke, *The Renaissance*, Longmans, 1964, p. 152

from da Pistoia contained not only Platonic documents – such as he was specifically requested to acquire – but also the work of 3rd century Neoplatonists Plotinus, Porphyry and Iamblichus, the *Chaldean Oracles*, the *Orphic Hymns*, and a curious body of fourteen books which would come to be known as the *Corpus Hermeticum*. Ficino, who was presently busying himself with the translations of Plato, was asked to temporarily set these aside in favor of the newly discovered documents, which de' Medici and Ficino believed to be representative of the *prisci theologia*, or "ancient theology", the true theological doctrine, given by God to man, and common to all world religions[307], as we had briefly discussed in the preceding section.

The authorship of the *Corpus Hermeticum* was attributed to the euhemeristic Hermes Trismegistus (Greek: Ἑρμῆς ὁ Τρισμέγιστος), an avatar of the Greek god Hermes, messenger and *psychopompos*, and the Egyptian Thoth, inventor of writing, magic and music.[308] During the Renaissance, it was widely accepted that Hermes Trismegistus was a contemporary of Moses and that his writings constituted an unparalleled body of ancient wisdom literature – a claim that was to be challenged by Isaac Casaubon, who dated the material to no earlier than the 2nd century CE. The texts deal with a wide range of subjects such as cosmology, astrology and the art of inspiriting statuary, amulets and talismans by means of astral magic and alchemy, thus informing the entire body of Renaissance-era Hermetic astrology in the court de' Medici and, in some ways, culminating in the work of Italian Hermetic astrologer, magician and Dominican friar, Giordano Bruno (1548-1600 CE), who said…

> *Like [the] Egyptians, magicians today formulate images, written symbols and ceremonies, which consist of certain actions and cults, and through which they make known their wishes with certain signals. This is the language of the gods.[309]*

---

307   Yates, *Giordano Bruno and the Hermetic Tradition*, University of Chicago Press, 1964, pp. 14-18

308   Bartlett, *The Civilization of the Italian Renaissance: A Sourcebook*, University of Toronto Press, 2011, p. 98

309   Bruno, as quoted in: Blackwell & de Lucca (eds.), *Giordano Bruno: Cause, Principle and Unity: Essays on Magic*, Cambridge University Press, 1998, p. 115

Engraving of Mercurius Trismegistus, Mussard, 1675

The production of astrological talismans and amulets is in keeping with a central magical principle identified by the eminent Scottish anthropologist and folklorist, J.G. Frazer (1854-1941), which he categorized as the *Law of Contagion*. This may be seen as the magical mechanism underlying operations such as amulet and talisman production. These objects, being consecrated and ritualistically exposed to the subtle influences of planetary, zodiacal and decanic light, were considered to have retained the cosmic powers through their exposure – a contagion resulting in a magical "battery" of sorts.

If we analyze the principles of thought on which magic is based, they will probably be found to resolve themselves into two: first, that like produces like, or that an effect resembles its cause; and, second, that things which have once been in contact with each other continue to act on each other at a distance after the physical contact has been severed. The former principle may be called the Law of Similarity, the latter the Law of Contact or Contagion. From the first of these principles, namely the Law of Similarity, the magician infers that he can produce any effect he desires merely by imitating it: from the second he infers that whatever he does to a material object will affect equally the person with whom the object was once in contact, whether it formed part of his body or not.[310]

The *Orphic Hymns* were a series of poems, ostensibly composed by the mythical hero Orpheus, and were used in his Mysteries and funerary rites. According to Taylor, the foremost translator of the Hymns into English, they were written by several authors, pseudepigraphically writing under the name *Orpheus*, among them the Athenian compiler of oracles, Onomacritus (Greek: Ὀνομάκριτος; 530-480 BCE). According to Taylor, the hymns were carried forward under the custodianship of the Neoplatonists.[311] During the Italian Renaissance, these hymns were used by Marsilio Ficino who, as we had discussed in the section on music, famously accompanied himself on a recreation of an Orphic lyre – for the purposes of conducting processes of natural magic to focus and direct the subtle planetary influences corresponding to each day.

The body of Orphic literature included "Sun hymns, or Jupiter hymns, or Venus hymns attuned to those planets, and this, being re-enforced by the invocation of their names and powers, was a way of drawing down their influences."[312] Several of the *Orphic Hymns* may be used for planetary invocations to be performed on their corresponding weekday ("To the Moon" on Monday, "To Mars" on Tuesday, etc.). Invocative practices such as these are performed in a conscious effort to hermetically draw upon the subtle

---

310   Frazer, *The Golden Bough: A Study in Comparative Religion*, MacMillan & Co., 1894, III:1

311   Taylor (trans.), *The Hymns of Orpheus*, London: White & Son, 1792, pp. 11-12

312   Yates, *Giordano Bruno and the Hermetic Tradition*, University of Chicago Press, 1964, p. 78

influence of the planetary bodies governing certain days and hours-of-the-day (see Appendix C). The following excerpts are taken from Thomas Taylor's 1792 translation of the *Hymns*.[313] These comprise the Hymns corresponding to the seven classical planets, including the sphere of the fixed stars (the firmament, or celestial sphere upon which the zodiac is fixed), and are presented below in their Chaldean order. The qabalist will note that these are also in the order of the *sephiroth* ascending the *Etz Chaim*: *Yesod* - the Moon, *Hod* - Mercury, *Netzach* - Venus, *Tiphareth* - the Sun, *Geburah* - Mars, *Chesed* - Jupiter, *Binah* - Saturn and *Chokmah* - the fixed stars (see Appendix B).

To the Moon:

HEAR, Goddess queen, diffusing silver light, Bullhorn'd and wand'ring thro' the gloom of Night. With stars surrounded, and with circuit wide Night's torch extending, thro' the heav'ns you ride: Female and Male with borrow'd rays you shine, And now full-orb'd, now tending to decline. Mother of ages, fruit-producing Moon, Whose amber orb makes Night's reflected noon: Lover of horses, splendid, queen of Night, All-seeing pow'r bedeck'd with starry light. Lover of vigilance, the foe of strife, In peace rejoicing, and a prudent life: Fair lamp of Night, its ornament and friend, Who giv'st to Nature's works their destin'd end. Queen of the stars, all-wife Diana hail! Deck'd with a graceful robe and shining veil; Come, blessed Goddess, prudent, starry, bright, Come moony-lamp with chaste and splendid light, Shine on these sacred rites with prosp'rous rays, And pleas'd accept thy suppliant's mystic praise.[314]

---

313   Taylor (trans.), *The Hymns of Orpheus*, London: White & Son, 1792
314   Ibid., pp. 124-126

To Mercury:

HERMES, draw near, and to my pray'r incline, Angel of Jove, and Maia's son divine; Studious of contests, ruler of mankind, With heart almighty, and a prudent mind. Celestial messenger, of various skill, Whose pow'rful arts could watchful Argus kill: With winged feet, 'tis thine thro' air to course, O friend of man, and prophet of discourse: Great life-supporter, to rejoice is thine, In arts gymnastic, and in fraud divine: With pow'r endu'd all language to explain, Of care the loos'ner, and the source of gain. Whose hand contains of blameless peace the rod, Corucian, blessed, profitable God; Of various speech, whose aid in works we find, And in necessities to mortals kind: Dire weapon of the tongue, which men revere, Be present, Hermes, and thy suppliant hear; Assist my works, conclude my life with peace, Give graceful speech, and me memory's increase.[315]

To Venus:

HEAV'NLY, illustrious, laughter-loving queen, Sea-born, night-loving, of an awful mien; Crafty, from whom necessity first came, Producing, nightly, all-connecting dame: 'Tis thine the world with harmony to join, For all things spring from thee, O pow'r divine. The triple Fates are rul'd by thy decree, And all productions yield alike to thee: Whate'er the heav'ns, encircling all contain, Earth fruit-producing, and the stormy main, Thy sway confesses, and obeys thy nod, Awful attendant of the brumal God: Goddess of marriage, charming to the sight, Mother of Loves, whom banquetings delight; Source of persuasion, secret, fav'ring queen, Illustrious born, apparent and unseen: Spousal, lupercal, and to men inclin'd, Prolific,

---

315   Ibid., pp. 152-153

most-desir'd, life-giving., kind: Great sceptre-bearer of the Gods, 'tis thine, Mortals in necessary bands to join; And ev'ry tribe of savage monsters dire In magic chains to bind, thro' mad desire. Come, Cyprus-born, and to my pray'r incline, Whether exalted in the heav'ns you shine, Or pleas'd in Syria's temple to preside, Or o'er th' Egyptian plains thy car to guide, Fashion'd of gold; and near its sacred flood, Fertile and fam'd to fix thy blest abode; Or if rejoicing in the azure shores, Near where the sea with foaming billows roars, The circling choirs of mortals, thy delight, Or beauteous nymphs, with eyes cerulean bright, Pleas'd by the dusty banks renown'd of old, To drive thy rapid, two-yok'd car of gold; Or if in Cyprus with thy mother fair, Where married females praise thee ev'ry year, And beauteous virgins in the chorus join, Adonis pure to sing and thee divine; Come, all-attractive to my pray'r inclin'd, For thee, I call, with holy, reverent mind.[316]

To the Sun:

HEAR golden Titan, whose eternal eye With broad survey, illumines all the sky. Self-born, unwearied in diffusing light, And to all eyes the mirrour of delight: Lord of the seasons, with thy fiery car. And leaping coursers, beaming light from far: With thy right hand the source of morning light, And with thy left the father of the night. Agile and vig'rous, venerable Sun, Fiery and bright around the heav'ns you run. Foe to the wicked, but the good man's guide, O'er all his steps propitious you preside: With various founding, golden lyre, 'tis mine To fill the world with harmony divine. Father of ages, guide of prosp'rous deeds, The world's commander, borne by lucid steeds, Immortal Jove, all-searching, bearing light, Source of existence, pure and fiery bright Bearer of fruit, almighty lord of years, Agil and warm, whom ev'ry pow'r reveres. Great eye of Nature and the starry skies, Doom'd with immortal flames to set and rise Dispensing justice, lover of the stream, The world's great despot, and o'er all supreme. Faithful defender, and the eye of right, Of steeds the ruler, and of life the light: With founding whip four fiery steeds you guide, When in the car of day you glorious ride. Propitious on these mystic labours shine, And bless thy suppliants with a life divine.[317]

To Mars:

Magnanimous, unconquer'd, boisterous Mars, In darts rejoicing, and in bloody wars. Fierce and untam'd, whose mighty pow'r can make The strongest walls from their foundations shake: Mortal destroying king, defil'd with gore, Pleas'd with war's dreadful and tumultuous roar: Thee, human blood, and swords, and spears delight, And the dire ruin of mad savage fight. Stay, furious contests, and avenging strife, Whose works with woe, embitter human life; To lovely Venus, and to Bacchus yield, To Ceres give the weapons of the field; Encourage peace, to gentle works inclin'd, And give abundance, with benignant mind.[318]

To Jupiter:

O Jove much-honor'd, Jove supremely great, To thee our holy rites we consecrate, Our pray'rs and expiations, king divine, For all things round thy head exalted shine. The earth is thine, and mountains swelling high, The sea profound, and all within the sky. Saturnian king, descending from above, Magnanimous, commanding, sceptred Jove; All-parent, principle and end of all, Whose pow'r almighty, shakes this earthly ball; Ev'n Nature trembles at thy mighty

317   Ibid., pp. 122-123
318   Ibid., pp. 196-197

nod, Loud-sounding, arm'd with light'ning, thund'ring God. Source of abundance, purifying king, O various-form'd from whom all natures spring; Propitious hear my pray'r, give blameless health, With peace divine, and necessary wealth. [319]

To Saturn:

ETHERIAL father, mighty Titan, hear, 1 Great fire of Gods and men, whom all revere: Endu'd with various council, pure and strong, To whom perfection and decrease belong. Consum'd by thee all forms that hourly die, By thee restor'd, their former place supply; The world immense in everlasting chains, Strong and ineffable thy pow'r contains Father of vast eternity, divine, O mighty Saturn, various speech is thine: Blossom of earth and of the starry skies, Husband of Rhea, and Prometheus wife. Obstetric Nature, venerable root, From which the various forms of being shoot; No parts peculiar can thy pow'r enclose, Diffus'd thro' all, from which the world arose, O, best of beings, of a subtle mind, Propitious hear to holy pray'rs inclin'd; The sacred rites benevolent attend, And grant a blameless life, a blessed end. [320]

To the Stars:

WITH holy voice I call the stars on high, Pure sacred lights and genii of the sky. Celestial stars, the progeny of Night, In whirling circles beaming far your light, Refulgent rays around the heav'ns ye throw, Eternal fires, the source of all below. With flames significant of Fate ye shine, And aptly rule for men a path divine. In seven bright zones ye run

---

319   Ibid., pp. 139-140
320   Ibid., pp. 136-137

with wand'ring flames, And heaven and earth compose
your lucid frames: With course unwearied, pure and fiery
bright. Forever shining thro' the veil of Night. Hail twin-
kling, joyful, ever wakeful fires! Propitious shine on all my just
desires; These sacred rites regard with conscious rays, And end
our works devoted to your praise.[321]

The Egyptian astronomers of the 10th Dynasty (around 2100 BCE) were the first to identify the thirty-six decans, which were small constellations marking a 10° arc of the ecliptic.[322] These were eventually catalogued, along with other astronomical data, in a series of texts referred to as the *Book of Nut* (12th Dynasty). In the texts, the heliacal risings of the thirty-six decans, or *horoscopes* (from the Greek: *horoskopoi*, meaning "watchers of the hours"), were shown to mark each decanic "hour" and were used as a stellar clock, which marked the nocturnal hours. It was this system which eventually lead to the twelve hours of day and night, which varied in length due to the time of year – with the twelve nighttime hours being compressed during the long days of summer, for example. In time, the system of twelve equinoctial hours was established; in this system, the length of the day and night hours are considered equal, as they are on the vernal and autumnal equinoxes.[323] Due to the Earth's annual revolution, the Sun appears to rise in a different decan every ten days, thereby dividing the 360° ecliptic into three 10° arc segments. After the Babylonian concept of the zodiac was introduced to Egypt, around the 1st century BCE, these two systems were synthesized and each sign was further subdivided into three decans (from the Greek: *dekanoi*, δεκανοί), or "faces" (from the Greek: *prosopon*). Many decan configurations, names and images are given, from those in the Dynastic *Book of Nut* to the Hellenistic *Hermetica*, from Late Antiquity in Julius Firmicus Maternus' *Matheseos libri octo* (4th century CE)[324] to their medieval appearance in Arabic works on astrology, such as the *Picatrix*. The decan names and images as they are found in the *Picatrix* appear to be the source for Agrippa's rendering in Book II

---

321   Ibid., pp. 121-122

322   von Bomhard, *Egyptian Calendar a Work for Eternity*, London, 1999, p. 51

323   Neugebauer, "The Egyptian 'Decans'", *Astronomy and History: Selected Essays*, New York: Springer, pp. 205-209

324   Quasten, Burghardt & Lawlor (eds.), "Life of Firmicus", *Firmicus Maternus: The Error of the Pagan Religions*, Issue 37, 1970

of his *De occulta philosophia*. While, in Dynastic Egypt, the decans were hieroglyphically depicted on coffin lids and in stellar clocks[325], by the Middle Ages, particularly in the Muslim World, they had become to garner elaborate definitions and attributes, often leading to convoluted descriptions that would be delivered by Agrippa to Renaissance magicians such as Giordano Bruno. For example, in Agrippa, we read that...

> *[...i]n the first face of Taurus ascendeth a naked man, an Archer, Harvester or Husbandman, and goeth forth to sow, plough, build, people, and divide the earth, according to the rules of Geometry.*

And, in the second face of Gemini...

> *[...] ascendeth a man in whose hand is a Pipe, and another being bowed down, digging the earth: and they signifie infamous and dishonest agility, as that of Jesters and Juglers; it also signifies labours and painful searchings.*[326]

The decans could be enumerated two ways: first, by the diurnal rotation of the Earth on its axis, whereby a new decanic "hour" is introduced on the horizon every 40 minutes, since each zodiacal sign spans 120 minutes and there are three decans per sign; second, by the annual revolution of the Earth around the Sun, whereby a new decanic "week" is introduced every 10 days since each zodiacal sign spans about 30 days and there are three decans per sign. Just as each sign of the zodiac has a ruling planet, and each planet is exalted in a certain sign, a planet is allotted to each decan as its ruler; this rulership applies to the decanic hours and weeks. The planetary rulers of the decans are distributed in the Chaldean order, beginning with Mars who rules the first decan of Aries...[327]

---

325   Symons, Cockcroft, Bettencourt & Koykka, *Ancient Egyptian Astronomy*, 2013, retrieved at: physics.mcmaster.ca

326   Agrippa, *De occulta philosophia libri tres* (*Three Books Concerning Occult Philosophy*), Book II, "Celestial Magic", Cologne 1533

327   Lilly, *Christian Astrology*, London, 1647, pp. 104-105

Sign	*First Decan*	*Second Decan*	*Third Decan*
Aries	Mars	The Sun	Venus
Taurus	Mercury	The Moon	Saturn
Gemini	Jupiter	Mars	The Sun
Cancer	Venus	Mercury	The Moon
Leo	Saturn	Jupiter	Mars
Virgo	The Sun	Venus	Mercury
Libra	The Moon	Saturn	Jupiter
Scorpio	Mars	The Sun	Venus
Sagittarius	Mercury	The Moon	Saturn
Capricorn	Jupiter	Mars	The Sun
Aquarius	Venus	Mercury	The Moon
Pisces	Saturn	Jupiter	Mars

Using Monday, January 11th at 10:20 a.m. as an example, we may begin by noting that Pisces is the ascendant at that hour and, at twenty minutes past, we are still in the first decan, which is ruled by Saturn; according to Agrippa's table (see Appendix C), the equinoctial ten o'clock hour on a Monday is ruled by the Sun; on the 11th of the month (the 21st day of the zodiacal month), we are in the third decanic week of Capricorn, which is ruled by the Sun; finally, the zodiacal sign of Capricorn is ruled by Saturn. Therefore, the complete planetary rulerships for Monday, January 11th at 10:20 a.m. are: Saturn (decanic hour), the Sun (planetary hour), the Sun (decanic week) and Saturn (zodiacal month). Qabalistically, the Sun and Saturn correspond to the *sephiroth Tiphareth* and *Binah* which are connected by the 17th path on the *Etz Chaim* (see Appendix B). The Hebrew letter associated with this path is *zayin*, which means "sword" and may refer to matters of the intellect. This is strengthened when we consider that the zodiacal sign of Gemini – an air sign, also associated with reason and the intellect – is assigned to this path. According to Agrippa's description of the third decan of Capricorn, a chaste and wise woman and a banker gathering his money sit at a table, signifying that one should govern in prudence and beware covetousness of money. This sense of being chained to materiality, evoked by the monetary symbolism, is also reflected in the Devil XV Tarot card, which is associated with the sign of Capricorn, and is ruled by Saturn. Perhaps the subject (or his *significator* in this analysis: *Adam Qadmon*) must learn to utilize his intellect in order to discern between the solar maiden clutching his heart (*Tiphareth*) and the saturnian crone, her hand over his right shoulder (*Binah*), as they are depicted flanking him on the Lovers VI Tarot (*Tarot de Marseilles*). The maiden also guards his heart from Eros' arrow while the crone seems to distract him. Might the crone represent the shackles of finance which distract the mind from its object? The gematriac value for *zayin* is seven – this may signify the need for the subject's initiatory ascent through the spheres, or via the seven liberal arts on the Staircase, as a means of sharpening the sword of the intellect. Thereby he may arrive at the supercelestial *ogdoad*, beyond the crone's saturnal sphere, in the sephirah of *Chokmah* ("Wisdom").

The zodiac (from the Greek: *zodiakos kyklo*, ζῳδιακός κύκλος, meaning "circle of little animals")[328] is defined as "an imaginary band in the heavens centered on the ecliptic that encompasses the apparent paths of all the planets [...]".[329] It extends about 9° of celestial latitude north and south of the ecliptic and is divided into twelve arc segments, each of 30° celestial longitude and containing a constellation denominating it.[330] Ancient Babylonian and Egyptian star catalogues preceded the zodiac and by about the 5th century BCE had begun to be divided into twelve signs denoting stellar months; this concept entered Hellenistic astronomy in about the 4th century BCE.[331]

328   Entry: "Zodiac", *Online Etymology Dictionary*, retrieved at: etymonline.com
329   Entry: "Zodiac", *Merriam-Webster Dictionary*, retrieved at: merriam-webster.com
330   Noble, "Papers communicated to the Association. The Signs of the Zodiac", *Journal of the British Astronomical Association*, 1902, pp. 242-244
331   Rogers, "Origins of the Ancient Constellations: I. The Mesopotamian Traditions", *Journal of the British Astronomical Assoc.*, 1998, pp. 9-28

Dendera zodiac ca. 1ˢᵗ century CE

The Dendera zodiac is perhaps the most widely known of the Hellenistic period. It dates from sometime in the 1ˢᵗ century BCE is located in the Osirian *pronaos* of the Hathor Temple at Dendera, Egypt. Though the temple itself was built during the Late Ptolemaic Period, the *pronaos* was a later addition still, probably dating from near the turn of the millennium.[332] This planispherical bas-relief depicts both the standard zodiacal and the parazodiacal constellations in, relative position, and is temporally oriented to the helical rising of *Sothis* (Sirius). The relief also depicts the planets and the thirty-six decans, as personified first-magnitude stars around the perimeter of the plane projection. The Dendera zodiac is the only known circular zodiac from Egyptian antiquity, as zodiacs of the time were generally square or rectangular. As a whole, the image is that of a 360-day year, which was, of course, imported from Sumerian astronomy, via the Babylonians. These 360 days *are* the 360° degrees of a circle, the astronomical basis for a geometrical quantification.

The zodiac, as we know it today, and the geocentric model of the cosmos were canonized in a 2ⁿᵈ century CE astronomical treatise written by

---

332   Marchant, "Decoding the Ancient Egyptian's Stone Sky Map", *New Scientist*, 2010

Claudius Ptolemy known as the *Almagest* (originally entitled *Mathēmatikē Syntaxis*; colloquial name from the Arabic: *al-majisṭī*, المجسطي). Much of the stellar and zodiacal content of the work is a compendium of horoscopic precedents in Hellenistic and Babylonian astronomy, with the northern zodiacal constellations (Aries through Virgo) being detailed in Book VII, and the southern constellations (Libra through Pisces) in Book VIII.[333] Other than the Ptolemaic order of the planets (identical to the Chaldean order and that of the *sephiroth*), the main point of interest in the work, from the perspective of the Western Esoteric Tradition, is Ptolemy's cosmology, which is laid out in a series of five postulates: the celestial realm is spherical; the Earth is a sphere; the Earth is at the center of the cosmos; the Earth, relative to the distance of the fixed stars, has no appreciable size and is considered as a mathematical point; and, the Earth does not move.[334] The *Almagest* was widely influential and was considered the authoritative work on the subject until the Copernican Revolution in the 16th century CE.

> *It is requisite that we should here say something of Magick, which is so linked to Astrology, as being her near Kinswoman, that whoever professes Magick without Astrology, does nothing, but is altogether out of the way. [...] So requisite is the use of Astrology to the Arts of Divination, as it were the Key that opens the door of all their Mysteries.* [335]

As natural magic is concerned with elemental processes on the terrestrial plane; and ceremonial, or theological magic is concerned with theurgy and angelic hierarchies on the divine plane; celestial, or "mathematicall magick" (Agrippa) is concerned with planetary, decanic and zodiacal magic, which is active in the middle of the three worlds. The qabalist could compare this with elemental magic performed in the *Assiahic* world, planetary magic performed in the *Yetziric* world, and theological magic performed in the *Briahic* and *Aztiluthic* worlds. While the documented origins of celestial magic can be traced as far back as the aforementioned Mesopotamian

---

333   van der Waerden, "History of the Zodiac", *Archiv für Orientforschung*, Volume 16, 1953, pp. 216-230, pdf retrieved at: cern.ch

334   Paraphrased from Toomer (trans.), *Ptolemy's Almagest*, Princeton University Press, 1998, pdf retrieved at: isidore.co

335   Agrippa, *The Vanity of the Arts and Sciences*, J.C. for Samuel Speed, 1676, Chapters XL & XLI, retrieved at: umich.edu

omenic literature and the astrological *nam-bur-bi* rites[336], megalithic sites such as Göbekli Tepe and Nabta Playa suggest a date which may be anterior by several millennia. Due to their astronomical orientation – as well as zodiacal carvings, in the case of Göbekli Tepe – these sites, and others like them, demonstrate the deliberate use of astronomical data in terrestrial constructions meant to symbolically and ritualistically affect microcosmic events.[337]

In 5th century BCE Persia, the ancient Iranian spiritual leader, Zoroaster (from the Greek: ζωρός *zōros*, meaning "undiluted" and ἄστρον *astron*, meaning "star"), whose very name alludes to his association with astronomy and astral magic, was considered a sorcerer-astrologer who, like Thoth-Hermes, had created the arts of astrology and magic.[338] The priests of Zoroastrianism were called *magi* (from the Old Persian *magush*, meaning "magician, astrologer"), which has a shared etymology with the English word *magic*.[339] Beginning in about the 3rd century BCE, astrological and magical works pseudepigraphically attributed to Zoroaster begin to appear. This "mass of literature", written in Greek, Aramaic, Syriac, Coptic and Latin, read as attempts to legitimize a font of ancient wisdom alien to the Hellenistic milieu. The pseudopigraphic use of exotic personages such as the Persian Zoroaster and the Egyptian Hermes Trismegistus tended to lend credence to claims of remote antiquity and the presence of revelatory wisdom in the otherwise standard issue astro-magical fare of the period.[340]

---

336   Hunger & Pingree, *Astral Sciences in Mesopotamia*, Brill, 1999, pp. 1-33

337   Yirka, "Ancient stone pillars offer clues of comet strike that changed human history", *Phys.org*, 2017

338   Beck, "Thus Spake Not Zarathushtra: Zoroastrian Pseudepigrapha of the Greco-Roman World", *A History of Zoroastrianism*, Brill Publishers, 1991, pp. 491-565

339   Entry: "Magi", *Online Etymological Dictionary*, retrieved at: etymonline.com

340   Beck, "Thus Spake Not Zarathushtra: Zoroastrian Pseudepigrapha of the Greco-Roman World", *A History of Zoroastrianism*, Brill Publishers, 1991, pp. 491-565

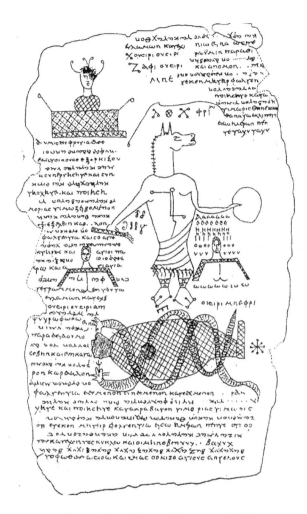

From the Papyri Graecae Magicae ca. 400 CE

As the art of astrology spread outward from Mesopotamia and Egypt, we begin to see concepts associated with celestial magic appearing in Hellenistic texts such as the aforementioned *Corpus Hermeticum*, which contain the astrological and magical books attributed to Hermes Trismegistus, and in the *Greek Magical Papyri*, wherein the "Eighth Book of Moses" instructs the magician call upon the "god of the hours of the day" (see Appendix C).[341] Over the course of several centuries, this body of knowledge

341   *Greek Magical Papyri*, PGM XIII 345, Betz (trans.), p. 182

passed from civilization to civilization and from culture to culture; Babylon's planetary and zodiacal astrology was integrated with the decanic astrology of Egypt resulting in the horoscopic astrology of the Greeks; various amalgamations had taken place as the mythological archetypes and narratives associated with the planets, stars and constellations were subsumed and conflated, revealing an eerily similar manifestation of astrolatry across cultures.

By the early Middle Ages, extant works of Hermetic astrology, alchemy and magic were being concentrated in the Islamic Middle East, resulting in works such as al-Khwarizmi's *Zij al-Sindhind* (9th century CE), al-Farghani's *Kitab fi Jawami* (9th century CE), the Sabian mathematician and astronomer, Thābit ibn Qurrah's *De Imaginibus* (9th century CE) and, of course, the *Picatrix*. As these volumes were translated into Latin, this magical current, which had previously been under the custodianship of the Muslim world, blossomed into medieval Europe's grimoire tradition. This period saw the production of works such as the *Sefer Raziel Ha-Malakh* (13th century CE), the *Sworn Book of Honorius* (13th century CE), the *Heptaremon* (15th century CE), *Clavicula Salomonis* (16th century CE) and *The Lesser Key of Solomon* (17th century CE), also known as the *Lemegeton*. The latter volume is principally concerned with *goëtic* magic – that is magic which involves the evocation of the seventy-two goëtic dæmons who are each assigned to one of the quinances, or 5° arc segments of the ecliptic. Just as each 10° decan is assigned a particular image, so too are the quinances assigned a dæmon. These goëtic dæmons – stellar personifications, not evil spirits, *per se* – are given titles such as "Duke" and "Emperor" and "Wandering Prince" in the second book of the *Legemeton*, *Ars theurgia goetia*, and are tied to certain points on the compass through which their astral ray might be concentrated.[342] The third book, known as the *Ars paulina*, contains horary and zodiacal magical material in the form of "four and twenty Angells" – one for each hour of the day – and details the 360 spirits of the zodiac, or the *Monomoiria* of Hellenistic astrology.[343]

342   Waite, *The Book of Ceremonial Magic*, Part I, Chapter III, section 2: "The Lesser Key of Solomon", London, 1913

343   Jones, *Astronomical Papyri from Oxyrhynchus*, Volumes I & II, American Philosophical Society, 1999, pp. 11, 284-289

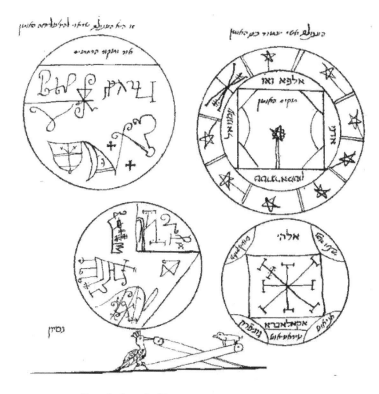

Pentacles from the Clavicula Salomonis, ca. 17ᵗʰ century

Astrology in the Abrahamic religions has always been somewhat of a problematic affair. Though Islam, in the Middle Ages, seemed to be particularly friendly to astronomy, astrology, alchemy and magic, Judaism and Christianity have historically frowned upon the Hermetic Arts, particularly any form of astrolatry. In Deuteronomy, the fifth book of the *Torah*, the prohibition and the penalty are laid out in no uncertain terms.

> *And beware lest you raise your eyes to heaven, and when you see the sun and the moon and the stars, all the host of heaven, you be drawn away and bow down to them and serve them, things that the* LORD *your God has allotted to all the peoples under the whole heaven.[344]*

---

344   *The Holy Bible*, KJV, Deuteronomy 4:19

And later…

> *If there be found among you, within any of thy gates which the LORD thy God giveth thee, man or woman, that hath wrought wickedness in the sight of the LORD thy God, in transgressing his covenant, And hath gone and served other gods, and worshipped them, either the sun, or moon, or any of the host of heaven, which I have not commanded; And it be told thee, and thou hast heard of it, and inquired diligently, and, behold, it be true, and the thing certain, that such abomination is wrought in Israel: Then shalt thou bring forth that man or that woman, which have committed that wicked thing, unto thy gates, even that man or that woman, and shalt stone them with stones, till they die. At the mouth of two witnesses, or three witnesses, shall he that is worthy of death be put to death; but at the mouth of one witness he shall not be put to death. The hands of the witnesses shall be first upon him to put him to death, and afterward the hands of all the people. So thou shalt put the evil away from among you.[345]*

This foreboding sentiment is contradicted in Genesis, however, where we read that the Supreme Being has given us the "lights in the firmament" as wise counsel; he has also given us the Sun to rule the day and the Moon to rule the night and all the stars and planets to "give light upon the earth".

> *And God said, Let there be lights in the firmament of the heaven to divide the day from the night; and let them be for signs, and for seasons, and for days, and years: And let them be for lights in the firmament of the heaven to give light upon the earth: and it was so. And God made two great lights; the greater light to rule the day, and the lesser light to rule the night: he made the stars also. And God set them in the firmament of the heaven to give light upon the earth, And to rule*

---

345   *The Holy Bible*, KJV, Deuteronomy 17:2-7

*over the day and over the night, and to divide the light from
the darkness.*[346]

In the Book of Job, the circle of the zodiac was referred to as the
Mazzaroth (Hebrew: מַזָּרוֹת, meaning "a garland of crowns").[347] The word
appears but once in the Tanakh but, in time, evolved to mean not merely
the "zodiac" but also "astrology" in general. Etymologically, the word *Mazzaroth* survives in the expression *mazel tov*, meaning "good luck".[348] The
Lord asks Job, "Canst thou bind the sweet influences of Pleiades, or loose
the bands of Orion? Canst thou bring forth Mazzaroth in his season? Or
canst thou guide Arcturus with his sons?"[349] Certainly *binding the influences*
and/or *loosening the bands* of a constellation refer to operations of celestial
magic; *binding the influences* speaks directly to the process of evoking decanic spirits into a talisman or amulet, while *loosening the bands* is reminiscent
of the *nam-bur-bi* – literally "evil loosening" – from the *Omen Compendia*.[350]
The idea of "bring[ing] forth the Mazzaroth in his season" may refer to
the Latin Vulgate translation, in which the word *Mazzaroth* is rendered as
Luciferum, meaning "morning star", likely in reference to the planet Venus.
Arcturus, or *Alpha Boötis*, is the brightest star in the constellation Boötes.
The name *Arcturus* (Greek: Ἀρκτοῦρος) means "Guardian of the Bear"[351],
as the star has been called since at least Hesiod's time.[352] Arcturus, due to
its proximity to Ursa Major (the "Greater She-Bear"), is associated with
the myth of Arcas, the son of Zeus and Callisto. Hera, very upset at the
state of affairs, as per usual, turned Callisto into a bear. Zeus spared his son,
Arcas, of Hera's wrath by secreting him away in Pan's wilderness, which
would come to be called Arcadia, in honor of the boy-hero. Arcas, who
had grown and become king of Arcadia, was an avid hunter and, one day,
while on an expedition encountered his mother, Callisto, in bear form.
She, not having seen her son in years, ran forward to embrace him. Arcas,

---

346   *The Holy Bible*, KJV, Genesis 1:14-18

347   Habel, *The Book of Job: A Commentary*, Westminster John Knox Press, 1985, p. 523

348   Entry: "Astrology"; Jastrow, Blau & Kohler, *Jewish Encyclopedia*, 1906, retrieved at:
jewishencyclopedia.com

349   *The Holy Bible*, KJV, Job 38:31-32

350   Hunger & Pingree, *Astral Sciences in Mesopotamia*, Brill, 1999, pp. 1-33

351   Entry: "Ἀρκτοῦρος", Liddell & Scott, *A Greek-English Lexicon*, Clarendon Press,
1940, retrieved at: tufts.edu

352   Rogers, "Origins of the Ancient Constellations: II. The Mediterranean Traditions",
Journal of the British Astronomical Association, 1998, pp. 79-89

alarmed as he was by the attacking she-bear, did not recognize her as his mother. He strung an arrow and took aim but Zeus, who couldn't bear to watch the tragic scene unfold, intervened, turning Arcas into a bear. He then pulled them both into the stars, where they are now the big and little bears, Ursa Major and Ursa Minor.

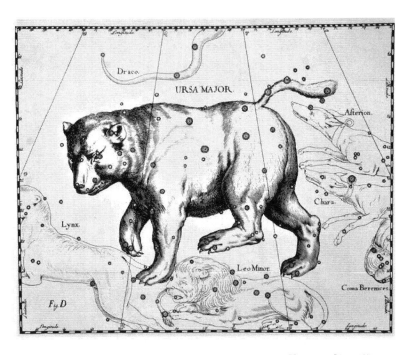

Ursa Major from Hevelius' Firmamentum Sobiescianum sive Uranographia, 1687

There is a section of the apocryphal Book of Enoch, colloquially known as the "Astronomical Book" (2nd century BCE), which was written in Aramaic and contains material not found in later versions of the book.[353] Ostensibly, the Astronomical Book was revealed to Enoch by the archangel Uriel, or Auriel, who is notable as being the angel of the North, the Earth and the zodiacal sign of Taurus in the correspondences used by the Hermetic Order of the Golden Dawn. Enoch is credited with the discovery of "the knowledge of the zodiac, and the course of the heavens"[354],

---

353   Martinez & Tigchelaar (eds.), *The Dead Sea Scrolls: Study Edition*, Brill/Eerdmans, 1997, pp. 430-443

354   Dwyer, *Revolution of the Luminaries*, Design of Time, 2016, pdf retrieved at: design-of-time.com

which is in keeping with his fulfilling of the Hermetic role in the Abrahamic tradition.[355] The Astronomical Book describes and catalogues the movement of "heavenly luminaries" against the firmament and through the "Gates of Heaven".

> *The Book of the Revolutions of the Lights of Heaven. Each as it is; according to their classes, according to their period of rule and their times, according to their names and places of origin, and according to their months. That Uriel, the Holy Angel who was with me, and is their leader, showed to me. And he showed me all their regulations, exactly as they are, for each year of the world and for ever, until the new creation shall be made which will last forever. And this is the First Law of the Lights. The light called the Sun; its rising is in the Gates of Heaven that are towards the east, and its setting is in the western Gates of Heaven.*[356]

The three Abrahamic religions – Judaism, Christianity and Islam – each observe a particular holy day of the week, which corresponds to a planet that has, in various ways, affected the symbolism of the religion. For instance, Saturday is the holy day in Judaism. It is known as the *Shabbat* (Hebrew: שבת; *Shabbat*, meaning "rest" or "cessation"), a day of rest, commemorative of the seventh day of Creation, when God rested. The etymological root of the word *Saturday* is the Latin *Saturni Dies*, or "day of Saturn", which was assigned by the Babylonian astronomers.[357] The Hebrew word for Saturn is *Shabtai* (Hebrew: שבתאי) and is related to the Jewish Sabbath through the same Babylonian planetary association.[358] The Star of David, or the *Magen David* (Hebrew: מָגֵן דָּוִד), is a hexagram which was adopted as a symbol of Judaism during the First Zionist Congress in 1897.[359] The hexagram had previously been used by medieval qabalists who had inherited it from Arabic magical and talismanic literature, wherein it was referred to as the Seal of Solomon, relating to the king's dominion over

355   Yates, *Giordano Bruno and the Hermetic Tradition*, University of Chicago Press, 1964, p. 52

356   *The Book of Enoch*, McCracken (trans), XIV:72:1-2

357   Entry: "Saturday"; *Online Etymological Dictionary*, retrieved at: etymonline.com

358   Sela, *Saturn and the Jews*, University of Pennsylvania, 2017, retrieved at: katz.sas.upenn.edu

359   Scholem, "The Curious History of the Six-Pointed Star. How the 'Magen David' Became the Jewish Symbol", *Commentary*, Vol. 8, 1949, pp. 251

the *djinn*.[360] During 1981's Voyager mission, a persistent hexagonal cloud at Saturn's North Pole was observed[361], thereby uniting both the geometrical and the planetary symbolism of Judaism in one cosmic event. David Origanus, a 17th-century professor of mathematics, wrote that "'Saturn is the significator of the Jews' [...] The identification of Saturn as the 'Star of Israel' and [the assertion of] its 'domination of the Judaic religion' has been made in a different context [...]".[362]

Sunday, from the Old English *Sunnandæg*, meaning "day of the Sun"[363], is recognized as the Sabbath in most Christian traditions. In 321 CE, Emperor Constantine I officially decreed Sunday to be the Roman day of rest corresponding to the seventh day of Creation.[364] In reference to the vestiges of Greco-Roman paganism, the Church Father, Saint Jerome, said: "If pagans call [the Lord's Day] the 'day of the sun,' we willingly agree, for today the light of the world is raised, today is revealed the sun of justice with healing in his rays."[365] The reclassification of Sunday is typical of Christianity's widespread adaptation and subsumation of pagan rituals, feast days and symbolism. The solar motif permeates the Christian narrative; precessional, zodiacal and diurnal solar allusions – too numerous to mention – may be discerned in the tradition. In the Gospel of Matthew, for example, *magoi* (Greek: μάγοι, meaning "astrologers") from the East – presumably Zoroastrian astronomers[366] – followed a rising star to Bethlehem (Hebrew: בֵּית לֶחֶם, meaning "House of Bread"), in what has been theorized to be an astrotheological myth involving the three stars in Orion's belt (the "wise men") following Venus (a "rising star") to the constellation Virgo (Bethlehem, the "house of bread") to the birth of the Sun (Jesus, the "Son").[367]

360   Leet, "The Hexagram and Hebraic Sacred Science", *The Secret Doctrine of the Kabbalah*, 1999, pp. 212-217

361   Caldwell, Turgeon, Hua, Barnet & Westphal, "The Drift of Saturn's North Polar Spot Observed by the Hubble Space Telescope", *Science*, 1993, pp. 326-329

362   Thorndike, *A History of Magic and Experimental Science*, New York: Columbia Univ. Press, 1934, vol. 7, pp. 145-146

363   Entry: "Sunday", *Online Etymological Dictionary*, retrieved at: etymonline.com

364   Zerubavel, *The Seven Day Circle: The History and Meaning of the Week*, University of Chicago Press, 1989, p. 45

365   St. Jerome, Pasch.: CCL 78, 550, as quoted in: *Catechism of the Catholic Church*, 1166

366   Axworthy, *A History of Iran*, Basic Books, 2008, pp. 31-43

367   See: Stowe, *Stowe's Bible Astrology*, Health Research, 1907 and Murdock (Acharya S.), *The Christ Con: The Greatest Story Ever Sold*, Adventures Unlimited, 1999

In the time of King Herod, after Jesus was born in Bethlehem of Judea, wise men from the East came to Jerusalem, asking, "Where is the child who has been born king of the Jews? For we observed his star at its rising, and have come to pay him homage." [368]

The IΧΘΥΣ acrostic, the *vesical piscis* ("fish bladder") and other ichthyic symbols may be seen as being in reference to the Piscean precessional age. Similarly, that Jesus is considered both the "lamb of god"[369] and the "fisher of men"[370] may be a precessional allusion to his birth marking the transition from the Arian Age (the first sign of the zodiac) to the Piscean Age (the last sign of the zodiac), also making him the zodiacal "Alpha and Omega, the beginning and the end, the first and the last".[371]

Jesus in a vesica piscis, surrounded by the Tetramorph

368   *The Holy Bible*, KJV, Matthew 2:1-2
369   *The Holy Bible*, KJV, John 1:29
370   *The Holy Bible*, KJV, Matthew 4:19
371   *The Holy Bible*, KJV, Revelation 22:13

Friday, from the Old English *Frigedæg*, meaning "day of Frigga"[372], is the Germanic translation of the late Latin *Veneris dies*, or "day of Venus". Friday is also the holy day in Islam, as the *Salaat-ul-Jumu'ah*, or "Friday Prayer", is a central religious obligation.[373] *Salat*, or "prayer" in general is the second of the five pillars of Islam; specifically, it prescribes the performance of prayers at five stages of the Sun's diurnal transit: *Fajr* (dawn), *Dhuhr* (midday), *Asr* (afternoon), *Maghrib* (sunset) and *Isha* (night). The *Jumu'ah* prayer is performed at equinoctial noon (*Dhuhr*) every Friday. According to Agrippa's planetary hours, and those widely used by Renaissance astrologers and magicians, equinoctial noon on a Friday is a solar hour, which may be said to be the highest "concentration" or "luminescence" of venerean influence (see Appendix C). Green, which is considered a sacred color in Islam[374], is the color associated with the planet Venus in the Hermetic, alchemical and qabalistic philosophies, probably due to the oxidation of copper resulting in a blue-green patina, or *verdigris*. Further support for this metallurgical interpretation may be seen in the etymological evolution of the English word *copper*, which also reinforces the association with the planet Venus, as it comes from *cuprum*, the Latinized name of the Greek island Cyprus, a major cult center of Aphrodite (Venus), "the Cyprian". [375] The star and crescent is the most ubiquitous symbol of Islam in modern times.[376] From an astronomical perspective, it is a depiction of an event known as the lunar occultation of Venus; this occurs when Venus is obscured by the Moon. This phenomenon is particularly striking during a waxing or waning crescent Moon as Venus seems to disappear when occulted by the shadowed portion of the Moon. Venerean influences become veiled or otherwise mediated by the saline and aquatic lunar forces, *just as fertility is governed by the menstrual cycle*. Venus and the Moon are both symbolic of feminine archetypes, but of a very different type; they may, however, be integrated and synchronized. Qabalistically, the *sephirah* of Venus (*Netzach*) and that of the Moon (*Yesod*) are connected by the 28th path on the *Etz Chaim*; Fittingly, the color attributed to *Netzach* is green, also, the mean of a lunar orbit (27.3 days) and a complete lunar phase (29.5 days) is 28.4 days[377], which rounds to 28, the number of the path

---

372   Entry: "Friday", *Online Etymological Dictionary*, retrieved at: etymonline.com

373   "Hashemi, Kamran", *Religious Legal Traditions, International Human Rights Law and Muslim States*, vol. 7, Brill, 2008

374   Lamborn Wilson, "Cloud Papers for Philip Taafe", *Critical Commentary*, retrieved at: philiptaaffe.info

375   Entry: "Copper", *Online Etymology Dictionary*, retrieved at: etymonline.com

376   Entry: "Moon", Glassé, *The New Encyclopedia of Islam*, p. 314

377   "Moon Phase Calculator", *Star Date*, retrieved at: stardate.org

connecting the two *sephiroth* (see Appendix B). The Tarot card attributed to this path is The Star XVII, which depicts an Aquarian woman pouring out two pitchers of water – one onto the earth, as if as a libation to the fertile mother, the other back into the body of water from whence it came, as a tribute to the cosmic mother who reflects our memory and, as the *anima*, guards the portal to the unconscious. The eight-pointed star – symbolic of Ishtar, the Venus of the Akkadians – hangs in the firmament among the "seven sisters" of the Pleiades. The Pleiades are a particularly important piece of this astrological symbol set in that the seven sisters live in the constellation of Taurus, which is ruled by Venus and in which the Moon is exalted. Thus, the venerean star and the lunar crescent are synthesized by the 28th path of the *Etz Chaim*, and the Aquarian integration of the spatial (the fertile Venus) and the temporal (the cyclic Moon) is achieved.

The Nebra Sky Disc, ca. 1600 BCE

The *Nebra* sky disc is a Bronze Age astronomical artifact found near Nebra, Germany, dating from about 1600 BCE, making it the oldest known depiction of the cosmos.[378] The disc is about one foot in diameter and composed of green, patinized bronze (due to the oxidation of its copper content) with gold inlays. It depicts a crescent Moon, the Pleiades star cluster and an orb usually interpreted to be the Sun, amidst other, smaller stellar objects. Two golden arcs, which were added to the disc at an undetermined later date (one being currently lost), span the disc at an angle of 82° – indicating the distance between the summer and winter solstices at 51°N (the southern border of Germany).[379] It is unknown whether the *verdigris*, or blue-green patina was meant to convey venerean symbolism or whether it was an intentional design element at all. However, the symbolic components of the artifact and its composition certainly lend themselves to a venereo-lunar interpretation; and the presence of the Pleiades seems to, again, indicate the stellar integration of Venus and the Moon in a manner evocative of the both The Star XVII Tarot card and the 28th path, to which it is attributed on the *Etz Chaim* (see Appendix B).

In specific systems within the broader framework of Western Esotericism, such as the *Societas Rosicriciana in Civitatibus Foederatis* and the Hermetic Order of the Golden Dawn, a firm elemental foundation (fire, air, water and earth, as they pertain to the qabalistic world of *Assiah*) is built upon with planetary (world of *Yetzirah*), decanic and zodiacal (world of *Briah*) occult theory. In the Second, or Inner Order grades of the aforementioned societies, the substance of this theoretical foundation is utilized by *Adepti* in operations of practical magic. Elemental, planetary, decanic and zodiacal correspondences are not only fundamental to developing a sound theoretical foundation in Western occultism, but they are also integral to a sufficiently developed interpretive perspective in Freemasonry. Additionally, a developed astromythological, or astrotheological perspective is an extremely valuable vantage point from which to survey the symbolism and ritual of the Craft. The astrologically-illuminated Freemason need look no further than the Three Lesser Lights, who represent the Sun, the Moon and the Master of the Lodge; the act of circumambulation, which is a terrestrial imitation of a celestial phenomenon; the Blazing Star, which may be interpreted to represent either Venus or Sirius equally convincingly; the Weeping Virgin of the Third Degree, with its obvious allusions to the constellation Virgo, the *kore* Persephone, and the conflation

378   "Nebra Sky Disc", *Memory of the World*, 2013, retrieved at: unesco.org
379   McIntosh, *Lost Treasures; Civilization's Great Riches Rediscovered*, London: Carlton Books, 2010, p. 16

of Chronos and Cronus (Saturn); the Four Veils of the Tabernacle, upon which is depicted the four fixed zodiacal signs; the keystone of the Royal Arch, which is an obvious allusion to the summer solstice; or the Hiramic Tragedy, a solar allegory; in order to begin to see how an understanding of, say, zodiacal and stellar lore would deepen and expand his appreciation of the Craft's symbolism.[380]

For what is the goal of our learning but that it may be used to enrich our experiences, our lives, and the lives of those around us? That we might develop our personal and cultural reference point in order to get more out of not merely art, literature, architecture, music, the theater and the cinema, but also a deeper appreciation of the initiatic experience? Of the world in which we live? Of life itself? That we might begin to perceive those underlying patterns which are the criteria by which the true, the good and the beautiful are judged? That we might, one day, progress beyond the theoretical and begin to have an authentic and unmediated experience of the world, on its own terms? That we might become active participants in the act of Creation, as opposed to merely passive observers? These are the aims of the occult sciences – when theory becomes applicable in a praxis that affords us access to a new paradigm of understanding and a new depth of experience. It is in this way that an ever-developing understanding of the seven liberal arts and sciences benefits us.

---

380   Lamb, *Myth, Magick & Masonry: Occult Perspectives in Freemasonry*, The Laudable Pursuit, 2018, Section II

CHAPTER IX

∴

THE WAGES OF A FELLOW CRAFT
&
THE JEWELS OF A FELLOW CRAFT

THE WAGES OF A FELLOW CRAFT

You have now arrived at the Middle Chamber where you are received and recorded a Fellow Craft. You are now en-titled to wages, as such; which are, the Corn of nourishment, the Wine of refreshment, and the Oil of joy, which denote peace, harmony, and strength.[1]

Having ascended the Winding Staircase, the Fellow Craft Mason finds himself at the door of the Middle Chamber of K∴S∴T∴, there to receive the wages of a Fellow Craft, which are corn, wine and oil. After a brief explanation of each, he is informed that, symbolically, they denote "peace, harmony and strength". Mackey, in his *Encyclopedia*, states that "[c]orn, wine and oil were most important productions of Eastern countries, they constituted the wealth of the people, and were esteemed as the supports of life and the means of refreshment."[2] This is the end of their discussion in ritual until we again encounter corn, wine and oil in the context of a cornerstone laying ceremony. In the *Holy Bible*, these three ancient

1 *Duncan's Masonic Ritual and Monitor* (1866), New York: Crown Publishers, 1986, p. 77
2 Mackey, *An Encyclopedia of Freemasonry and its Kindred Sciences*, Everts & Co., 1884, p. 187

commodities are commonly referenced together, both in terms of being paid out as wages and offered as alms or tithings; corn, wine and oil appear in Deuteronomy 11:14, 12:17, 14:23, 18:4, 28:51, Chronicles 31:5, 32:28, Nehemiah 10:39, 13:5, 13:12, Hosea 2:8, 2:22, Joel 2:19, 2:24, and Haggai 1:11.[3] From the perspective of the Western Esoteric Tradition, we find that the wages of a Fellow Craft symbolize the *tria prima*, or three philosophical principles of alchemy – salt, sulfur and mercury.

Corn, meaning "seed of a cereal plant; seeds of cereal plants generally; plants which produce corn when growing in the field", was used to refer to oats, wheat, barley and others, generally. Etymologically, the word stems from the proto-Germanic *kurnam*, meaning "small seed".[4] As a verb, the word *corn* is defined as "to preserve or season with salt in grains [...] to cure or preserve in brine containing preservatives and often seasonings."[5] In Preston's time, the word *corn* was often substituted for *salt*, due to the manner in which meat and fish were cured, or preserved, such as *corned* beef.[6] Up until the middle of the 20th century, either dry salt, or a brine solution was used in this process which inhibited the growth of micro-organisms and allowed for the dry storage of surplus foods. Specifically regarding the use of salt as wages, we find that the very word *salary* is derived from the Latin *salarium*, or "salt money, soldier's allowance for the purchase of salt".[7] Thus, *corn* may be very reasonably conflated with *salt*.

Wine production can be traced back to at least 6,000 years ago, developing roughly concurrently in Georgia, Armenia, Iran and Sicily.[8] The process involves the fermentation of grapes, when yeast consumes the glucose and fructose content and converts it into ethanol.[9] Wine has been used in religious rituals such as those of cult of Dionysus, the *Bacchanalia* of the Romans, the *Kiddush* in Judaism and in the Christian Eucharist. In medieval alchemy, wine was associated with the mercurial "spirit", or the alcohol content of the grape, and was often used as the universal Vegetable Kingdom solvent in spagyric operations, along with its further distillation, brandy.

3   Leilich, "Salt, Wine and Oil", *Knight Templar Magazine*, Feb. 2018

4   Entry: "Corn", *Online Etymological Dictionary*, retrieved at: etymonline.com

5   Entry: "Corn", *Merriam Webster Dictionary*, retrieved at: merriam-webster.com

6   Leilich, "Salt, Wine and Oil", *Knight Templar Magazine*, Feb. 2018

7   Entry: "Salary", *Online Etymological Dictionary*, retrieved at: etymonline.com

8   Hames, *Alcohol in World History*, Routledge, 2010, p. 17

9   Alba-Lois, et al., "Yeast Fermentation and the Making of Beer and Wine", *Nature*, retrieved at: nature.com

*First, the grapes are "sacrificed" or crushed to release their es-
sences in the juice. Then, Putrefaction begins as the juice is allowed to decompose and rot. Next, a white layer of digesting
bacteria arises that begins the process of Fermentation. This
phase is also sometimes marked by waxy substance the alchemists called the Ferment and an oily film known as the Pea-
cock's Tail. Finally, the new life force "conquers" the original
identity of the grape juice and supplants it with a new and
higher presence or life. This higher presence is release during the
next operation (Distillation), which produces the true Spirit of Wine (its alcohol), which contains the purified essence of
grapes.[10]*

Aromatic oils have been used in ritualistic anointing ceremonies for
millennia, usually conferring honor, protection or consecrating the anointed. In the Abrahamic traditions, we encounter this practice in the stories of
Aaron, the *Messiah* (Hebrew: מָשִׁיחַ) and the *Christ* (Greek: Χριστός), both
words meaning "the Anointed One".[11] Generally, essential oils are distilled
from some organic material using steam and condensation. Leaves, flowers, roots, seeds, bark and peels are most commonly used in the distillation
process, wherein the material is put in an alembic over simmering water.
The volatile compounds are vaporized and allowed to pass through the
neck of the alembic; the steam carrying the oils is then condensed back
into liquid form and collected. This oil/water mix, or *hydrosol*, may be used
in this state or further separated by simmering the water off.[12] Oil fulfills
the role of sulfur because it may be burned in lamps and heaters and is, like
sulfur ("brimstone"), associated with elemental fire and the "soul" principle; and also because almost all of the elemental sulfur in the world today
is produced as a byproduct of "sour" or crude oil.[13]

10   Hauck, "Searching for the Cosmic Quintessence: How Medieval Alchemists
Meditated", *The Rose+Croix Journal*, retrieved at: academia.org
11   Baynes (ed.), "Anointing", *Encyclopædia Britannica* (9th ed.), New York: Charles
Scribner's Sons, 1878, p. 90
12   Lattin, "What is the Role of Chemistry in Aromatherapy?", *American College of
Healthcare Sciences*, 2016, retrieved at: achs.edu
13   "Sulfur (content)", *Energy Insights*. McKinsey, retrieved at: mckinseyenergyinsights.
com

The tria prima: salt, sulfur and mercury, from Nazari, Il metamorfosi metallico et humano, 1572

The *tria prima* of Paracelsian, or spagyric alchemy consists of salt, sulfur and mercury. These are the *soma*, *psyche* and *pneuma* of the Greeks; the *corpus*, *anima* and *spiritus* of the Romans; and the body, mind and spirit of modern metaphysics. These three philosophical principles also correspond to the wages of a Fellow Craft: corn, wine and oil. The separation (*solve*), purification and reintegration (*coagula*) of these three principles, results in their alchemical perfection and, as we have learned, when this process is performed in the outer operative lab, there is a hermetically corresponding inner transformation and integration happening within the alchemist –

this is the defining factor differentiating alchemy from chemistry. Another way we may begin to synthesize these three principles is through qabalistic and tarotic contemplation – in order to do this, we must first translate the *tria prima* into the language of Hermetic Qabalah.

Having addressed the numbers three, five and seven, their symbolism, and their relationship to the courses of steps on the Winding Staircase in the foregoing, we will now place these numbers within the scheme of alchemy and the Western Esoteric Tradition by applying a qabalistic proof. We will begin by locating these numbers on the *Etz Chaim* and in the Tarot. According to the established correspondences used in modern Hermetic Qabalah (see Appendix A), the number three is the gematriac value of the Hebrew letter *gimel* (ג; meaning "camel"), which is attributed to the High Priestess II card; the number five is the gematriac value of the Hebrew letter *heh* (ה; meaning "window"), which is attributed to the Emperor IV card; the number seven is the gematriac value of the Hebrew letter *zayin* (ז; meaning "sword"), which is attributed to the Lovers VI card.

Each Hebrew letter and, consequently, each card in the Major Arcana, is associated with a certain path on the *Etz Chaim* (see Appendix B). Each path connects two *sephiroth* and thereby represents the dynamic activity of their relationship. The letter *gimel* (3) is assigned to 13th path, which connects *Kether* to *Tiphareth*; the letter *heh* (5) is assigned to 15th path, which connects *Chokmah* to *Tiphareth*; and the letter *zayin* (7) is assigned to 17th path, which connects *Binah* to *Tiphareth*. When this is viewed in the context of the *Etz Chaim*, we see the emergence a very interesting and symmetrical pattern. The supernals – *Kether*, *Chokmah* and *Binah* – are very deliberately emanating the numbers three, five and seven into *Tiphareth*, which is the place of devotion to the Great Work, or *Magnum Opus*. Furthermore, when we analyze the three Tarot cards in this operation, we find that they represent none other than the alchemical *tria prima*: salt, sulfur and mercury. We will explain how and why this is the case in the following terms of our proof…

The High Priestess II card corresponds to salt because she represents the sea; she is the *Stella Maris*, or "Star of the Sea" (Latin: *mare*; root of marine, *La Mer*, Mary, etc.); her robes flow into the crashing oceanic waves, which seem to be compelled to agitation by the waxing crescent Moon at her feet, just as the saltwater tides are in a constant dialogue with, and subject to the gravitational attraction of *Luna*, the Moon, who reacts specifically to the presence of these oceanic salts.[14] The color associated with

---

14   "Tide Formation – Gravitational Pull", *Exploring Our Fluid Earth*, retrieved at: manoa.hawaii.edu

this card and its path on the *Etz Chaim* is blue, the color of the briny ocean. The High Priestess II is also seated on a white, cubical stone, which further accentuates her saline character as, atomically, salt forms a cubic, crystal lattice.[15] She carries the supernal Light from the Crown to its manifestation in the Beauty of *Tiphareth*, like the dromedary who carries its precious store of water across the abysmal desert to a beautiful oasis.

The Emperor IV Tarot corresponds to sulfur because of its association with Martial fire. In the hieroglyphical language of the Tarot, this card represents the zodiacal sign of Aries – a fire sign which is ruled by Mars (Greek: *Ares*), the God of War. Biblically, sulfur was known as "brimstone"[16], which means "burning stone"[17], and represents YHVH's fury and wrath, as well as destruction and combustibility, in general. The color associated with this card and its path on the *Etz Chaim* is red, the color of Mars and iron oxide. Alchemically, the glyph representing sulfur is a cross topped with an upward facing, elemental fire triangle – the fire of Mars and of Aries, the primary member of the astrological fire triplicity. The zodiacal flame of Wisdom is carried forth by the warlike Emperor, laying siege to the *Civitas Solis*[18], the Adocentyan[19] middle-kingdom of *Tiphareth*.

The Lovers VI card corresponds to mercury because of its attribution to the zodiacal sign of Gemini, which is ruled by Mercury; also, the color associated with this card and its path on the *Etz Chaim* is orange, which is the color of the mercurial *sephirah* of *Hod*. The man and woman depicted on the card, when taken together, may be said to represent the hermaphrodite (Hermes-Mercury and Aphrodite-Venus), or the divine androgyne of Heinrich Khunrath (1560-1605 CE) in his *Amphitheatrum sapientiae aeternae* (1595). They appear to be in the ritual-process of their Hermetic Marriage – united in the universal, mercurial solvent – presided over by the Archangel Raphael who, standing before Sol, guides the androgynic couple from the sorrow and leaden heaviness of the Saturnal *sephirah* of *Binah* to solar *Tiphareth*'s blazing light of perfection (which, in the Rider-Waite Tarot, is labelled with the number *VI*, further emphasizing this orb's identification with the sixth *sephirah*, *Tiphareth*), wherein the Archangel himself resides.

---

15   "Sodium Chloride: NaCl - Salt of the Earth", *American Chemistry Council*, 2003, retrieved at: chlorine.americanchemistry.com

16   Greenwood & Earnshaw, *Chemistry of the Elements* (2nd ed.), Oxford: Butterworth-Heinemann, 1997

17   Chisholm (ed.), Entry: "Brimstone", *Encyclopædia Britannica*, Cambridge University Press, 1911, p. 571

18   See: Campanella, 1602

19   See: *Ġāyat al-Ḥakīm* (a.k.a. *Picatrix*), Book IV

The High Priestess, the Emperor and the Lovers, Rider-Waite Tarot, Rider & Sons, 1909,
From the private collection of William S. Burkle

These three Tarot cards, which are gematriacally associated with the numbers three (*gimel*), five (*heh*) and seven (*zayin*), thereby guide the three supernal potencies from *Kether*, *Chokmah* and *Binah* to their manifestation in *Tiphareth*, wherein we see the completion of the *Magnum Opus* (see Appendix B). Analogously, in *spagyric* or Paracelsian alchemy performed in the Vegetable Kingdom, the salt, sulfur and mercury of any plant or herb is divided (Latin: *solve*) into its three alchemical constituents: its calcined ash (salt; body), its distilled essential oils (sulfur; soul), and its fermented alcohol content (mercury; spirit). These three philosophical principles – the *tria prima* – are then recombined (Latin: *coagula*) into an alchemically purified and essentialized tincture, which may be used medicinally or magically. When this process is performed by the alchemist, the external operation is believed to be hermetically mirrored in the operator – i.e. the microcosm and the microcosm are sympathetically engaged in the alchemical dialogue of transformation.

For those interested in this field of research, and its operative experimentation, a simple spagyric tincture preparation will be here provided as a practicum:

Materials needed

¼ cup – 1 cup of the preferred plant material

Mortar and pestle

Clean, glass jar with lid

Grain alcohol

Plastic wrap

Muslin, or cheesecloth

Small kitchen funnel

Pyrex, or similar, baking dish

Tincture bottle with dropper

A spagyric operation is a vegetable kingdom alchemical process usually consisting of the separation, purification and recombination of a root, herb or flower's three alchemical principles: salt, sulfur and mercury. The word, which comes from the Greek *spao* (to draw out) and *ageiro* (to gather), is believed to have been coined by Paracelsus in his *Liber Paragranum*. The processes involved are: distillation of the essential oils (the sulfur, or "soul" of the plant), fermentation to render the alcohol content (the mercury, or "spirit" of the plant), and extraction of the mineral content (the salt, or "body" of the plant). After these three principles are isolated and purified, they are recombined in a tincture which may be used for medicinal, ritualistic or magical purposes. Spagyric tinctures differ from common alcohol tinctures in that they contain the basic salts rendered from the calcined plant matter.

A spagyric tincture corresponding to each day of the week may be chosen by consulting a table listing which plants, herbs or roots are ruled by which classical planet (the Moon, Mercury, Venus, the Sun, Mars, Jupiter & Saturn); lists such as these are readily available online and in some books on astrology, but *Cunningham's Encyclopedia of Magical Herbs* (Cunningham, Llewelyn, 1985) is a particularly excellent reference. Every stage of the operation should be considered deliberately and performed ritualistically, as these operations are intended to have an effect on the operator as well as the plant material. This dynamic is analogous to that of astronomy and astrology, both of which measure and chronicle the movements and cycles of celestial bodies – astrology, however, is differentiated from astronomy in that there is the accompanying belief that these macrocosmic cycles have a causal effect on microcosmic man. Similarly, alchemy is differentiated from chemistry in that the microcosmic alchemical operation is believed to have an effect on the macrocosmic operator. Consideration of this dynamic, along with utilizing the subtle influences of cosmic sympathies, is integral to practical alchemy.

Ultimately, one would harvest the plant material on a weekday and hour corresponding to the plant's planetary ruler (see Appendix C). The plant, root or herb is then dried and cut into small pieces. These small, dried pieces are ground in a mortar and pestle as finely as possible. Deposit this material into a clean, glass jar. Ideally, you would want to have a ¼ cup – 1 cup of dried and ground plant material.

In the simple spagyric method, and for beginners in this art, the use of a universal vegetable kingdom mercury, such as grain alcohol, is recommended. Fermentation for the mercury of the plant material itself is more time and labor intensive, and also typically yields very little mercury. Since vegetable kingdom mercury is universal across this domain, using grain alcohol amounts to the very same principle – grain alcohol itself being a vegetable kingdom mercury. Slowly add the grain alcohol to the jar containing the dried and ground plant material until it is covered by about an inch. Seal the mouth of the jar with plastic wrap and apply the lid. The plastic wrap prevents the tincture from coming into contact with the metallic lid. Mark the jar with the name of the plant material and also with the planetary glyph corresponding to the plant matter. Place the jar in a dark, warm place for forty days (one alchemical month), shaking to stir up the sediment at least every few days.

Then Jesus was led up by the Spirit into the wilderness to be tempted by the devil. And after fasting forty days and forty nights, he was hungry. And the tempter came and said to him, "If you are the Son of God, command these stones to become loaves of bread." But he answered, "It is written, 'Man shall not live by bread alone, but by every word that comes from the mouth of God.'" Then the devil took him to the holy city and set him on the pinnacle of the temple.[20]

---

20   *The Holy Bible*, KJV, Matthew 4:1-25

At the next day and hour corresponding to the plant, after one full alchemical month, remove the lid and the plastic wrap. If your plant material is ruled by Mars, for example, you would do this on the first Tuesday *after the forty-day period*, preferably in the first hour after sunrise. Again, this should be done deliberately and ritualistically – perhaps by lighting a red candle, listening to "Mars, Bringer of War" from Holst's *The Planets*, and after meditating on, say, the Emperor IV (zodiacal Mars) or the Tower XVI (planetary Mars) Tarot card. The essential oils (sulfur) will have infused into the alcohol (mercury) and these should be either siphoned off and/or poured through a small kitchen funnel packed with muslin cheese-cloth into a tincture bottle with dropper. Set the sulfur and mercury tincture aside.

The alcohol-soaked plant material, which has been depleted of its essential oils, should be transferred to a Pyrex (or similar) baking dish. Take the dish outside and touch a match to the material; this is the process of calcination. It should burn to ash without much tending. Depending on the chosen plant material, the ash will be anywhere from black to grey and, rarely, to completely white. The goal at this stage is to render white ash. You may need to return the dish to the broiler on your stove – this will further calcinate the matter. The white ash (containing the mineral salts) should be brought back to the mortar and pestle and ground into a fine powder.

> *Every man's work shall be made manifest: for the day shall declare it, because it shall be revealed by fire; and the fire shall try every man's work of what sort it is. If any man's work abide which he hath built thereupon, he shall receive a reward. If any man's work shall be burned, he shall suffer loss: but he himself shall be saved; yet so as by fire. Know ye not that ye are the temple of God, and that the Spirit of God dwelleth in you?*[21]

There is an optional process at this stage: you may simply add the powdered body (salt) to your alcohol (mercury) and essential oil (sulfur) tincture now, or you may transfer the white ash to a shallow glass, or petri dish, cover it with a small amount of distilled water and allow it to evaporate on a window sill. This will further purify your salt and, if you are fortunate, it will render the crystalized salt alkaloids – a white stone.

---

21   *The Holy Bible*, KJV, Corinthians 3:13-16

He who has an ear, let him hear what the Spirit says to the churches. To the one who conquers I will give some of the hidden manna, and I will give him a white stone, with a new name written on the stone that no one knows except the one who receives it.[22]

These purified salts may then be added to your mercury and sulfur tincture. Either way, you have separated (*solve*) the three alchemical principles of your plant material, purified them, and recombined (*coagula*) them in their perfected form in a potable spagyric tincture.

May my teaching drop as the rain, my speech distill as the dew, like gentle rain upon the tender grass, and like showers upon the herb.[23]

This tincture may be ingested on the day of the plant's planetary ruler, preferably at an hour ruled by that planet. You may also choose to ingest the tincture at a time when you would like to draw on the subtle cosmic influence of that particular planet. For instance, you may ingest a mercurial tincture to enhance intellectual pursuits, a venerean tincture to further romantic interests, a jupiterian tincture to stimulate financial ventures.

And as soon as he came near the camp and saw the calf and the dancing, Moses' anger burned hot, and he threw the tablets out of his hands and broke them at the foot of the mountain. He took the calf that they had made and burned it with fire and ground it to powder and scattered it on the water and made the people of Israel drink it.[24]

As we have seen, the wages of a Fellow Craft may be seen to represent the alchemical *tria prima*: the three philosophical principles which, speculatively, represent the body (salt, corn, *soma*, *corpus*), the mind (sulfur, oil, *psyche*, *anima*) and the spirit (mercury, wine, *pneuma*, *spiritus*). These three

---

22   *The Holy Bible*, KJV, Revelation 2:17

23   *The Holy Bible*, KJV, Deuteronomy 32:2

24   *The Holy Bible*, KJV, Exodus 32:19-20

principles represent the tripartite nature of man – renowned in Western Occultism, since time immemorial – and must be separated and recombined in their refined state, balanced and working in concert, integrated through the operations of speculative alchemy. However, *we must do the operative work*; this is the only way to utilize the hermetic sympathies between the microcosm and the macrocosm, as we have abundantly illustrated throughout the present volume. The work must be completed in the outer to affect the inner – for this is the basis of all the Hermetic Arts, and likewise of Freemasonry.

Having addressed the physical wages and their exoteric, superficial interpretations, as described in the Fellow Craft lecture (see Appendix D) – as well as having unpacked the meaning and application of their alchemical correlatives – we will presently disclose the occult value of undertaking such a syllabus. We will see how the seven liberal arts and sciences purify and prepare us, in a very deliberate developmental sequence, for the subjects of philosophy and theology. For, only after the mind has been sufficiently organized and disciplined by the trivial and quadrivial subjects, is the student adequately prepared to execute the work laid out for them on the metaphysical trestleboard.

Giovanni Pico della Mirandola (Johannes Picus Mirandulanus)

But indeed not only the Mosaic and Christian mysteries but also the theology of the ancients show us the benefits and value of the liberal arts [...] For what else did the degrees of the initiates observed in the mysteries of the Greeks mean? For they arrived at a perception of these mysteries when they had first been purified through those expiatory sciences, as it were, moral philosophy and dialectic. What else can that perception possibly be than an interpretation of occult nature by means of philosophy? Then at length to those who were so disposed came that ΕΠΟΠΤΕΙΑ, that is to say, the observation of things divine by the light of theology. Who would not long to be initiated into such sacred rites?[25]

---

25   Pico della Mirandola, *De hominis dignitate* (English: *Oration on the Dignity of Man*), 1486

In the above excerpt, Pico likens the classical syllabus of seven liberal arts and sciences to a philosophical Mystery tradition in their own right. Extrapolating on this theme, one may view each of the subjects representing a grade, or degree; and the trivium and quadrivium representing the lesser and greater Mysteries, respectively. Ultimately, the wages are an understanding of the Hermetic Arts and of theurgy. One is given the occult keys to their own destiny. The fruition of a goal is but an equation, or algebraic expression, with variables to be plugged in and solved; the vision of the sum and the cultivation of a hermetic resonance with our objective; we partake in Creation. No longer subject to the whims of chance, we cultivate and refine the focus of the will, which is projected through space and time thereby inseminating the future with our imagination. These are the wages. Yet they may only be responsibly and effectively employed by those who have refined their will, and that refinement requires an understanding of the world, phenomenal and noumenal, and the curriculum for this process is the seven liberal arts and sciences.

THE JEWELS OF A FELLOW CRAFT

You are also entitled to the jewels of a Fellow Craft; which are, an attentive ear, an instructive tongue, and faithful breast. The attentive ear receives the sound from the instructive tongue, and the mysteries of Masonry are safely lodged in the repository of faithful breasts.[26]

As we have illustrated in the foregoing, the prescribed sequence of the Fellow Craft lecture (see Appendix D) – and, especially, that of the seven liberal arts and sciences – is intentional and represents a culmination of the collective wisdom of mankind, *spanning many millennia*. We have stood on the porch of the Temple; we have passed through the Brazen Pillars; we have ascended a flight of stairs, consisting of three, five and seven steps; and, finally, we have we have arrived the door to the Middle Chamber – a door which represents the liminal threshold between the physical and the

26   *Duncan's Masonic Ritual and Monitor* (1866), New York: Crown Publishers, 1986, p. 77

metaphysical worlds. It is here that we are to receive the Jewels of a Fellow Craft – these are: an attentive ear, an instructive tongue, and a faithful breast.

The attentive ear teaches us the value of effective listening. Hearing and listening are separate operations; generally, hearing is passive and listening is active. Entering a conversation with an agenda to express or a bias to confirm is almost always a detriment; these positions impede effective listening. In conversation, the mind should be made as clear as possible and put in a state of readiness to receive new information. Strive to comprehend; this sometimes means asking clarifying, open-ended questions – listen to the response. It is important to note that which is not being verbalized as well – this can sometimes tell us more than that which is openly communicated. Be mindful of non-verbal cues, body language and gesticulation, and how these color the meaning of the spoken word. Often, in conversation, as our thoughts are stimulated by points as they are raised by our interlocutor; in this case, we may find ourselves formulating our responses and thinking of our contributions to the conversation rather than actively listening. Effective listening is a skill that, like any other skill, can be developed and refined; we become better listeners with practice.[27,28]

The instructive tongue affords us the opportunity to apply what we have learned in the *artes sermocinales* (language arts) of the trivium – grammar, rhetoric and logic, or dialectic. These arts arm us with a capacity for critical thought, the ability to persuade through discourse, the ability to recognize and circumvent logical fallacies, and the ability to communicate compelling arguments and hypotheses. In conversation or debate, the trivial arts prepare us to organize and articulate our thoughts in a meaningful and impactful way. They also help us to decide whether to offer input or commentary at all; for, sometimes, the best response is silence. A certain economy of speech is cultivated as we learn to distinguish between "wise counsel" and unsolicited advice; and it is by the observance of this distinction that our contributions appreciate in weight and value. By a similar token, the weakness or strength of our personal will is directly proportionate to how well we keep our word. For instance, the more one fails to honor a verbal commitment, the less one's word means the next time – not only to the one to whom the promise was made, but also to oneself, which is always to the detriment of one's will.

27   Tartakovsky, "7 Tips to Becoming a Better Listener", *Psych Central*, 2018, retrieved at: psychcentral.com

28   Nemko, "How to Become a Better Listener", *Psychology Today*, 2014, retrieved at: psychologytoday.com

That the "mysteries of Masonry are safely lodged in the repository of faithful breasts" is essential to the maintenance of the Craft. To maintain the secrecy of our Mysteries is not only paramount but Obligatory to the Freemason. In fact, this commitment to keeping our Mysteries inviolate has made Freemasonry a synonym for secrecy. Apropos the safeguarding of the Romany language among the Gypsies, for example, it was said that they observed "a kind of freemasonry among them,"[29] their language being a part of that which bound them together as a people and was, consequently, jealously guarded from outsiders. Similarly, of the early Christians, it was observed that "[p]roscription always strengthens fellowship among the proscribed, and the persecution of the early Christians created a kind of freemasonry among them".[30] Using the sphinx (composed of the tetramorphic creatures: bull, lion, eagle and man) as a simile for the perfected man, *Éliphas* Lévi attributed initiatic silence to one of the "four words of the Magus" as follows…

> *To attain the SANCTUM REGNUM, in other words, the knowledge and power of the Magi, there are four indispensable conditions—an intelligence illuminated by study, an intrepidity which nothing can check, a will which cannot be broken, and a prudence which nothing can corrupt and nothing intoxicate. TO KNOW, TO DARE, TO WILL, TO KEEP SILENCE—such are the four words of the Magus, inscribed upon the four symbolical forms of the sphinx.*[31]

29   Mercer, "About Gipsies", *To-Day*, Howard House, 1896

30   "Christian Fellowship", *The Christian Advocate*, McCutcheon & Co., 1908, p. 454

31   Lévi, *Dogme et Rituel de la Haute Magie* (English: *Dogma and Ritual of High Magic*), published in two volumes in 1854 and 1856

Éliphas Lévi's Cherubim of Ezekiel, 1854

CHAPTER X

∴

THE LETTER G
&
SUMMARY

THE LETTER G

I shall now direct your attention to the letter "G", which is the initial of geometry, the fifth science, it being that on which this Degree was principally founded. Geometry, the first and noblest of sciences, is the basis upon which the superstructure of Masonry is erected. By geometry, we may curiously trace nature through her various windings to her most concealed recesses. By it we discover the power, the wisdom, and the goodness of the Grand Artificer of the Universe, and view with delight the proportions which connect this vast machine. By it we discover how the planets move in their different orbits, and demonstrate their various revolutions. By it we account for the return of the seasons, and the variety of scenes which each season displays to the discerning eye. Numerous worlds are around us, all formed by the same Divine Artist, and which roll through the vast expanse, and are all conducted by the same unerring law of nature. A survey of nature, and the observation of her beautiful proportions, first determined man to imitate the Divine plan, and study symmetry and order.[1]

---

1 *Duncan's Masonic Ritual and Monitor* (1866), New York: Crown Publishers, 1986, pp. 77-78

The Fellow Craft lecture is concluded with an exposition on the Masonic concepts embodied by the letter *G* (see Appendix E). At first, the candidate is explicitly told that the letter's significance stems from it being the initial of the word *geometry*; but he is soon afterward informed by the Worshipful Master that the letter *G* has a higher signification – that of alluding to the "sacred name of Deity".[2] Being that we are referencing English-speaking ritual, we may presume that the Worshipful Master is referring either to "God" or to the "Grand Architect (or Artificer) of the Universe" (often abbreviated as G∴A∴O∴T∴U). The candidate is informed that it was by man's observation of the celestial bodies and his study of the laws of nature, her symmetry and proportions, that he was inspired to imitate the "Divine Artist" in his own, terrestrial works. In essence, man, having learned a little of Deity's creative *modus operandi*, was set at liberty to utilize His methods. He has reverse-engineered the Divine Works of the G∴A∴O∴T∴U and has learned to recreate them in the microcosm. Man has extrapolated the laws of geometry from nature Herself and utilized them – in the form of astronomy, navigation, radio propagation, echolocation, etc. – to penetrate the Earth and space.

Conversely, it has been argued that systems such as geometry, number, time, and even space itself, are merely man's projections into reality – his way of qualifying and quantifying his experience, of understanding the relationship between objects, and so forth. This idealistic stance was notably explored by the German, Enlightenment-era philosopher, Immanuel Kant (1724-1804), "the central figure of modern philosophy"[3], who posited the following…

> *Space is not something objective and real, neither substance, nor accident, nor relation; but subjective and ideal, arising by fixed law from the nature of the mind like an outline for the mutual co-ordination of all external sensations whatsoever. Those who defend the reality of space either conceive of it as an absolute and immense receptacle of possible things, an opinion which, besides the English, pleases most geometricians, or they contend for its being the relation of existing things itself, which clearly vanishes in the removal of things and is thinkable only in actual things […] The first inane fiction of the*

2   *Duncan's Masonic Ritual and Monitor* (1866), New York: Crown Publishers, 1986, p. 78
3   Rohlf, "Immanuel Kant", *Stanford Encyclopedia of Philosophy*, 2016, retrieved at: plato.stanford.edu

reason, imagining true infinite relation without any mutually related things, pertains to the world of fable. But the adherents of the second opinion fall into a much worse error. Whilst the former only cast an obstacle in the way of some rational or noumenal concepts, otherwise most recondite, such as questions concerning the spiritual world, omnipresence, etc., the latter place themselves in fiat opposition to the very phenomena, and to the most faithful interpreter of all phenomena, to geometry. For, not to enlarge upon the obvious circle in which they become involved in defining space, they cast forth geometry, thrown down from the pinnacle of certitude, into the number of those sciences whose principles are empirical. If we have obtained all the properties of space by experience from external relations only, geometrical axioms have only comparative universality, such as is acquired by induction. They have universality evident as far as observed, but neither necessity, except as far as the laws of nature may be established, nor precision, except what is arbitrarily made. There is hope, as in empirical sciences, that a space may some time be discovered endowed with other primary properties, perchance even a rectilinear figure of two lines.[4]

Kant's critique of time followed similar logic, concluding that it is a human construct, as opposed to a clockwork, or some Newtonian "stream" in which we move and have our being but, rather, a feature of human cognition without an objective correlative in the world. In making this connection, it could be said that Kant, in conjoining space and time as subjective abstractions, arrived at the notion of space-time being a unified whole over one hundred years before Einstein had, in his special theory of relativity (1905). So, it may be said that these conventional methods, which man has devised in his various attempts to understand the world, represent his *ideas* of the world – not necessarily the world itself. It is his theory, his critique, and his methodology. From this perspective, it may be that the underlying geometry and the patterns that man finds in Creation are precisely the things that are obscuring a true and immediate apprehension of reality, in the Platonic, or idealistic sense. Does a geometrical interpretation of Deity's Creation merely veil His Works, leaving man yet one more step

---

4   Eckoff (trans.), *Kant's Inaugural Dissertation of 1770*, 1894, Section III, par. 15, D

removed from the direct appreciation of his Divine Source? Nevertheless, we, as human beings, have found these systems and concepts to be useful in our processing and navigation of experience; geometry, in particular, has been especially valuable and truly may be said to be the foundation upon which so many other useful arts and sciences rest.

The idea of "numerous worlds"[5], as stated in "the G Lecture" sequence of the Fellow Craft degree in Preston-Webb Masonic ritual, is reminiscent of what was considered by the Roman Catholic Church to be a heretical concept when it was introduced by the Dominican friar, philosopher and hermetic occultist, Giordano Bruno (1548-1600). Influenced by the recently (re)discovered[6] heliocentric model of Copernicus, Bruno believed that, not only was the Sun at the center of the planetary spheres – an idea already considered heretical in his time – but that it was merely a star among countless stars, and that each star, out of the thousands that cluttered the firmament, hosting planets in orbit about it in an arrangement similar to our own, with this arrangement disappearing in an infinite, fractal expanse.

> *The universe was infinite, animate and populated by numberless solar systems. It was also eternal. As such, it exhibited all possibilities at any given moment, and all parts of it assumed all possibilities over time, thereby constituting a cognizable manifestation of a timeless and absolute principle, God, conceived as the sole being who truly existed. In keeping with these ideas, Bruno proposed versions of metempsychosis, polygenism, panpsychism and, renouncing Christian emphases on human imperfection, advocated a morality that exhorted individuals to perfect their intellectual powers.*[7]

The Church was to take issue with Bruno's cosmology on three points: the implication that an infinite universe can have no center, thus displacing God; that these other planets hosted intelligent life, a position known as cosmic pluralism; and that his theory subverted the established Aristote-

---

5   Duncan's Masonic Ritual and Monitor (1866), New York: Crown Publishers, 1986, pp. 77-78

6   An observation first attributed to Aristarchus in Archimedes's *The Sand Reckoner*. Dreyer, *A History of Astronomy from Thales to Kepler*, Dover Publications, 1953, pp. 135-148

7   Knox, "Giordano Bruno", *Stanford Encyclopedia of Philosophy*, 2018, retrieved at: plato.stanford.edu

lian and Ptolemaic models, upon which the scholastically-leaning dogma of the Church rested. Due to these transgressions – in the company of many others, such as his denial of eternal damnation, of Christ's divinity, of transubstantiation, his pantheism and his belief in metempsychosis – Giordano Bruno was tried and condemned by the Inquisition to be burned at the stake in 1600 at Rome's Campo de' Fiori. Considering that Bruno was martyred for his Hermeticism and intrepid scientific and philosophical spirit, even in the face of mortal dangers, perhaps the letter *G* should also stand for "Giordano".

Jordanus Brunus.

Eja age sublimes tentet natura recessus,
Nam tangente Deo fervidus ignis eris!

Engraving of Giordano Bruno from ca. 1830

The invention of the letter *G* is credited to Roman freedman, Spurius Carvilius Ruga (3rd century BCE) when a vacancy was created by either the supplanting of the letter *K* by the hard Latin *C*, or when the Phoenician letter *Z*, originally in the seventh position (as evidenced by its gematriac value: *zayin* = 7), was supplanted by *G*.[8] Of the letter *G*, Mackey, in his *Encyclopedia*, wrote the following:

> *It is, in fact, a corruption of the old Hebrew Kabbalistic symbol, the letter yod, by which the sacred name of God – in fact, the most sacred name, the Tetragrammaton – is expressed. This letter, yod, is the initial letter of the word הוהי, or Jehovah, and is constantly to be met with among Hebrew writers, as the abbreviation or symbol of that most holy name, which, indeed, was never written at length. Now, as G is in like manner the initial of God, the English equivalent of the Hebrew Jehovah, the letter has been adopted as a symbol intended to supply to modern Lodges the place of the Hebrew symbol. [...] The letter G, then, has in Masonry the same force and signification that the letter yod had among the Kabbalists. It is only a symbol of the Hebrew letter, and, as that is a symbol of God, the letter G is only a symbol of a symbol.*[9]

The problem with Mackey's interpretation is that the Latin (and English) letter *G* corresponds not to the Hebrew letter *yod*, but to *gimel*. Furthermore, *gimel* corresponds to the Greek letter *gamma*, which is the first letter of the word γεωμετρία, meaning "geometry". This seems to almost irrefutably connect the Masonic letter *G* with the art of geometry, as is first stated in the ritual, as opposed to God. It is also Masonically significant that, in Greek, the letter *G* is called *gamma* (Γ), which forms a square – an angle of ninety degrees, or "the fourth part of a circle".

It is fitting to end our study of the letter *G* with its significance vis-à-vis the Hebrew letter *gimel*, its gematriac value of three, and its corresponding Tarot card, the High Priestess II. On the scroll she is holding (Rider-Waite), is written *TORA*, or "Law". As we had briefly discussed in Chapter II, some of the anagrammatic modes of the word TORA are: ROTA, TARO, ORAT, TORA, and ATOR (corroborated by the Wheel of Fortune X Tarot card). These modes, if read sequentially, form a quasi-Latin sentence, which may be interpreted to read: "The wheel of Tarot speaks the law of Hathor".[10]

8   Gnanadesikan, *The Writing Revolution: Cuneiform to the Internet*, John Wiley & Sons, 2011

9   Mackey, *An Encyclopedia of Freemasonry and its Kindred Sciences*, Everts & Co., 1884, p. 302

10   Greer, *Tarot for Your Self: A Workbook for Personal Transformation*, Weiser, 1984, p. 27

The High Priestess II of the Rider-Waite Tarot deck is replete with archetypally feminine imagery. The card depicts a woman between two pillars, holding the scroll of Law, wearing blue flowing robes and a silver crown reminiscent of those worn by the goddesses Hathor and Selene (Greek: Σελήνη), and a crescent Moon at her feet. In the case of Hathor, the crescent Moon motif is implied by the horns of a bull – a likely allusion to the Taurian precessional age, the period from whence her worship commenced. In the Taurian age (approximately 4000-2000 BCE, a period whose commencement corresponds to the Masonic *Anno Lucis*)[11], Predynastic Egypt consisted of a loose coalition of agrarian cultures and cattle cults which likely led to the deification of Hathor in her bovine form. The robes, demeanor and crescent Moon at the High Priestess' feet are also prominent features in Marian symbolism.[12] Her watery, flowing blue robes symbolize the sea – an idea is corroborated by the etymology of the words *marine*, *Stella Maris*, from the Latin *mare*, meaning both "sea" and "broad, dark area of the moon" – and allude to the sympathetic relationship between the Moon's phases and the sea's tides, another example of cosmic sympathies and their earthly resonance.[13] Astronomically, this sympathetic tidal/lunar activity is largely due to the presence of oceanic salts, strengthening the Marian association with the incarnate body.[14] In mythological, alchemical and occult symbolism, woman seems to be at the fulcrum between the sea and the Moon – a position embodied by the menstrual cycle. For, what is the menstrual cycle but a microcosmic model of the macrocosmic lunar phases? The very etymology of the word supports their essential unity, converging on the Proto-Indo-European *menses*, or "moon, month".[15] Similarly, the ebb and flow of the saltwater tides, themselves linked to the lunar phases, seem to symbolically intercede for the feminine reproductive cycle.

---

11   Lamb, *Myth, Magick & Masonry: Occult Perspectives in Freemasonry*, The Laudable Pursuit, 2018, Section II

12   Roten, *Marian Symbolism of the Crescent Moon*, University of Dayton, retrieved at: udayton.edu

13   Entry: "Mare" (n. 2), *Online Etymology Dictionary*, retrieved at: etymonline.com

14   "Tide Formation – Gravitational Pull", *Exploring Our Fluid Earth*, retrieved at: manoa.hawaii.edu

15   Entries: "Menstrual" & "Moon"; *Online Etymology Dictionary*, retrieved at: etymonline.com

The letter G, from Mackey's Manual of the Lodge, 1891

SUMMARY

In the foregoing, we have examined the entirety of the Fellow Craft degree lecture – from the porch, where we learned of the distinction between the operative and speculative denominations of Masonry and encountered the Brazen Pillars; to the Winding Staircase, where we learned of the immense value attributed to each step, of the human experience in and of the world, as well as the refinement of those experiences through the application of the seven liberal arts and sciences. We have passed to the Middle Chamber of K∴S∴T∴, where we received the wages and jewels of a Fellow Craft, and unraveled some of the mystery of the letter *G.* Part of the genius of this lecture is in its sequence – a sequence to which we have remained faithful – as each of these subjects are contingent upon their predecessor. As was stated in the Introduction, it was our intention to highlight the contents of the lecture primarily through the lenses of Western astrology, classical mythology, Neoplatonism, Hermeticism, Qabalah, Rosicrucianism, operative and speculative alchemy, Tarot symbolism and, of course, Freemasonry – in essence, from the perspective of the Western Esoteric Tradition, as a whole. All the while, understanding that it is helpful to have a developed reference point in these subjects in order to effectively apply their interpretive perspective and, with that in mind, endeavoring to provide some insight on these theoretical perspectives, in context and in the footnotes, as well as providing several comprehensive resources in the Suggested Reading section, for those who wish to dig deeper into these invaluable aids to a deeper understanding of the Fellow Craft lecture's occult substratum.

It has been the author's objective to endeavor to supplement this wealth of material with which we are presented, but upon which we are given no further elucidation beyond the lecture itself. As was stated in the Introduction, the author identified this as a glaring deficit in Masonic pedagogy needing to be addressed, hence the writing of the present volume. It was not the author's intention to compose a textbook or workbook, nor to instruct anyone in the practical minutiæ of these arts and sciences – the intention was merely to provide a broad overview of the subjects as referenced in the Fellow Craft degree lecture, predominantly from an esoteric or occult perspective. However, the reader is encouraged to take on a more academically rigorous study of these arts and sciences, if possible, as these are prescribed in our ritual for the purpose of personal betterment and, perhaps most especially, in the interest of developing a broader foundation of knowledge upon which may be erected more lofty philosophical and theological structures – as was the principle purpose of the curriculum from its initial codification in the ancient world to its adoption in the ritual of Freemasonry.

Though the immense scope of our subjects has precluded our going exhaustively deep into any one of them without spilling over into multiple volumes, it is the author's hope that some portion of the innumerable revelations and insights, which were unveiled to him during the conceptualization, research, composition, editing and revision processes, and culminating in the realization of the present volume, have been rendered communicable to the reader and that the reader, particularly those who have been passed to the degree of Fellow Craft, may have found value in his labors.

APPENDICES

Appendix A: *Qabalistic, Tarotic and Astrological Correspondences*[1]

Letter	Name	Meaning	Value	Tarot	Astrology	Path
א	*Aleph*	Ox	1	0 Fool	*	11
ב	*Beth*	House	2	I Magician	Mercury	12
ג	*Gimel*	Camel	3	II High Priestess	Moon	13
ד	*Daleth*	Door	4	III Empress	Venus	14
ה	*Heh*	Window	5	IV Emperor	Aries	15
ו	*Vau*	Nail	6	V Hierophant	Taurus	16
ז	*Zayin*	Sword	7	VI Lovers	Gemini	17
ח	*Cheth*	Fence, Field	8	VII Chariot	Cancer	18
ט	*Teth*	Serpent	9	VIII Strength	Leo	19
י	*Yod*	Hand	10	IX Hermit	Virgo	20
כ,ך	*Kaph*	Palm	20, 500	X Wheel of Fortune	Jupiter	21
ל	*Lamed*	Ox-goad	30	XI Justice	Libra	22
מ,ם	*Mem*	Water	40, 600	XII Hanged Man	*	23
נ,ן	*Nun*	Fish	50, 700	XIII Death	Scorpio	24
ס	*Samech*	Prop	60	XIV Temperance	Sagittarius	25
ע	*Ayin*	Eye	70	XV Devil	Capricorn	26
פ,ף	*Peh*	Mouth	80, 800	XVI Tower	Mars	27
צ,ץ	*Tzaddi*	Fish Hook	90, 900	XVII Star	Aquarius	28
ק	*Qoph*	Back of Head	100	XVIII Moon	Pisces	29
ר	*Resh*	Head	200	XIX Sun	Sun	30
ש	*Shin*	Tooth	300	XX Judgement	*	31
ת	*Tau*	Cross	400	XXI World	Saturn	32

* Astrologically, the three mother letters, *Aleph*, *Mem* and *Shin*, may be assigned to the three quadriplicities (fixed, mutable and cardinal) or to the planets Uranus, Neptune and Pluto, respectively, though these correspondences are not standardized.

---

1 Küntz (editor), *The Complete Golden Dawn Cipher Manuscript*, Holmes Publishing, 1996, pp. 59 and 116

Appendix B: The Etz Chaim, Sephiroth and Paths

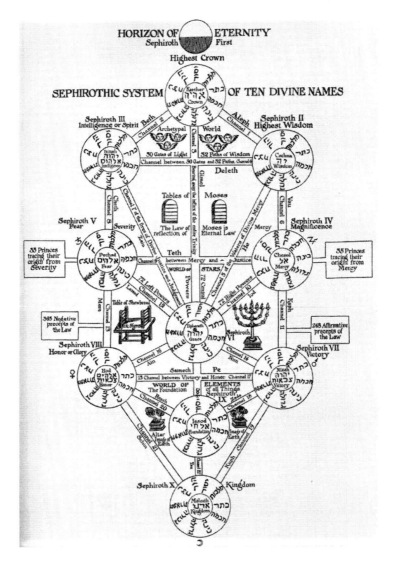

English translation of Kircher's Etz Chaim, from Œdipus Ægyptiacus, 1652

Appendix C: *Agrippa's Table of Planetary Hours*

Daytime Hour	Sunday	Monday	Tuesday	Wednesday	Thursday	Friday	Saturday
1 (Sunrise)	Sun	Moon	Mars	Mercury	Jupiter	Venus	Saturn
2	Venus	Saturn	Sun	Moon	Mars	Mercury	Jupiter
3	Mercury	Jupiter	Venus	Saturn	Sun	Moon	Mars
4	Moon	Mars	Mercury	Jupiter	Venus	Saturn	Sun
5	Saturn	Sun	Moon	Mars	Mercury	Jupiter	Venus
6	Jupiter	Venus	Saturn	Sun	Moon	Mars	Mercury
7	Mars	Mercury	Jupiter	Venus	Saturn	Sun	Moon
8	Sun	Moon	Mars	Mercury	Jupiter	Venus	Saturn
9	Venus	Saturn	Sun	Moon	Mars	Mercury	Jupiter
10	Mercury	Jupiter	Venus	Saturn	Sun	Moon	Mars
11	Moon	Mars	Mercury	Jupiter	Venus	Saturn	Sun
12	Saturn	Sun	Moon	Mars	Mercury	Jupiter	Venus

Nighttime Hour	Sunday	Monday	Tuesday	Wednesday	Thursday	Friday	Saturday
1 (Sunset)	Jupiter	Venus	Saturn	Sun	Moon	Mars	Mercury
2	Mars	Mercury	Jupiter	Venus	Saturn	Sun	Moon
3	Sun	Moon	Mars	Mercury	Jupiter	Venus	Saturn
4	Venus	Saturn	Sun	Moon	Mars	Mercury	Jupiter
5	Mercury	Jupiter	Venus	Saturn	Sun	Moon	Mars
6	Moon	Mars	Mercury	Jupiter	Venus	Saturn	Sun
7	Saturn	Sun	Moon	Mars	Mercury	Jupiter	Venus
8	Jupiter	Venus	Saturn	Sun	Moon	Mars	Mercury
9	Mars	Mercury	Jupiter	Venus	Saturn	Sun	Moon
10	Sun	Moon	Mars	Mercury	Jupiter	Venus	Saturn
11	Venus	Saturn	Sun	Moon	Mars	Mercury	Jupiter
12	Mercury	Jupiter	Venus	Saturn	Sun	Moon	Mars

Chapter XXXIV: Of the true motion of the heavenly bodies to be observed in the eight sphere, and of the ground of Planetary hours

Whosoever will work according to the Celestiall opportunity, ought to observe both or one of them, namely the motion of the Stars, or their times; I say their motions, when they are in their dignities or dejections, either essential or accidentall; but I call their times, dayes and hours distributed to their Dominions. Concerning all these, it is abundantly taught in the books of Astrologers; but in this place two things especially are to be considered and observed by us. One that we observe the motions and ascensions and windings of Stars, even as they are in truth in the eight sphere, through the neglect of which it happeneth that many err in fabricating the Celestiall Images, and are defrauded of their desired effect; the other thing we ought to observe, is about the times of choosing the planetary hours; for almost all Astrologers divide all that space of time from the Sun rising to setting into twelve equall parts, and call them the twelve hours of the day; then the time which followeth from the setting to the rising, in like manner being divided into twelve equall parts, they call the twelve hours of the night, and then distribute each of those hours to every one of the Planets according to the order of their successions, giving alwayes the first hour of the day to the Lord of that day, then to every one by order, even to the end of twenty four hours; and in this distribution the Magicians agree with them; but in the partition of the hours some do different, saying, that the space of the rising and setting is not to be divided into equall parts, and that those hours are not therefore called unequal because the diurnal are unequal to the nocturnall, but because both the diurnal and nocturnal are even unequall amongst themselves; therefore the partition of unequall or Planetary hours hath a different reason of their measure observed by Magicians, which is of this sort; for as in artificiall hours, which are alwayes equall to themselves, the ascensions of fifteen degrees in the equinoctiall, constituteth an artificial hour: so also in planetary hours the ascensions of fifteen degrees in the Eclipticke constituteth an unequall or planetary hour, whose measure we ought to enquire and find out by the tables of the oblique ascensions of every region.[2]

---

2 Agrippa, *Three Books of Occult Philosophy*, 1531, Book II, Chapter 34

Appendix D: *The Fellow Craft Degree Lecture*

[...W]*e are now about to make an ascent through a porch, by a flight of winding stairs, consisting of three, five, and seven steps, to a place representing the Middle Chamber of King Solomon's Temple, there to receive instructions relative to the wages due, and jewels of a Fellow Craft.*

Masonry is considered under two denominations – namely, Operative and Speculative. By Operative Masonry, we allude to the proper application of the useful rules of architecture, whence a structure will derive figure, strength, and beauty; and whence will result a due proportion and a just correspondence in all its parts. It furnishes us with dwellings, and convenient shelters from the vicissitudes and inclemencies of the seasons; and while it displays the effects of human wisdom, as well in the choice as in the arrangement of the sundry materials of which an edifice is composed, it demonstrates that a fund of science and industry is implanted in man, for the best, most salutary, and beneficent purposes.

By Speculative Masonry, we learn to subdue the passions, act upon the square, keep a tongue of good report, maintain secrecy, and practise charity. It is so far interwoven with religion as to lay us under obligations to pay that rational homage to the Deity, which at once constitutes our duty and our happiness. It leads the contemplative to view with reverence and admiration the glorious works of creation, and inspires him with the most exalted ideas of the perfections of his Divine Creator.

Our ancient brethren worked at both Operative and Speculative Masonry; they worked at the building of King Solomon's Temple, besides numerous other Masonic edifices. They wrought six days, but did not work on the seventh (7th), for in six days God created the heavens and the earth, and rested on the seventh day; therefore our ancient brethren consecrated this day as a day of rest from their labors; thereby enjoying frequent opportunities to contemplate the glorious works of creation, and to adore their great Creator.

Brother, the first thing that particularly attracts our attention are [...] two large brazen pillars *[...] one on the right and one on the left hand. The name of the one on the left hand is Boaz, and signifies strength; the name of the one on the right is Jachin, and denotes establishment; they, collectively, denote establishment and strength, and allude to a passage in Scripture: "In strength shall this house be established." These are representations of the two pillars erected at the outer porch of King Solomon's Temple. They are said to have been in height thirty-five (35) cubits, twelve in circumference, and four in diameter; they are said to have been adorned with two large chapiters of five cubits each, making their entire height forty (40) cubits. These chapiters were ornamented with a representation of net-work, lily-work, and pomegranates, and are said to denote Unity, Peace, and Plenty The network, from its connection, denotes unity; the lily-work, from its whiteness, and the retired place in which it grows, purity and peace; the pomegranates, from the exuberance of their seed, denote plenty. These chapiters have on the top of each a globe, or ball; these globes are two artificial spherical bodies; on the convex surfaces of which are represented the countries, seas, and various parts of the earth, the face of the heavens, the planetary revolutions; and are said to be thus extensive, to denote the universality of Masonry, and that a Mason's charity ought to be equally extensive. The principal use of these globes, besides serving as maps, to distinguish the outward parts of the earth, and the situation of the fixed stars, is to illustrate and explain the phenomena arising from the annual revolution and the diurnal rotation of the earth around its own axis. They are the noblest instruments for improving the mind, and giving it the most distinct idea of any problem or proposition, as well as enabling it to solve the same.*

Contemplating these bodies, we are inspired with a due reverence for the Deity and his works and are induced to encourage the studies of astronomy, geography, navigation, and the arts dependent on them, by which society has been so much benefited.

The composition of these pillars is molten or cast brass; they were cast whole, on the banks of the river Jordan, in the clay grounds between SUCCOTH and ZAREDATHA, where King Solomon ordered these and all holy vessels to be cast.

They were cast hollow, and were four inches or a hand's breadth thick. They were cast hollow the better to withstand inundation and conflagrations, and are said to have contained the archives of Masonry.

[...] *The next thing that attracts our attention are the winding stairs which lead to the Middle Chamber of King Solomon's Temple, consisting of three, five, and seven steps.*

The first three allude to the three principal stages of human life, namely, youth, manhood, and old age. In youth, as Entered Apprentices, we ought industriously to occupy our minds in the attainment of useful knowledge; in manhood, as Fellow Crafts, we should apply our knowledge to the discharge of our respective duties to God, our neighbors, and ourselves; so that in old age, as Master Masons, we may enjoy the happy reflections consequent on a well-spent life, and die in the hope of a glorious immortality.

They also allude to the three principal supports in Masonry, namely, Wisdom, Strength. and Beauty; for it is necessary that there should be wisdom to contrive, strength to support, and beauty to adorn all great and important undertakings.

They further allude to the three principal officers of the Lodge, viz.: Master, and Senior and Junior Wardens. [...]

The five steps allude to the five orders of architecture and the five human senses.

The five orders of architecture are Tuscan, Doric, Ionic, Corinthian, and Composite. [...]

The five human senses are hearing, seeing, feeling, smelling, and tasting, the first three of which have ever been highly es-teemed among Masons: hearing, to hear the word; seeing, to see the sign; feeling, to feel the grip, whereby one Mason may know another in the dark as well as in the light. [...]

The seven steps allude to the seven Sabbatical years, seven years of famine, seven years in building the Temple, seven golden candlesticks, seven wonders of the world, seven wise men of the east, seven planets; but, more especially, the seven liberal arts and sciences, which are grammar, rhetoric, logic, arithmetic, geometry, music, and astronomy. For this and many other reasons the number seven has ever been held in high estimation among Masons.

[...Y]ou have now arrived at the place representing the Middle Chamber of King Solomon's Temple, where you will be received and recorded as a Fellow Craft. [...]

The first thing that particularly attracted your attention on your passage here, was a representation of two brazen pillars, one on the left hand and the other on the right, which was explained to you by your conductor; after passing the pillars you passed a flight of winding stairs, consisting of three, five, and seven steps, which was likewise explained to you; after passing the stairs, you arrived at the outer door of the Middle Chamber, which you found closely guarded by the Junior Warden, who demanded of you the pass and token of the pass of a Fellow Craft; you next arrived at the inner door of the Middle Chamber, which you found guarded by the Senior Warden, who demanded of you the grip and word of a Fellow Craft. You have now arrived at the Middle Chamber where you are received and recorded a Fellow Craft. You are now entitled to wages, as such; which are, the Corn of nourishment, the Wine of refreshment, and the Oil of joy, which denote peace, harmony, and strength. You are also entitled to the jewels of a Fellow Craft; which are, an attentive ear, an instructive tongue, and faithful breast. The attentive ear receives the sound from the instructive tongue, and the mysteries of Masonry are safely lodged in the repository of faithful breasts. ³

Appendix E: *The G Lecture*

I shall now direct your attention to the letter "G" [...] which is the initial of geometry, the fifth science, it being that on which this Degree was principally founded.

Geometry, the first and noblest of sciences, is the basis upon which the superstructure of Masonry is erected. By geometry, we may curiously trace nature through her various windings to her most concealed recesses. By it we discover the power, the wisdom, and the goodness of the Grand Artificer of the Universe, and view with delight the proportions which connect this vast machine. By it we discover how the planets move in their different orbits, and demonstrate their various revolutions. By it we account for the return of the seasons, and the variety of scenes which each season displays to the discerning eye. Numerous worlds are around us, all formed by the same Divine Artist, and which roll through the vast expanse, and are all conducted by the same unerring law of nature. A survey

3   *Duncan's Masonic Ritual and Monitor* (1866), New York: Crown Publishers, 1986, pp. 72-77

of nature, and the observation of her beautiful proportions, first determined man to imitate the Divine plan, and study symmetry and order. This gave rise to societies, and birth to every useful art. The architect began to design, and the plans which he laid down, being improved by experience and time, have produced works which are the admiration of every age.

The lapse of time, the ruthless hand of ignorance, and the devastations of war have laid waste and destroyed many valuable monuments of antiquity on which the utmost exertions of human genius have been employed. Even the Temple of Solomon, so spacious and magnificent, and constructed by so many celebrated artists, escaped not the unsparing ravages of barbarous force. Freemasonry, notwithstanding, has still survived. The attentive ear receives the sound from the instructive tongue, and the mysteries of Masonry are safely lodged in the repository of faithful breasts. Tools and implements of architecture are selected by the fraternity, to imprint on the memory wise and serious truths; and thus, through a succession of ages, are transmitted unimpaired the excellent tenets of our institution.

[…T]his letter has a higher signification; it alludes to the sacred name of Deity […] to whom we should all, from the youngest Entered Apprentice, who stands in the northeast corner, to the Worshipful Master, who presides in the east, with all sincerity humbly bow.[4]

---

4   *Duncan's Masonic Ritual and Monitor* (1866), New York: Crown Publishers, 1986, pp. 77-78

SUGGESTED READING

Agrippa, *Three Books of Occult Philosophy*, 1531 (Llewelyn, 2014)

Angus, *The Mystery Religions*, London: Murray, 1928

Bartlett, *Real Alchemy*, Ibis Press, 2007

Bey, *T.A.Z. The Temporary Autonomous Zone,* Autonomedia, 1985

Campbell, *The Hero with a Thousand Faces*, Pantheon, 1949

Case, *Tarot: A Key to the Wisdom of the Ages*, Macoy Publishing, 1947

Cassirer (et al.), *The Renaissance Philosophy of Man*, University of Chicago Press, 1948

Chevalier (et al.), *Penguin Dictionary of Symbols*, Penguin, 1969

Copenhaver (trans.), *The Book of Magic: From Antiquity to the Enlightenment*, Penguin, 2015

Crowley, *Magick: Liber ABA: Book IV*, 1913 (Weiser, 1994)

Cunningham, *Cunningham's Encyclopedia of Magical Herbs*, Llewelyn, 1985

Debord, *Society of the Spectacle*, Black & Red, 1970

Durant, *The Story of Philosophy*, Simon & Schuster, 1926

Goodrick-Clarke, *The Western Esoteric Traditions: A Historical Introduction,* Oxford University Press, 2008

Fortune, *The Mystical Qabalah*, London: Society of Inner Light, 1935

Frater Albertus, *Alchemist's Handbook*, Weiser, 1974

Frater YShY, *Adept Magic in the Golden Dawn Tradition*, Kerubim Press, 2014

Frazer, *The Golden Bough*, Macmillan, 1890

Gilbert, *The Golden Dawn Companion*, Aquarian Press, 1986

Greer & Warnock (trans.), *The Complete Picatrix*, Adocentyn Press, 2011

Hall, *The Secret Teachings of All Ages*, Crocker Co., 1928 (Dover, 2010)

Hamilton, *Mythology*, 1948 (Grand Central, 2011)

Herzberg, *Myths and their Meaning*, Allyn & Bacon, 1966

Hewitt-Brown, *Stellar Theology & Masonic Astronomy*, 1882

Higgins, *Hermetic Masonry*, 1916 (Kessinger, 2010)

Jung (et al.), *Man and his Symbols*, Doubleday, 1964

Küntz (editor), *The Complete Golden Dawn Cipher Manuscript*, Holmes Publishing, 1996

Küntz (editor), *The Golden Dawn Source Book*, Holmes Publishing, 1996

Lamb, *Myth, Magick & Masonry: Occult Perspectives in Freemasonry*, The Laudable Pursuit, 2018

Lévi, *Dogma and Ritual of High Magic*, two volumes in 1854 & 1856

Lévi, *The History of Magic*, Rider & Son, 1922

Lévi, *The Key to the Great Mysteries* (*La Clef Des Grands Mystères*), Paris: Bailliere, 1861

Mackey, *An Encyclopedia of Freemasonry and its Kindred Sciences*, Everts & Co., 1884

Mackey, *The Symbolism of Freemasonry*, Clark & Maynard, 1869

Mathers (trans.), *Kabbalah Unveiled*, London: Redway, 1887

Newman, *Alchemically Stoned: The Psychedelic Secret of Freemasonry*, The Laudable Pursuit, 2017

Newton, *The Builders*, Torch Press, 1914

Nichols, *Jung and Tarot*, Weiser, 1980

Preston (Oliver, commentary), *Illustrations of Masonry*, Masonic Publishing and Manufacturing Co., 1867

Regardie, *The Golden Dawn*, Llewelyn, 1971

Roob, *Alchemy & Mysticism*, Taschen, 2011

Ruck (et al.), *Mushrooms, Myth & Mithras*, City Lights, 2011

Salaman (et al.), *The Way of Hermes: New Translations of the Corpus Hermeticum*, Inner Traditions, 2000

Tester, *A History of Western Astrology*, Ballantine, 1987

Van Gennep, *Rites of Passage*, Paris: Émile Nourry, 191

Vaughan, *Renaissance Man and Mason*, Rose Circle, 2016

Waite, *The Pictorial Key to the Tarot*, 1911 (U.S. Games, 1971)

Westcott (trans.), *Collecteana Hermetica*, vols. I-X, 1893-1896

Westcott (trans.), *Sepher Yetzirah*, London: The Theosophical Publishing Society, 1887

Yates, *Giordano Bruno and the Hermetic Tradition*, University of Chicago Press, 1964

Yates, *The Rosicrucian Enlightenment*, Routledge, 1972

This list is by no means exhaustive, nor is it a comprehensive bibliography to the present volume; it represents merely a few of the works that I have personally found indispensable in developing the critical and theoretical frame of reference employed throughout this book. JPL.

INDEX

Symbols

47th Problem of Euclid, 107, 269, 273

A

Abrasax, Abraxas, 139, 248

Acacia, 97, 123

Agrippa, Heinrich Cornelius, 71, 78, 87, 104, 105, 146, 177, 184, 185, 216, 220, 221, 275, 365–368, 370, 381

AIQ BKR, 223

Alberti, Leone Battista, 317, 318

Alchemy, 33, 34, 44–46, 64, 71, 107, 112, 113, 198, 203, 204, 213, 214, 275, 297, 302, 357, 373, 374

al-Farabi, 219

al-Khidr, 150–152

Alpha et Omega, 277

Ancient and Accepted Scottish Rite, 45, 63, 64, 125, 134, 187, 273

Androsphinxes, 61, 342

Anno Lucis, 66, 309, 411

Anubis, 99, 164

Aphrodite, 76, 78, 85, 108, 158, 200, 202, 287, 350, 351, 381

Apollo, 92, 102, 123, 270, 304, 315

Apollonius of Tyana, 305, 323

Aquinas, Thomas, 110

Arcas, 376, 377

Archimedes of Syracuse, 274

C

F

G

ABOUT THE AUTHOR

Jaime Paul Lamb is the author of *MYTH, MAGICK & MASON-RY: Occult Perspectives in Freemasonry* (The Laudable Pursuit, August, 2018). He is a member of Old Well-Saint John's Lodge no. 6, F.&A.M., a charter member of Ascension Lodge no. 89, F.&A.M., a *Frater* of both the Arizona College of the *Societas Rosicruciana in Civitatibus Foederatis* and the Hermetic Society of the G ∴ D ∴, and is a Past Master of Arizona Research Lodge no. 1 for the year 2016. Lamb has been writing and lecturing on Masonic and occult subjects since 2014. His work has been published in *Ad Lucem*: the official organ of the *Societas Rosicruciana in Civitatibus Foederatis, Knight Templar* magazine, *Royal Arch Mason*

magazine, Southern California Research Lodge's *Fraternal Review*, the *Journal of the Masonic Society*, the *Square*, and many other online and print Masonic publications. He has been featured on Masonic and occult podcasts such as *Whence Came You?* and *Thoth-Hermes*, and has presented his work at conferences and symposia nationwide. Lamb currently resides in Phoenix, Arizona with his wife, Stephanie, and too many animals.

To inquire about speaking engagements, lecture presentations, podcast/radio appearances, article solicitations or other opportunities, please email the author directly at: jaimepaullamb@hotmail.com.

Made in the USA
Columbia, SC
15 November 2020